D0975278

THE
ROMAN
SEARCH FOR WISDOM

ALSO BY MICHAEL K. KELLOGG

The Greek Search for Wisdom

Three Questions We Never Stop Asking

THE
ROMAN
SEARCH FOR WISDOM

MICHAEL K. KELLOGG

 Prometheus Books

59 John Glenn Drive
Amherst, New York 14228

Published 2014 by Prometheus Books

Cover image © Bigstock®
Cover design by Grace M. Conti-Zilsberger

Inquiries should be addressed to
Prometheus Books
59 John Glenn Drive
Amherst, New York 14228
VOICE: 716–691–0133
FAX: 716–691–0137
WWW.PROMETHEUSBOOKS.COM

18 17 16 15 14   5 4 3 2 1

Library of Congress Cataloging-in-Publication Data

Kellogg, Michael K., 1954-
    The Roman search for wisdom / By Michael K. Kellogg.
        pages cm
    Includes bibliographical references and index.
    ISBN 978-1-61614-925-3 (hardback)
    ISBN 978-1-61614-926-0 (ebook)
    1. Conduct of life. 2. Wisdom. 3. Philosophy, Ancient. I. Title.

BJ1589.K455 2014
870.9'001—dc23
                                                            2013047303

Printed in the United States of America

For Baird

Macte nova virtute, puer, sic itur ad astra.
—Virgil, *Aeneid*, 9.641

CONTENTS

PREFACE

A reader familiar with the classics of ancient Greece might turn to the Romans with some trepidation. The Greeks, after all, perfected epic poetry and invented history, tragedy, comedy, and philosophy, as well as democracy. What would the Romans have to say that was not just a pale imitation? Ancient Rome was a military juggernaut, famous for its balanced constitution, its regard for the rule of law, and its vast empire. The Romans made original contributions to architecture and engineering, not to poetry and philosophy. Besides, after the fall of the republic, the ruling emperors had only limited (and sometimes no) tolerance for independent thought.

Fortunately and delightfully, that concern is misplaced. To be sure, the first Roman efforts in literature were simply Latin translations from the Greek. The Romans absorbed Greek culture as readily as they absorbed Greek lands. As Horace aptly put it, "Captive Greece took its Roman captor captive, / Invading uncouth Latium with its arts."[1] But, starting as early as Plautus, in the third century BCE, the Romans began adapting Greek models to meet their own needs and circumstances. Plautus did not slavishly follow Menander; he created new works out of old material and laid the critical foundations for much of modern comedy. He still seems refreshingly modern in a way that recovered fragments of Menander do not.

Cicero summarized and preserved a great deal of ancient philosophy that would otherwise be lost to us, but he also made original contributions in political and legal philosophy. Lucretius's *De Rerum Natura* (*On the Nature of Things*) is the greatest philosophical poem ever written, and it still carries tremendous intellectual and emotional power. Virgil belongs with Homer and Dante as the three indispensable epic poets. Horace brought lyric poetry to its most perfect form in Latin. Ovid is like no one else, a wry master of the love elegy and the mythological trope. Even Seneca's tragedies—largely spurned and unread today—were strikingly original and had a critical influence on Elizabethan drama, including Shakespeare. Livy and Tacitus can readily stand with Herodotus and Thucydides as the greatest ancient historians.

There is no question that the Roman writers suffered from what the contemporary critic Harold Bloom would call "the anxiety of influence."[2] They could not ignore their towering Greek predecessors. Instead, they absorbed what the Greeks had to teach them and created new works of art and thought that withstand comparison. After the Greeks, no one else could invent the basic genres. But the Romans did, as all great artists do, reinvent them and use them to say something that is still for us today urgent and compelling, beautiful and harrowing.

THE GRANDEUR THAT WAS ROME

On desperate seas long wont to roam,
Thy hyacinth hair, thy classic face,
Thy Naiad airs have brought me home
To the glory that was Greece,
And the grandeur that was Rome.

—Edgar Allan Poe, "To Helen"

There can surely be nobody so petty or so apathetic in his outlook that
he has no desire to discover by what means and under what system
of government the Romans succeeded in less than fifty-three years in
bringing under their rule almost the whole of the inhabited world, an
achievement which is without parallel in human history.

—Polybius, *The Rise of the Roman Empire*

No one is well educated who is ignorant of our literature.

—Cicero, *On Moral Ends*

FROM MYTH TO HISTORY

I t is hardly surprising that the second great civilization in the Western tradition developed an origination myth to rival that of the first. The Romans traced their heritage to the losing side in the Trojan War, so the ultimate military conquest and cultural absorption of Greece by Rome turned the tables in more ways than one. According to the ancient legend, Aeneas, son of the Trojan Anchises and the goddess Aphrodite (renamed Venus in Latin), escaped the destruction of Troy in 1153 BCE,[1] carrying his aged father and his household gods upon his back. After many trials and battles, he and his followers settled in Latium, where his son Ascanius ruled in the city of Alba Longa for thirty years, followed by a succession of kings of mixed Trojan and Latin ancestry.

Aeneas's founding of a new homeland is the basis for Virgil's epic poem, the *Aeneid*, and in somewhat different form also begins Livy's history of Rome—though Livy acknowledged that he was purveying "old tales with more of the charm of poetry than of a sound historical record."[2] This Trojan tale mixes uneasily—both thematically and chronologically—with the myth of Rome's founding by Romulus and Remus. In Livy's account, Numitor—the rightful king of Alba Longa in the Trojan succession—was deposed by his younger brother Amulius, who then killed Numitor's sons and forced his daughter to become a priestess at the temple of Vesta. There, she was impregnated by Mars, the god of war, and bore him twins: "perhaps she believed it, perhaps she was merely hoping by the pretence to palliate her guilt," Livy remarks.[3] Cast out of the temple and exposed to the elements, the twins were suckled by a she-wolf and later raised by a shepherd. Eventually, they learned their true identities, killed Amulius, and helped their grandfather to regain the throne. Then, in 753 (the traditional date of the founding of Rome), they decided to build a city of their own on the Tiber with the overflow population from Alba Longa. Romulus built an outpost on one of the seven hills in the area (the Palatine) and Remus on another (the Aventine). Inevitably they quarreled over precedence, and Romulus killed Remus, a harbinger of the fratricidal civil wars that would plague Rome for centuries.

Romulus established the twin guarantors of order upon which Rome would depend for the next millennium: elaborate religious rituals and the rule of law. To ensure respect for his own person, he was accompanied everywhere by twelve *lictors* (attendants) who bore with them *fasces* (a bundle of rods, which symbolized the power of the king over life and death, and which gave us the modern term *fascism*). In order to grow the population, Romulus turned the city into a place of asylum for refugees, riffraff, and criminals of every sort. Anyone who settled there was granted Roman citizenship. But they lacked women. After his overtures to surrounding communities were unsurprisingly rebuffed—even ancient parents did not relish having their daughters marry outlaws and social outcasts—Romulus grew proactive. He celebrated a festival in honor of Neptune and invited the neighboring settlements to attend a great spectacle. When the show began, a signal was given, and the able-bodied, unattached men of Rome seized and carried off the young women, a large number of whom were Sabines.

The parents fled in the confusion. The terrified young women were reassured personally by Romulus that they would be treated with respect as lawful wives and (soon-to-be) mothers. When the Sabines and other towns finally marshaled their forces to attack Rome, the now-reconciled women interposed themselves and pled with both sides to spare, respectively, their fathers and their husbands and to avoid shedding kindred blood. An uneasy peace ensued, at least for a time, and Rome continued to grow in numbers and in strength. The rape (abduction) of the Sabine women and their subsequent pleas for peace became a favorite subject in art from the Renaissance to Picasso.

One day, while reviewing his troops, Romulus was enveloped in a thick mist and carried off to join the gods above. (Plutarch suggests that the story was concocted to cover up his murder by jealous rivals.) Romulus was the first in a series of seven legendary kings, each of whom reigned for an average of thirty-five years. For the next two centuries, Rome continued to conquer and absorb neighboring towns. And it continued to welcome new citizens. In 616, a settler from Tarquinii in Tuscany maneuvered his way into the kingship under the name Tarquin and began an aggressive and successful policy of expansion. But the sons of Tarquin's predecessor were resentful of his usurpation and, once they were adults, engineered his assassination. Tarquin's death was kept a secret until Servius Tullius, who had been raised in the palace, was able to drive off the assassins and establish himself as the natural successor. To forestall objections from Tarquin's sons, he married his two daughters to the two princes.

That turned out not to be a good idea. Both of the daughters were named Tullia—after the Roman custom of giving all daughters the feminine form of the father's family name—but they were opposites in temper. The younger was as vicious as the older was mild-mannered. Yet the younger Tullia was married to the bland, unambitious Arruns, while the older was married to the fiery Lucius Tarquinius, who went by his father's name, Tarquin. Tarquin and the younger Tullia conspired together, arranged the deaths of their respective partners, and then married one another. The surviving Tullia played the role of Lady Macbeth in urging her husband to seize the throne. He finally did so. His hired thugs killed Servius Tullius in the street, and Tullia exultantly drove her carriage repeatedly over the body, splattering herself with her father's blood.

Thus began the reign of Tarquinius Superbus—Tarquin the Proud, as he was called—the last of Rome's kings. He was a successful warrior but an arrogant tyrant at home, and resentment against him rose steadily. When his son Sextus Tarquinius raped Lucretia, a virtuous young woman, she made her father and his friends promise to avenge her before plunging a knife into her own heart. One of those friends, Lucius Junius Brutus (the ancestor of Gaius Julius Caesar's leading assassin), immediately led a revolt and drove the Tarquins from the city. The year was 509, and the republic was at hand. "The whole period of monarchical government," Livy writes, "from the founding of Rome to its liberation, was 244 years."[4]

THE REPUBLIC

Brutus convinced all the citizens of Rome to swear an oath never to tolerate another king. Under his guidance, they established a mixed constitution of the sort recommended by Aristotle, with elements of monarchy (two consuls, each elected for one year and rarely serving more than one term), oligarchy (the Senate, drawn at first almost exclusively from noble families and effectively given life tenure), and democracy (the popular assembly, which had exclusive authority to pass laws and elect officials). This balancing of powers—like that of our own government—was expressly designed to make change difficult and to neutralize the efforts of any one person or group to dominate the body politic. Recognizing, however, that emergencies could occur in which decisive action was required, the constitution also allowed the consuls, in consultation with the Senate, to appoint a dictator for a period of up to six months.

The mixed Roman constitution, which evolved over time, was much celebrated by Cicero, Polybius, and others. But, in fact, it heavily favored the aristocracy. Voting was by groups (known as "centuries," though the numbers in each group could vary widely) and the well-to-do had many centuries, while the plebeians were lumped into a very few and hence had little ultimate say. A general strike in 494—known as the Succession of the Plebs—led to the creation of a new position, the Tribunes of the People, who were given veto power (*intercessio*) over any action taken by the government.

Another critical reform—the most important political development in Western history after the Greek invention of democracy—was the creation of a written legal code and a strong commitment to the rule of law. The so-called Twelve Tables were drawn up by a group of commissioners circa 450 to provide transparency and a clear structure in which everyday life was free to unfold. Inscribed on ivory tablets and placed in the Forum for all to see and read, the Twelve Tables touched upon property, torts, contracts, family relationships, and crimes. Citizens could, for the first time, know with some clarity the rules that governed their actions. The security provided by the rule of law has been crucial to every free and successful society since Rome. Schoolboys learned the Twelve Tables by heart down to the time of Cicero, three hundred years later, though the original tablets were destroyed in 390 by marauding Gauls (as the Romans referred to the Celts from what is now France and northern Italy).

Religion was also important in the republic; indeed, there was little separation between politics and religion, and leading politicians also presided over sacrifices and festivals. The Greek gods were given Latin names (Jupiter, Juno, Mars, Minerva, etc.) and joined a pantheon of local deities. Religious rituals, sacrifices, and festivals were an essential part of daily life, and few important actions (either public or personal) were commenced without some attempt by the priestly augurs to take the auspices and thereby determine the will of the gods, such as by watching the flights of birds or examining their entrails. Cicero, though no believer in such prophecies, nonetheless served as an augur and found it highly convenient to declare certain days inauspicious for public action in order to defuse tension or to defer open conflicts.

Another distinctive feature of the Roman genius was displayed in engineering and architecture. Through the centuries, the same Roman emphasis on discipline, order, and efficiency that animated their military conquests and their code of laws was also reflected in their widespread system of paved roads, their triumphal arches and domes, and their public baths and multistory cement apartment buildings, as well as in their grand palaces and other landmarks, such as the Coliseum and the Pantheon. The Romans built everything to last. The *Ten Books on Architecture* by Vitruvius Pollio are still required reading for first-year students of architecture.

Most important of all, though—at least to those writing nostalgically toward the end of the republic—were the severe personal discipline, courage, self-sacrifice, and love of liberty and country that animated the early Romans. The Romans made a fetish of teaching virtue through exemplars (from the Latin *exempla*); just as they had a pantheon of gods, so too they had an even more important pantheon of republican heroes, starting with Lucretia and Brutus.

Brutus exemplified the Roman trait of placing duty ahead of personal feelings. Once the Tarquins had been banished, they convinced the kings of various neighboring towns to attack Rome and return them to the throne. Brutus's own sons conspired with the Tarquins to betray the city. When the plot was uncovered, Brutus, who was one of the two consuls, rejected the lesser punishment of banishment and unhesitatingly had the boys condemned. His personal anguish was evident to all as his sons were bound to the stake, stripped, flogged, and beheaded in his presence. But duty took precedence. Brutus himself died shortly thereafter, in a cavalry battle against the Tarquins and their allies, when he recklessly threw himself into the midst of the fighting, killing one of Tarquin's sons, even as he himself was killed.

Horatius Cocles earned his fame when an army of Etruscans led by Porsena, king of Clusium, was about to sweep into Rome over the sole bridge leading across the Tiber River. Horatius and two others took a stand at the end of the bridge, in a desperate effort to buy time, while those behind sought frantically to dismantle it. After sending the other two back to safety, Horatius fought on alone until he heard the sound of the bridge crashing into the water behind him and then dove into the river and swam to the Roman shore.

Porsena settled down to a siege that threatened to starve out the Romans. Gaius Mucius volunteered to infiltrate the enemy's camp and assassinate the king. Unfortunately—not being in a position to ask for a positive identification—he killed the king's secretary instead. Porsena threatened to burn him alive if he did not reveal all the details of the plot. Gaius Mucius thrust his own right hand into the fire and held it there in defiance, without uttering a sound. Suitably impressed, Porsena freed him. Gaius Mucius returned the favor by warning the king (falsely) that three hundred other Romans—equally determined—had also vowed each to make an assassination attempt in turn; Gaius Mucius was simply the first. The shaken king abandoned the siege and his support for the Tarquins and became a trusted ally of Rome.

The hopes of the Tarquins were finally, and decisively, crushed in a battle at Lake Regillus, in which the Roman forces were allegedly aided by the twin gods Castor and Pollux (the Dioscuri), sons of Jupiter and brothers of Helen of Troy. But Rome's wars with its neighbors did not cease: Sabines, Samnites, Volscians, Aequians, Veientes, Latins, and Hernici, among others, repeatedly but unsuccessfully sought to check the growing power of the republic. The early history of the republic, as recounted by Livy, is a numbing litany of battles, enlivened by indelible individual portraits.

Coriolanus was an enormously successful commander in these wars, particularly against the Volscians. But his arrogance and contempt for the masses led to his banishment; he sought refuge with the Volscians and led their army against Rome in 491. His mother, accompanied by his wife and children, went out of the city to confront him. She bitterly lamented having borne a son who had become an enemy of her country and a threat to its freedom. Coriolanus kissed his mother, his wife, and his two children and withdrew his army, knowing that he thereby ensured his own death at the hands of the Volscians. Shakespeare would base his tragedy *Coriolanus* on Plutarch's account of this tale.

Perhaps the most storied exemplar of republican virtue was Lucius Quinctius Cincinnatus, who, after serving as consul, retired to a three-acre farm outside Rome. A Roman legion was besieged by the Aequians in 458 and was in danger of annihilation. Cincinnatus was appointed dictator for a period of six months. The senators who went to fetch him found him at the plow. Cincinnatus relieved the legion, defeated and made peace with the Aequians, and returned to his farm, all within fifteen days. He responded to his country's call and asked for nothing in return, voluntarily relinquishing power, as George Washington—whose veterans and their descendants formed the Society of the Cincinnati—would do after his second term in office.

Not all were so selfless, however. The Board of Ten commissioners (*decemvirs*) charged with establishing the legal code unconstitutionally sought to retain power, displacing both consuls and tribunes. Each was now accompanied by his own set of twelve *lictors*, who became bodyguards and enforcers and added axes to the *fasces* they carried. But their leader, Appius Claudius, was ultimately felled by the same lust that led to the overthrow of the Tarquins. He had a pimp seize Verginia, the daughter of a distinguished centurion, and claim that she was the pimp's slave so that Appius could have his way with her. But the man's attempt to carry off the girl was thwarted when her nurse cried for help and gathered a crowd. The issue was brought before Appius, who falsely ruled that she was indeed a slave and was to be handed over to Appius's factotum. The centurion, Lucius Verginius, plunged a dagger into his own daughter's heart rather than allow her to be taken by force. The incident galvanized disgust with the *decemvirs*. They were driven from office, and Appius was thrown into prison, where he committed suicide before he could be tried and executed. The consuls and the tribunes were restored, but individual attempts to grab extraconstitutional power would continue to plague the republic.

WARS OF CONQUEST

In 390 (or in 387, according to some accounts), Rome was sacked by a horde of invading Gauls. Having defeated a hastily assembled and outnumbered Roman army outside the city, the Gauls descended on the largely undefended Rome. Those capable of bearing arms took refuge, with their women and children, on the fortified Capitoline Hill. Others fled the city, which was pillaged and largely destroyed. But those on the hill held out. In Livy's romanticized account, the sacred geese raised an alarm when the Gauls attempted a nighttime assault up the steep slopes. The Senate sent a messenger to Marcus Furius Camillus, a brilliant commander who earlier had been exiled on false charges, appointing him dictator. Camillus raised an army, and the Gauls were driven off (in some accounts, bought off). The Romans rebuilt their city, and not until the fifth century CE would Rome fall again.

The Romans steadily expanded their borders, conquering the Latins in 338 and razing the ancient town of Alba Longa. The successful commander in that war, Titus Manlius, executed his own son for disobeying orders by engaging in successful single combat with a rival cavalry officer who had taunted him during a reconnaissance. After the battle of Sentinum in 295, in which Rome defeated a coalition of Samnites, Etruscans, and others, central Italy was firmly within its control. In a stroke of genius, the Romans offered these conquered peoples civic rights and a share in the spoils of future conquests. As a result, each such encounter enhanced the size and power of their forces.

This virtually inexhaustible supply of manpower proved critical in Rome's battles with Tarentum, a city in southern Italy. Tarentum sought foreign help from Pyrrhus, king of Epirus and (briefly) Macedon, who fancied himself a world conqueror in the mold of his second cousin, Alexander the Great. Pyrrhus was indeed a talented general, and he narrowly defeated the Romans in hard-fought battles at Asculum in 279 and Malventum in 275. But his losses were heavy and his forces depleted. He famously remarked after Asculum, "Another such victory and we shall be lost,"[5] and thus gave us the term *Pyrrhic victory*. Pyrrhus had no reinforcements available, while the Romans quickly replenished their losses, and he departed after Malventum, leaving southern Italy to the Romans.

Following this consolidation, Rome rapidly moved from regional to world power. In 264, Rome set its sights on Sicily, which was already in the sphere of influence of Carthage, a Phoenician trading settlement in North Africa that had grown to dominate the western Mediterranean. The First Punic War (from *Poeni*, the Latin name for the Phoenicians who founded Carthage) lasted twenty-three years, until 241. Rome's superior land forces were constantly stymied, in part by the brilliance of the Carthaginian commander Hamilcar Barca but mainly by Carthage's superiority at sea. Eventually, in their typically thorough way, the Romans built a navy from scratch based on captured Carthaginian vessels and taught their men to sail. They even invented the grapnel, which allowed them to lock onto opposing vessels and fight as if on land. After a number of embarrassing defeats, the Romans finally mastered the art of war at sea, and Carthage sued for a peace that gave Rome a substantial indemnity and control over Sicily. Rome later annexed Sardinia and Corsica as well. Carthage, with its navy and trade power still intact, turned its attention to Spain.

Hamilcar Barca and his son Hannibal were extremely successful in their conquest of the Iberian Peninsula. But, when they besieged the town of Sagentum (near modern Valencia), the Romans (falsely) claimed a treaty violation and declared war. The Second Punic War lasted from 218 to 201 and was very nearly disastrous for Rome. Hannibal marched from Spain across the Alps and invaded Italy. Though he lost half of his forces and most of his famous elephants on the journey, he was able to recruit fresh troops among the Gauls in northern Italy. He then proceeded to bedevil the Romans in a series of victories so brilliant that the Romans feared to engage him. He thrashed the Romans at the Trebia River in 218 (killing more than twenty thousand), at Lake Trasimene in 217 (fifteen thousand), and again at Cannae in 216 (where as many as seventy thousand Roman soldiers lost their lives). Fabius Maximus, known as Cunctator, or the Delayer, took over the Roman command and merely shadowed and harassed Hannibal while avoiding any broader engagement. That strategy, although it annoyed many at Rome, proved inspired.

For whatever reason, Hannibal never attacked Rome itself. Perhaps he thought it too heavily defended; certainly, his genius as a commander was for open warfare rather than for siege tactics. Regardless, Hannibal instead sought to convince the various Roman allies in Italy to revolt and join forces with him. He portrayed himself as a liberator. But the allies were too wary of Rome's resilience to throw in their lot with a foreign army that would undoubtedly leave, later if not sooner. Moreover, Hannibal's army was hardly welcome as it pillaged the countryside and lived off of land belonging to others. Nor did Hannibal get reinforcements from Spain as expected. The Roman commander Publius Cornelius Scipio defeated Hamilcar Barca in Spain, and a relief force led by Hannibal's brother, Hasdrubal, was defeated in 207 before he even reunited with Hannibal. Hasdrubal's head was placed in a sack and thrown into his brother's camp to underscore Hannibal's isolation.

Hannibal literally ran circles around Rome for sixteen years. The devastation was great, but in the end had limited tactical value. Rome continued to harry rather than engage Hannibal, and Scipio, who would acquire the nickname Scipio Africanus, was dispatched to attack Carthage in 204. Hannibal was finally recalled and decisively beaten at the battle of Zama in 202. Carthage capitulated, turned over its navy, and became a client state of Rome, restricted to its existing boundaries. After a failed attempt to seize power, Hannibal was driven from home, then hounded by Rome in Asia Minor until he was cornered and committed suicide in 183.

Yet there was a Third Punic War from 149 to 146. Marcus Porcius Cato, known as Cato the Censor, was a severe, humorless farmer/soldier/statesman. Despite Carthage's compliance with the treaty and its unfailing support as an ally of Rome, Cato was concerned that Carthage was again growing in prosperity and power and could pose a future threat. He ended every speech in the Senate with the words *Ceterum censeo Carthaginem esse delendam* ("Moreover, it is my belief that Carthage must be destroyed."). Eventually, Rome seized on a pretext and did just that. In 146, Carthage was burned to the ground and its people killed, sold into slavery, or driven into exile. Like Troy before it, a great city simply ceased to exist.

THE REPUBLIC IN CRISIS

With the defeat of Carthage, Rome had no rival in the western Mediterranean. The devastation in the Italian countryside wreaked by Hannibal was rapidly repaired, and Rome began an aggressive policy of eastward expansion, spreading her influence into Macedonia, Greece, Thrace, and Asia Minor. Roman coinage appeared throughout the empire, even as taxes and plunder poured into the capital. But increasing riches brought increasing troubles. Corruption among provincial governors was widespread. Bribery at home swayed elections and determined plum appointments. Most significant, the plebeian population in Rome swelled with returning soldiers and peasants displaced from their land as huge, slave-worked estates replaced the smaller, less efficient farms of an earlier era.

The people clamored for land reform and greater political rights, while the nobles clung fiercely to their lucrative prerogatives. A new breed of politicians emerged, known as *populares*. They were led by the Gracchi brothers, grandsons of Scipio Africanus. Tiberius Gracchus was elected tribune in 133. When he introduced a land-redistribution scheme, he was assassinated at the instigation of the *optimates* (those supporting the nobles) that same year. His younger brother, Gaius Gracchus, was tribune in 124 and again in 122. Gaius pressed for land reform, a grain dole, and the resettlement of veterans on conquered lands, and he too was killed.

Rome at this time had no police force, no public prosecutors, and very few permanent bureaucrats. Public riots and political violence by armed groups of thugs grew increasingly common. Into this power vacuum stepped two very different strongmen. Gaius Marius was a brilliant commander with notable successes in North Africa and Gaul. He reorganized the military structure—eliminating any property qualification for service and introducing a silver eagle carried on a pole as the standard of the legions. With strong popular support, Marius served as counsel six times in succession. But, although he stretched existing constitutional restrictions, he did not shatter them.

No such compunction balked his younger rival, Lucius Cornelius Sulla, a thorough *optimate* and every bit as brilliant a general as Marius. Sulla commanded successfully in North Africa and in the Social War (91–88), in which Italian allies, known as the *Socii*, fought for greater rights. Ultimately, Rome granted full citizenship to all those south of the Po River. (The northernmost portion of Italy was still largely controlled by Gauls.) Elected consul in 88, Sulla departed to deal with the troublesome King Mithridates VI in Pontus, on the southern coast of the Black Sea. No sooner had he left, however, than allies of Marius and the *populares* rescinded his appointment and gave it to Marius. Sulla, still in Italy, simply turned back with his army and marched on Rome. Bringing troops into the capital with hostile intent was considered a sacrilege. Sulla's officers abandoned him, but his men did not. Sulla drove Marius and his followers from the city, annulled the legislation revoking his appointment, and went off to deal with Mithridates.

The precedent having been set, Marius and his followers gathered an army and returned to Rome the following year. A significant number of *optimates* were killed, but Marius's seventh consulship was cut short by his own illness and death. His colleague, Lucius Cornelius Cinna, took control and pushed through a number of reforms, including debt forgiveness. Sulla, after dealing with Mithridates and other issues in the East, returned with his army in 82 and marched for a second time on Rome. He defeated Cinna and his allies at the battle of the Colline Gate and established himself as dictator. Sulla reversed many reforms, strengthened the power and numbers of the Senate, and published a proscription, with political opponents named as enemies of the state who were to be killed on sight and have their property forfeited. Sulla stepped down in 80 and retired to the country, restoring the republic. But the damage had been done. The path to power for ruthless commanders was clear, and the republic's days were already numbered.

Successful military commanders often were granted a "triumph," in which they paraded their army into Rome accompanied by prisoners and plunder. (A triumph was the only occasion on which an army could lawfully be brought into the capital.) The general rode in his adorned chariot—Caesar once had his chariot emblazoned with the words *Veni, vidi, vice*—"I came, I saw, I conquered"—accompanied by a slave who constantly whispered into his ear, "Remember, you are only a man," or, more profoundly, *Memento mori* ("Remember that you will die."). Such reminders, however, proved increasingly ineffective. Gaius Julius Caesar and Gnaeus Pompeius Magnus (Pompey the Great) would soon reenact, in even more deadly form, the battles of Marius and Sulla.

But, first, there were slaves to contend with. Rome increasingly depended on slaves as domestic servants, prostitutes (both male and female), tutors (especially if they were Greek), mine workers, farm laborers, and even gladiators to fight and die in the ring. In the first century, there were more than two million slaves in Italy, perhaps one-third of the entire population. Slaves had no rights: they could be sold, abused, and even killed without consequence. Their testimony was not accepted in court unless exacted under torture. Interestingly, though, slaves who had purchased their freedom or were freed by their masters automatically became citizens. Some freedmen played important roles in the arts—Terence was a freedman; Horace was the son of a freedman—and some even became wealthy, like the character Trimalchio, in Petronius's *Satyricon*. Others were simply cast out when they had no further use. There was a series of slave revolts, the most significant of which was led by the Thracian gladiator Spartacus in 73. He attracted 150,000 followers and defeated three separate Roman armies sent against him over a period of two years. The revolt was finally and brutally suppressed in 71 by the Roman general Marcus Licinius Crassus, who crucified six thousand recaptured slaves along the Appian Way to Rome from the Bay of Naples.

In 60, Crassus became the junior partner with Pompey and Caesar in an unofficial political alliance that became known as the First Triumvirate. Pompey, a protégé of Sulla, had led armies in Sicily, in North Africa, in Spain, against pirates in the Mediterranean, and against Mithridates in Asia Minor. Caesar's military successes came first in Spain and, later, in Gaul and Britain. Both men thirsted for power beyond the one-year consulship. Sulla had planned to eliminate Caesar, but after others successfully interceded on Caesar's behalf, Sulla warned them: "Never forget that the man whom you want me to spare will one day prove the ruin of the party which you and I have so long defended. There are many Mariuses in this fellow Caesar."[6]

The First Triumvirate retained republican forms, seeking election to various positions or operating through proxy officials, but effectively exercised control for a decade. Crassus was killed fighting the Parthians (from ancient Persia) in 53. Caesar spent ten years conquering Gaul, including a foray into Britain. He amassed tremendous wealth, which he used to pay for massive building projects in Rome as well as games and spectacles on an immense scale. He treated his troops with equal generosity, and they were fiercely loyal to him. Caesar intended to return to Rome as consul in 50, but, with Pompey's backing, the *optimates* in the Senate blocked his election. On January 10 in the year 49, Caesar and his men crossed the Rubicon River, a small stream in northeastern Italy that marked the southern limit of his command, and marched on Rome. Once over the river, he noted, there was no turning back: "The die is cast."[7] Civil war had begun.

PAX ET PRINCEPS[8]

Rather than face Caesar at Rome, Pompey fled to Greece, where he gathered an army. Many prominent Romans—including Cato the Younger, Marcus Junius Brutus (descendant of the Brutus who led the revolt against Tarquinius Superbus), and, for a time, the philosopher and statesman Marcus Tullius Cicero—rallied to his standard. But Caesar defeated Pompey at Pharsalus in Greece in 48. Pompey fled to Egypt, where he was beheaded by a young pharaoh hoping to curry favor with Caesar. When the remnants of Pompey's army were cornered in North Africa, Cato—an emblem of stern, old-fashioned Roman virtue—became a martyr to the fallen republic by committing suicide rather than accepting the clemency of Caesar. Cicero, Brutus, and Brutus's brother-in-law Gaius Cassius were less particular; they sought pardons and quickly accommodated themselves to the new order, while quietly nursing their grievances and ambitions.

Scattered fighting continued until 45. After dallying with Cleopatra in Egypt, Caesar returned to Rome and had himself declared dictator for life, which turned out to be not very long. He was stabbed to death in the Senate house on the Ides (15th) of March 44 by a group of senators that included the recently forgiven Brutus and Cassius. Cicero, while not part of the plot, heartily applauded the result.

Despite great hopes, the death of Caesar did not bring back the republic. Instead, it brought a second civil war. Following the unfortunate example of Pompey, the assassins fled to Greece to raise an army. Meanwhile, Octavian, Caesar's great nephew and adopted heir, formed an alliance with Caesar's chief lieutenant, Mark Antony, and one of Caesar's other supporters, Marcus Aemilius Lepidus. This Second Triumvirate defeated the republican forces at Philippi in October 42. Roman freedom and the republic both died at Philippi. Brutus and Cassius now followed the example of Cato and committed suicide. Cicero was murdered along with half the Senate in a widespread proscription.

Octavian and Antony narrowly avoided open conflict with one another by agreeing to split the empire in a treaty forged at Brundisium in 40: Octavian took the west and Antony the east (in a foreshadowing of the later split into an eastern and a western empire). Lepidus, who was largely an afterthought, accepted North Africa. Antony moved to Alexandria, where he fell in with the adaptable Cleopatra and adopted the luxurious and decadent ways of an Eastern potentate. Octavian quietly, steadily, and efficiently enhanced his own power base. He found an excuse to dismiss Lepidus in 36, but he bided his time in dealing with Antony.

A third civil war started in 32 and was quickly ended the following year at the Battle of Actium. There, Octavian (in reality, his brilliant general Agrippa) defeated the combined forces of Antony and Cleopatra at sea. Octavian hounded them back to Egypt, where first Antony and then Cleopatra committed suicide rather than be taken captive. In 27, Octavian was declared emperor under the name Augustus Caesar, though he preferred to be considered the *princeps*, or "first citizen." He kept some republican formalities but maintained strict control over all aspects of government. Most welcomed the change. After sixty years of almost constant and devastating strife—the Social War, the struggles between Sulla and Marius, the slave revolts, and three civil wars—Rome was at peace. Although he secured Spain to the west, pushed Roman influence to the banks of the Rhine and the Danube to the north, and annexed Judea to the east, the Augustan Age was largely a time of consolidation and improved administration rather than new conquests. The army was loyal to him, and his vast personal wealth secured the support of the people.

Under his liberal patronage and remarkable tolerance of free speech, up to a point, poetry and the fine arts flourished. Rome itself became the true world capital. Augustus restored temples and put up imposing buildings at a rapid pace. In a rare boast, he claimed that he found Rome a city of brick and left it a city of marble. Augustus also sought to correct what he viewed as the lax, urban morals of contemporary Rome. He rewarded marriage and the begetting of children. He passed laws against adultery (which he himself apparently honored in the breach). Both his daughter and his granddaughter were banished for serial adultery (and, at least in the latter case, political intrigue).

Augustus also emphasized the importance of religious rituals and customs and tried to restore the old Roman gods to a prominent place in everyday life. Perhaps this was simply a method of crowd control—as were his grain doles and public games—but he certainly understood that he himself would be worshipped as a god after his death. In many places outside Rome, he was deified, and temples were built to him even while he was still living. The month of July had been named for his great-uncle, Julius Caesar (who had reformed the calendar); August soon bore his name. Yet he himself lived modestly on the Palatine Hill.

Augustus's most important legacies were order, stability, prosperity, and the *Pax Romana* that descended over much of the known world and lasted for centuries. When Augustus died in 14 CE, at the age of seventy-six, he expressed his "hope that these foundations which I have established for the State will abide secure."[9] They did, indeed, abide for many years, but there were three variables he could not control.

First was biology. Augustus left no son, and although he determined his own successor, he chose badly, and others after him chose even worse. Rome became a cauldron of violent intrigue. Second was the Praetorian Guard of nine thousand, which he established to serve as a highly compensated private army to protect and serve the will of the emperor. Soon, emperors would serve the will of and even be chosen by that army. Third, surprisingly enough, not everyone welcomed the *Pax Romana*. The Caledonian chieftain Calgacus famously remarked in 86 CE, *Auferre, trucidare, rapere, falsis nominibus imperium; atque, ubi solitudinem faciunt, pacem appellant* ("They plunder, they butcher, they ravish, and call it by the lying name of 'empire.' They make a desert and call it 'peace.'").[10] Conquered peoples rebelled, while Persian warriors from the east and Germanic tribes from north of the Rhine and the Danube constantly probed the boundaries of the empire, eventually finding and exploiting the weak spots as internal dissension weakened external defenses.

DECLINE AND FALL

Rome in the several decades after Augustus became a grotesque and gruesome soap opera, wonderfully presented in Robert Graves's two historical novels, *I, Claudius* and *Claudius the God*. More contemporary—but still compulsively readable— accounts are offered by the Roman historian Tacitus in his *Histories* and *Annals*, and by Suetonius in *The Twelve Caesars*, which consists of compact biographies starting with Julius Caesar and ending with Domitian, who was emperor from 81 to 96 CE. With respect to each emperor, Suetonius sought to present not only an account of his reign but also "a brief description of his appearance, personal habits, dress, character, and conduct in peace and war."[11]

After Augustus, the royal bloodlines became almost comically complicated and were further compounded by adoption, murder, incest, and usurpation. What follows is a simplified version. Augustus married his only child, Julia, to his accomplished general and close friend, Agrippa. She gave Agrippa three sons (Gaius, Lucius Caesar, and Agrippa Postumus) and two daughters (Julia and Agrippina) before his untimely death. Gaius and Lucius Caesar both died young, one from natural causes and the other in battle. Agrippa Postumus, for reasons that are still unclear (some suggest mental instability, others that he too actively intrigued for the throne), was banished to a remote island and killed at the time of the emperor's own death.

With no direct male heir, Augustus had adopted Tiberius Claudius, his wife Livia's older son from a prior marriage. (As a result, the line of emperors from Julius Caesar to Nero are commonly known as the Julio-Claudians.) Tiberius, who had an outstanding military career and showed promise as an administrator, was emperor from 14 to 37. He had two potential heirs: his real son, Drusus, and his adopted son, Germanicus (the son of Tiberius's younger brother, also named Drusus, and the grandson of Mark Antony and Augustus's sister, Octavia). But both Drusus and Germanicus, who Suetonius notes was "everywhere described as having been of outstanding physical and moral excellence,"[12] died in suspicious circumstances. They may have been poisoned. Tiberius withdrew to the island of Capri, where he grew increasingly paranoid, vicious, and debauched. He was murdered in 37 by Caligula (Germanicus's surviving son), who was paranoid, vicious, debauched, and also totally mad. Suetonius suggests that Tiberius deliberately chose to inflict Caligula on Rome: "I am nursing a viper for the Roman people," he boasted.[13]

Caligula engaged in open incest with his sisters and planned to have his horse named as consul. He also exhausted the state treasury and imposed heavy and unpopular taxes to replenish it. He, his wife, and his young daughter were all murdered by the Praetorian Guard in 41, which then proclaimed Claudius as emperor. Claudius, the younger brother of Germanicus, limped and stuttered and had limited control over his limbs. He was thought to be mentally deficient, and yet he was at least a better emperor than his predecessors and successors, in addition to being an accomplished historian. Claudius's biggest mistake was to marry Agrippina (the daughter of Agrippina the Elder and Germanicus and hence great-granddaughter of Augustus) and adopt her son, Nero, the great-great-grandson of Augustus. Claudius also had a surviving son of his own by way of an earlier marriage, as well as two daughters, one named Octavia for her great-grandmother. The boy was named Tiberius Claudius Germanicus but was later given the name Britannicus in honor of his father's military triumph there in 43, in which he extended the inroads made by Julius Caesar. Nero married his stepsister, Octavia, and was named co-heir with his stepbrother and now brother-in-law, the young Britannicus. Agrippina grew tired of Claudius and fed him poisoned mushrooms to advance her son. Nero, in turn, poisoned Britannicus and became sole emperor. Apparently Nero managed to evade the royal food tasters by having the poison added when Britannicus called for a hot drink to be cooled.

Notwithstanding this brutal seizure of power, Nero's reign (54–68) was at first both stable and prosperous. He was advised by, among others, the philosopher and tragedian Seneca. But he eventually tired of being controlled. When a carefully staged boating accident failed of its desired effect, Nero had his mother, Agrippina, murdered with special instructions that she be stabbed in the womb. He also got rid of his advisors. Seneca was at first allowed to retire but later was ordered to commit suicide; so too was Seneca's nephew, the promising young poet Lucan, as well as the satirical novelist Petronius. Nero proved recklessly extravagant, as well as arbitrarily cruel. In 64, a great fire destroyed much of the capital. Nero began building a massive palace on the ruins, leading to the rumor that he himself had set the fire in order to clear the ground. Some even alleged that he stood on the balcony of his former residence, playing the lyre and singing about the sack of Troy while the city burned. In fact, he was probably not even in the capital at the time. But, in an effort to divert blame, Nero began to persecute an obscure and tiny sect whose members followed the teachings of a Jewish prophet, one Jesus of Galilee, born in the reign of Herod and crucified by order of the Roman governor Pontius Pilate in 36. His followers called him Christ (the Messiah) and themselves Christians. The persecution of Christians, starting with the execution of Paul of Tarsus, was perhaps Nero's only lasting legacy. Faced with almost certain deposition by several of his commanders, Nero killed himself in 68. The line of succession of the Julio-Claudian emperors thereby came to an end.

Nero was followed by three insignificant and quickly deposed rival commanders, each supported by a different segment of the army (Galba, by the troops in Spain; Otho, by the Praetorian Guard; and Vitellius, by the troops in Germany), who seized but could not hold power. Titus Flavius Vespasianus (r. 69–79), a commander of the army in Asia, finally established some stability. The so-called Flavian dynasty extended to his sons Titus (r. 79–81) and Domitian (r. 81–96). But that dynasty ended when Domitian was murdered by his own guards; he was so thoroughly hated that even his wife joined in the conspiracy. The only lasting legacy of the Flavians was the massive amphitheater in Rome, the Coliseum, which was completed in 80. Their reign also saw the eruption of Mount Vesuvius in 79, which buried and thus preserved the cities of Pompeii and Herculaneum.

The remarkable fact is that the Roman Empire itself was mostly unaffected by eight decades of these disastrous rulers. There were some internal revolts—in Britain, North Africa, Gaul, and Judea—but they were mostly over taxes and were readily suppressed. Augustus had indeed established firm and enduring foundations.

A group that Machiavelli would call the "Five Good Emperors" followed the Flavians: Nerva (r. 96–98), Trajan (r. 98–117), Hadrian (r. 117–138), Antoninus Pius (r. 138–161), and Marcus Aurelius (r. 161–180), the warrior-philosopher. They helped to restore the finances, maintain order, and solidify the borders. After Nerva's overthrow of Domitian, he and his successors determined succession by adoption, rather than birth, and each chose wisely. Hadrian toured the empire from Britain and Spain in the west to the Black Sea, the Red Sea, and the Euphrates River in the east, a continuous expanse never to be matched again. Edward Gibbon, the great eighteenth-century historian of Rome's decline and fall, concurred in Machiavelli's judgment on this interlude:

> If a man were called to fix the period in the history of the world during which the condition of the human race was most happy and prosperous, he would, without hesitation, name that which elapsed from the death of Domitian to the accession of Commodus [the tyrant son of Marcus Aurelius].[14]

The Western Roman Empire lasted almost three hundred years after Marcus Aurelius, but the ancient world in literature and thought effectively ended with his reign. Forces of dissolution, both internal and external, continued to build. The empire increasingly and perhaps unwisely relied on hired barbarian troops to expel barbarian invaders. Borders began to fray, particularly in Germany and Asia Minor. Diocletian (r. 284–305) started the process by which the empire was divided into west and east. He also commenced in 303 what became known as the Great Persecution, during which the Christian church was outlawed in large portions of the empire.

The persecution eased following Diocletian's death, and the emperor Constantine—who founded Constantinople on the site of ancient Byzantium—converted to Christianity in 312. Constantine donated vast amounts of money to build and support churches. But, as leaders who mix religion and politics are wont to do, Constantine started to get involved in doctrinal disputes. He established the Nicene Creed in 325 as the fundamental statement of Christian faith, transforming what had been a cult into an institutional religion. He also began persecuting perceived heretics, such as the Arians (who portrayed Christ as a separate, lesser divinity).

By 395, the split between the western and eastern empires, with separate emperors for each, was largely complete. So were the seeds of the western empire's destruction. Visigoths, pressured by roving bands of Huns from Mongolia, poured across the Danube and were allowed to settle in Roman territory in 376. They were promised funds for their support (really, a bribe to remain peaceful). When the funds did not materialize, the Visigoth king Alaric led them to sack Rome in 410. It was not yet the official end of the western empire but certainly was close to it.

Attila united the Huns and invaded Gaul and Italy in 451–52. Rome was saved only by plague, which halted the advance, and Attila himself died the following year. But the aptly self-named Romulus Augustus, the last western emperor, was deposed in 476 by the German chieftain Odoacer. Remarkably, the eastern empire lasted almost another thousand years, until the fall of Constantinople in 1453 at the hands of the growing Ottoman Empire. In the West, the ancient world was at an end, and the Dark Ages had begun.

TEN ROMAN AUTHORS

The ten Roman authors who are the focus of this book were, for the most part, an easy choice. **Plautus (ca. 254–184)** is the father of modern comedy and the first Roman author from whom we have substantial surviving works. His younger contemporary Terence (ca. 195–159) is more appreciated by modern scholars, but Plautus was by far the more popular and productive playwright. Accordingly, although I discuss Terence, my principal focus is on Plautus.

The Epicurean poet **Lucretius (ca. 99–55)** and the philosopher/statesman **Cicero (106–43)** are the towering figures of the republic in crisis. Catullus (ca. 84–54), an important contemporary love poet, is discussed in the chapters on Cicero and Lucretius. Two historians of Rome from this same period, Julius Caesar (100–44) and Sallust (86–ca. 35), are treated in the chapter titled "Tacitus and the Roman Historians," along with Polybius (ca. 200–ca. 118), a Greek who wrote of the Punic Wars.

During the reign of Augustus, the major poets were incontestably **Virgil (70–19)**, **Horace (65–8)**, and **Ovid (43 BCE–17/18 CE)**. The historian Livy (ca. 59 BCE–ca. 17 CE), who shares the romantic sensibility of Virgil and Horace, is discussed in the chapter on Tacitus. Other less significant poets, such as Tibullus (ca. 55–ca. 19) and Sextus Propertius (ca. 48–ca. 16), are considered briefly in the chapter on Ovid. With the death of Ovid, what was known as the golden age of Roman literature came to an end.

During the so-called silver age that followed, I have chosen to focus on **Seneca (4 BCE–65 CE)**, **Plutarch (46–ca. 120)**, **Tacitus (ca. 56–ca. 117)**, and **Marcus Aurelius (121–180)**, the emperor and Stoic philosopher discussed in the final chapter along with the Greek slave **Epictetus (55–ca. 135)**. Plutarch was also Greek and wrote in Greek. But his work on the lives of distinguished Romans and his comparisons between Greek and Roman figures make him essential both to an understanding of ancient Rome and to a treatment of moral thought during the period of empire.

Other writers of the silver age are regrettably afforded little or no coverage. They include Lucan (39–65)—nephew of Seneca, author of an epic poem known as the *Pharsalia*—Martial (ca. 40–ca. 103), creator of the modern epigram, and the satirist Juvenal (ca. 55–ca. 130), who coined the phrase "bread and circuses" to explain how emperors sought to keep the masses in line.[15] The imperial biographer Suetonius (ca. 70–ca. 130) is discussed all too briefly in the chapter on Tacitus. Less than their due is also afforded to Pliny the Elder (23–79), a writer on natural history who attempted to survey all of human knowledge and who was killed when he got too close while studying the eruption of Vesuvius, and his nephew, Pliny the Younger (61–ca. 112), a prolific writer of letters about contemporary politics, life, and morals. The younger Pliny wrote of his uncle, "He believed that any time not devoted to study was wasted."[16] The works of Petronius (ca. 27–66), author of the first great picaresque comic novel, the *Satyricon* (which survives only in fragments); Apuleius, author of another picaresque novel, *The Golden Ass*; and the minor poets Statius and Persius, unfortunately, are not discussed at all.

In order to be faithful to the evolution of Roman thought, I have treated the ten authors in chronological order, based on date of birth. Each chapter can be read as a stand-alone unit. Although Plutarch, Tacitus, and the other ancient historians are usually discussed after authors from the periods about which they are writing, there is enough historical background in the introduction and within each chapter to set the context. Plutarch may have written about early Romans and Tacitus about the Augustan Age, but their sensibilities are quite different from the periods they studied. Since the intellectual milieu changed rapidly, I preferred modest repetition to anachronism. Readers new to Roman history may find the abbreviated chronology at the back of the book useful in placing authors and events in context.

I defer any discussion of explicitly Christian writers to my next book, which I plan to begin with the gospels and follow such authors as Augustine and Boethius through Dante and Chaucer to the first stirrings of the Renaissance.

CHAPTER 1

PLAUTUS AND ROMAN COMEDY

The first known literary work in Latin was a translation of the *Odyssey* by the Greek-born tragedian Livius Andronicus (ca. 284–ca. 204). At the time, translation was itself a new art form. Before Andronicus, Latin readers either learned Greek or went without; after Andronicus, Roman schoolboys could read Homer in their native language. Thus began a tradition of the translation, adaptation, and gradual transformation of Greek originals into the foundations of a distinctly Roman literature. Rome absorbed Greek culture as aggressively and systematically as it conquered the Mediterranean world.

For us, Roman literature begins with Titus Maccius Plautus (ca. 254–184). The tragedies of Andronicus and Quintus Ennius (239–169), based on Greek models, were more highly regarded and praised in antiquity than Plautus's comedies. So, too, was Ennius's epic poem of Rome's founding, the *Annales*. Yet Plautus is the first Roman author whose writings have survived. We possess twenty complete or nearly complete comedies by Plautus and six by his successor, Publius Terentius Afer (ca. 195–159), known to us as Terence.

It is ironic, and yet somehow fitting, that Roman literature begins with comedy. When we think of Rome, we think of brutal conquests abroad and ruthless power struggles at home. During the era of Plautus and Terence, Rome was fighting for its very existence in the Punic Wars that ultimately resulted in the complete destruction of Carthage, Rome's rival for hegemony in the Mediterranean. The Roman Republic was dominated by aristocratic senators, most particularly Marcus Porcius Cato (ca. 234–149), known as Cato the Censor, who enforced the principal Roman virtues—valor (*virtus*), dutifulness (*pietas*), industry (*industria*), and frugality (*frugalitas*)—within a strict and repressive social hierarchy that was

31

heavily dependent upon slave labor and that treated women and children as just another form of property.

The military and political spheres are wholly absent from the plays of Plautus and Terence. They wrote domestic comedies modeled on the "new comedies" of Menander and his Hellenistic contemporaries. Plautus and Terence, too, set their plays in Greece, mostly at Athens. Romans viewed the Greeks then rather as the Germans view contemporary Greeks today—as querulous, duplicitous, pleasure-loving, profligate, and lazy—and Plautus in particular capitalizes on those stereotypes. And yet his characters regularly remind the audience that the Athenian setting is just a pretense. What we are seeing is a portrait of contemporary Romans at home; not the official, stern portrait of the Roman military republic, but a funhouse mirror in which everyday life is distorted and turned topsy-turvy.

Plautus caricatured and subverted the standard roles in Roman society (fathers and mothers, sons and lovers, soldiers and slaves). He presented these types in their most ridiculous aspect, and through the catharsis of laughter, the rigors of Roman life became more palatable. Plautus humanized the Romans and in doing so brings us closer to them. Just beneath their serious and pompous exteriors lie the endless possibilities of farce. Indeed, it is precisely the serious, pompous exteriors that so readily lend themselves to farce. Without Plautus, ancient Rome would be intolerable. His comedies make clear that the order, hierarchy, and strict obedience touted by Rome could not have been so absolute. After Plautus, it is impossible to take the Romans as seriously as we might otherwise have done. In the process, we find that we cannot take ourselves quite as seriously either.

Plato argued in the *Laws* that it will be "impossible to understand the serious side of things in isolation from their ridiculous aspect."[1] Plautus helps us to understand the full complexity of Roman life and how ridiculous each of us becomes when we attempt to squeeze ourselves into an established mold. Like the Romans, we play various parts in the world, but we have little self-knowledge. We publicly tout the virtues of courage, piety, industry, and frugality, but our behavior reveals a wide gap between what we say and what we do. We propose to control ourselves and our fate. But in his comedies of mistaken identity—of children lost at birth and identical twins: real, imagined, and divine—Plautus shows that error, deception, and chance are the gods that truly rule our existence. Plautus used farce to illuminate the underlying human condition. He found wisdom in laughter.

THE GOLDEN AGE OF ROMAN DRAMA

The first dramatic performance in Rome took place in 240, one year after the end of the First Punic War (264–241). It was a tragedy written by Livius Andronicus, based on a Greek model. Andronicus was considered the father of Roman literature by Cicero, Horace, and others, and the period from 240 to the death of Terence in 159 was by common consent the golden age of Roman drama. Yet only the merest fragments of Andronicus's many plays survive. Equally unavailable to us are the plays of Gnaeus Naevius (ca. 270–ca. 201), who tested the bounds of censorship with a comedy that mocked one of the aristocratic families in Rome. Rome was not Greece, and Naevius did not enjoy the immunity of Aristophanes. Personal criticism of the powerful was forbidden, and he was thrown into prison. Naevius wrote two more plays in prison and was then released after apologizing for his indiscretion, but a second episode led to his banishment and eventual suicide. Quintus Ennius had a more successful and discreet career, but no greater luck with the survival of his plays. Even his great epic poem on the founding of Rome, which was mandatory reading for all Roman schoolboys, survives only in fragmentary lines.

Thus, Roman drama, as we know it, consists of the plays of Plautus and Terence. Plautus was born in Umbria circa 254. He was a free citizen and moved to Rome as a young man, where he started working in the theater. He is said to have lost an early fortune in a shipping venture, and he began writing plays himself at the age of forty-five, during the Second Punic War (218–201). He was both prolific and wildly successful, writing, by one account, as many as 130 plays before his death in 184. It is difficult to determine the precise number, however, because revivals were common after his death, and many plays were falsely attributed to him in order to attract a larger audience. The scholar Marcus Varro (116–27) made a definitive list of twenty-one plays in the first century BCE, which became the standard edition of Plautus into the Middle Ages. One of those plays—*Vidularia*, alphabetically the last and hence the most exposed in the manuscript—survives only in fragments, but the others are all or mostly intact.

Plautus's successor, Terence, was born in Carthage circa 195 (though possibly as much as ten years later) and brought to Rome as a slave at a young age. Showing early promise, he was educated and later freed, ultimately finding acceptance among the aristocratic circles of Rome. He wrote only six plays before his untimely death in 159, but all have survived. Terence was better appreciated after his death than during his lifetime. As the prologue to his *Hecyra* plaintively explains, his audience—used to the raucous fun and verbal pyrotechnics of Plautus—was inclined to drift off to watch boxers, gladiators, and tightrope walkers, rather than enjoy his more intricate plots, more subtle characters, and more complex moral dilemmas.[2] Although Terence's plays are perhaps better read than performed, they have been justly praised for their realism, their elegance, and the sympathy displayed throughout. A famous line from *The Self-Tormentor* has often been applied to Terence himself: *homo sum: humani nil a me alienum puto* ("I am a man: nothing that is human is foreign to my interests.").[3]

Together, the twenty-six plays of Plautus and Terence provide the foundations of modern comedy. Shakespeare, Ben Jonson, Congreve, Molière, and innumerable others modeled plays on Roman originals. Even the television situation comedy, with its domestic setting and constant puncturing of pretensions, is a direct descendant of Roman comedy.

Roman comedy itself, of course, drew upon the increasing knowledge of Greek culture that came with Rome's expanding influence over the Mediterranean world. But it combined those Greek sources with more native forms of farce, music, and jesting that were already common in Rome. And it adapted its blend of comic elements to the domestic concerns of contemporary Romans. Social and political criticisms were never explicit. And, as Naevius discovered to his sorrow, personal attacks would not be tolerated. But otherwise, there was extraordinary license—enabled by the distancing convention of setting the plays in Athens—to mock and subvert what was otherwise held inviolate.

Four festivals each year were devoted to theater, though athletic contests, gladiatorial shows, and circus acts were also part of the mix. The plays—both tragedies and comedies—were commissioned by public officials. Small troupes of five or six actors, run by a producer/lead actor, would purchase the play from its author and then perform it, with individual actors (always men) playing more than one part. The troupes were paid out of public funds, and no charge was made for admission. Performances might be repeated, but without further remuneration for the author.

The stages in this era were temporary wooden structures, open to the air, with limited seating. We know little of early staging beyond what we can imaginatively reconstruct from the words themselves. For Plautus in particular, much depended on the actors, and there was clearly ample leeway for stage business. The costumes were Greek, and the players likely wore masks (which would have helped with the doubling of parts and were undoubtedly crucial to portraying the identical "twins" in plays such as *Amphitryo* and *The Brothers Menaechmus*).

The stage was very large, as wide as sixty yards. Overhearings, asides, and soliloquies were common. Every thought was spoken aloud, and eavesdropping by others on stage was crucial to several plays. The action was continuous. The plays were not divided into acts and scenes by their authors; such notations are the product of later editors such as Varro. As a result, there were no changes in scenery. The standard setting was a street in front of two or three houses, and players would either emerge from one of the houses or from the wings: by convention, stage left (to the spectators' right) led to the town and stage right to the country. Occasionally, "indoor" scenes would be enacted by bringing furniture out of one of the houses. But, for the most part, any offstage action was simply described by the characters through monologue or dialogue.

There are three distinctive features of Plautus's plays that warrant mention. First, the plays usually contain prologues to request the audience's attention and to set the stage for the action to follow. Since Plautus's plots are full of errors, deceptions, and mistaken identities, the comedy frequently depends on the audience knowing in advance what the characters will discover only during the course of the play, such as that the young maiden whom Daemones will protect in the course of *Rudens* (The Rope) is his own lost daughter, captured by pirates and sold to a pimp; or that the gods Jupiter and Mercury have taken the visage of Amphitryo and his slave, Sosia, so that Jupiter can sleep with Amphitryo's wife. The element of surprise is not lost, for the audience doesn't know exactly how the plot will unfold. But the prologues allow for irony without spoiling the fun.

Second, Plautus's characters sing. Indeed, as much as 15 percent of the lines in Plautus are from songs, which makes his plays forerunners of modern musical comedies. Thus, the modern musical adaptation of Plautus, *A Funny Thing Happened on the Way to the Forum*, with Stephen Sondheim's brilliant lyrics, is very much in keeping with the original.

Third, Plautian characters, often the slaves, do not hesitate to remind the audience members that they are watching a play. In monologues, they will report the course of events offstage; in soliloquies, they will reveal their emotional states.[4] In *Amphitryo*, when the god Mercury, disguised as the slave Sosia, rushes on stage, ordering everyone to stand aside, he stops to explain to the audience:

Well, I suppose a god can order people about if a slave can; you know—those slaves in a comedy, who rush in to announce that the ship has just come in or the angry old man is on his way. I'm here on Jupiter's orders and business, so I can surely expect people to get out of my way and let me pass.[5]

In *Casina*, Cleostrata decides to forgive her husband "to keep a long play from running any longer."[6] Plautian characters will even enlist the audience's assistance, as when Euclio pleads with his audience to reveal who has stolen his gold, and suggests that someone from the audience may have done so. This shattering of the dramatic illusion, so carefully cultivated by other playwrights, hearkens back to Aristophanes and underscores Plautus's point that we are always performing, in life as well as on the stage, insofar as we try to fulfill the roles in society to which we are born or bred or into which we have somehow drifted.

FOUR "EDIFYING" PLAYS

Plautus died in 184, the same year that Cato became censor. As Plutarch explains,

> Ten years after his consulship, Cato stood for the office of censor, which was indeed the summit of all honour, and in a manner the highest step in civil affairs; for besides all other power, it had also that of an inquisition into every one's life and manners. For the Romans thought that no marriage, or rearing of children, nay, no feast or drinking-bout, ought to be permitted according to every one's appetite or fancy, without being examined and inquired into; being indeed of opinion that a man's character was much sooner perceived in things of this sort than in what is done publicly and in open day.[7]

Cato sought to inquire into and regulate precisely those domestic affairs that were the province of comedy. The censor had many fine qualities—he was austere, exacting, uncompromising, parsimonious, and litigious—but humor does not appear to have been among them. He despised the growing influence of Greek culture, which he considered effeminate and luxury-loving. He sought to reverse the decline of traditional Roman morality through sumptuary laws that limited expenditures on dress, the numbers of guests at dinner parties, and other signs of personal indulgence. As the first writer of Latin prose, his history of Rome expunged all references to prominent individuals in order to celebrate the collective triumph.

Given that Rome was constantly at war during his lifetime—the Punic Wars were only the most prominent—Cato's severity is perhaps understandable. But so too—and certainly more appealing—is Plautus's countervailing levity. Plautus mocks narrow, simplistic moralizing of the sort at which Cato excelled. Yet his plays have a moral force of their own. Indeed, several are deliberately structured to explore traditional Roman virtues, albeit with a twist. We will briefly discuss four of these "edifying" plays.

A Three-Dollar Day is full of Catonian moralizing. The elderly Megaronides opens the action with a dire warning: "There is a plague of wickedness rife in this city, destroying all the laws of morality; indeed most of them are by now a dead letter, and while morality withers wickedness flourishes like a well-watered plant."[8] Another old gentleman, Philto, offers a series of Polonius-style nostrums to his son, prefacing them with the injunction, "Oh, it makes me weep to think I should have lived to see such a generation. . . . Stick to the good old ways, my boy, and do as I tell you."[9] Even the slave Stasimus laments, "Law has about as much control over morals as parents have over their children!"[10]

The occasion for such pronouncements is the profligate, luxury-loving, foolishly generous Lesbonicus, who has squandered the family fortune in the absence of his father, Charmides. Lesbonicus has even sold his family's house to fund his riotous living. The new owner, Callicles, was charged by his friend Charmides with watching over the young Lesbonicus. Megaronides accordingly reproaches Callicles not only for letting Lesbonicus go to ruin but also for hastening the process by giving him ready money for the house and then profiting from the exchange. Yet Megaronides, despite his moral certainty, is completely mistaken.

When Charmides left Athens to secure his fortune overseas, he told Callicles that he was leaving a treasure of gold in the house, but charged him to keep the secret from his son, Lesbonicus, lest the son spend the gold. Accordingly, when Lesbonicus decided to sell the house, Callicles stepped in to buy it in order to preserve the gold. Challenged by Megaronides, Callicles explains that he could not both do the right thing and avoid public suspicion. "My conscience is in my own keeping; but as for suspicion, that's something in another man's mind."[11] Callicles prefers to take the right action even if it brings social condemnation.

Not all the other characters feel the same way. Lysiteles wants to marry Lesbonicus's sister and is willing to forgo any dowry to do so. Lesbonicus, however, refuses because such a course would put him in the wrong. He prefers to sell his last remaining asset, the family farm, to provide the dowry so that he might salvage his pride. Lysiteles will not accept a dowry; Lesbonicus will not give his sister without one. "It's no favour to do something for a person against his will," explains Lesbonicus.[12] "I'm perfectly clear as to what I ought to do; I am in my right mind; I know what public opinion is and I intend to respect it, and nothing you can say will prevent me." One wants to play the loyal, generous friend; the other would be the noble brother and penitent spendthrift. Each reproaches the other for a false show of virtue. They reach an impasse and all but come to blows. The welfare of the sister is altogether forgotten.

Callicles resolves the dilemma with a fake letter from Charmides that purports to send money to provide a dowry for his daughter—a dowry Callicles will himself furnish out of the hidden treasure. Comic complications ensue when Charmides himself arrives home and intercepts the letter. But the play ends happily. Lysiteles marries the now properly dowried sister, and Lesbonicus obtains his father's forgiveness and agrees to marry Callicles's daughter and "as many more as you like to mention, father."[13] Charmides explains that "one penance is enough for one man."[14] But Callicles interjects, "Not for him it isn't. A hundred wives would be no more than he deserves for all his misdeeds."[15]

Despite this conventional ending, with an already-tired joke about difficult wives and long-suffering husbands, the play grapples with the question of where virtue lies and with the gap between public morality and private action. So, too, in a quite different way does *The Pot of Gold*, which involves another hidden treasure, buried under the hearth by the grandfather of Euclio, the current owner of the house. The grandfather failed to tell his own son about the gold. But the hearth god, Lar Familiaris, who provides the prologue, allowed the grandson to find it because of the kindness and attentiveness of Euclio's daughter, Phaedria. Discovery of the gold, however, changed Euclio from a hardworking, self-reliant, parsimonious farmer (a veritable Cato) into a paranoid and miserable miser, blind to the welfare of his own daughter.

Phaedria was ravished on Harvest Night by a drunken young nobleman, Lyconides. She is about to give birth when the play opens. Ignorant of this fact, Euclio betroths Phaedria to his rich neighbor, Megadorus, who wants to marry a girl of modest means and modest demeanor. "Let her bring me her virtue and good name," he says; "that's dowry enough."[16]

Megadorus sends cooks to the house of Euclio to prepare the marriage feast, and Euclio, fearful that his gold will be discovered, takes it away for safekeeping. But a slave of Lyconides overhears Euclio talking to himself about where he will hide the gold and promptly steals it. Lyconides, meanwhile, has confessed his violation of Phaedria to Megadorus, who happens to be his uncle and who urges Lyconides to press his own suit for the girl directly to Euclio.

Euclio, who has just learned that his gold is missing, is in despair. "What has life left for me," he asks, "now I have lost the treasure which I guarded with such loving care?"[17] He is oblivious to the birth pains of his daughter, his true treasure, a short distance away. Lyconides approaches to beg forgiveness for his "wicked deed,"[18] a confession that Euclio immediately assumes concerns his gold, rather than his daughter. The cross-purposed conversation that ensues is strikingly funny, and Molière adapted it for *The Miser*. Euclio's laments, once he learns that both his gold and his daughter are lost, are also echoed in Shylock's cry: "My daughter! O my ducats!"[19]

Lyconides convinces the servant to return the gold to Euclio in exchange for his freedom. Lyconides feels some qualms about rewarding the servant for his theft, and himself benefiting from it, but Megadorus—like Callicles—is no Cato.

> My boy, your scruples do you credit. But if you take my advice, you will trouble your head less, at this moment, about the niceties of strict morality, and more about what is to the best interests of all concerned. After all, what is money, apart from what it can buy? And when was money more harmlessly employed than when used to purchase the happiness and contentment of at least three people at once?[20]

Euclio blesses the marriage and gives the couple the pot of gold as a dowry. "If that money can go where it will do some good," he explains, "I shall be the happiest man in the world, instead of the most miserable, which is what I have been ever since it came into my possession. Day or night, I've not had a moment's peace with that treasure on my mind. . . . Now at last—I'm going to sleep."[21]

Amphitryo is the only mythological play we have from Plautus. It tells the traditional story of Jupiter, his love for Alcmena, and the birth of the Greek hero Hercules. Mercury, Jupiter's attendant god, delivers the prologue. He explains that the play cannot be a comedy, since the gods themselves will appear in it. Yet neither is it a tragedy, since lowly characters, and even a slave, also have a part. Here, Plautus is deliberately tweaking Aristotle, who pronounced that tragedies must present characters who are better than the average, while comedies deal with characters of "the meaner sort."[22] Mercury, in a bow to the importance of stagecraft, insists that he can take a tragedy and "easily make it a comedy, and never alter a line."[23] "I'm a god, after all," he explains,[24] and, indeed, many of the speeches that follow are appropriate to tragedy but rendered comic by their context. In this case, however, he will present a "tragic-comedy" (a term of Plautus's own devising).

The Greek general Amphitryo has been many months at war. In his absence, Jupiter has appeared in the guise of Amphitryo and made love to Alcmena, who is now pregnant with two children, one from Amphitryo and one from Jupiter.

Jupiter is enjoying a final night of pleasure with Alcmena—which he has prolonged by bidding Night to hold in place—before the real Amphitryo returns. Mercury, disguised as the slave Sosia, stands guard outside. He promises to wear a feather in his bonnet, while Jupiter will have a gold tassel on his, so that the audience can tell them from their mortal counterparts.

Sosia comes home to encounter Mercury claiming to be Sosia. It is a remarkable scene, as Sosia confronts himself and suffers a crisis of identity. "I can't understand it . . . I'm sure I'm the same man I always was."[25] "So help me gods, where did I lose myself? Where was I translated? . . . Have I gone and left myself at the harbour by mistake?"[26] With Sosia driven off to find his master so as to reassure himself of his own existence, Jupiter and Alcmena emerge for a tearful parting, as Jupiter (cum Amphitryo) explains that he must rejoin his troops immediately. Alcmena plays the part of the exemplary Roman wife. She loves her husband and sorrows at his absence, but can endure it if he comes back in glory.

> If this is my reward—to see my husband
> Hailed victor, crowned with laurels, borne in triumph.
> It is enough. There is no greater gift
> Than valour. Valour is all. Valour protects
> Our life, our liberty, our health, our wealth,
> Our home, our kith and kin. Valour is all,
> And he hath all that hath it![27]

Yet now, just as she has tearfully reconciled herself to his absence, the real Amphitryo returns, expecting a hero's welcome from, and a passionate reunion with, his wife. Alcmena shows a certain understandable impatience with his return: "What on earth has he come back for, after saying he couldn't stay a minute longer? . . . Well, it's his house; I suppose he can come back if he wants to."[28]

Amphitryo is appalled by her bland reception. She, in turn, is mystified and then annoyed by his claim to have just returned after a lengthy absence. When she explains that they just spent the night together, Amphitryo is outraged and accuses her of infidelity. Alcmena fiercely defends her honor and resolves to leave him for questioning it. "And what is my dowry? Not that treasure which the world calls dowry. What is it if not honour and purity and temperance, fear of the gods, love of my parents, the happiness of my family, and the will to love and obey you, to be good to all good friends and helpful to all honest men."[29]

The play ends happily, of course. Jupiter explains that Alcmena is innocent and has unwittingly borne a child "begotten by me [who] will live to make you famous forever by his deeds."[30] In fact, she bears twins, one the child of Amphitryo, the other Hercules, who immediately demonstrates his godly prowess by strangling two snakes sent by a jealous Juno. Amphitryo accepts the verdict of the gods. But after the play lingers the question that Mercury, disguised as Sosia, asked of Amphitryo: "Who are you, anyway?"[31] It is indeed the perennial question of Plautian comedy. And even Alcmena, clinging passionately to her set role as a faithful Roman wife, is not immune to it.

The question of true identity versus social identity is explored even further in *The Prisoners*, Plautus's penetrating portrait of slavery. Slavery was an accepted, commonplace institution in ancient Greece and Rome, critical to both economies and to the leisure that made their cultural outpourings possible. Even the great philosophers—Plato, Aristotle, Epicurus, Cicero—did not think to question it. Indeed, Aristotle was inclined to treat slavery as a natural condition of inferior beings. Plautus, however, focused on the common humanity of the slave, the cruelty of the institution, and the serendipity that caused one man to belong, not to himself, but to another.

The play revolves around Tyndarus, son of Hegio of Aetolia, who was stolen as a boy by a runaway slave and sold to be a slave to the father of Philocrates in Ellis. Philocrates and Tyndarus have been companions since boyhood. Now they have been captured in a war with Aetolia and sold as slaves to none other than Hegio. Neither father nor son recognizes the other, however. Moreover, Hegio's other son, Philopolemus, was captured in Ellis, and Hegio is looking for leverage to make a trade.

Tyndarus and Philocrates change places, with Tyndarus pretending to be the master and Philocrates the slave. In this way, Tyndarus (as Philocrates) ensures his master's freedom by proposing that Hegio send Philocrates (as the slave Tyndarus) to negotiate the trade with Philocrates's father. Tyndarus (as Philocrates) will remain in Hegio's control until Philocrates (as Tyndarus) returns with Philopolemus. Tyndarus sends Philocrates off with a heartfelt plea:

> Remember this above all: you are being allowed to go home on bail, on my responsibility; I remain here, staking my life on your return. You will not forget me, I hope, as soon as you are out of my sight . . . you will not forget me, left here to slave it out for your sake . . . while you count yourself a free man, breaking your bond, and never giving another thought to your task of saving me by bringing this man's son home.[32]

The plan unravels, however, when Hegio brings home another Elian captive, Aristophantes, who immediately greets Tyndarus by his true name. Oblivious to all signals from Tyndarus and outraged that Tyndarus, a mere slave, is pretending to be Philocrates, the self-righteous and decidedly stupid Aristophantes finally convinces Hegio of Tyndarus's true identity. Furious at the deception, and believing that he has lost his chance to recover his son, Hegio has Tyndarus bound in heavy chains and sent off to the quarries, where he will be beaten, starved, and forced to dig up half again as much as the usual daily quota of stones. The standard comic convention—by which clever slaves are threatened with such harms but never in fact suffer them—is shattered.

True to his word, however, Philocrates returns with the ransomed Philopolemus and with the very slave who ran off with Tyndarus as a child, Stalagmus. Stalagmus, under threat of a whipping, reveals all. Hegio rejoices at the restoration of both his sons even as he sorrows at the inhuman treatment to which he subjected Tyndarus. "To have done so much more, yet so much less, than I had the right to do! My heart bleeds for what I have made him suffer; oh that I could undo what has been done."[33]

Hegio did "so much less" than the law gave him a right to do in punishing his slave; yet he did "so much more" to his son than morality and conscience and affection would countenance. Who is slave and who is free depends upon chance and circumstance. "Man is a thing of nought," the prologue tells us.[34] Unless all men are treated as having value, none have value. Yet Stalagmus is of course shackled with the same chains taken from Tyndarus and threatened with hanging; he will be lucky if he lands in the quarries instead. The bad slave is duly punished and the good slave (who was, in fact, freeborn) is freed and restored to his family. But a sense of injustice and arbitrary wrongdoing remains. The epilogue is decidedly tongue-in-cheek, celebrating "a highly edifying play,"[35] as if the underlying message were not decidedly subversive.

A ROGUE'S GALLERY

The plays of Plautus are full of standard types—characters well known to Roman audiences and referred to even in the prologues by their roles rather than their names. Thus, in *Casina*, the prologue brings onto the stage an old man; his jealous wife; their son; a young girl, abandoned by her mother sixteen years before and now the object of desire of both the father and the son; and two slaves—one acting on behalf of the father and one for the son. After that setup, the plot pretty much unfolds of its own accord. Terence, in his prologue to *The Self-Tormentor*, makes gentle fun of this practice, by hoping the audience will not be disappointed if he presents "a play which doesn't depend on action" and which doesn't involve stock characters such as "a running slave, angry old man, greedy sponger, shameless imposter and rapacious pimp."[36]

Yet Plautus gives a life to his characters that both capitalizes upon and transcends their stick-figure aspects. He shows that we relate to one another, and even to ourselves, as types. But when those established roles are shattered by absence, by chance and circumstance, or by deliberate deception, we no longer know who we are, what we should be, or how we must act. "Who am I, then, if I am not myself?" asked the long-absent Charmides in *A Three-Dollar Day*.[37] The question that confronted Amphitryo upon his return—"Who are you, anyway?"—continues to confront us all.

Plautus's plays, like Shakespeare's, contain a cornucopia of minor, colorful characters: usurers, lawyers, fishermen, and cooks, to name a few. There are men of business, such as Lyco the banker, who explains, after going over his books, "I see I'm rich, if I don't pay what I owe; if I do, I'll be in the red."[38] And there is that curious Roman character, the parasite—the man who would come to dinner—who lives as a hanger-on, to flatter and amuse his patron in exchange for a good meal.

Among the more substantial of the frequent roles is the braggart soldier (*Miles gloriosus*), who strikes heroic poses but is inevitably the butt of ridicule and deception. He is "all boasting and bellowing,"[39] but, like Therapontigonus in *Curculio*, finds he cannot even outface a lowly pimp:

> THERAPONTIGONUS: What's this? A pimp trying to scare me, veteran of
> hundreds of battles? I swear by my sword and shield, my battlefield com-
> rades, if you don't listen to me and hand over the girl, I'll reduce you to
> crumbs the ants can carry away.
> CAPPADOX: I too swear, by my tweezers, comb, mirror, my curling-iron, scis-
> sors, and towel, that your bragging and posturing mean no more to me than
> the woman who cleans my privy.[40]

The pimp or slave dealer (*Leno*) gets an even less sympathetic hearing. Dordalus, in *The Persian*, is tricked into buying a fake Persian slave. He then loses his money and gets a beating as well when the slave's father claims her as freeborn. The pimps in Plautus think nothing of lying and cheating, and, hence, others think nothing of deceiving them in turn. "My tongue hath sworn—the rest is up to me," explains Labrax in *The Rope*.[41]

The courtesan (*Meretrix*) tends to be more formidable. Arena, in *The Little Box*, reproached for prostituting her daughter rather than arranging a marriage for her, protests, "Hey, wait! She's married every day, one man today, / Another one tonight. I never let her sleep alone. / If she didn't marry morning and night, you'd be / Mourning our little family, dead of starvation."[42] Cleareta, the equally hard-nosed madam in *Asinaria*, explains, "The girl who gives it away hasn't got a future."[43]

The two sisters in *Two Sisters Named Bacchis* are charming but wholly mercenary, and their two young lovers are willing to pay any price for love. Planesium, in *Curculio*, says to her hapless young man, "If you love me, buy me; no more questions. Get to work and get the job done."[44] But Phronesium, in the *Truculentus*, is easily the worst (or best) of the lot, juggling three suitors and extracting from each as much money as possible, and even pretending to give birth in order to fool the solider Stratophanes into believing the child is his own. The suitors know that Phronesium is interested only in money and cannot be trusted. But they are captives regardless and willing victims whose "passion is to ruin [themselves] with passion."[45] As the maid Astaphium explains, "A lover is like an enemy town . . . the sooner he can be sacked, the better it is for his mistress."[46]

The *Senex* (old man) is a staple of every Plautian comedy. As a father, the *Senex* is sometimes indulgent—recognizing his own youthful passions—and sometimes severe. In the latter case, his son usually wishes him dead or away, when he is not trying to extract money from him. Either way, the fathers are easily duped and get very little of the respect ordinarily considered their due. "I'd sooner sell my father," announces Philolaches in *The Ghost*,[47] than not have sufficient money for his lover. Better still: "If only someone would come and tell me my father is dead. I'd disinherit myself and make her his legatee."[48] Sometimes the *Senex* is a would-be lover (*Senex amator*) and rival to his own son, a position that is exposed as altogether ridiculous. Thus, in *Asinaria*, the father aids his son in buying for a year the favors of the girl whom the boy loves by tricking money out of his wife, but then he expects to share the girl's favors. The son cheerfully agrees, but the father is dragged away by his now-watchful wife.

The *Matrona* (wife) is often the butt of bad jokes and asides that have little or nothing to do with the plot. Thus, in *A Three-Dollar Day*, the otherwise serious and upright Callicles urges his offstage wife to "pray that our house may be ever righteous, happy, fortunate, and blessed," and then adds "and that your death may be not long delayed."[49] In an early version of a Henny Youngman routine ("Take my wife—please!"), Callicles and Megaronides each congratulate the other on the health of his wife, and each bemoans the same ("Is she well?" "Too well.") and offers to exchange.[50] When Cleostrata uncovers and thwarts her husband's attempted infidelity in *Casina*, she remarks, "You shall be the death of me!" and her husband responds (again, in an aside), "If only it were true!"[51]

The Brothers Menaechmus is the story of two long-separated, identical twins. The brother who arrives new to town is constantly mistaken for his counterpart by the latter's wife, mistress, and slave. The play was the model for Shakespeare's *Comedy of Errors* (though Shakespeare doubled both master and slave, as in *Amphitryo*). Here, too, the wife who tries to stop her husband's infidelity and the constant giving of presents to his mistress gets little sympathy, even from her own father: "I've told you dozens of times; it's your business to try to please your husband, not keep spying on everything he does, always wanting to know where he's going and what he's up to."[52]

But not all the wives in Plautus are portrayed as "untamed shrews."[53] Alcmena is noble and faithful. The two sisters in *Stichus* are married to two long-absent brothers who have gone off in an effort to repair their failing fortunes. The wives resist their father's urging that they divorce the men. As one explains,

> I'm perfectly happy with my beggar,
> And will love him as much in our current poverty
> As I did in our earlier prosperity.
> It was to the man, not his money, you married me.[54]

They are vindicated when reunited with their again-wealthy husbands. And even Cleostrata, in *Casina*, is a heroine of sorts. Her husband lusts after the beloved of his son. But the son is not present to protect his own interests. As the prologue explains, "That son who went abroad won't make it back today. / Plautus changed his mind and dropped him from our play, / by washing out a bridge that lay upon his way."[55] Cleostrata arranges to substitute her son's male slave for the girl in what would become a classic "bed trick" that teaches the straying husband and lecherous father a lesson and preserves the girl for her son.

The *Adulescens* (young man) in Plautus is invariably in love and tends to be fatuous, dim-witted, hapless, and penniless. "Fixed and fettered by love, that's me," proudly announces Pistoclerus in *Two Sisters Named Bacchis*.[56] Alcesimarchus, in *The Little Box*, dissects his situation more minutely: "I'm blown / This way and that, torn to pieces, riven, driven, / With my head all groggy and my thoughts all foggy. / Where I am, there I am not; where I am not, / There my soul is sure to be—an omniplex / Of conflicting desires!"[57] Lysiteles is less kind about his friend Lesbonicus in *A Three-Dollar Day*: "Love . . . robs him of all sense and sanity, makes him detest what's good for him and run after what is forbidden, covet what is scarce and despise what is common. . . . You're lost and damned once you take lodgings at Love's hotel."[58] That is also the theme of Lydus, Pistoclerus's tutor, who calls the door to the Bacchis sisters' house a door to hell and warns, "No one comes this way unless he has abandoned all hope who enters here."[59] Dante would later adapt that line (in Italian) for the sign displayed at the entrance of his inferno.[60]

Money has no inherent value for the *Adulescens*; it is to be squandered on pleasure and his *Uirgo* (young girl). Indeed, the squandering is itself a form of pleasure. "I agree he bought a girl while you were away," explains Tranio in *The Ghost*. "I agree he borrowed money; and I can tell you he spent every penny of it. Has he done anything that isn't done in all the best families?"[61] How to get and keep the girl—without money and in the face of an intransigent older man, whether father, soldier, or pimp—is the constant dilemma of the young man, a dilemma he himself can never solve without help.

That is where the clever slave (*Servus callidus*) makes his entrance. The slave in many of Plautus's comedies drives the action as if he were himself the author of the play. He confronts his young master's dilemma by weaving a manic web of illusion and deception that sweeps everyone from the order of everyday life into a chaos of his own devising. At his best—Pseudolus (*Pseudolus*), Tranio (*The Ghost*), Palaestrio (*The Swaggering Soldier*)—the slave is, as Gian Biagio Conte, the foremost expert on Latin literature, explains, "a true demiurge, an artist of fraud, a poet who stages the event before everyone's eyes."[62]

The slave is lively, talkative, and impudent. Tranio's words in *The Ghost* are the hallmark of the clever slave: "They say the best lie is a thumping lie. That's it—I'll say what the gods put into my mouth."[63] The clever slave is equal to any occasion. Epidicus, in the play that bears his name, is typically reassuring: "We'll find a way. I'll get us out of this. Don't worry, pal; I've got a thousand plans."[64] Even when Tranio recognizes that he has "no hope of keeping the master in the dark indefinitely and there's no one I can . . . shift the blame on to,"[65] he is not at a loss. "A man that's not able to show a brave heart in a tight place is not worth two pins."[66] So "come what may, I must carry on and try to cause more confusion."[67]

Yet the slave's creation, like Tranio's, often gets away from him, as events spin out of control, and the ultimate triumph and restoration of order depends heavily on *Tyche* (luck or fortune), in ways the slave himself could not have foreseen: mistaken identities are resolved; lost children (kidnapped long ago and sold as slaves) regain their parents and their rightful place in society; and severe fathers recollect their own youthful follies and relent. The obstacles are overcome, but often as much by chance as through the cleverness of the slave.

Regardless, for a brief time, the social hierarchy is turned upside down, and the lowest person socially (the slave) becomes the most important figure in the drama.[68] Master is suppliant, relying on the superior resources of the slave. "Tranio," says Philolaches, "I commit all my life and hope into your hands."[69] The slave orchestrates, and the master meekly follows the score. Occasionally, a master will assert himself with threats of whippings and other punishments, including banishment to the quarries or the mill. But the slave rarely takes the threats seriously, and they are not carried out (except in *The Prisoners*). He enjoys an impunity that is lacking in everyday life.

THREE COMIC MASTERPIECES

The Swaggering Soldier begins not with a prologue but with a short vignette to introduce Captain Pyrgopolynices, the dreadful, wonderful, antihero of the play. This *Miles gloriosus* is accompanied by his attendant, Artotrogus ("Here, at his master's heels, close to his hero, his brave, his blessed, his royal, his doughty warrior— whose valour Mars himself could hardly challenge or outshine.").[70] Pyrgopolynices struts and primps in front of his house in Ephesus, while prompting Artotrogus for a steady outpouring of ever more outrageous praise. Even more than martial prowess, Pyrgopolynices relishes amatory conquests: women falling at his feet, unable to resist his handsome mien. "It really is a bore to be so good-looking," he purports to lament.[71] Clearly, though, the soldier is no hero to his valet, whose main object is to fill his own stomach by keeping his master's ears stuffed with nonsense. Artotrogus punctuates his plaudits with asides such as, "If anyone ever saw a bigger liar or more conceited braggart than this one, he can have me for keeps."[72]

Pyrgopolynices leaves the stage to gather troops for the king, while the real hero, the slave Palaestrio, comes to tell us the plot. This delayed prologue is ingenious, giving us just enough of Pyrgopolynices to whet our appetites for his downfall and to sustain our interest through the plot twists that follow before Pyrgopolynices reappears. Palaestrio explains that he was once the servant to a young man in Athens, Pleusicles, who was enamored of a young woman named Philocomasium. While

Pleusicles was away on a diplomatic mission, Pyrgopolynices arrived in Athens and began to curry favor with Philocomasium's mother, bringing her wine and jewels and delicacies. Abusing the confidence thus gained, he abducted the young girl and brought her to Ephesus. Palaestrio immediately set sail to alert his master but was captured by pirates who (you guessed it!) gave him to Pyrgopolynices. Accordingly, both Palaestrio and Philocomasium are slaves and prisoners in the same house. But, together, they conspired to send word to Pleusicles, who has now arrived in Ephesus and is staying next door at the home of Periplectomenus, a friend of Pleusicles's father. Palaestrio contrives to cut an opening through the common wall so the lovers can meet.

Palaestrio now has two dilemmas to resolve. The first is relatively straightforward. Sceledrus, a servant charged with guarding Philocomasium, has climbed upon the roof and seen Philocomasium embracing Pleusicles. Accordingly, Palaestrio must trick the slave into believing that he didn't see her.[73] This he readily achieves by concocting a story that Philocomasium's mother and identical twin sister have just arrived in Ephesus with the latter's lover, and are staying with Periplectomenus. By slipping back and forth between the houses through the secret passage, Philocomasium— appearing from one house as herself and from the other as her sister, Honoria— utterly befuddles Sceledrus, who tries to guard each door in turn. In the guise of Honoria, she feigns complete ignorance of Sceledrus and Palaestrio, prompting the usual Plautian identity crisis. "It looks as if . . . we've mislaid ourselves somewhere," groans Sceledrus. "She says she doesn't know either of us."[74] Palaestrio fuels these fears by responding, "We must get to the bottom of this, Sceledrus, and find out whether we are ourselves or somebody else's selves."[75] Sceledrus's response to this conundrum is to retreat to the cellar, where he stupefies himself with his master's wine.

Palaestrio must now design a second ruse "for trimming Captain Curlylocks and assisting our loving friend in his design of abducting and possessing his beloved Philocomasium."[76] For this feat, a more complex play-within-the-play is required, and Palaestrio sets about casting the additional parts. He of course enlists Pleusicles, though with some reluctance, for as he explains to Periplectomenus, "My master, let me tell you, is a man wrapped up in an elephant's hide; he has no more intelligence than a stone."[77] "I am aware of that," the old neighbor responds. Periplectomenus, a perennial bachelor, is in turn charged with recruiting a woman "in the business"— "as attractive as possible, and as young as possible"[78]—to pretend to be his wife. Periplectomenus happens to know just the person, Acroteleutium, who readily agrees to fool the captain. "Who doesn't know that public pest, that big-mouthed menace to women, that scent-reeking hairdresser's delight?"[79]

With the proper cast assembled, Palaestrio, in the classic reversal of slave turned master, carefully rehearses and directs each of the actors in his or her part. "A pleasure to command such loyal subjects," he notes.[80] To Pleusicles he is particularly insistent: "Try to keep your mind on your instructions!"[81] Palaestrio's plan is for Acroteleutium, using her maid Milphidippa as a go-between, to pretend to be enamored of Pyrgopolynices and to seek his favors. It is not a fair fight. As Acroteleutium explains, "When we pool our talents for mischief-making, there will be no fear of our being outwitted by anyone else's low cunning,"[82] and certainly not by the gullible captain. Pyrgopolynices is thoroughly taken in and ready to believe that Acroteleutium as well as her maid are both hopelessly in love with him. His only concern is how to get Philocomasium out of the way so that he may enjoy his new love. Palaestrio advises him to take advantage of the fact that her sister and her mother have just arrived in Ephesus looking for her. He can send her home. But, to avoid any hard feelings, Palaestrio suggests that she be allowed to keep her jewelry and all the other gifts Pyrgopolynices has given her.

Philocomasium, who, unlike her lover, is no fool, plays her part to perfection, resisting and feigning great sorrow at the prospect of being parted from such a master. She ultimately gives way, but only after Pyrgopolynices also agrees to let her take Palaestrio with her. It is now Palaestrio's turn to lament such a bitter blow. "How can I ever live without you, master?" he asks.[83] Indeed, Palaestrio—apparently feeling upstaged by Philocomasium—rather overplays his hand. He almost convinces Pyrgopolynices not to part with him and must backpedal furiously. Pleusicles then arrives disguised as a ship's captain, who says they must sail immediately. Unable to control himself, Pleusicles repeatedly embraces Philocomasium and all but gives the game away. But eventually they depart with all of Philocomasium's baggage in tow and with Palaestrio enjoining the captain to remember this day and who served him best.

Pyrgopolynices then enters Acroteleutium's house to embrace his new love, only to be trapped by Periplectomenus and his servants, who give him a sound beating and even take away the costume (tunic, cloak, and sword) that identified him as a soldier. When Sceledrus arrives from the harbor to report that the alleged "ship's captain" was really Philocomasium's lover, the humiliation is complete. "Now I see what an ass they've made of me," the great captain laments, "and it was Palaestrio, the double-dyed villain, that lured me into the trap."[84]

Pyrgopolynices is absurd. His comic counterpart to the *hubris* of the heroes of Greek tragedy makes his downfall inevitable. He has none of the wit and humor of Shakespeare's Falstaff, the greatest of his many successors in the role of braggart soldier and would-be lover. All the laughter is at his expense, and justifiably so. Yet one cannot help but feel, at the end of this play, a faint stirring of the hollowness that awaits us after Hal's mock but anticipatory repudiation of his companion in *Henry IV, Part I* ("FALSTAFF: . . . banish plump Jack, and banish all the world! PRINCE: I do, I will.").[85] This, too, is intended by Plautus. He presents us with a delightful play-within-the-play. But the moral for Palaestrio's comedy, which Pyrgopolynices gamely attempts to draw (". . . justice has been done. Serve all lechers so . . ."[86]), is not the moral of Plautus's play.[87] After the laughter settles, Plautus leaves us not with a clear moral but rather with a lingering feeling of unease and an uncertainty as to whom we are and whom we want to be.

Pseudolus was one of Plautus's last plays, presented in 191, when he was about sixty-three years old. Cicero cites it in his short book *Cato the Elder: On Old Age* as an example of the "supreme satisfaction" of remaining intellectually keen and productive.[88] It is said to have been Plautus's own favorite, and for good reason. In it he revels in his virtuosity as a showman.

All the standard Plautine types are on steroids in this play. Calidorus, the young man hopelessly in love with his Phoenicium, is the epitome of the hapless, penniless, and mindless lover. When told he must shape up and be sensible, he protests: "That's absurd. A lover must behave like a fool or there's no fun in it."[89] Ballio, the pimp who owns Phoenicium, relishes his own role as the villain and enjoys the abuse showered upon him. When another character says to him, "The man I'm looking for is a lawless, shameless, faithless, godless sinner," he readily responds, "Must be me. I answer to all those epithets."[90] Simo is the stern father who conveniently forgets that his own youthful "sins and extravagances were numerous enough to be distributed round the whole population, one per man."[91]

But it is Pseudolus, the eponymous hero, who self-consciously steals the show of his own creation. He is the apotheosis of the clever slave, "a living marvel,"[92] or, less kindly, "the most audacious rogue alive."[93] He is that tightrope walker who spoiled spectators for the plays of Terence. Pseudolus's mission, of course, is to get Phoenicium away from Ballio and drop her into Calidorus's waiting lap. But Ballio has already sold her to a captain for 2,000 drachmas. He was paid 1,500 on account, and will hand over the girl when the captain's factotum arrives with his seal and the remaining 500.

The task seems almost too easy for Pseudolus. Accordingly, he immediately makes it harder, like a magician who loads himself with chains and locks and dangers to make his escape ever more marvelous. When confronted by Simo, he readily admits that he plans to get from him the 2,000 drachmas needed to buy

Phoenicium. "Well I am warning you; take care," he advises.[94] "That's my advice; take care. Take care. Before the end of this day, you'll be giving me money with those very hands." Then he explains to Simo that he will also get Ballio to hand over the girl. Simo foolishly bets Pseudolus 2,000 drachmas that he cannot accomplish such a feat, and rushes off to warn Ballio. Even the audience is warned directly by Pseudolus "to be on their guard . . . against me . . . and not to trust a word I say."[95] Everyone is now prepared for his tricks, but Pseudolus is unconcerned. "Lord love you, you know what I can do when I wave my magic wand, what a dust I can stir up when I set about it."[96]

But when Calidorus presses to know his plan, Pseudolus puts him off. "I'll tell you when the time comes. No point in going over it twice—plays are long enough as it is."[97] In fact, he doesn't know yet what his plan might be, as he confesses as soon as he is alone.

> Pseudolus, you haven't a clue, which end to start weaving or where to finish off. Well, after all, when a poet sits down to write, he has to start by looking for something which doesn't exist on this earth, and somehow or other he finds it; he makes a fiction look very much like a fact. That's what I'll do; I'll be a poet; I'll invent two thousand drachmas, which at present don't exist anywhere on earth.[98]

Having deliberately equated himself with the author of the play, Pseudolus gives himself time to compose the script and then returns to the stage to announce to the audience that he has a foolproof plan. But we never learn what that plan was, because it immediately changes when Harpax, the captain's factotum, arrives on set. "I shall have to change my tactics now," Pseudolus explains. "This alters the situation. This'll have to be dealt with first and all my previous plans shelved."[99]

Pseudolus pretends to be Ballio's servant. Harpax gives him the letter bearing the agreed-upon seal. But he won't give up the 500 drachmas except directly into Ballio's hands. So Pseudolus sends him off and says he will call for him when Ballio returns. He then induces a friend of Calidorus to loan him 500 drachmas and a servant to dress up in the part of Harpax. The friend, like a good producer, underwrites the drama and provides the actors and costumes. The self-conscious theatricality is maintained when Calidorus asks Pseudolus how he got the sealed letter, but Pseudolus declines to answer. "Well, look, this play is being acted for the benefit of the audience; they know what happened because they saw it happen. I'll tell you about it some other time."[100]

The friend's servant proves a match for Pseudolus himself and readily obtains

Phoenicium from Ballio, who is mightily relieved to have the girl off his hands so that he is now impervious to whatever tricks Pseudolus might devise. He even boasts of his success to Simo and spontaneously offers to pay him 2,000 drachmas if Pseudolus succeeds in fooling him. Harpax then arrives and is assumed by both to be an imposter sent by Pseudolus. When the truth is finally unraveled, Ballio is thoroughly vanquished: he loses the girl and must repay the captain as well as his bet to Simo. Calidorus has his Phoenicium, and Simo owes 2,000 drachmas to Pseudolus. The two—master and slave—go off to drink together, but when Simo suggests they invite the audience, Pseudolus demurs. "My God, no! They never invite me anywhere; I'm not inviting them. But . . . if you will please to show your kind appreciation of our company and our play . . . we will invite you here again . . . tomorrow."[101]

Plautus and Pseudolus are one. Watch what I can do to marvel and delight you, they tell the audience. However clearly you are warned and closely you are watching, I can still "bring some new kind of surprise on to the stage."[102] Yet there is also a frank acknowledgment of the role of chance and luck in any success. However clever the plans, circumstances may change them and require an ad lib response; however well written the play, the spontaneous interpretations of the actors and the circumstances of its presentation are (as Terence found to his sorrow) critical to success. With flexibility and cleverness and considerable good luck, we may win through. But, 2,200 years before Nassim Taleb, Plautus cum Pseudolus emphasized that we are, all of us, fools of randomness.

> The best laid plans of a hundred skilled men can be knocked sideways by one single goddess, the Lady Luck. It's a fact; it's only being on good terms with Dame Fortune that makes a man successful and gives him the reputation of being a clever fellow; and we, as soon as we hear of someone striking it lucky, we admire his shrewdness, and laugh at the folly of the poor devil who's having a run of bad luck. For that matter, we're all fools though we don't know it, for running so hard after this or that, as if we could possibly tell for ourselves what's good for us and what isn't. We lose the certainties while seeking for uncertainties; and so we go on, in toil and trouble, until death creeps up on us.[103]

The Rope, Plautus's most enchanting and enchanted play, is about holding onto those certainties as to a lifeline. The play clearly influenced Shakespeare in both the mood and the setting of The Tempest. Daemones, an elderly Athenian, is living in exile with his wife, Daedalis, on the remote and rocky coast of Cyrene. Like

Prospero, he is now embittered and a recluse, but his exile and lost fortune were due—so the god Arcturus, who speaks the prologue, explains—to no fault of his own but rather to his good nature and excessive generosity.

Daemones and his wife also lost a young daughter, who was captured by pirates and sold long ago to a trafficker in women. Her name is Palaestra, and a tempest will soon bring her to shore near where the couple lives. Palaestra is loved by Plesidippus, a young man of Athenian birth who is living in Cyrene. He paid a deposit for her to the pimp Labrax. But, convinced by a fellow rogue that he could get more for girls in Sicily, Labrax set sail with Palaestra, her friend Ampelisca, and a trunk containing all his wealth. Arcturus sent the storm to wreck both the ship and Labrax's plans.

Palaestra and Ampelisca spend a perilous night in a small lifeboat before being cast into the water and separately making their way to shore. Palaestra's first words, like those of Odysseus far from home on Calypso's islands, are words of lamentation.

> What have I done
> That the gods should treat me thus? Cast me ashore
> Like this in an unknown country? Oh poor me,
> Is this what I was born for? What a reward
> For my good life! Have I ever been undutiful
> To gods or parents? If so, then I deserve it,
> And I can bear it. Have I not been as careful
> As anyone could be, never to offend them?
> Then what a cruel, wicked, and unjust
> Thing you have done to me, gods. If this is the way
> You treat the innocent, how will the guilty learn?[104]

There is irony in her heartfelt lament. The god Arcturus claims to have sent the storm precisely to help Palaestra and to punish Labrax. And that will be its ultimate effect. But the ready moral—that the gods reward virtue and punish vice—is not fully borne out in the play.

Palaestra's acute distress is relieved by her joyful reunion with Ampelisca, who speaks for both when she says, "Oh now I can touch you I really want to live again."[105] But one source of sorrow remains. Palaestra had a little box with tokens that would make her known to her parents. Labrax took it from her and locked it in his trunk, which is now, presumably, at the bottom of the sea.

The two girls seek refuge at the nearby shrine of Venus, where they are given food and shelter by the elderly priestess and caretaker. But Labrax, who has also struggled ashore, tracks them there and attempts to drag them from the shrine and claim them as the sole means of rebuilding his fortune. They are rescued by Daemones and his beefy servants, who subdue Labrax and set him under guard. But Daemones does not recognize his long-lost daughter.

Plesidippus arrives and drags Labrax off to the magistrate for having stolen his deposit, while the two girls are taken into Daemones's cottage. A fisherman and slave of Daemones, named Gripus, then comes on stage pulling a heavily loaded net. In it is the trunk of Labrax, which he has fished from the sea. Trachalio, the slave of Plesidippus, grabs one end of the rope and offers to help, for a price. He will not reveal the catch to the true owner if Gripus will split the contents with him. Gripus, a sturdy but simple fellow, is outraged. The two trade comical legalisms over ownership and whether a trunk caught at sea is the equivalent of a fish. They nearly come to blows, but the smaller Trachalio holds to the rope with all his might, and they ultimately appeal to Daemones as arbitrator.

At this point, Trachalio reveals that he wants nothing in the trunk but a little box of trinkets to restore to Palaestra so that she might find her parents. "O my beloved parents," she explains, "this is you in here. Here I have kept all my help and hope of finding you."[106] Gripus suspects a fraud. "As soon as I show it to them, they'll immediately say they recognize it, naturally."[107] But Palaestra identifies each object in the little box sight unseen, including a little gold sword with her parents' names inscribed upon it: Daemones and Daedalis. "The gods are good to me!" exclaims Daemones, as he embraces his daughter. "Not to me they aren't!" grumbles Gripus.[108]

Once her identity is established, the denouement is swift. Palaestra will marry Plesidippus. Ampelisca and Trachalio will both be freed and allowed to marry one another. Even Labrax will have his trunk restored, minus 2,000 drachmas—1,000 to pay for the freedom of Gripus, and the other to be returned to Labrax in exchange for the freedom of Ampelisca.

Daemones draws a straightforward moral: it is better to be poor and honest and favored by the gods than to have any part in immoral dealing. Gripus is less sure.

> I've heard actors in comedies spouting that sort of stuff, telling people how to behave, and getting applause for it. But I never heard of any of the audience behaving any the better for it, after they got home.[109]

The play is full of ready morality, often misused by characters to justify their actions.[110] In the end, Labrax maintains most of his wealth, despite his misdeeds. Gripus may have his freedom but will continue his hard life as a fisherman. The reunion of Palaestra with her parents and her beloved Plesidippus seems more a product of chance and circumstance than of divine plan, notwithstanding the prologue. And whether that reunion makes up for the long, intervening years of loss and sorrow is itself unclear. The morality of the universe is more complex than simplistic maxims will allow. We must cling to what Pseudolus called "the certainties," as Trachalio clings to the rope and Palaestra to her little box. In an uncertain world, our ties to one another are our only real support. If there was a moral to the play, it was spoken by Ampelisca: "Oh now I can touch you I really want to live again."

Cicero, Horace, and others would look back to the era of Cato the Censor as a lost golden age of the republic in which men were governed by a simple, straightforward morality. What they should really have mourned was the loss of Plautus to keep them honest and fully human.

CHAPTER 2

MARCUS TULLIUS CICERO, THE GOOD CITIZEN

The Roman state stands upon the morals and men of old.
—Quintus Ennius (239–169)[1]

Marcus Tullius Cicero lived in the waning days of the Roman Republic. He was unrivaled as an orator and as a prose stylist. He wrote extensively on political and moral philosophy. He served with distinction in the highest offices of the state, despite his modest background. He was intimate with Gnaeus Pompey and Gaius Julius Caesar as well as Marcus Brutus and Gaius Cassius. He mentored the young Octavian, the future Augustus Caesar. He courageously attacked Mark Antony in a series of philippics that defended liberty against tyranny, a defense all the more stirring because it would cost him his life. By the time of Cicero's murder, at the age of sixty-three, the republic had been torn apart by corruption and civil strife, and the age of the emperors was at hand. Yet no one had fought harder to preserve that republic and the ideal of civic virtue captured so well by the poet of the early days of Rome, whom Cicero called "our noble Ennius."[2]

Cicero is still read today for many reasons. He is an invaluable source of historical information about the late republic. His extensive and candid correspondence (of which 914 letters survive) and his fifty-eight extant speeches paint a remarkable portrait of contemporary Roman life and political developments. He was also an inexhaustible synthesizer and adapter of Greek philosophy, preserving large swaths of Hellenistic thought that would have perished otherwise and developing much of the terminology that dominated philosophy in the Middle Ages. Indeed, the Latin words he invented for Greek concepts (such as *probabile*, *moralis*, *qualitas*, and *moderatio*) are integral parts of our vocabulary today.

But those are reasons for historians and scholars to read Cicero. We should read him because his vision of man as a free citizen of a republic is still compelling and still fragile, threatened today by some of the same forces against which he struggled. We owe to Cicero a very modern conception of the *dignitas* of each individual, whose sphere of autonomy—whose ability to fashion his own life and safeguard his possessions—is preserved against both tyranny and mob rule by a balanced constitution designed to keep competing forces and interests in check. He was the first and perhaps greatest proponent of the rule of law as a means of securing life, liberty, and property, at a time when all three were constantly in peril.

We owe to Cicero, in short, the foundations of humanism and the liberal tradition in social and political thought. Cicero was called "the Father of his Country" for his success in preserving the republic against the Catilinarian conspiracy.[3] In many ways, he is the father of our country as well. His writings reached through the centuries to guide our founders.

But Cicero was more complex and more interesting than this pedigree alone would suggest. He emphasized not just the natural rights of individuals to pursue their own version of happiness but also the inherent duties we have as citizens and the ideals of justice that must animate any legitimate constitution. For Cicero, to study philosophy was to learn how to live. With his own peculiar blend of stoicism and skepticism, he explored personal virtue, the good life, friendship, old age, and death. But civic virtue was always his preeminent and overriding concern. Indeed, he did not separate at all the sphere of the moral from the sphere of the political. Cicero presented a unified vision of what we owe to one another and to the state. He admitted no gap between the two, any more than he admitted a gap between his own political and intellectual pursuits. His writings continued and complemented his public service. Cicero was, first and last, in both his life and his death, a citizen of the ideal Roman Republic for which he longed.

THE NEW MAN

Cicero was born on January 3 in the year 106, in Arpinum, a town about seventy miles from Rome, which was at that time a journey of two to three days. His family was part of the local aristocracy, but that provincial distinction was of limited value in Rome. He was not of the highest rank, the *nobiles*, the Roman nobility from whom senators and consuls were traditionally drawn. Rather, Cicero qualified as one of the *equites* (equestrians), a growing upper-middle class with substantial landed capital. That would prove enough for his purposes. His family was linked by ties of marriage to some of the ruling families in Rome. Another resident of Arpinum, Caius Marius, had translated his success as a soldier into the consulship, which he held an unprecedented seven times, notwithstanding his lack of nobility. Cicero had no military talent, but he would fight his way along the path trod by Marius with the power of his oratory.

By the time of Cicero's birth, the Roman Republic was already in crisis. In theory, the balanced constitution protected all interests. Two consuls, drawn from among the senators, were elected by the people and held office for a single year. They provided executive authority with the advice of the full Senate. The Senate established policy, but legislation was passed by the people at the popular assembly, whose interests were further protected by tribunes with critical veto power over any action that was considered contrary to the interests of the people.

Yet the Roman state was still dominated by, and run largely for the benefit of, the narrow group of *optimates*, and other citizens chafed under their rule, particularly as the spoils of empire increased. Voting took place by groups, varying greatly in size, with more groups reserved for the upper class. Moreover, because all voting was in person, those nominal citizens who lived outside Rome were effectively disenfranchised.

The Gracchi brothers, Tiberius and Gaius, who were tribunes in 133 and 123–122, respectively, sought enhanced power by appealing to the people directly with a land-redistribution scheme. Known as *populares*, these politicians introduced an element of instability into the political system. Tiberius, the elder Gracchus, was assassinated at the instigation of *optimates*, but popular reforms were still pressed by his younger brother and by later politicians. It was this uneasy mix of reactionary *optimates* and restless, disenchanted *populares* that provided ambitious *equites* such as Cicero with their opportunity to serve the republic. Yet it would also provide an opening for unscrupulous military commanders—Cornelius Sulla, Caesar, and Octavian—seeking personal power and wealth.

Cicero received a thorough education in Greek classics as well as in law, oratory, and debate. He studied in Rome alongside Caesar (to whom he was distantly related) and Titus Pomponius, subsequently known as Atticus for his long sojourn in Attica, the city-state formed around Athens. Atticus was Cicero's longest and closest friend, with whom he corresponded regularly. The two men form an interesting contrast: Cicero, with his driving ambition and partisan preferences; Atticus, with his life of leisured wealth and an easy, apolitical disposition that left him on good terms with all sides, while committed to none.

The Rome of Cicero's day had a population of several hundred thousand, a quarter of whom were slaves. Riots and assassinations fueled by disputes between *optimates* and *populares* led to such chaos that, in 82, the military commander Sulla brought his troops into Rome (which had no police force or other means of keeping order) and established himself as dictator. He published a proscription, a list of thousands of prominent citizens whose lives and property were forfeited to the state. Sulla restored order in the capital and rolled back a number of earlier reforms so as to increase the power of the Senate at the expense of the tribunes and the popular assembly.

In 80, several of Sulla's allies falsely accused Sextus Roscius of parricide as a means of appropriating his property. Cicero, at the age of twenty-six, was the only lawyer willing to take the case, and his successful defense led to many subsequent commissions. Cicero worried about reprisals from Sulla—and even found it prudent to visit Athens for six months, where he began his close study of Greek philosophy—but none were forthcoming, and, when Sulla resigned the dictatorship in 78, the republic was restored.

This change opened the way for Cicero's own political career. Age limits for officeholders marked a natural progression on the ladder of political ambition in Rome, and Cicero sought and attained each office—*quaestor* (age thirty), *aedile* (thirty-six), *praetor* (thirty-nine), and *consul* (forty-two)—at the earliest possible age.

He was among the twenty *quaestors* (tax collectors) elected in 75, and he was one of two sent to oversee the collection of taxes in Sicily. There, to the shock and delight of the Sicilians, he behaved honestly, without demanding illegal commissions or accepting illicit bribes. Political offices, particularly those positions overseeing the vast holdings of the empire, were often used largely as a means of self-enrichment, a form of corruption Cicero deplored. In 70, he successfully prosecuted Verres, a notoriously corrupt former governor of Sicily. The case established him as the greatest advocate of his day. The poet Catullus called Cicero "silver-tongued among the sons of Rome" and "a prince of lawyers."[4]

A lawyer could not accept pay directly, but clients were expected to show their gratitude through legacies and other gifts. Cicero grew wealthy and built a number of country homes, most famously at Tusculum, outside Rome. As a former *quaestor*, Cicero was automatically enrolled as a senator for life, and there he debated the issues of the day with his roughly six hundred fellow senators. His speeches were applauded, and his biting quips—to which he was addicted, sometimes to his own peril—were both celebrated and feared. He married Terentia, who came from a prominent family, and they had a daughter, Tullia (from the feminine form of his middle name), and later a son named Marcus. Cicero built a beautiful house on the Palatine Hill, the most fashionable area of Rome, just above the Forum where he argued in the courts and debated in the Senate.

The loyalty he had won in Sicily was highly useful when he was elected *aedile* in 69. The four *aediles* oversaw the capital city, including the upkeep of temples and buildings, the food supply, and the presentation of public games. His contacts in Sicily ensured that he always had adequate supplies of grain and adequate funds to put on gladiatorial contests and chariot races.

In 67, at the age of thirty-nine, Cicero became one of the eight *praetors* who carried the symbols of *imperium* (the sovereign power of the state over the individual in matters of war and the enforcement of the laws) and who acted as judges in the courts and administrators of provinces. Cicero finished his praetorship in 66 and sought the consulship a little more than two years later, after the required waiting period had expired. There were six candidates, but Cicero won easily with the most votes of anyone. It was a remarkable achievement for the young lawyer. Not only was he the first "new man" (i.e., nonmember of the hereditary aristocracy) elected to the highest office in at least three decades, but he did it with limited connections and no military experience. Cicero talked his way to power.

The consulship, for which only senators were eligible, lasted a single year, and it was rare for any individual to hold it more than once, Marius notwithstanding. The consuls could veto any proposals brought before the Senate, and, in political emergencies, a consul might assume a temporary dictatorship for a maximum of six months. But the powers of the position were limited largely by the desire of the senators to preserve their own prerogatives and to prevent any one among them from seizing too much power. There were no political parties, but there were political spoils, and they were jealously guarded. Bribery of voters was widespread, and ex-consuls often sought lucrative governorships to replenish their depleted coffers.

Cicero's fellow consul had precisely that agenda and hence agreed to stand aside in exchange for a rich governorship after the end of his term, leaving Cicero, in effect, the sole consul. He tried to strike a balance between the *optimates* and the *populares*, and was accordingly mistrusted by both. Throughout his career, Cicero was a proponent of moderate reform to relieve the tensions of a highly stratified society. He was also a fierce opponent of corruption and the abuse of power. He was, from the perspective of more than two thousand years, touchingly naive.

But he was also a tough and decisive consul when he needed to be. Lucius Sergius Catilina (Catiline, in English), twice defeated in his own efforts to become consul, tried to launch a coup in 63 and have Cicero and leading members of the

Senate assassinated. Cicero, with the help of informants, ferreted out the plot, presented convincing evidence of the conspiracy to the Senate, and had five leading conspirators arrested. (There were no prisons in Rome, so the conspirators were held under guard at the houses of individual senators.) Catiline fled the capital and tried to raise an army. Cicero convinced the Senate to put the five conspirators to death without trial. Catiline's army then largely dissolved, and he was easily defeated and killed. It was for these actions that his contemporary, Marcus Porcius Cato—commonly known as Cato the Younger to distinguish him from his great-grandfather, Cato the Censor (234–149)—dubbed Cicero *Pater patriae* ("the Father of his Country"). But Cicero had little chance to bask in his glory. The Catilinarian conspiracy proved to be just one act in a larger, unfolding drama. Within a few years, Cicero himself was in exile and under a sentence of death.

The true threat to the republic was posed not by Catiline but by Pompey and Caesar. Cicero feared Pompey less than he feared Caesar, and he tried to convince Pompey to seek power by constitutional means. But Pompey ultimately allied with Caesar and with Licinius Crassus, a former supporter of Sulla, who had suppressed the slave revolt led by Spartacus. Crassus was no friend of Cicero, for Cicero had accused him of being part of the Catilinarian conspiracy. Pompey, Caesar, and Crassus reached a secret agreement in 59 to support each other and exercise complete control in Rome. Thus was formed the so-called First Triumvirate, which lasted for a decade, until it dissolved into civil war.

The triumvirate instituted various popular reforms, including the distribution of free grain. They also made calculated use of violence through local political "clubs," which were little more than gangs of thugs that could sway affairs in the absence of any police force. They maintained some semblance of republican government, seeking "election" to various positions or operating through proxy officials. Even Cicero was slow to realize the threat posed by the three. But, ultimately, he publicly attacked the triumvirate as inconsistent with republican principles. They tried to co-opt Cicero with various offers of high office, but he refused them all.

The triumvirate exacted its revenge through the indirect medium of Clodius Pulcher. Clodius and his sister Clodia (who was both celebrated and excoriated by the infatuated Catullus, and with whom Clodius himself was rumored to be in love) were famous in Rome for their licentious behavior. Clodius was once discovered in Caesar's house disguised as a woman during a sacred festival for women only (a case of life imitating Aristophanes's *Women at Thesmophoria Festival*). Apparently, he had designs on Caesar's wife. Caesar dismissed the allegations as absurd but divorced his wife regardless, with the famous remark: "Caesar's wife must be above suspicion."[5] Clodius was prosecuted for sacrilege, and Cicero testified against him by refuting his claimed alibi. Clodius successfully bribed the jury and escaped conviction, but he and his sister were thereafter the objects of a number of barbed quips from Cicero.

Once Cicero publicly attacked the triumvirate, Caesar, with the blessing of Pompey and Crassus, supported Clodius as tribune in 58. Clodius promptly brought charges against Cicero for putting the Catilinarian conspirators to death without trial. Cicero was even attacked in the streets by Clodius's thugs. He fled the city at night and was condemned in absentia. His goods and some of his houses were confiscated, including his house on the Palatine Hill, which was razed and replaced by a temple. Cicero settled in Thessalonica, where he wrote despairing letters second-guessing his decision to flee and reproaching himself for not having the courage to commit suicide. "Neither practical wisdom nor philosophical teaching," he wrote to his brother, Quintus, "is sufficiently strong to be able to endure such great sorrow."[6]

But Clodius proved a difficult and recalcitrant ally for the triumvirate. Riots and open fighting were common in Rome. Pompey decided to back Cicero, after having done nothing to help him before; in the end, Caesar agreed to do the same. Accordingly, Cicero was recalled and returned in 57 to great acclaim from the Roman people. Clodius himself was eventually murdered in a pitched street battle, and Cicero successfully defended the alleged murderer.

At this point, Cicero reached an accommodation with the triumvirate. It was not his finest hour, but his acquiescence may have been necessary to preserve his life. He spent more time on literary and philosophical pursuits, as he had urged himself to do two years earlier in a letter to Atticus:

> Why do these [contemporary political] issues preoccupy me, when I am eager to abandon them, and to devote all my energy and attention to philosophy? This, I declare, is my intention. I only wish that I had done it from the outset. But now, having learnt by experience how empty are the pursuits I considered glorious, I plan to take account of all the Muses.[7]

Cicero accordingly turned his thoughts from the decayed republic of his day to the ideal republic of his imaginings. Between 55 and 51, he produced a series of major works: *On Oratory* (*De Oratore*), *The Republic* (*De Republica*), and *The Laws* (*De Legibus*), the latter two ambitiously named after works of Plato.

Yet Cicero could not let go of the idea that noble service to the republic (such as his own) should be accompanied by great fame and an honorable retirement, and he tried to create such a reality for himself. As Plutarch explained, Cicero "was always excessively pleased with his own praise, and continued to the very last to be passionately fond of glory; which often interfered with the prosecution of his wisest resolutions."[8] Cicero even urged a fellow writer to compose an epic poem celebrating Cicero's consulship. When that failed, he wrote one himself, *On His Own Times*, which occasioned much ridicule but, fortunately for Cicero, has not survived. Tacitus acidly wrote: "Caesar and Brutus also wrote poetry—no better than Cicero, but with better luck, for fewer people know that they did."[9]

DE REPUBLICA (THE REPUBLIC)

We possess only about a quarter of the full text of *The Republic*. We would not have even that much but for a much-tattered manuscript discovered in the Vatican archives in 1820. Before then, only fragments and one discrete section had survived. We now have most of books 1 and 2, along with bits and pieces of the next three books and a significant portion of book 6.

The work is written in dialogue form, and, as in Plato's *Republic*, the conversation begins on a festival day and involves multiple generations who discourse upon the nature of justice and the ideal state. The principal speaker is Publius Cornelius Scipio, who conquered Carthage in 146 to end the Third Punic War. (His grandfather by way of adoption, Scipio Africanus, defeated Hannibal in 202.) Scipio was in many ways Cicero's ideal citizen and ideal man. He was a respected thinker as well as a statesman and a soldier. He exercised great military power but was content to operate within the confines of the constitution, serving twice as consul. The other participants are also figures from Rome's past—the "wisest and most distinguished of our countrymen" at that time, Cicero calls them[10]—and the multigenerational dialogue serves as a passing on of wisdom and the traditions of good governance.

The dialogue is set in 129, following the aborted reforms and assassination of Tiberius Gracchus. The Roman Republic would suffer a steady downward trajectory from that point onward, so it is only fitting that Cicero sets his dialogue at this tipping point in Roman history, to remind his readers of what they are in danger of losing as well as the principles and virtues that are essential to preserving a republican government. Cicero's philosopher-statesmen are far more practical than Plato's. They start from an existing government and develop their account of justice and the ideal constitution with that government firmly in mind. They propose improvements rather than a wholesale makeover.

Cicero's *Republic* begins, however, with the question whether it is even worthwhile for a good man to devote his energies to political life. Faced with instability and mob violence, more and more Romans were, like Cicero's friend Atticus, withdrawing from political life in favor of a life of contemplation and private pleasure among friends. Cicero accordingly precedes the dialogue with a polemical preface designed "to get rid of people's scruples about entering public life."[11]

Cicero argues that each of us has, by nature, an innate fellow-feeling that spurs us on to do good and "to defend the well-being of the community."[12] Such virtue manifests itself only in practice, however, and its most important field of practice "is in the government of a state, and in the achievement (in reality, not just in words) of those things which our friends in their shady nooks [a dig at "the Garden" where Epicurus taught and his followers gathered] make such a noise about."[13] The statesman has practical, not merely theoretical, wisdom. It is the statesman who gives us law, justice, education, and the customs and values that shape our lives and our community.

Cicero chides those who have abandoned the republic at the time of its greatest need: We owe our lives and our well-being to our country. We cannot expect "a safe haven for our leisure and a quiet place for our relaxation" without actively working to preserve it.[14] We must give to our country "the largest and most numerous portions of our loyalty, ability, and sagacity, leaving to us for our private use only what might be surplus to its needs."[15]

There is a certain amount of special pleading in this polemic. As previously noted, Cicero was excessively fond of glory, and he often praised duty as a screen for his own ambition, seeking a principled justification for what he wanted to do anyway. Yet his call to public service is nonetheless stirring. More important, his actual practice in office confirmed his high ideals. Cicero put country ahead of self, promoted the stability of the state, and tried to shape its laws as a force for good.

Yet Cicero himself was plainly still ambivalent—and for good reason, given his own career. He follows his preface with homage to the philosophic life by Scipio, the hero of his dialogue. Politics may be a grim duty, Scipio explains, but true excellence and fulfillment lie in philosophic wisdom. He notes that his grandfather Africanus used to say "that he was never doing more than when he was doing nothing, and was never less alone than when alone."[16] The philosopher, in his retirement, can "share the company . . . of the greatest minds by enjoying their discoveries and writings" and "can truly claim everything as his in virtue, not of the citizen's, but of the wise man's right."[17] Power, office, and wealth are of small account when compared to such wisdom.

The value of the philosophic life versus the political life is constantly revisited in Cicero's work, and it is never fully resolved. Scipio, of course, as well as his grandfather Africanus, answered the call of their country notwithstanding their preference for a quiet retirement. So, too, did Cicero. His abiding belief, preserved in a fragment and reflected in his own life, is that "there is for good men no limit or end of looking out for one's country."[18] But the lasting value of his writings belies any suggestion that only active participation in politics can benefit the state. We have all benefitted more from Cicero's periods of enforced retirement than from his unsuccessful efforts to preserve the Roman Republic. To paraphrase the American jurist Oliver Wendell Holmes Jr., to think is not less than to do. Sometimes, as with Cicero, it is a great deal more.

Cicero's vision of justice is closely tied to his defense of the political life. We come together as a community not just for mutual protection but also because it fulfills our nature to do so. Cicero echoes Aristotle in suggesting that man has an "innate desire" to form communities.[19] A community is not just a collection of individuals huddling together; moral consensus and a partnership for the common good are needed to bind us together as a society. Thus, a community must be held together by agreement with respect to justice. But justice, for Cicero, is not merely conventional, a matter of contract. It is eternal, absolute, and universal, and it is knowable through the application of reason. We have a natural inclination toward justice, but that inclination must be cultivated and expanded through reason. Cicero thus stressed the importance of speech (*oratio*) both to seek reason and to join men together with shared values, shared institutions, and a shared cultural heritage.

Justice and the common interest, then, are the twin foundations of the state. Our sense of justice must be reflected in our laws and our institutions, and it must be clear that power is entrusted to our leaders only for the good of the public. That is what legitimizes any form of government. For Cicero, the *res publica* (literally, the public thing) must also be a *res populi* (a thing of and for the people).

Cicero was not a populist, however. He thought justice could be trampled by an unconstrained mob as readily as by an unconstrained tyrant. Indeed, one often leads to the other. Cicero's conception of justice accordingly stresses respect for the life, liberty, and property—the individual autonomy—of our fellow men. These fundamental rights (our founders would call them "self-evident" and "unalienable"[20]) both define and set limits on what we owe to one another as citizens and on the legitimate authority of government. They are guaranteed and protected by the ideal constitution. They recognize and defend the *dignitas*, the fundamental moral worth, of each individual.

Cicero was a staunch defender of private property (and opponent of schemes for its redistribution) even as he decried the use of public office for the pursuit of personal wealth. Personal wealth, like personal rights, provides a bulwark between the individual and the state, a sphere in which freedom and autonomy are possible. The pursuit of economic self-interest is accordingly both understandable and consistent with the demands of morality, provided it is done fairly and with justice toward others and is not pursued to the exclusion of one's duties as a citizen.

Like Plato, Cicero believed that the justice of the state is found in the harmony of its various constituents. But Cicero's actual proposal draws more on Aristotle and the Greek historian of early Rome, Polybius, than on Plato. Aristotle had catalogued the three pure types of state (monarchy, aristocracy, and democracy) and their three depraved counterparts (tyranny, oligarchy, and mob rule). He argued that each pure type tends to degenerate into its opposite and that the various depraved states are themselves unstable. He therefore advocated a mixed constitution, one that judiciously combines the best elements of each system. Only such a mixed constitution, he argued, provides an opportunity for a stable commonwealth. Polybius, in his history, argued that the Roman constitution, developed over centuries, was itself the embodiment of such a mixed constitution.

Cicero molds the idea of a mixed constitution into the system of checks and balances that so influenced our own founders. The consuls (monarchy), the Senate (aristocracy), and the popular assembly (democracy) each have a distinct role to play in the government, and any two provide a check against too much concentration of power in the third. "So a state, by adjusting the proportions between the highest, lowest, and intermediate classes, as if they were musical notes, achieves harmony."[21]

In Cicero's system, the Senate performs the crucial middle role. The Senate keeps the consuls from overstepping their authority, while guiding and controlling the leveling impulses of the assembly. Cicero feared tyranny, but at the same time he did not trust unvarnished, unfiltered, unchanneled democracy any more than our own founders did. That is why he places so much power in the hands of the Senate and so much (unrealistic) emphasis on the need for senators to be free from self-interest and to rule for the benefit of all. Government, for Cicero, was a sacred trust at a time when so many of his fellow senators were either focused on spoils and influence-trading or had simply abdicated their responsibility to the commonwealth. In his ideal republic, the senators are wise and selfless, and the people are respectful and willing to be led by the best citizens.

Cicero was not completely naive. He recognized the difference between his ideal government and the reality of contemporary politics, even criticizing his fellow senator Cato the Younger for his failure to be sufficiently pragmatic: "As for our Cato, your affection for him is no greater than mine. Yet in spite of his exemplary attitude and total integrity, he sometimes inflicts damage on the state, for he delivers speeches as if he were in Plato's republic and not in Romulus' cesspit."[22] But, from Cicero's perspective, history provided a powerful argument in favor of his ideal state. Like Polybius, he looked back to the heyday of the Roman Republic and concluded that "no form of government is comparable in its structure, its assignment of functions, or its discipline, to the one which our fathers received from their forebears and have handed down to us."[23] He sought not dramatic change but a return to the old ways in an idealized form. "The very mind that envisages the future," he explains, "recalls the past."[24]

In book 2, accordingly, Scipio traces the development of Rome from its founding to the emergence of the republic, from the rule of kings to the growth of democratic institutions and controls. The republic, he argues, was the product not of abstract thought or the plan of any single person, but of the collective experience and wisdom of many great men. Institutions and practices evolved and became better over time "by a kind of natural process."[25] This organic growth, guided by collective wisdom, was a key concept for Cicero and would later underwrite the British and American common-law traditions, in which legal doctrines accreted and were adjusted over time in the crucible of actual cases, rather than being laid down once and for all at the outset. Scipio explains:

> Cato [the Censor] used to say that our own constitution . . . had been established not by one man's ability but by that of many, not in the course of one man's life but over several ages and generations. He used to say that no genius of such magnitude had ever existed that he could be sure of overlooking nothing; and that no collection of able people at a single point of time could have sufficient foresight to take account of everything; there had to be practical experience over a long period of history.[26]

Scipio's view of history is deliberately idealized for inspiration and edification. But Cicero clearly believed that the senators of Rome's republican glory were great statesmen ruling, with wisdom and moderation, for the benefit of a grateful people. If only the men of today "continued to live by our forefathers' principles and values,"[27] the republic would be saved and would evolve with steady but modest reforms toward an ideal state. "It is because of our own moral failings," he laments, "that we are left with the name of the republic, having long since lost its substance."[28]

DE LEGIBUS (THE LAWS)

In order to recover that substance, to reclaim the ideal republic of his imagining, Cicero turns, as Plato did before him, to the law. Plato's *Laws* was a consciously second-best approach to statecraft, presenting a more pragmatic and pedestrian alternative to his utopian vision of the perfect society. Not so for Cicero. His account is designed to show how near the ideal is to us, provided the law properly educates and trains the citizens, "calling people to their duty by its commands and deterring them from wrong-doing by its prohibitions."[29] Some compromise is inevitable as the demands of justice and reason are adapted to practical realities. But, for Cicero, the statesman is superior to the philosopher because he develops a framework of laws and institutions that embodies ideals that the philosopher can only contemplate, and that provide the best possible life for the republic's citizens. Law is to be derived, he tells us, "from the deepest recesses of philosophy,"[30] but its overriding aim is "to ensure the safety of citizens, the security of states, and the peaceful happy life of human beings."[31]

Cicero's *Laws* survives only in fragments, which makes for frustrating but still fruitful reading. In keeping with its more pragmatic focus, its participants are not from Rome's heroic past but from its uncertain present. The book records a one-day conversation between Cicero, his brother, Quintus, and his friend Atticus. The description of Rome's legal system, even with Cicero's modest innovations, is of largely historical interest. But three features of the book stand out.

First, Cicero takes a very broad view of law as "a code of living and a system of training for nations and individuals alike."[32] What he calls "civil law"—our common law of contracts, torts, and property—forms but a small, though critical, portion of his discussion. Cicero starts with universal principles of justice (echoing his treatment in *The Republic*) and works down from there. He discusses religious laws and includes customs and moral codes, as well as the constitution of the state. Nothing that shapes the lives of citizens is outside the scope of his mandate, not even "the laws of music," which he notes cannot be changed without bringing a change in the character of the people. Indeed, anticipating modern parents, he laments the fact that, instead of the "agreeable plainness" of traditional, decorous tunes, "audiences now rock to and fro jerking their necks and eyes in time with the inflexions of the singer's voice."[33] Predictably, where religion too is concerned, Cicero insists that the Roman people preserve the rituals and beliefs of their family and forebears—not necessarily because those beliefs are correct or the rituals efficacious—but simply because they are part of the traditions of the state. Like his conservative successor, Edmund Burke, Cicero is suspicious of any radical change. The very fact that a practice has survived through centuries is a strong argument in its favor.

Second, despite the all-encompassing, intrusive focus of Cicero's conception of law, he still emphasizes the importance of the rule of law as a bulwark of personal freedom and autonomy. The rule of law not only binds citizens together in their obligations but also safeguards individuals in their rights. "A man can inherit an estate from his father," he notes, "but a good title to the estate, that is, freedom from anxiety and litigation, he inherits not from his father but from the law."[34] The rule of law preserves life, liberty, and property, thereby allowing citizens "to live happy and honourable lives."[35] The law, moreover, must treat all citizens equally. It is, by definition, "something enjoined and binding on everyone."[36] "If the equalization of wealth is rejected," and Cicero certainly rejects it, and if "the equalization of everybody's abilities is impossible," which Cicero also believes, "legal rights at least must be equal among those who live as fellow-citizens in the same state."[37] These twin notions—the rule of law as the bulwark of freedom, and equality before the law—are the foundations of the modern, liberal state, and we owe them most to Cicero.

Third, all true law is natural law, which is universal and eternal. "There will not be one such law in Rome and another in Athens, one now and another in the future, but all peoples at all times will be embraced by a single and eternal and unchangeable law."[38] Natural law, Cicero explains, is "right reason in harmony with nature."[39] What he means is that we are inclined by nature to draw together into communities and to have regard for one another. Natural law springs from, and builds upon, that inclination. For Cicero, "nothing is more vital than the clear realization that we are born for justice, and that what is just is based, not on opinion, but on nature."[40]

If law were purely conventional, based only on opinion, it would be arbitrary, a matter of power rather than reason. Instead, the law allows man to reach his fullest potential as part of a community. Natural law is the set of general principles that makes civilization possible. It is a reflection of the common kinship of man, just as "moral excellence is nothing other than the completion and perfection of nature."[41] Thus, one who denies natural law turns his back on his own best nature as a human being. Cicero explains that "human nature is such that a kind of civil code mediates the individual and the human race."[42] The essential elements of this civil code respect the bonds of "civic friendship" between citizens: do not hurt others (the law of torts); respect private and common property (laws governing property); and keep one's promises (the law of contracts). With respect to each of these matters, law is "right reason in commanding and forbidding."[43]

Cicero's account of natural law has been remarkably influential and enduring. As noted, it underwrites the common-law tradition in England and America. So much so, indeed, that Oliver Wendell Holmes Jr., a legal realist, was led to protest that "the common law is not a brooding omnipresence."[44] For Cicero, though, it was very much like that. The proper principles of law (like those of morality) are something we are trying to discover, not to invent. We are using our particular human gifts—reason and speech—to work our way to a right result in each case, testing our conclusions over time and in a variety of circumstances. That, in fact, is very much the experience of those working in the common-law tradition. Certainly, it is an appropriate ideal, and Cicero treats it as such, even as he elsewhere rejects the Stoic attempt to base natural law on divine providence. Cicero is courageously, if perhaps vulnerably, humanist in his outlook. As a result, his conception of natural law and a life according to nature seem to float adrift. Yet that is not necessarily a failing for one who believes that justice and morality are rooted not in abstract reasoning from first principles or in the commands of an all-powerful god but in human nature itself. This pragmatic approach also drives his discussion of duty and the good life.

DE OFFICIIS (ON DUTIES)

The triumvirate of Caesar, Pompey, and Crassus devolved into civil war after Crassus was killed in 53 while fighting the Parthians. Cicero favored Pompey and even joined his camp briefly in central Greece, where Pompey had gone to muster his troops. But, when Pompey was decisively defeated in August of 48 near the town of Pharsalus, Cicero returned to Rome and Caesar's clemency. Pompey fled to Egypt, hoping to raise a new army in Asia Minor, but he was assassinated there on orders of the Egyptian king, Ptolemy XIII. Continued pockets of resistance gradually dissolved or were mopped up by Caesar. (Cato the Younger, who had also joined Pompey, became a Stoic hero by committing suicide in 46 after the battle of Thapsus rather than accept Caesar's pardon.)

With Caesar in sole command of the state, the Senate played only a limited role in politics. Cicero accordingly began another fruitful period of retirement at Tusculum. His time for private study was both marred and intensified by the death of his beloved daughter, Tullia, in early 45. But, from 46 to 44, he wrote many of his most important works, including *On Duties, On Moral Ends, Discussions at Tusculum, On Friendship*, and *Cato the Elder: On Old Age*. As Tadeusz Zieliński, a Polish classical philologist who died during World War II, explained, "The history of civilisation knows few moments equal in importance to the sojourn of Cicero at his houses in the country during the brief period of Caesar's sole rule."[45]

Instead of continuing to focus on the ideal state and its laws, Cicero now began to contemplate the moral life of individuals, though still within the context of the state. Written in the form of advice to his son, Marcus, *On Duties* is a manual of sorts for the good citizen. "No part of life," he explains to his son, "neither public affairs nor private, neither in the forum nor at home, neither when acting on your own nor in dealings with another, can be free from duty. Everything that is honourable in a life depends upon its cultivation, and everything dishonourable upon its neglect."[46] *On Duties* focuses on practical ethics rather than philosophical theories. It outlines a social and political morality in which civic virtue still reigns supreme. *On Duties* is Cicero's apologia, his defense and justification, for his own career of public service.

For Cicero, duty comes under four headings (derived from the four Greek virtues, but with a decidedly Roman twist): wisdom (*prudentia*), justice (*justitia*), courage (*fortitude*), and temperance (*temperantia*).

Wisdom is the search for truth and for good sense. Cicero rejects both dogmatism and the senseless refinements of abstract thought. His view of wisdom is highly pragmatic. "Nothing can be securely grasped," he suggests; we can only approach the truth through trial and error, by testing our ideas constantly against those of others, as Plato did in his *Dialogues*.[47] Absolute, certain knowledge of human affairs is impossible. But there is nothing wrong with living according to one's best, considered judgment, subject always to revision in light of changing circumstances. Cicero adopts not a corrosive skepticism but a constructive one; he is committed, but he retains an open mind guided by the best principles as he currently sees and understands them. It is a view that rejects first principles in favor of close attention to actual human life.

As always, though, for Cicero, virtue lies primarily in action, not in thought. And it is upon action that the three remaining virtues are focused. Courage and moderation form an importantly matched set. Courage celebrates "the greatness and strength of a lofty and unconquered spirit."[48] Courage sets aside both desire and fear, disdaining safety and riches while undertaking honorable tasks that are both great and beneficial to the state. (Cicero, ever mindful of his own example, is careful to point out that courage is not limited to the military sphere, but also manifests itself in oratory and statesmanship.) The problem with a lofty spirit, however, is that it all too easily falls into willfulness and an excessive desire for preeminence. Courage wants payment in glory and power. Hence, there is also a need for moderation, for a "limit in everything that is said and done."[49] Modesty and restraint are among the "gentler virtues" that temper the lofty spirit and allow one to serve the state without endangering it.

Justice, though, is "the most illustrious of the virtues,"[50] and paramount in its demands upon us. Justice is concerned "with preserving fellowship among men, with assigning to each his own, and with faithfulness to agreements one has made."[51] This capsule definition of *justice* may be as good as anyone has ever offered. For Cicero, the key precepts of justice are that no man should harm another and that private property must be respected. But there is also an affirmative aspect of justice that requires us not just to refrain from inflicting injury but also to deflect injury being imposed on others and, even more, to affirm what Ennius called the "sacred fellowship" among men.[52] For Cicero, justice includes kindness, liberality, and beneficence, not simply a strict adherence to precepts. And it must be directed at all men, low as well as high, strangers as well as kin. Wisdom, courage, and moderation are of value primarily because they allow us to pursue such a broad conception of justice.

Cicero recognizes, however, that in everyday life we have a hierarchy of duties. We owe some form of justice to all men in all places. But there are "degrees of fellowship among men."[53] Those of the "same race, tribe, and tongue" have a higher call upon our affections, as do those who live in the same city, those with whom we have business dealings, our relations, our friends, and the members of our households. Thus, "moving from that vast fellowship of the human race we end up with a confined and limited one" that places greater claims on our time and attention.[54] As we shall see, the friendship of honorable men holds a special place in Cicero's scheme of values. So, too, does "the bonding of blood," which "holds men together by goodwill and love; for it is a great thing to have the same ancestral memorials, to practise the same religious rites, and to share common ancestral tombs."[55] But the "first fellowship exists within marriage itself, and the next with one's children."[56] Cicero, like Aristotle, sees "the one house in which everything is shared" as the basic unit of society upon which the political community is grounded.[57] And, yet, it is still the fellowship of the republic that claims our greatest allegiance. "Parents are dear, and children, relatives and acquaintances are dear, but our country has on its own embraced all the affections of all of us."[58]

It is unclear how young Marcus—who was, frankly, a disappointment to his father—took this advice. One can imagine him giving it no more heed than Laertes gave to the banal nostrums of his own father, Polonius, poured upon him like bath-water before his departure for Paris in act 1 of *Hamlet*. Yet, as the great critic Lionel Trilling has noted, even Polonius had "a moment of self-transcendence, of grace and truth,"[59] at the end of his speech, in which he exhorted his son:

> This above all: to thine own self be true,
> And it must follow, as the night the day,
> Thou canst not then be false to any man.[60]

Cicero is no Polonius. His counsel combines wisdom with experience and paints an indelible portrait of the duties of a Roman citizen. Yet Cicero, too, has a moment of grace in which he transcends his times and the traditional views of virtue that he has preserved and molded with such skill. He urges his son to evaluate his own talents and best qualities and to weave them into a seamless whole. Nothing is more beautiful, he remarks, "than an evenness both of one's whole life and of one's individual actions. You cannot preserve that if you copy someone else's nature and ignore your own."[61] This idea of being true to one's own nature is very modern and un-Roman. Two millennia later, it would become Nietzsche's ultimate injunction: "Become who you are!"[62] Yet who we are, both Cicero and Nietzsche recognized, is something that is not inside us but high above us. The ideal to which we aspire is a construct of what we most admire. "First of all," Cicero explains, "we must decide who and what we wish to be, and what kind of life we want."[63] Only then, and based on that ideal, can we "[establish] our whole way of life."[64]

ON THE GOOD LIFE

Cicero confronts "our whole way of life" in both *On Moral Ends* (*De Finibus Boni et Mali*) and *Discussions at Tusculum*. The former is theoretical; the latter—written during the waning days of Caesar's rule and dedicated to Brutus, who would soon lead Caesar's assassination—is highly practical. Yet in both dialogues Cicero proceeds, as usual, by considering and criticizing positions that are one-sided and therefore stray from the full truth. Specifically, Cicero juxtaposes Epicureanism and Stoicism. He vigorously rejects the former, but, although his own views are closely aligned with the latter, he also advocates a softer, more pragmatic version of Stoicism.

Cicero agrees with both Hellenistic schools, however, that "the whole aim of philosophy is to lead us to a happy life."[65] He lauds Socrates, the inspiration for the Epicureans and the Stoics, for bringing philosophy down from the heavens to focus on "how one ought to live and behave, and what is good and what is bad."[66] Abstract arguments and endless refinements are of limited value. Philosophy is a guide to living. It is, Epicurus stressed, a form of therapy, in which our desires are purified and our fears eliminated. As such, philosophy builds character and self-sufficiency, allowing us to "face all of life with equanimity."[67]

We discuss Epicurus and his doctrines in the next chapter, in the context of Lucretius's *De Rerum Natura* (*On the Nature of Things*), a poem read and privately praised by Cicero. But it is important, here, to anticipate the two, interrelated aspects of Epicureanism that so worried and inflamed Cicero that he spent the better part of two works criticizing the school. First, Epicurus argued that plea-sure, not virtue, is the highest good. This does not mean that Epicurus advocated riotous living and moral license; quite the contrary. Epicurus valued peace of mind (*ataraxia*) and the absence of pain above all things. He accordingly urged that our desires be reduced to the minimum necessary to sustain life and health and that we practice virtue to avoid mental agitation and fear. Second, as a natural consequence of the first point, he urged his disciples to withdraw from any political involvement in favor of a quiet life of contemplation and retirement: "We must free ourselves from the prison of everyday affairs and politics."[68]

For Cicero, who valued duty and public service above all things, both doc-trines were anathema. As he explains to one of his Epicurean interlocutors, "If I can show that there is a morality worth seeking for its own essence and its own sake, then your whole system collapses."[69] His initial argument, however, seems more ad hominem than logical. He points to the lives and actions of those we most admire. Pleasure cannot be the highest good, he contends, in light of "the dangers, the efforts, and, yes, the pain that the very best people endure for the sake of their country and family. Far from courting pleasure, such people renounce it entirely, preferring in the end to bear any kind of pain rather than neglect any part of their duty."[70] Our mutually accepted definition of the good depends upon virtue, not advantage. We often act "for no other reason than that it is the decent, right and honourable thing to do."[71]

Of course, Epicurus's proposed definition of the highest good is prescriptive rather than descriptive. Epicurus is arguing for a new way of conceiving the good life. But Cicero is not begging the question. He bases his view of the good life, as he did his conception of justice and the state, not in convention but in man's inmost nature. Our mutually accepted definition of the good is grounded in our nature as social beings who care about and feel responsibility for others.

In this sense, Cicero follows the Stoics, for whom a life of virtue is a life lived in harmony with nature. For the Stoics, however, living according to nature meant living according to a divine plan. Cicero pays lip service to such a view, but religion seems to have had little personal importance for him. He acknowledges the role of traditional piety in the family and the state, but he is dismissive of divination, oracles, omens, and astrology. (Ironically, Cicero was appointed augur in 53, though he viewed the position simply as an opportunity to defuse political tensions or thwart legislation he disfavored by pronouncing that the signs were "unfavorable" for meetings of the Senate or the assembly.) Cicero's faith lay in the republic of Rome and in man's innate capacity for goodness and self-sacrifice.

Without such grounding in human nature, morality would be meaningless. "It is obvious," he wrote, "that if fairness, honesty and justice do not originate in nature, and all merely serve utility, then there is nobody good to be found."[72] The very resonance of words such as *wisdom, courage, justice,* and *temperance*—words seldom used by Epicurus—inspire in men a longing for virtue that is the greatest guarantor of individual happiness and fulfillment. As Cicero told his son, "we must decide who and what we wish to be, and what kind of life we want." Cicero's point is that an exclusive focus on utility is a debasement of man's inherent nobility and civility. That is not what we wish to be, for "if pleasure is the standard by which all things are judged then there is no room for either virtue or friendship."[73]

At the same time, Cicero rejects the Stoic conviction that "in order to live a happy life the only thing we need is moral goodness."[74] As expressed by Cato the Younger in *Discussions at Tusculum*, the Stoic position is that nothing but virtue is to be sought or counted as good. Pleasure, health, beauty, riches, honors, family, and friends are not goods; nor are pain, illness, deformity, poverty, disgrace, and isolation to be considered evils. The only evil is a lack of moral virtue. Cato does not deny either the "formidable hazards" of fortune or "the feebleness and frailty of mankind."[75] But he contends that "if such a thing as moral goodness really exists . . . then it surely possesses the ability to rise above the accidents that can befall human beings."[76] All the hazards and accidents of life are endurable. Instead of blaming circumstances for any unhappiness, we should blame "a deficiency in our own character."[77] Wise men are "entirely self-sufficient,"[78] and "nothing that there is the slightest possibility of eventually losing can be regarded as an ingredient of the happy life."[79] The Stoic philosopher must look only to himself and to philosophy for "every possible guarantee for a satisfactory and happy life."[80]

This rigid, Stoic position is also rejected by Cicero. Pleasure is not everything, but neither is it nothing. "In declaring what is moral to be the only good," he chides the Stoics, "you do away with concern for one's health, care of one's household, public service, the conduct of business and the duties of life."[81] A man should value virtue above all other things, but that is not to say that these other ingredients of a good life may be wholly disregarded. We should, through moral fortitude, rise as much as possible above the bludgeonings of chance, but cruel sorrows (such as the recent loss of his daughter) are not to be dismissed as insignificant to human happiness. The "mind is not some strange immaterial entity (a concept I find unintelligible) but is itself a species of body," and therefore desires pleasure and freedom from pain.[82] The Stoic contention that moral goodness alone is sufficient for happiness is as silly as the Epicurean argument that pleasure alone has value. Cicero, as always, occupies a more balanced, middle ground.

For Cicero, the good life, like the good constitution, is a mixture of elements. It involves public service and private contemplation, active morality as well as personal pleasure. Most of all, it involves the bonds that connect us to one another: bonds of country, laws, language, and traditions; familial bonds; and the bonds of friendship. "Take away the bond of kindly feeling from the world," he wrote, "and no house or city can stand."[83]

ON FRIENDSHIP

Cicero's life was buoyed by many friendships, but none lasted longer or was more intimate and essential to his well-being than that with Atticus, his lifelong correspondent and advisor, whom he called "that affectionate and wise friend with whom I can converse without hypocrisy, pretence, or reserve."[84] Cicero dedicated *On Friendship* to Atticus, and it is one of the most profound and moving tributes ever written on the subject, unequaled until at least the sixteenth century, when Montaigne wrote of his love for the deceased Étienne de La Boétie.

Cicero's treatment is set in 129 in the form of a discourse by Gaius Laelius Sapiens, a Roman consul, soldier, and orator, who had lost his closest friend, Scipio Africanus the Younger, just a few days earlier. The tone, in keeping with the prevailing Roman Stoicism, is more abstract and didactic than Montaigne's personal outpouring. Yet it is equally effective in conveying the overwhelming importance of friendship to a full and rich life.

Indeed, Cicero urges his readers to place friendship above every other human concern. Beside it, honors, riches, and pleasures are of small account. "Nothing else in the whole world," he writes, "is so completely in harmony with nature, and nothing so utterly right, in prosperity and adversity alike."[85] Nature itself creates the ties that bind us to one another, and without such mutual affection "life can hold no joys."[86] Unlimited wealth and power would be empty without friends, without mutual trust and the assurance of enduring goodwill. "Whatever gifts of mind and character we may possess, we only reap their finest fruits when we are able to share them with our nearest and dearest."[87]

As this last quotation indicates, for Cicero friendship stems from strength and not weakness; it is an overflowing of generous feelings toward another, "an inclination of the heart."[88] There can be no element of calculation in it. Our capacity for friendship is measured not by our need but by our self-sufficiency. We should do more for our friends than we are willing to do for ourselves, and even more than we are willing to have them do for us. Cicero thus disputes the standard Roman idea of *amicitia*, friendship based on mutual services and support. Friendship brings the greatest of all possible benefits, but that is not the reason we enter into it. We cannot be watching to see if we give or receive more, weighing utility in the scales like a shopkeeper. We will do anything for a friend except what is wrong. Only virtue and duty to our country have a superior call upon us.

For this reason, "friendship is only possible between good men."[89] It is based upon trust and a common commitment to virtue. "Without goodness, it cannot even exist."[90] Friends must be open about their concerns, their plans, and their goals. More, there must be a baring of souls to one another. No secrets can be kept from a friend; we must share our inmost being. Flattery is to be shunned. Advice and even criticism are an obligation of friendship, which "must be truthful if it is to have any meaning at all."[91] Otherwise, enemies would be more valuable than friends, for they can at least be counted upon to expose our failings.

Such an intimate investment in another human being will inevitably involve distress in the face of life's vicissitudes. This is another respect in which Cicero distances himself from both Epicureans and Stoics, who pledged their highest fealty to *ataraxia*, the former seeking it in the absence of pain, the latter in the allegedly impregnable fortress of virtue. One should try to maintain peace of mind, argued Cicero, but that is not itself the end of life. In order to engage fully in the world and with family and friends, *ataraxia* must be sacrificed to the bonds that draw us to one another and will therefore inevitably expose us to pain and suffering. Friendship is worth that cost. Through all of life's changes, friendship is our most durable asset, and old friends, of course, are dearest, "like a wine that has improved with age."[92] "Without friendship," Cicero concludes, "life does not deserve the name."[93]

ON OLD AGE

Everyone wants to live to an old age, Cicero notes; when it comes they all complain. But "the evils for which ignorant people blame old age are really their own faults and deficiencies."[94] And those unable to find happiness and fulfillment in their final years will have found every age wearisome. We must follow nature and accept the joys and consolations peculiar to each stage of life. Old age is a time of final ripening, as the fruit gets ready to fall from the tree. We can only embrace it, for nature will follow its course regardless.

That is the sort of old age Cicero envisioned: "the tranquil and serene evening of a life spent in peaceful, blameless, enlightened pursuits."[95] He chose Cato the Censor—farmer, soldier, and statesman—as his spokesman. Cato the Elder, as he was also sometimes known, was eighty-four years old when the dialogue is set, and this paragon of traditional Roman virtue directly confronts the four reasons commonly given for viewing old age as necessarily unhappy: that it takes us away from active work, that it weakens the body, that it deprives us of physical pleasures, and that it is not far from death.

There are proper occupations for each stage of life, and old age has its own appropriate tasks. Indeed, "there is nothing of which old age should be more wary than yielding itself to idleness and inactivity."[96] The old may find solace in study, writing, friendship, and quiet contemplation; in farming and observing nature through the changing seasons; in mentoring the young; and in providing wise counsel to the republic. Money, property, and position are all helpful in such a life, but these are neither necessary nor sufficient for "decent, enlightened living."[97] The crucial point is that we must keep ourselves so usefully occupied that we do not even notice the "gradual process of extinction."[98]

As for physical infirmity, "exercise and self-control enable a man to preserve a good deal of his former strength even after he has become old."[99] We can husband our powers and exert them according to our capacity. Yet the state of our body is less important than the state of our character. Mind and spirit require our closest attention. The faults of character traditionally associated with advanced years—irritability, churlishness, moroseness, avariciousness—"need vigilant resistance."[100]

"To be respected is the crowning glory of old age."[101] Honor is properly given to the wisdom of elders. And old age can offer advantages in toughness and courage because it has less to lose. But the foundations for such respect must be well laid in early life; white hair and wrinkles alone will not bring authority. In advice that would have later benefitted King Lear, Cato notes, "Age will only be respected if it fights for itself, maintains its own rights, avoids dependence, and asserts control over its own sphere as long as life lasts. For just as I like a young man to have something old about him, so I approve of the old man who has a touch of youth."[102] For such a man, "whatever the age of his body, in spirit he will never be old."[103]

Old age also frees us from youth's most dangerous failing, the lustful pleasures that "cloud a man's judgment, obstruct his reasoning capacity, and blind his intelligence."[104] For the old, conversation and companionship are more important than sex. Enjoyment of food and drink need not be lacking, but that, too, diminishes with age. We can set aside such sensual pleasures along with ambition, rivalry, quarreling, and all other passions in favor of a quieter, more tranquil life.

Cato argues, finally, that death is of no account, and "the wisest people are those who die with greatest equanimity."[105] For if death "removes the soul to some place of eternal life," then "its coming is greatly to be desired."[106] If, as seems more likely, death entails complete destruction of soul as well as body, then, while there is nothing good in it, there is nothing to be feared in it either because all thought and sensation ceases. Nature gives us a temporary dwelling place but has also marked out the limits of all things, life among them. In light of its end, no life can be considered long; but at least the old have achieved that for which their juniors hope. We should enjoy what we have but not cling too greedily to the remnants of life.[107] "Now that my race is run," Cato concludes, "I have no desire to be called back from the finish to the starting point!"[108]

DEATH

Cicero was only sixty-two years old when he wrote *On Old Age*. He hoped that his remaining years would pass in just the way Cato describes. What he got instead was a chance to die in service to his country. "The time which ought to have been the most serene and tranquil of my life," he wrote, "proved exactly the opposite, producing a more pressing horde of vexations and tempestuous storms than I had ever experienced in all my days."[109]

With the assassination of Caesar on the Ides of March in 44, Cicero returned to active politics. Brutus and Cassius, who led the conspiracy, proved oddly paralyzed afterward and, instead of moving quickly to restore the republic, fled to Greece to raise an army. Cicero attempted to fill the void in Rome. His most bitter antagonist was Caesar's second-in-command, Mark Antony, who sought to rally Caesar's troops and impose a new tyranny. Cicero complained in a letter to Brutus that the assassination was only "half done" because they left Mark Antony alive. To Cassius he wrote, "I only wish that you had invited me to the dinner on the Ides of March; there would have been nothing left over."[110]

Cicero's desperate efforts to restore the republic nearly succeeded. He mentored, supported, and advised the young Octavian, Caesar's great-nephew and adopted son, in hopes that he would be a malleable counterweight to Antony. Between the fall of 44 and the spring of 43, Cicero organized and encouraged republican forces, and he launched a series of fourteen philippics (named for the speeches of the Greek orator Demosthenes directed against Philip of Macedon) to rally opposition to Antony.

On the cusp of victory, however, Cicero was betrayed by Octavian, who cut a deal with Antony and abandoned the republic. A second triumvirate of Octavian, Antony, and another of Caesar's generals, Marcus Lepidus, was formed in November of the year 43. Cicero and his family were proscribed, along with three hundred other senators and two thousand *equites*. Cicero first attempted to flee the proscription and boarded a boat for Macedonia. Yet, inexplicably, he insisted on disembarking and began walking back toward Rome. Finally dissuaded from this course, his servants carried him to his villa near Formiae, on the coast halfway between Rome and Naples. There, he was overtaken by agents of the triumvirate. Cicero declined to run farther, waited patiently for them to approach while reclining on his litter, and then stretched out his neck to the executioner's sword. His severed head and the hand that had written the philippics were carried back to Rome and nailed up in the Forum for all to see.

In his second philippic, Cicero had anticipated his own end and hoped that at least it would serve the cause of the republic. Addressing Antony, he declared:

> When I was a young man I defended our state: in my old age I shall not abandon it. Having scorned the swords of Catiline, I shall not be intimidated by yours. On the contrary, I would gladly offer my own body, if my death could redeem the

freedom of our nation—if it could cause the long-suffering people of Rome to find final relief from its labours.[111]

It was not to be; the battle of Philippi in 42 ended in the defeat of the republicans, and Brutus and Cassius committed suicide. Lepidus was quickly pushed aside, and Antony and Octavian divided the world. Twelve years later, Antony himself would be dead, along with his Cleopatra, and Octavian would be crowned as Augustus Caesar, emperor of Rome.

Yet the vision of the aging Cicero trudging his way on the road back to Rome and certain death is an indelible symbol of the last days of the republic. And his writings continue to celebrate the dignity of the individual and the importance of the rule of law as a guarantor of freedom. Caesar himself said of Cicero that he was the "winner of a greater laurel wreath than any gained from a triumph, inasmuch as it is greater to have advanced the frontiers of the Roman genius than those of the Roman Empire."[112]

Cicero wrote that, in addition to natural endowments, to attain greatness, "you need just one thing: enthusiasm—a passion little short of love! Without such a passion, no one is going to achieve anything outstanding in life."[113] Cicero had such a passion for his beloved republic and for the teachings of philosophy, and he strove to remain true to both.

CHAPTER 3

LUCRETIUS AND THE POETRY OF NATURE

The verses of sublime Lucretius are destined to perish only when a single day will consign the world to destruction.
　　　　　—Ovid, *Amores*

Despite Ovid's confidence, the great poem of Titus Lucretius Carus, *De Rerum Natura* (*On the Nature of Things*), barely survived the destruction of the Roman Empire and the Dark Ages that followed. As dramatically told in Stephen Greenblatt's *The Swerve*, Poggio Bracciolini, a scholar and papal scribe, discovered a copy of the text at a remote monastery in Germany in 1417 and had it transcribed. Further copies were made, and the poem ultimately had an enormous influence on Renaissance and Enlightenment thinking as well as the growth of science at this time.[1]

A contemporary of Cicero, Lucretius lived through the same period of corruption, civic violence, and civil war. But he had a very different reaction to these events. While Cicero stressed the duty of all Romans to support the republic, even at the cost of their own lives, Lucretius urged his readers to abandon ambition and politics, to shun violence and avarice, and to seek instead a life of quiet contemplation and pleasure away from the madding crowd. As Michel de Montaigne, who lived through a similar period of violence and strife, would conclude: "Not being able to govern events, I govern myself."[2]

Lucretius was a follower of the Greek philosopher Epicurus, and he devoted his life to a poetic presentation of the master's ideas. Chief among those ideas was the belief that a proper understanding of natural phenomena and human mortality would free us from superstition and fear, from destructive passion, and from the frenetic quest for wealth and power that Lucretius likened to pouring water into a sieve.

During the time of Cato the Censor, the predominant philosophy of the Roman Republic was Stoicism. But Epicureanism grew steadily in importance during the crisis that would lead to the dissolution of the republic in the first century. Precisely for that reason, Cicero worked furiously to combat Epicureanism's message of political apathy and its advocacy of pleasure over duty. Yet even Cicero admitted to his brother, Quintus, somewhat reluctantly perhaps, that *De Rerum Natura* was a poem of great art with flashes of genius.

If anything, Cicero's praise was too modest. *De Rerum Natura* is undoubtedly the most important explicitly philosophical poem ever written. It had a profound influence on later Latin poetry, especially on Virgil, who, in the great debate between Cicero and Lucretius, opted for different answers at different times, and yet was always indebted to Lucretius as a poet. The materialist and antireligious message of the poem, seeking natural explanations for natural phenomena, has been of overriding importance to philosophy and science since the Renaissance. Its description of the evolutionary development of community, civilization, and culture anticipated modern social science. And its constant reminder that not all change is progress— that with the development of civilization also came enhanced and more organized forms of warfare and oppression—is a lesson perhaps not fully absorbed until the twentieth century. Yet the greatest thing about the poem—and the reason we should read it today—lies in the vivid and uncompromising beauty of its descriptions of nature and human relationships, stripped of superstition and false comforts. As George Santayana noted, "We seem to be reading not the poetry of a poet about things, but the poetry of things themselves."[3] By demythologizing the natural world, and making clear that humans are fully a part of that world, Lucretius created a new, naturalist poetry that has greatly enhanced our appreciation of nature and our understanding of what it is to be human. It may be true, as the deconstructionists are wont to say, that every decoding is another encoding. But Lucretius's new encoding of nature and the human soul in a poetry that spurns romantic and religious illusions and yet inspires joy is one of the pivotal feats of Western thought.

EPICURUS

The Greek philosopher Epicurus was born in 341 on the island of Samos in the eastern Aegean. His father, although an Athenian citizen, had gone there five years earlier as a colonist. In the turmoil following the death of Alexander the Great in 323, the Athenians were expelled from Samos, and Epicurus spent some years studying philosophy on the Ionian coast of Asia Minor. In 311, at the age of thirty, he moved to Mytilene, on the island of Lesbos, and opened his own school. From there, he and his disciples went to Athens in 306, where he purchased a house with a kitchen garden. All were welcome as students: men and women, citizens and slaves. They formed a small but close-knit commune, withdrawn from the broader world, supported by members with the means to do so, and connected by ties of friendship to one another and by respect bordering on worship for the master. The school became known as "the Garden." Epicurus lived, taught, and wrote prolifically there until his death in 271 at the age of seventy.

The little we know about Epicurus comes largely from Diogenes Laertius, whose multivolume *Lives and Opinions of Eminent Philosophers*, written in the third century CE, is an invaluable (if sometimes unreliable) source for Greek philosophy. In addition to a brief biography and a list of some three dozen works, Laertius includes three letters written by Epicurus setting forth his philosophy and forty "Principal Doctrines," short maxims of a single sentence or, at most, a paragraph. Those materials, along with some additional fragments and the so-called Vatican Sayings, which were discovered in the Vatican library in 1888, are all that remain of his vast outpouring—fewer than one hundred total pages.

Yet the basic outlines of Epicurus's philosophy are clear. Epicurus founded one of the three Hellenistic schools that dominated philosophy from the death of Alexander to the coming of Christianity; the other two were Stoicism and, of lesser importance, Skepticism (which evolved from the radical withholding of belief by Pyrrho of Ellis to the more pragmatic approach of the New Academy, the latter drawing its inspiration from the constant questioning and nondogmatic open mindedness of Plato's early dialogues). For all three schools, philosophy was not a body of knowledge but a way of life and, indeed, a form of therapy for turbulent emotions, fretful desires, and false beliefs. As Epicurus wrote, "Vain is the word of a philosopher, by which no mortal suffering is healed. Just as medicine confers no benefit if it does not drive away bodily disease, so is philosophy useless if it does not drive away the suffering of the mind."[4]

For Epicurus, as for the Stoics, the goal of philosophy was tranquility or peace of mind. But the two schools took very different approaches to achieve that end. The Stoics disdained natural science and focused on the cultivation of virtue as an impregnable fortress against the hazards of fortune. Epicurus thought that a proper understanding of science would relieve us of superstition and fear, allowing us to enjoy our lives, free from mental disturbance.

Epicurus was an empiricist. He believed that all of our knowledge comes from the senses and that we form concepts based on that experience. He therefore rejected the Platonic view that the material world is but a pale copy of an ideal world accessible to reason and philosophy. Reason itself depends on sensation for the raw material of its concepts. Epicurus was also a materialist; he believed that the world was composed only of material objects. He thus rejected the notion that minds or the soul or the gods or ideas have some separate, immaterial existence. Whatever exists, he taught, is composed of atoms—tiny, indivisible, and indestructible particles that join together and break apart in an endless process of formation and dissolution.

Some have seen a paradox in Epicurus's reliance on sense impressions to infer the existence of particles too small to be detected by the senses. Yet the scientific method properly relies upon careful observation to develop theories about the ultimate constituents of the universe. "Only let mythical explanations not be admitted," Epicurus wrote, "and they will not be, if we make inferences about the unseen by attending closely to the visible."[5]

Epicurus's atomic theory was derived from two Ionian philosophers of the fifth century: Leucippus (ca. 430) and Democritus (ca. 420). None of the former's writings survived, and only fragments of the latter's did. But we do have Democritus's most famous maxim: "By convention sweet, by convention bitter, by convention hot, by convention cold, by convention colour: but in reality, atoms and void."[6]

Epicurus departs from earlier atomic theory in at least one critical respect. Although he is an empiricist and a materialist, he is not a determinist. That is, he does not assume a rigid chain of cause and effect that determines everything that will happen in the universe based on the current position, motion, and velocity of elementary particles. Epicurus introduces an element of randomness in the motions of the atoms—the "swerve"—that makes them in some ways unpredictable. It is an intriguing, if random, anticipation of modern quantum mechanics. But Epicurus's reason for the innovation was to account for free will. We experience the reality of free will, in his view, and therefore atoms must swerve and all actions and events cannot be predetermined. "It would be better to accept the myth about the gods," he writes, "than to be a slave to the determinism of the physicists."[7]

We will explore the parameters of Epicurean physics in our discussion of Lucretius, who presents its fullest exposition. Here, we should simply note three conclusions that Epicurus draws from his scientific approach to nature.

First, Epicurus rejects the gods of myth. Surprisingly, he accepts the existence of gods, though, like everything else, they are made of atoms. They are an exception to the general rule that everything that comes to be also falls apart. Their atoms somehow perpetually regenerate. Yet he effectively eliminates them from human consideration. He rejects the superstition that the gods play any part in human affairs. They did not create the world. They neither punish nor reward humans. They lead a blessed existence wholly apart from our concerns, and all phenomena commonly attributed to the gods (dreams, thunderbolts, earthquakes, plagues) have a natural, rather than a supernatural, cause.[8] Epicurus rejects teleological explanations for events; he rejects any suggestion that nature follows a divine plan or has some hidden purpose. Individual humans can devise purposes for themselves and their fellows, but the universe unfolds without purpose through the chance interaction, accretion, and dissolution of atoms. Atoms are not moved by prayers and sacrifices.

Second, Epicurus rejects the immateriality and hence the immortality of the soul. "Those who claim that the soul is incorporeal are talking rubbish," he notes, "for the soul would not be able to act or be acted upon if that were so.[9] The soul must dissolve with the body. "It is not possible to imagine the soul existing and having sensation without the body."[10] Accordingly, "death is nothing to us, since every good and evil lie in sensation."[11] There is no afterlife and therefore no system of rewards and punishments. While we exist, death is not present; when death is present, we do not exist. "It is nothing either to the living or the dead, since it does not exist for the living, and the dead no longer are."[12]

Third, Epicurus held that "pleasure is the beginning and the goal of a happy life."[13] Our love of pleasure is natural and inborn. So, too, is our avoidance of pain. "I do not know how I shall conceive the good," Epicurus explains to the shock of puritans everywhere, "if I take away the pleasures of taste, if I take away sexual pleasure, if I take away the pleasure of hearing, and if I take away the sweet emotions that are caused by the sight of a beautiful form."[14]

Although pleasure for Epicurus is the highest good, not every pleasure is to be chosen. Some pleasures (food, drink, warmth) are both natural and necessary for life. Others, such as sex, are natural but not necessary and hence may be enjoyed in moderation, provided we do not harm ourselves or others. Still other pleasures—such as the enjoyment of luxuries, the exercise of power, and the accumulation of wealth—are neither necessary nor natural and should be avoided, as these foster desires that are never satisfied and therefore leave pain and dissatisfaction in their wake. The wise man needs very little to be happy, but "nothing is sufficient for the man to whom the sufficient is too little."[15] The richest man is he with the fewest needs. By all accounts, Epicurus himself lived a life of great simplicity, subsisting largely on bread and water and occasional bits of cheese.

Epicurus further distinguishes between bodily pleasure and mental pleasure. The satisfaction of physical needs is vital to life. But *ataraxia*, mental tranquility, is vital to happiness. Accordingly, Epicurus is more interested in the pleasures of thought than in carnal desire. He is more interested in avoiding disturbance than in actively seeking pleasure. "It is better for you to be free of fear and lying on a bed of straw than to own a couch of gold and a lavish table and yet have no peace of mind."[16] By reducing our needs, we reduce our vulnerability to pain and mental anguish. We should "refer every choice and avoidance to the health of the body or the calm of the soul, since this is the goal of a happy life."[17]

In particular, he stressed, "We must free ourselves from the prison of everyday affairs and politics."[18] Fear of death and the gods causes restlessness, anxiety, and insecurity that find their incomplete outlets in ambition and in avarice. But the wise man avoids all "actions that bring strife in their wake."[19] Epicurus thus considers prudence to be the highest virtue, since prudence teaches us that it is impossible "to live pleasantly without living wisely, virtuously, and justly."[20] In other words, virtue and justice are not inherently good, but they have utilitarian value. They are part of the human compact that prevents one from harming others and being harmed in turn. They free us from strife and allow us to live a quiet life of contemplation.

To one who adopts his philosophy, Epicurus promises: "You shall be disturbed neither waking nor sleeping, and you shall live as a god among men."[21] Of course, Epicurus's gods are indifferent to human beings, and Epicurus appears to advocate such indifference so as to minimize our vulnerability. If we care deeply about other people, our mental equilibrium is hostage to their fortunes. Yet, surprisingly, Epicurus stresses the importance of friendship to the good life almost as much as Cicero does. "Of all the things that wisdom provides for living one's entire life in happiness," Epicurus writes, "the greatest by far is the possession of friendship."[22] "It is necessary even to run risks for friendship's sake," he explains.[23] In this instance, the pleasures of friendship—particularly the friendship of like-minded disciples of Epicureanism—outweigh the pains that are the inevitable result of our commitment to others.

POET AND PHILOSOPHER

One of Epicurus's maxims was "Live your life without attracting attention."[24] Lucretius seems to have taken it to heart, for if little is known about the life of Epicurus, even less is known about the author of *De Rerum Natura*. From his writing, we can likely infer that he was a highly educated Roman aristocrat with a villa in the country, where he spent much of his time. The poem shows great learning and sophistication; it addresses former tribune and fellow poet Gaius Memmius as an equal; and it reflects a deep love and familiarity with country life. Scholars place Lucretius's birth around 99, when Cicero was seven years old, and his death in 55, a year before that of the poet Catullus. But those dates are conjectures. And, beyond that, we know nothing specific, despite a scurrilous and spurious suggestion by Saint Jerome, four hundred years later, that Lucretius was driven mad by a love potion, wrote his poem in his brief intervals of sanity, and then committed suicide, after which the poem was prepared for publication by Cicero.

We do know, however, that Lucretius lived through a time of constant and terrible strife: the Social War, the civil war between Sulla and Marius, the slave revolt of Spartacus, the proscriptions of Sulla, and the beginning of the end of the republic during the First Triumvirate. "In this evil hour of my country's history," he wrote, he could not, like the gods, stand "aloof and detached from our affairs."[25] Accordingly, he saw it as his mission to bring, if not civil peace, then mental peace to the hearts of his fellows. "This it is that leads me to stay awake through the quiet of the night, studying how by choice of words and the poet's art I can display before your mind a clear light by which you can gaze into the heart of hidden things."[26]

Following Epicurus, Lucretius thought the road to wisdom and inner peace was through a proper understanding of the natural world and man's place within it. He structured his poem accordingly, with a linear development from the simplest to the most complex elements of the universe, including man and his institutions, showing how the latter arise out of the former and can be explained thereby. The poem was divided by Lucretius himself (not by later scholars) into six books. The first two books explain the basic atomic elements out of which all things are composed. Atoms are in constant motion in the void, and their chance collisions lead to compounds of atoms that develop and dissolve over time. The next two books deal with man, particularly with his mind and spirit, with his sensations and thoughts, and with the material nature of the soul composed, like all else, out of atoms and hence, like all else, mortal. The fifth and sixth books deal with the evolution of the world and its wonders, with explanations for natural phenomena and for the growth of civilization and culture, all within the context of naturalism and without need for divine intervention. The three pairs of books form a triptych, in which the central panel, dealing with man, is most important to the poem, and is placed in its proper natural context by the other two.[27]

Lucretius drew freely for substance on his master's writings, especially the now lost, lengthy treatise known as *On Nature*. Lucretius wrote in dactylic hexameter, the standard six-foot meter of much Greek and Latin poetry, with unrhymed lines consisting of six stresses, each followed by two short syllables or one long one. It was the same meter used by Hesiod (ca. 700) in his *Theogony* and by Empedocles (ca. 450) in *On Nature*, two earlier didactic poems in Greek that served as models for Lucretius. Empedocles is explicitly mentioned and criticized in Lucretius for his theory that everything is made of four elements—fire, air, earth, and water. But his quasi-mythological contention that two forces—Love and Strife—cause the movements and combinations and dissolutions of these elements exercised a profound influence on Lucretius. Empedocles and his Ionian counterparts were the last Greek writers to employ poetry to present their natural philosophies.

Dactylic hexameter was also used by Homer (ca. 725) in his two great epic poems, the *Iliad* and the *Odyssey*. And it was used in Latin poetry both before Lucretius, by Ennius, and after him, by Virgil, in their epics on the founding of Rome. That, too, is fitting, for Lucretius is writing an epic as well as a didactic poem. He is writing the epic of Epicurus, the "glory of the Grecian race," who lived "a life worthy of the gods."[28] Hercules, the greatest hero of Greek mythology, fought and conquered such mythical beasts as the Nemean lion, with its impenetrable golden fur; the many-headed Hydra; and the man-eating, fire-breathing horses of Diomedes. But such creatures are nothing compared to the monsters of our own souls. "Pride, lust, aggressive behaviour, self-indulgence, indolence—what calamities they inflict! The man who has defeated all these enemies and banished them from his mind, by words not by weapons, is surely entitled to a place among the gods."[29]

Epicurus is the epic hero who diagnosed and cured our worst ailments, who showed us how to sweep our breasts clean of the most horrific and soul-destroying monsters. He "smash[ed] the constraining locks of nature's doors" and triumphed over superstition and religion.[30] "Fables of the gods did not crush him, nor the lightning flash and the growling menace of the sky."[31] He looked into the souls of men and "found aching hearts in every home, racked incessantly by pangs the mind was powerless to assuage, forced to vent themselves in recalcitrant repining."[32] "Therefore he purged men's breasts with words of truth."[33] He taught them to triumph over fear and untrammeled desire, over ambition and avarice, and pointed the way toward the highest good, a godlike inner calm, strong in its own resources, a sunlit haven among the stormy seas of life.

Epicurus himself disdained poetry and rhetoric in favor of plain, even crude, statements of his position. He thought poetry led men astray by enchanting and mythologizing the world and by fostering romantic illusions. It is ironic, then, that his greatest disciple presented Epicurean doctrines in verse. It is even more ironic that Lucretius begins his poem with a hymn to "life-giving Venus," mother of Aeneas and the Roman race, "delight of men and gods," through whom "all nature teems with life" and without whom "nothing emerges into the shining sunlit world to grow in joy and loveliness."[34] Venus is the goddess of spring and love and reproduction. She couples with and quiets Mars, the god of war and strife. Even in a prose translation, the beauty of the poetic invocation shines through.

> For you the inventive earth flings up sweet flowers. For you the ocean levels laugh, the sky is calmed and glows with diffused radiance. When first the day puts on the aspect of spring, when in all its force the fertilizing breath of Zephyr is unleashed, then, great goddess, the birds of air give the first intimation of your entry; for yours is the power that has pierced them to the heart. Next the wild beasts and farm animals alike run wild, frisk through the lush pastures and swim the swift-flowing streams. Spellbound by your charm, they follow your lead with fierce desire. So throughout seas and uplands, rushing torrents, verdurous meadows and the leafy shelters of the birds, into the breasts of one and all you instill alluring love, so that with passionate longing they reproduce their several breeds.[35]

More is at work here than the traditional, obligatory invocation of Lucretius's particular muse: "yours is the partnership I seek in striving to compose these lines."[36] More is at work here than a tribute to Empedocles, with his fundamental forces of Love and Strife, of whom Lucretius writes: "the songs that took shape in his divine breast proclaim in ringing tones such glorious discoveries that he scarcely seems a scion of mortal stock."[37] More is at work here than even an effort to administer philosophy "in the dulcet strains of poesy" as physicians smear the rim of a cup of medicine with honey so that children are "lured by the sweetness at their lips into swallowing the bitter draught."[38]

The poetry is in fact integral to the philosophy and cannot be viewed separately from it. Lucretius rejects mythology, even as he recognizes its allure. "If anyone elects to call the sea Neptune and the crops Ceres and would rather take Bacchus' name in vain than denote grape juice by its proper title," he writes, "we may allow him to refer to the earth as the Mother of the Gods, provided that he genuinely refrains from polluting his mind with the foul taint of superstition."[39] Lucretius does not believe in the poetry of the gods. But he believes in the inherent poetry of nature. We might even say that he demythologizes the natural world in order to remythologize it without the gods. Lucretius finds sufficient wonder in the material world that he feels no need to create an immaterial world to which it is subordinate. Lucretius comes to nature in the same posture of romance that others approached the gods, and yet without sentimentality. Nature warrants clear-eyed study and a considered effort to see with fresh, unjaded eyes:

> Take first the pure and undimmed lustre of the sky and all that it enshrines: the stars that roam across its surface, the moon and the surpassing splendour of the sunlight. If all these sights were now displayed to mortal view for the first time by a swift unforeseen revelation, what miracle could be recounted greater than this?[40]

We have no need of the false beauty of mythology. Reality is infinitely more precious and full of poetry.

ATOMS AND THE VOID

Lucretius tackles "the problem of how things are created and occasioned without the aid of the gods."[41] Since he will brook no supernatural explanations for phenomena, Lucretius begins his discussion of the physical world with the proposition that nothing is created out of nothing.[42] All things must be explained by the combination and dissolution of existing elements. The corollary of this proposition is that nature never reduces anything to nothing.[43] Things fall apart, but the basic building blocks of matter must survive: "something must remain changeless, or everything would be absolutely annihilated."[44] This "something" is the atom, from the Greek word *atomos*, meaning indivisible.[45] Atoms are the invisible and indestructible seeds of which all things are composed.

Atoms are in constant motion in the void. Lucretius's conception of motion—which is altered only by some counteraction—would not be adopted by modern science until the time of Galileo, but it was a significant advance over the Aristotelian insistence that motion requires a constant propulsive force. Even within apparently solid bodies there is empty space in which atoms are always moving, combining, and colliding. Density is simply a function of the amount of empty space within each object.

Atoms and the void: that is all there is and all there ever can be. Material objects, including all living things, are compounds of atoms and vacuity.[46] There are only a limited number of types of atoms in terms of shape and size. For example, no atoms are large enough to be visible. Yet the possible combinations are enormous. Lucretius draws a famous analogy between the letters that make up his poem and the atoms that make up the universe:

> Consider how in my verses, for instance, you see many letters common to many words; yet you must admit that different verses and words differ in substance and in audible sound. So much can be accomplished by letters through mere change of order. But the elements can bring more factors into play so as to create things in all their variety.[47]

Lucretius argues that the universe is not bounded in any direction.[48] "There is therefore a limitless abyss of space, such that even the dazzling flashes of lightning cannot traverse it in their course, racing through an interminable tract of time, nor can they even shorten the distance still to be covered."[49] Since space is infinite, matter must also be infinite; otherwise, matter would simply dissipate. "The supply of matter would be shaken loose from combination and swept through the vastness of the void in isolated particles; or rather, it would never have coalesced to form anything, since its scattered particles could never have been driven into union."[50]

Time is a function of matter and motion. "Time by itself does not exist; but from things themselves there results a sense of what has already taken place, what is now going on and what is to ensue."[51] Time cannot be sensed apart from change. Yet time has no beginning and no end because the motion of atoms in the void itself has no beginning and no end.

Given infinite matter in infinite space and infinite time, there must also be an infinite number of worlds.

> Granted, then, that empty space extends without limit in every direction and that seeds innumerable in number are rushing on countless courses through an unfathomable universe under the impulse of perpetual motion, it is in the highest degree unlikely that this earth and sky is the only one to have been created and that all those particles of matter outside are accomplishing nothing.[52]

Our world is just one among many that has come into being through the chance interaction of atoms. It had a beginning and will have an end, like all things composed of atoms: "sky and earth too had their birthday and will have their day of doom."[53]

No physical object—however substantial—can escape the ravages of time. Motion tears things apart just as it brings them together. "Dripping water hollows a stone."[54] Iron ploughshares and cobblestones in the highway are worn imperceptibly away. But one thing's dissolution is the new beginning for another, as atoms blindly rush together to form new compounds: "here they bring decay, there full bloom, but they do not settle."[55] Nothing is born without another's death. Decomposition is essential for any new flowering, in an endless process of creative destruction. Love and Strife—attraction and repulsion—are still, as in Empedocles, the fundamental forces that cause the coming together and the breaking apart of basic elements in a continuous cycle.

> So the sum of things is perpetually renewed. Mortals live by mutual interchange.
> One race increases by another's decrease. The generations of living things pass in
> swift succession and like runners hand on the torch of life.[56]

It is a beautiful and compelling image. As George Santayana wrote, Lucretius's conception of the indestructible building blocks of matter, endlessly mutating into new forms—"the swarming atoms, in their unintentional, perpetual fertility"—is "a very great thought, perhaps the greatest thought that mankind has ever hit upon."[57]

THE GODS

Lucretius adopts Epicurus's doctrine of the "swerve," by which atoms originate some new movement that will "snap the bonds of fate."[58] If the atoms followed fixed paths and did not swerve, they would not collide and form bodies. Hence, nothing could come into being. Nor could we swerve from our own course "at the bidding of our own hearts."[59] Lucretius believed that science could never provide a mechanistic explanation of the exact motion of atoms, much less of human choices, and, hence, he rejected a purely deterministic view of the universe.

Lucretius also rejected the operation of fate in a broader sense. Fate was a central tenet of Stoic philosophy, which taught that all things unfold pursuant to a divine plan. As Marcus Aurelius would later write, "If not a wise providence, then a mere jumble of atoms."[60] Lucretius opts for the atoms and finds no purpose or meaning in their chance coming together and breaking apart, other than the purposes that humans inject into the universe through their own choices and the meanings they create for themselves. "Certainly the atoms did not post themselves purposefully in due order by an act of intelligence, nor did they stipulate what movements each should perform."[61] Nor, he argues, were the atoms created or directed by any divinity. There is no divine plan, no first mover, no designer or creator. Lucretius flatly rejects the view that the world and its inhabitants could not have arisen and developed "without the guidance of the gods,"[62] and much of his poem is directed to finding naturalistic explanations for both the wonders (the sun and the stars, the changing seasons, life-giving rain) and the terrors (earthquakes, thunderbolts, plagues) of the world. He pays particular attention in book 5 to the natural evolution of man and the development of language, tools, and culture.

Lucretius does not reject the gods, though he views their existence as so amorphous and unrelated to human life that many readers consider him to be effectively an atheist. The gods of Lucretius are more akin to dream visions created by man than independent entities. But, if Lucretius's attitude toward the gods themselves is ambivalent, his fierce rejection of established religion is not. Citing the example of Iphigenia—the virgin daughter of Agamemnon who was sacrificed to ensure favorable winds for the Greek expeditionary force on the way to Troy: "a sinless victim to a sinful rite"[63]—Lucretius condemns religion as inherently blind and cruel. He anticipates Nietzsche in finding something dark and vengeful at the heart of the religious impulse. And he anticipates a bleak future of war, persecution, and mass murder committed for the greatness and glory of one god or another. The true impiety is not to expel the gods from human life, but rather to invoke their names in support of violence and aggression.

> Poor humanity, to saddle the gods with such responsibilities and throw in a vindictive temper! What griefs they hatched then for themselves, what festering sores for us, what tears for our posterity! This is not piety, this oft-repeated show of bowing a veiled head before a stone; this bustling to every altar; this kowtowing and prostration on the ground with palms outspread before the shrines of the gods; this deluging of altars with the blood of beasts; this heaping of vow on vow. True piety lies rather in the power to contemplate the universe with a quiet mind.[64]

Lucretius dismisses dreams and divination as so much superstition, born of ignorance of the laws of nature that govern events. It is a delusion to think that there are gods who watch out for us, who intervene in the world, and who are appeased by sacrifice or influenced in our favor by prayer. All of ancient mythology is a lie. So, too, is the official Roman religion, which is so often used as a tool of social and political power. Religion casts a dark shadow over human life; only a proper understanding of the nature of things will bring spiritual liberation and enlightenment.

DEATH

Since we are made of the same stuff as all other things that come into being and pass away, our atoms, too, will disperse in time. Death is unavoidable. Lucretius celebrates both mind, "the seat of intellect," and spirit, the "dominant force in the whole body," "where fear and alarm pulsate" and where "is felt the caressing touch of joy."[65] But he does not exempt them from his verdict. They are too integrally connected with one another and with the body to survive its dissolution. They are composed of material atoms, not some immaterial substance, and hence must break apart. Mind and spirit are no less a part of the body than hands or eyes.

Indeed, unless they were material, mind and spirit could not propel the limbs, change the expression of the face, or guide and steer the whole man. "It is surely crazy to couple a mortal object with an eternal and suppose that they can work in harmony and mutually interact."[66] Standing alone, neither mind nor body would enjoy the power of sensation: "it is by the interacting motions of the two combined that the flame of sentience is kindled in our flesh."[67] Our mind and body "are born together, grow up together and together grow old."[68]

> With the weak and delicate frame of wavering childhood goes a like infirmity of judgment. The robust vigour of ripening years is accompanied by a steadier resolve and a maturer strength of mind. Later, when the body is palsied by the potent forces of age and the limbs have collapsed with blunted vigour, the understanding limps, the tongue rambles and the mind totters: everything weakens and gives way at the same time.[69]

Since the mind dies with the body, there is no afterlife. There is no immortality, no hell or heaven, and no system of punishments or rewards. Accordingly, death should hold no fear for us. While dying may be an experience, death itself is not. To be dead is to have no sensations, no thoughts, and no feelings. "Nothing will have power to stir our senses, not though earth be fused with sea and sea with sky."[70] Whether our remains "moulder in the grave or fall a prey to flames or to the jaws of predatory beasts" makes no difference.[71] We will not be there to feel it. We will not be there to witness it: "there will be no other self alive to mourn [our] own decease."[72]

Yet we persist in mourning our own decease in advance. We are the only animals that can anticipate death. That makes us unique and sets us apart. But such knowledge is also a source of fear and anxiety, which can drive us to religion and render us unable to enjoy basic pleasures. We must accordingly remind ourselves that the fear of death is irrational. Death is literally nothing to us, just as the infinite period of our nonexistence before birth was nothing to us.

One will object that death separates us from loved ones, frustrates whatever plans we have conceived, and ends the very pleasurable sensations that Lucretius urges us to enjoy. We can properly fear death, not because of any supposed afterlife, but insofar as we love and cherish this life. Once born, we have a basic instinct to preserve our lives, exceeded perhaps only by our need to procreate. Thus, a hatred of, and resistance to, death is ingrained in us. We anticipate the loss of what we now enjoy.

Lucretius's response to this objection is both subtle and radical. He makes clear that the transitory nature of human life is itself the source of all value. We love life precisely because of its fragility. This sense of fragility infuses Lucretius's wondrous descriptions of burgeoning life, spring, love, the power of the mind, and the growth of civil society and culture, all of which are threatened by, and eventually succumb to, violence, natural disasters, and disease, or are simply worn away by time. All of these things will pass, and that is why we cherish them. "Death is the mother of beauty," Wallace Stevens would later write in "Sunday Morning," his Lucretian poem about living in a world without God.[73]

For Lucretius, the mortal, material world will do. It must, for that is all there is. We need not go in search of another, immaterial world, or fritter our time away in vain efforts to flee from our mortality. Only when we conquer fear and embrace mortality can we also embrace beauty and pleasure. Only then can we find delight and joy. More is not always better. "However many generations you may add to your store by living, there waits for you nonetheless the same eternal death."[74] Life unfolds in time and has a natural limitation. All our plans and our frantic desire to control events will not alter that limitation. We will die regardless. But our lives can be complete in each moment. If our life has been a source of joy, we should retire like a dinner guest who has eaten his full. If our life has grown distasteful, all the more reason not to cling to it.

It is because we fail to embrace the inevitability of death, Lucretius stresses, that the sufferings of the damned are still very much with us. "As for all those torments that are said to take place in the depths of Acheron," he writes, "they are actually present here and now, in our own lives."[75] The conscience-ridden mind finds its own hell on earth and "in terrified anticipation torments itself with its own goads and whips."[76] Sisyphus, driven by political ambition, continuously rolls his boulder uphill, only to see it roll back down, as he strives for a "profitless and never-granted prize."[77] Tityos, "prostrated by love," has his liver torn by birds of prey, "devoured by gnawing anxiety or rent by the fangs of some other passion," only to see it regenerate each night so that it may be torn again.[78] Greed, too, is never satisfied: "the circling seasons enrich us with their products and their ever-changing charms," but we are simply pouring water into a leaking vessel that is never filled.[79]

We feel a weight of depression in our breasts—a longing without object—that makes us restless and eager to throw off the load without the means to do so. Lucretius offers a telling portrait of the Roman aristocrat, bored at home, who ventures out only to return as speedily, and who then rushes off to his country seat "as though rushing to save a house on fire," but no sooner does he arrive than he courts oblivion in sleep or returns to town.[80] In all his frantic activities, he is simply running away from his own self and "the lot in store for mortals throughout the eternity that awaits them after death."[81] Death is the one fate we cannot escape, and so we distract ourselves with avarice, ambition, and love. "So long as the object of our craving is unattained," Lucretius writes, "it seems more precious than anything besides. Once it is ours, we crave for something else. So an unquenchable thirst for life keeps us always on the gasp."[82]

CIVILIZATION AND ITS DISCONTENTS

For Cicero and, to a lesser extent, Aristotle, the social and political virtues are innate. Men are born to live together in groups, and from this fact of nature the two philosophers derive laws that govern the proper organization of those groups. Cicero's commitment to natural law, in particular, is his commitment to a political order grounded in man's fundamental nature. For Cicero, justice is not just a duty that all persons owe to one another; it is also a form of personal fulfillment in which man realizes his highest nature.

Lucretius has a very different, less sentimental view of the state. The German philosopher Arthur Schopenhauer would later liken men to porcupines, huddling together for warmth but being careful to keep sufficient distance to avoid each other's sharp quills.[83] That image captures Lucretius's thoroughly pragmatic approach to politics. Justice, for Lucretius, is nothing more than an evolving social contract for mutual advantage, in which one agrees not to harm others so that others will not harm one in turn. Our social and political institutions are the product of this uneasy balance between need and fear.

In his justly famous account of man's origins and evolution, Lucretius depicts primitive humans eking out a brutish existence, living in the manner of wild beasts. They had not mastered fire or agriculture or even the use of skins to clothe their bodies. They slept in thickets or caves as shelter from wind and rain and protection from animals. They lived without any restraint of law or morals, and coupled as "mutual desire brought them together, or the male's mastering might and profligate lust, or a bribe of acorns or arbutus berries or choice pears."[84]

Yet gradually, through happenstance and by trial and error, they developed. They used stones and ponderous clubs to hunt. They built huts and donned skins to clothe themselves. They fashioned plows to work the land. There was no god Prometheus to give man fire, no god Bacchus to give him wine. All the arts were painstakingly acquired over time. Humans developed language out of the cries of animals. "Woman mated with man, moved into a single home and the laws of marriage were learnt as they watched over their joint progeny."[85]

After this mellowing, their development accelerated. They formed mutual alliances for their own protection. Cooperation appeared among men. "It was not possible to achieve perfect unity of purpose," Lucretius explains.[86] "Yet a substantial majority kept faith honestly. Otherwise the entire human race would have been wiped out there and then instead of being propagated, generation after generation, down to the present day."[87] Lucretius showed a remarkably prescient appreciation of the so-called prisoner's dilemma—how to ensure cooperation for mutual benefit while minimizing cheating—on which modern theories of social evolution and moral development are based.[88]

The strong governed the weak during these early years in the development of social organizations. Kings founded and ruled cities. But over time, laws of property were established, along with civil rights and duties. "Mankind, worn out by a life of violence and enfeebled by feuds, was the more ready to submit of its own free will to the bondage of laws and institutions."[89] A desire for peace and plenty led to an explosion of innovation and activity:

So we find that not only such arts as seafaring and agriculture, city walls and laws, weapons, roads and clothing, but also without exception the amenities and refinements of life, poetry, pictures and statues, artfully carved and polished, all were taught gradually by usage and the active mind's experiments as men groped their way forward step by step. So each particular development is brought gradually to the fore by the advance of time, and reason lifts it into the light of day. Men saw one notion after another take shape within their minds until by their arts they scaled the topmost peak.[90]

Many of these arts are still being perfected. The world is relatively new, and mankind is still in its youth. But not all developments are improvements. Mankind has learned ever more deadly and organized forms of warfare. Hands, nails, and teeth gave way to stones and branches, which were in turn replaced by iron and bronze. Men were gathered in ranks, the better to kill one another. "So tragic discord gave birth to one invention after another for the intimidation of the nation's fighting men and added daily increments to the horrors of war."[91] Religion, too, came into being as men formed gods in a more perfect image of themselves and then made all they could not understand dependent on the whim of those gods, even inventing an afterlife in which men would suffer torment. Thus, superstition, willful ignorance, and a fear that manifested itself in cruelty were born.

A restless discontent came upon men. They chafed under the restraints of civilization even as they benefited from them. Recognizing their own mortality, they sought refuge and distraction in acquiring wealth, in seeking even more refined and unnatural pleasures, and in a fruitless quest to dominate others through political and military means.

Material progress has been relatively steady, as man the innovator constantly sought improvements in his way of life. Nature was not designed for his comfort. He faced a harsh land with bad weather and wild animals and yet made steady progress. But he is not immune to natural disasters—floods, earthquakes, storms— or diseases that threaten that progress. There is no divine plan, no first mover, no designer or creator to protect humankind. Our evolution was not teleological; it was not driven by providence. It does not proceed in an inevitably positive direction. We may have "scaled the topmost peak," but there is no guarantee that life will become better rather than worse over time. The past is not a perfect guide to the future, and we enjoy no immunity from random disaster.

In book 6, Lucretius offers a description of the great plague that devastated Athens during the Peloponnesian War, a plague that slaughtered the good and the bad indiscriminately and shattered the social and moral bonds between citizens. Thucydides used the plague as a metaphor for civil war and its inherent lawlessness as men return to a more brutish existence. Lucretius uses the plague as a broader metaphor for the fragility of human life and progress. No higher power is looking out for us. Life can dissolve into chaos as readily as it can coalesce into order. Nothing abides forever but atoms and the void.

The civilization into which Lucretius was born appeared to be collapsing around him. Just as material progress is no guarantee against natural disasters; just as religious observance is no guarantee against the plague; so, too, natural law and abstract ideas of justice are no guarantee against the individuals and groups bent upon seizing political power. We can choose to adopt the social values needed for peaceful cooperation and coexistence. But aggression is barely held in check, and those values are easily overwhelmed. Indeed, the traditional Roman virtues (particularly the emphasis on honor and courage) that were essential to expanding the empire were also instrumental in tearing it apart, as successful military commanders conspired for more and more personal power and openly resorted to violence as a means to obtain it.

Lucretius laments "this evil hour of my country's history." He wishes we could live together in peace and safety without constant resort to violence. He seeks a human interaction, instead of a bestial one. But he recognizes that the restraint necessary to community breeds violence, a point Freud would develop in his book *Civilization and Its Discontents*. Our suppressed aggression—essential to surviving in a harsh world but at odds with civilization—augments our ambition and avarice. Disordered and troubled souls find their outlet in violence.

Lucretius, like Freud, seeks to tame these "monsters of the soul" through his therapeutic analysis of them. Unlike Cicero, however, he does not advocate active participation in politics to resist the dissolution of the republic. There is a deep fatalism in Lucretius's worldview. All things made by men are destined to come apart and dissolve, including the Roman Empire. Individual resistance is both fruitless and counterproductive to the mental peace he seeks to instill. "Far better," he writes, "to lead a quiet life in subjection than to long for sovereign authority and lordship over kingdoms."[92] As his reference to the myth of Sisyphus makes clear, political power is a vain pursuit even for the seemingly successful, all of whom will fall in turn. "So leave them to sweat blood in their wearisome, unprofitable struggle along the narrow pathway of ambition."[93]

Yet what of the noble Cicero, struggling along the narrow path back to Rome and certain death? Cicero sought to make the constitution better and more just and stable, preserving both freedom and peace for its citizens. Lucretius would consider that a fool's errand; Cicero should have continued on to Greece and devoted whatever life he had left to contemplation, pleasure, and friendship. Lucretius recognizes civic attachment but not civic duty. Politics is a prison to which we mistakenly commit ourselves. However pure we think our motives may be, they are corrupted by ambition and a deep-seated lust for power and honor. For Lucretius, our highest duty is to transform not the body politic but our own lives, and to save not the republic but our mortal souls.

SEX AND LOVE

Lucretius began his poem by urging Venus to enfold Mars, the god of war, in her arms and lull him to rest. Thus would Love overcome Strife and the people of Rome gain untroubled peace. As Lucretius well knew, the hope was a vain one. Indeed, his allegory itself suggests that Love and Strife are conjoined and that any hard-won peace would, at best, be fleeting.

Lucretius's analysis of love bears a striking resemblance to his analysis of political aggression. Whether Sisyphus pushes his rock uphill in search of power or romance, the result is the same: disappointment, frustration, and anger. For Lucretius, love is "that drop of Venus' honey that first drips into our heart, to be followed by icy heartache."[94] It begins—naturally, innocently, and joyfully—in attraction and sexual desire, but is fueled by false beliefs and by expectations that the object of such desire can never fulfill. We have made a religion of love, a new mythology that leads to obsession. We seek possession, even fusion, with our mate and, hence, are tormented by separation. Jealousy and violence are the result, as we are "goaded by an underlying impulse to hurt the thing, whatever it may be, that gives rise to these budding shoots of madness."[95]

Lucretius draws freely on Aristophanes's description of love in Plato's *Symposium*, in which he contends—half humorously, half seriously—that men and women were once joined together but were separated by the gods. In this riven state, "each one longed for its own other half."[96] They would throw their arms around one another and wish to grow together again, and be, as Lucretius puts it, "wholly absorbed, body in body; for sometimes it seems that that is what they are craving and striving to do, so hungrily do they cling together in Venus' fetters."[97] Such intense passion—the need to possess and devour the other—is always and forever unsatisfied because it seeks a union more than human. "Lovers' passion is storm-tossed, even in the moment of possession, by waves of delusion and incertitude."[98]

An even closer poetic analogy is to be found in the work of Lucretius's younger contemporary, Catullus (ca. 84–54). In his 116 surviving poems, Catullus writes of beauty, friendship, joy, despair, and culture. His highly personal, lyric poetry emphasizes private experience over public duty and eschews both the epic and didactic traditions. The poems seem artless and fresh and yet are literary and urbane.

Most memorably, Catullus's poems deal with love. Catullus was obsessed with Clodia, the half-sister of Clodius Pulcher. (It was Clodius who engineered Cicero's temporary banishment.) Referring to her by the pseudonym Lesbia, he writes of the bright days of their early love as the fulfillment of the best life has to offer. But Lesbia excites his jealousy, and his passion becomes bitter and dark: "nothing is left of me, each time I see her, . . . tongue numbed; arms, legs melting, on fire; drum drumming in ears; headlights gone black."[99] He protests that "what a woman tells her lover in desire should be written out on air and running water."[100] Yet her willful actions inflame rather than decrease the violence of his love. His constant need for her becomes all-consuming. "I hate and I love. And if you ask me how, I do not know: I only feel it, and I'm torn in two."[101] His mind is "drowned in its own devotion,"[102] and he wishes "only that the gods cure me of this disease and, as I once was whole, make me now whole again."[103] The illusion of wholeness in love, promised by Aristophanes, is in reality a self riven in two.

Lucretius, following Epicurus, undertakes to cure the disease of love. "Your only remedy," he writes, "is to lance the first wound with new incisions; to salve it, while it is still fresh, with promiscuous attachments or to guide the motions of your mind into a different direction."[104] In other words, before love takes root, seek refuge in promiscuity or distraction in other interests. Sexual pleasure is wonderful. But romantic love is a poetic illusion. It will never find fulfillment because its expectations are unrealistic. "Do not think that by avoiding romantic love you are missing the delights of sex. Rather, you are reaping the sort of profits that carry with them no penalty."[105] Epicurus himself was by all accounts kind, gentle, cheerful, and abstemious. Yet he was also an early advocate of free sex, in the sense of sex without attachment or possessiveness.

Lucretius, however, points to a third way, in which sex and demythologized love can coexist in a fruitful and lasting relationship. Recall that in his discussion of social evolution, he wrote how "woman mated with man, moved into a single home and the laws of marriage were learnt as they watched over their joint progeny." In such a bond, "love is built up bit by bit by mere usage."[106] Both the man and the woman accept need, dependence, and concern for one another as the inevitable concomitants of such a life, for it is better to "be called father [or mother] by delightful children" than to "live through a sexual life that yields no fruit."[107]

Even the bitter Catullus longs for such a relationship, while knowing he can never have it with Lesbia: "God let her mean what she says, from a candid heart, that our two lives may be linked in their length day to day, each to each, in a bond of sacred fidelity."[108] The false poetry of love has corrupted our desires and addicted us to strife. But we can still find our way back to the more quotidian but fulfilling and even more beautiful reality of quiet commitment.

ATARAXIA

Lucretius compares the Epicurean philosopher to a person safe on land while storm winds lash the waters, or to a noncombatant, free from peril, watching opposing hosts marshaled on the field of battle. The philosopher does not delight in the afflictions of others yet still finds pleasure in contemplating the troubles from which he is free.

> But this is the greatest joy of all: to possess a quiet sanctuary, stoutly fortified by the teaching of the wise, and to gaze down from that elevation on others wandering aimlessly in search of a way of life, pitting their wits one against another, disputing for precedence, struggling night and day with unstinted effort to scale the pinnacles of wealth and power.[109]

There is something distasteful about these metaphors of detachment and indifference, and of joy in one's assumed superiority. Yet we cannot so easily dismiss the portrait of men wandering aimlessly, with no true sense of purpose, all the while disputing for precedence and lusting after wealth and power. Lucretius's metaphor is a Roman variant of Plato's allegory of the cave, in which the philosopher breaks the chains that bind others, transcends the petty squabbles of everyday life, and ascends to the light of truth. In one form or another, such a metaphor has shaped the philosopher's job description for two millennia.

Yet Plato's philosopher returned to daily life in order to run the ideal republic of Plato's devising. The Lucretian philosopher does no such thing. Nor does he lay claim to truth in the Platonic sense of absolute and eternal ideas binding at all times and in all places. He knows only the random interaction of atoms in the void, and the fear and excessive desire that can blight our lives with frantic activity. The Lucretian philosopher does not wish to exercise political power over others. Indeed, he shuns any form of ambition as the unconscious by-product of one of the monsters of his own soul, however noble and Ciceronean it may appear on the surface. He looks first to cure himself by limiting his propensity to error and mis-guided activity.

Lucretius does not believe that advances in society, technology, or culture will make us happier. Only a fundamental change in our attitudes and beliefs will effect that result. Otherwise, we are simply pouring water into a sieve, feeding fears and desires that can never be satisfied and that are unworthy of our humanity. Superstition, false beliefs, and corrupt desires constantly threaten to negate the very values that can make life a source of pleasure and joy.

Lucretius's great poem begins with Venus, regeneration, and birth; it ends with the plague, dissolution, and death. Between the two stand our lives. We are made of the same material stuff as the universe. We appear in it by chance, and we will disap-pear from it just as other species have disappeared before us. We occupy no privi-leged place. The universe does not exist for our benefit. It simply is, just as we simply are. There is no guiding hand. No one is watching out for us. We are on our own.

And yet, we are not completely on our own. Lucretius does not advocate a godlike detachment from the world. He does not believe we can become invul-nerable to change like the gods. Nor should we wish to be, for the gods cannot enjoy those things—passing away even as they come into being—that are cher-ished precisely because they are temporal and finite and vulnerable. In his poem, Lucretius advocates steady, quiet attachments to spouse, children, friends, and even country. But these attachments recognize our limitations, our fallibilities, and our vulnerabilities.

For Lucretius, the beginning and the end of wisdom lies in such recognition. We live amid the random interaction of atoms in the void. Yet our very insignifi-cance and the randomness of our existence frees us for happiness. The world is an object of wonder and joy. With our minds "released from worry and fear,"[110] we can enjoy simple pleasures and a life enriched by contemplation, friendship, and love. We can find poetry and fulfillment in atoms and the void.

CHAPTER 4

VIRGIL— POET OF SHADOWS

The poet we know as Virgil was born Publius Vergilius Maro in the rural district of Andes, near Mantua, on October 15, in the year 70 BCE. Mantua was then part of the Roman military province of Cisalpine Gaul (that is, the portion of Gaul on "this"—the Italian—side of the Alps). Roman citizenship was not granted to its inhabitants until 49, when Virgil was already twenty-one years old.

Little is known of Virgil's life, and that little is often just an imaginative reconstruction by later biographers extrapolating from his writings. His father was apparently a modest farmer but successful enough to send his son first to Cremona, a small town on the Po River, and then to Milan and Rome to pursue his studies. Legend has it that Virgil studied law and rhetoric in Rome but proved too shy to plead cases in public. Regardless, he abandoned Rome and the law for Naples and the Epicurean philosopher Siro. A youthful poem attributed (probably falsely) to Virgil announces:

> Away with you, away now, hollow bombast of the rhetoricians. . . . I am setting sail for the havens of the blessed, to seek the wise words of great Siro, and will redeem my life from all care. Leave me, you Muses; yes, you too, I suppose, must leave me now, sweet Muses (for I will confess the truth; you have indeed been sweet):— and yet, revisit my pages, but modestly and rarely.[1]

Virgil bid farewell to the Muses because the Epicureans were suspicious of poetry as inimical to truth. Yet the Epicurean poetry of Lucretius, with which Virgil became deeply enchanted, must have convinced him otherwise, for his subsequent visits from the Muses were neither modest nor rare.

The pull of Epicureanism and the desire to "redeem [his] life from all care" were undoubtedly powerful. Virgil lived through two civil wars and the end of the republic, in addition to the many wars of conquest that cleared the Mediterranean of pirates and added Transalpine Gaul (modern France, Belgium, and parts of Germany, the Netherlands, and Switzerland) to the empire. It was a time of famine, proscription, dispossession, and violent unrest. Virgil may well have avoided any political commitment during the first civil war between Julius Caesar and Pompey. But after the assassination of Caesar and the onset of the second civil war, he was drawn through patrons into the orbit of Octavian, the future Caesar Augustus. Octavian defeated the combined forces of Mark Antony and Cleopatra in 31 at the sea battle of Actium. Virgil, along with many others, was grateful to Octavian for the time of peace and stability that followed. Some forms of the republic were even retained, although there was no doubt that Octavian was in absolute control. Yet Virgil somehow kept his independence of mind and spirit notwithstanding the patronage and the expectations of an emperor who liked to think of himself (and whom Virgil willingly celebrated) as a descendant of the gods.

Virgil produced only three works: reputedly, he spent three years on the *Eclogues*, seven on the *Georgics*, and twelve on the *Aeneid*, which was still, he thought, several years short of its final form at the time of his death. According to one account, Virgil dictated a number of lines each morning and spent the afternoon licking them into shape "as a she-bear licks her cubs."[2] Each of the poems is highly distinct in subject matter, yet each bears the unmistakable stamp of Virgil's elegiac sensibility and startling genius. The *Eclogues* created the genre of pastoral poetry; the *Georgics*, which some consider, with Dryden, "the best poem by the best poet,"[3] celebrates a life of steady work in harmony with nature; and the *Aeneid* is a conscious rival of both the *Iliad* and the *Odyssey* in its epic telling of the founding of Rome. All three poems, however, are, in the end, about the power of poetry to create its own higher reality, as both a haven and a heaven for the soul. It is not surprising that Virgil was the ancient poet of choice for later Christian writers.

In the year 19, at the age of fifty, Virgil embarked on an extended trip to Greece to lick his final cub, the *Aeneid*, into shape. But he took ill and died in Brundisium (Brindisi, in the heel of the boot area of southern Italy, then considered part of Calabria) on September 20. He gave instructions that his unfinished epic should be burned, instructions Augustus unhesitatingly overrode.

Virgil is said to have composed his own epitaph, which was inscribed on his tombstone in Naples: *Mantua me genuit; Calabri rapuere; tenet nunc Parthenope; cecini pascua, rura, duces* ("Mantua gave me birth; Calabria took me away; and now Naples holds me; I sang of pastures, farms, leaders.").

ECLOGUES

Virgil's *Eclogues* were cherished in the Middle Ages primarily for his alleged prophecy of the coming of Christ. In the fourth Eclogue, he writes of an anticipated "child by whom / The Age of Iron gives way to the Golden Age," and of the ensuing

> Commencement of the glory, freedom from
> Earth's bondage to its own perpetual fear.
> Our crimes are going to be erased at last.
> This child will share in the life of the gods and he
> ... will be the ruler of a world.[4]

Never mind that the anticipated child to whom he was likely referring was that of Mark Antony and Octavian's sister, a union that it was hoped would free Romans from the fear of social unrest, erase the crimes of fratricidal civil war, and produce a stable succession of political rather than spiritual leaders. That child, in any event, proved to be a daughter, and Mark Antony soon abandoned Octavian's sister for Cleopatra. But perhaps Virgil was anticipating a son born to Augustus himself. Still other candidates have been proposed. Regardless, the prophecy is broad enough and bold enough that one cannot blame the early Christians for embracing it as a foreshadowing of their savior.

Our interest in the poems lies elsewhere, however. The term *Eclogues*, which simply means "selections," was chosen by later editors. Virgil's own title was *Bucolica*, from the Greek *boukolika*, meaning herdsmen's songs. In this short collection, Virgil both perfected and transcended the genre of pastoral poetry begun by Theocritus, a Greek poet from Sicily who wrote in Alexandria circa 280–250. Several of Theocritus's *Idylls* have rural settings in Arcadia (a remote and mountainous region of the Peloponnese associated with Pan, the god of shepherds and rustic music) and tell of shepherds such as Thyrsis and Lycidas, lying in the shade by cool springs, singing of their often hopeless love for Amaryllis and other maidens.

The mood and setting of these poems is captured in the opening lines of Theocritus's first Idyll, a lament for Daphnis, the archetype of the bucolic singer:

> There is sweet music in that pine tree's whisper, goatherd,
> There by the spring. Sweet too is the music of your pipe;
> ...
> Begin, my Muses, begin the herdsman's song.[5]

The singers are at languid ease in their rural setting, but suffused with feelings of loss. Nature itself weeps for Daphnis.

Virgil wrote his bucolic poems from 41 to 38, revising them for publication as a unit. He used the hexameter meter of Homer, as adapted to Latin by earlier poets such as Ennius and Lucretius. But he uses this heroic meter to very different effect, as he explains in the opening of his sixth Eclogue:

> When I began to write, my Muse did not
> Disdain to play Sicilian games nor did
> She blush to live in the woods, and when I thought
> Of singing of kings and battles, the god Apollo
> Tweaked my ear and said to me, "A shepherd
> Should feed fat sheep and sing a slender song."[6]

Virgil eschewed epic grandeur for the Sicilian games of Theocritus. He wanted to "sing a slender song" of rural landscapes and rustic herdsmen, who gather their flocks in the remote countryside, far from kings and battles. Accompanied by reed pipes and flutes, Tityrus, Lycidas, and other herdsmen sing of the god Pan, of nymphs, of nature, of their dreams, and of their loves. As Paul Alpers, the most important commenter on the *Eclogues* and the pastoral tradition generally, explains, "The self-awareness and wit with which pastoral poets scale down their verse is a way of reclaiming a degree of strength relative to their world."[7]

But, of course, Virgil's shepherds bear no relationship to real shepherds. And the countryside they inhabit is one that does not exist and never did exist. It is an idealized landscape of the imagination that somehow seems more urgent, genuine, and natural than the world in which we actually live.

> You mossy spring, you grasses softer than sleep,
> Under the shade cast by the little tree,
> Protect my flock from the scorching heat of noon.
> Summer is coming on. The buds begin
> To swell and cluster on the spreading vines.[8]

It is a dream world of innocence and purity, an Eden in which Virgil's shepherds have ample leisure (*otium*) for love and song. Bruno Snell, in his famous chapter, "Arcadia: The Discovery of a Spiritual Landscape," explained that Virgil was creating a deliberate "poetic counterpart of reality."[9] Far from Rome, the poet has the freedom to indulge and develop his feelings, and out of his sensibility come "self-contained forms of beauty whose reality lies within themselves."[10] Virgil created a world in which, unsurprisingly, the most important personage is the poet himself.

> Inspired poet, the song you sing is such
> As sleep must be to the weary on the grass
> Or cool brook water quenching the thirst of summer.[11]

There is nothing simple or artless about pastoral poetry. It is, in fact, self-consciously artificial and literary. The herdsmen engage in song contests. They commemorate departed singers (such as Daphnis). They sing of nature and love and mythology. But mostly they sing about singing. This is poetry about the transformative power of poetry, and the spiritual clearing it creates in our lives. This is a poet writing for other poets about the leisure and solitude essential to art and about the realm of the personal, in which beauty and delicacy of feeling matter most of all.

It is for this reason that pastoral poetry is inherently elegiac. It is imbued with a feeling of separation from everyday life and attachment to an idealized, never-to-be-attained world. John Milton tapped into this elegiac tradition in the seventeenth century when he wrote his great short poem, "Lycidas," in honor of a fellow Cambridge student and poet who drowned in the Irish Sea.

> Yet once more, O ye laurels, and once more,
> Ye myrtles brown, with ivy never sere,
> I come to pluck your berries harsh and crude,
> And with forced fingers rude
> Shatter your leaves before the mellowing year.
> Bitter constraint, and sad occasion dear,
> Compels me to disturb your season due;
> For Lycidas is dead, dead ere his prime,
> Young Lycidas, and hath not left his peer.
> Who would not sing for Lycidas? he knew
> Himself to sing, and build the lofty rhyme.
> He must not float upon his watery bier
> Unwept, and welter to the parching wind,
> Without the meed of some melodious tear.[12]

The great critic Samuel Johnson, in his *Life of Milton* was harshly critical of this invocation of the pastoral. "'Lycidas,'" he wrote, "is not to be considered as the effusion of real passion; for passion runs not after remote allusions and obscure opinions. Passion plucks no berries from the myrtle and ivy, nor calls upon Arethuse and Mincius, nor tells of rough *satyrs* and *fauns with cloven heel*. Where there is leisure for fiction there is little grief."[13] With due respect, since it so rarely happened, Johnson missed the deeper point. By adopting the pastoral conventions, Milton's poem aches with a sense of loss, of what might have been, and what ought to be, that is ultimately more haunting than a seemingly unfiltered and more "natural" outpouring of grief (itself a conventional form requiring tremendous artistic control).

Virgil himself, however, recognizes the limitations of pastoral poetry. He perfected it, transcended it, and bid it farewell in the course of his ten Eclogues. The world of Rome intrudes upon even his first poem through the confiscation of land given to the veteran soldiers of Octavian who defeated Brutus and Cassius and their republican forces in the civil war that followed the assassination of Caesar.

In the first Eclogue, the poet/herdsman Tityrus has managed to retain his farm by appealing directly to a "young man" (presumably Octavian) in Rome. His land may be stony in places and marshy in others, but it is his, and he will find there "the cool of the shade" and familiar streams.[14] His fellow poet Meliboeus is not so lucky. His heartfelt lament is direct enough to satisfy Dr. Johnson:

> Oh, will it ever come to pass that I'll
> Come back, after many years, to look upon
> The turf roof of what had been my cottage
> And the little field of grain that once was mine,
> My own little kingdom. Have we done all this work
> Upon our planted and fallow fields so that
> Some godless barbarous soldier will enjoy it?
> This is what civil war has brought down upon us.
> So Meliboeus, carefully set out
> Your plants and pear trees, all in rows—for whom?
> For strangers, for others, we have farmed our land.[15]

The gratitude of Tityrus must be balanced against the bitterness of Meliboeus. One may stay, the other must go, but for arbitrary and unfair reasons. Tityrus offers Meliboeus a place of rest and plenty before he begins his exile. But Meliboeus makes no response to this small gesture of embarrassed kindness. He is unwilling to ease Tityrus's guilt.

The land around Mantua was indeed confiscated by Octavian and given to his soldiers. Some speculate—based on Virgil's identification with Tityrus elsewhere in the poems—that the farm of Virgil's father was spared through the intervention of a patron. Others suggest that Virgil's father was among the dispossessed. Regardless, Virgil's public sympathy with those who lost their land—"Heartbroken and beaten, since fortune will have it so"[16]—was courageous.

The more interesting point, though, is the poetic one. Politics should not be able to intrude upon an imaginary landscape in Arcadia. And yet it does. The spiritual landscape needed for poetry is being crowded out, dispossessed by political and social upheaval.[17] Poetry can give us both hope and comfort, but it is not proof against power and circumstance. For "what can music do / Against the weapons of soldiers?"[18]

More broadly, the expropriation of land is symbolic of the exhaustion of the pastoral motif itself. ("Time takes all we have away from us; / . . . I am forgetting all my songs; / My voice grows hoarse."[19]) The artificial world of pure art is too fragile to sustain our lives. Tityrus's final invitation, which Meliboeus does not answer, is to the consolations of poetry itself, which are no longer sufficient when divorced from the world in which we actually live. Palaemon—a neighbor—listens to and enjoys a song contest between two herdsmen. He praises both but declines to judge between them, noting that there is work to be done: "the time has come to close the sluices, boys, / For now the fields have drunk their fill of song."[20]

Ultimately, Virgil decides that the artificial shade of pastoral is bad for poetry itself. Poetry must leave Arcadia for the sunshine of his native Italy.

> Now we must go; the shade's not good for singers,
> The juniper shade's unwholesome; unwholesome too
> For the plants that need the sunshine is the shade.
> Go home, my full-fed goats, you've eaten your fill,
> The Evening Star is rising; it's time to go home.[21]

GEORGICS

The central motif of the *Eclogues* is the power and seductive appeal of love: *omnia uincit Amor: et nos cedamus Amori* ("Love conquers all; and let us all yield to Love.").[22] In the *Georgics*, work, not love, is what counts: *labor omnia vicit improbus*

("Hard labor conquered all.").[23] Ultimately, however, the two coalesce. For difficult labors properly performed are themselves manifestations of love, and in such work we find our highest fulfillment.

The *Georgics*, seven years in the making, was completed in 29, after the end of the second civil war. The scars of that war, and the many other wars through which Virgil lived, are evident throughout the poem.

> War everywhere in the world; crimes everywhere,
> . . .
> No honor at all is given to the plow;
> The fields are barren and empty, the farmers gone;
> The crooked sickles are beaten into swords;
> . . .
> Mars rages everywhere.[24]

Virgil longs for a time of healing after decades of disastrous strife, and he hopes that plows will again churn the fields where men fought and died.[25] He wants to grab hold of something simple and familiar and so turns to farming as a metaphor for the peace and plenty that has so long eluded Italy. Cincinnatus, that embodiment of traditional Roman virtue, was famously summoned from his small farm in 458 and given dictatorial powers in a military crisis when rival Italian tribes were threatening Rome. He defeated them decisively and, after sixteen days in power, gave up his position and returned to his plow. So, too, Virgil turns away from war, politics, and the self-seeking bustle of urban life and finds salvation in (re)attachment to the land.

> Far from the battlefield,
> Earth brings forth from herself in ample justice
> The simple means of life, simply enjoyed.
> . . .
> When Justice left the earth,
> She left her footprint here, among such people.[26]

The *Georgics* is both a paean and a guide to farming. In book 1, Virgil focuses on crops—"What's right for bringing abundance to the fields";[27] book 2 deals with trees and vines; book 3 with livestock; and book 4 with bees, the source of honey and hence (in a world still without sugar) of all sweetness.

Virgil follows the didactic tradition of the Greek poet Hesiod, whose *Works and Days* offered instruction out of his life as a small farmer on the slopes of Mount Helikon, living in harmony with the seasons.[28] Virgil resolves to "bring the Muses home from Helicon / To my own native country."[29] Yet, while the world of Hesiod—at the end of the eighth century—was indeed one of small farmers eking out a meager living, Virgil's Italy was increasingly dominated by large estates run by overseers and slaves, whose owners spent most of the year in Rome. Virgil's vision of the small, sturdy, independent farmer—like that invoked by politicians in our own day—was already more symbol than reality. Yet it was a powerful symbol for all that.

Virgil's farmer

> neither looks with pity on the poor
> Nor does he look with envy at the rich.
> He takes from his fields and from his orchard boughs
> What they have offered of their own free will,
> Nor does he have experience of the iron
> Hard-heartedness of the law, the Forum's madness,
> Insolence of bureaucratic office.[30]

Virgil's farmer is, in short, the embodiment of the Epicurean hero celebrated by Lucretius, who avoids entanglement in public affairs and looks to himself for his sufficiency. But there are two important differences. First, the farmer has no need of philosophical doctrine, and Virgil supplies him with none. Lucretius "has learned the causes of things, / And therefore under his feet subjugates fear / And the decrees of unrelenting fate."[31] The farmer is not so grand, and Virgil in his poem does not aspire to "mighty knowledge" but instead will "find delight in the rural fields / And the little brooks that make their way through valleys."[32] Second, the farmer is not detached from the world but rather connected to it in a more fundamental and natural way. He seeks not leisure and isolation but a deeper engagement through work.

Virgil follows Hesiod's (and, coincidentally, the Hebrew Bible's) conceit of a lost golden age when "men shared / All things together and Earth quite freely yielded / The gifts of herself she gave, being unasked."[33] According to Hesiod, unrelenting toil was a punishment imposed by Zeus for the theft of fire and other sins that exalted man. (In the Bible, the original sin was to eat the forbidden fruit of the tree of knowledge of good and evil.) Virgil, however, views work as man's greatest blessing.

> For Father Jupiter himself ordained
> That the way should not be easy. It was he
> Who first established the art of cultivation,
> Sharpening with their cares the skills of men,
> Forbidding the world he rules to slumber in ease.[34]

Work for Virgil is not a fall from grace but a path to meaning and purpose. Want is the "cause of human ingenuity, / And ingenuity the cause of arts."[35] Life is both hard and precarious. Thus, we have developed skills and arts. As we shall see, those skills and arts are no guarantor against the vagaries of nature and life. But they are, as the poet/translator David Slavitt has explained, "a solace and a reward."[36] "Work is what we are, and it is by our work that we assert and defend ourselves, if only temporarily, against the chaos and emptiness of the universe."[37] The *Georgics*, then, is a poem about the redemptive power of work, and the farmer a perfect "for instance."

Without unceasing toil on a farm "you will, alas, / End up, defeated, staring at your neighbor's / Granary full of corn, and in the woods / You'll shake the oak tree, frantic for something to eat."[38] The farmer's mission is to discipline and train the soil, to create order where there was none before.[39] "This is the work he does, and it sustains / His country, and his family."[40] But he must pay strict attention to, and even glory in, the minute but critical details of farming. Virgil includes an extended passage on the care a farmer must lavish upon his tools: his curved plow, heavy threshing-sledge, and ponderous hoes.[41] (A similar attention to detail, with similar effect, is to be found in the *Little House on the Prairie* series by Laura Ingalls Wilder and *The Growth of the Soil* by Knut Hamsun.) He must study the weather and the ways of the winds and "know / The history of the planting in that ground, / What crops will prosper there and what will not."[42] He must learn the many varieties of trees and vines, and the "appropriate way to cultivate each kind."[43] He must nurture his "worthy bullocks and his herd of cows,"[44] guard his sheep, and discipline his oxen to the plow. There is both plenty and pleasure to be found in such labor. Indeed, marking the worth of each detail (for the poet as well as the farmer) is an act of reverence and of love. The farmer tells off the seasons like the beads of a rosary.

> The farmer's labor circles back on him
> As the seasons of the year roll back around
> To where they were and walk in their own footsteps.[45]

Book 2 ends with Virgil's famous praise of the Italian countryside, with its vast fields, abundant crops, olive groves, "mighty lakes,"[46] and the spring rains "bringing to life the life waiting to live."[47] Virgil portrays a restored and peaceful Italy, in the early days of Augustus's rule, as a sort of earthly paradise. In David Ferry's lovely translation:

> I think it must have been that just such days
> As these were the shining days when the world was new;
> Everywhere it was spring, the whole world over;
> The East Wind held in check its winter winds;
> The beasts drank in the light of that first dawn;
> The first men, born of the earth, raised up their heads
> From the stony ground; the woods were stocked with game,
> And the first stars came out in the sky above.[48]

Yet Virgil recognizes that it cannot last (and thereby redeems himself from hagiography and naive optimism). Illness, war, old age, the passions that divide men, even death itself, can be deferred but not avoided. Entropy alone is sufficient to dissipate progress.

> All things by nature are ready to get worse,
> Lapse backward, fall away from what they were,
> Just as if one who struggles to row his little
> Boat upstream against a powerful current
> Should but for a moment relax his arms, the current
> Would carry him headlong back again downstream.[49]

Nature, which seems at times so beneficent, can turn against us in a moment. "Drought, or torrential rain, winds bringing the cold," "battering hailstones," earthquakes, and volcanic eruptions can all destroy what was so carefully and lovingly cultivated.[50] Virgil, following Thucydides and Lucretius, includes a detailed and gruesome description of the plague, focusing on its devastating effect on livestock. His account of the pervasive and destructive influence of sexual passion is equally Lucretian. *Amor omnibus idem*, he writes, "love is the same for all," and all living creatures, human and animal alike, "rush into the fire."[51] Whatever is alive is condemned to perish, often sooner and more violently than expected. According to his biographer, James Boswell, Samuel Johnson "often used to quote, with great pathos,"[52] these lines from the *Georgics*:

Optima quaeque dies miseris mortalibus aevi
Prima fugit; subeunt morbi tristisque senectus
Et labor, et durae rapit inclementia mortis.

The best days of life, for all poor mortal creatures,
Are the soonest to be gone; then illness comes,
And sad old age, and trouble; and pitiless death
Soon carries us away.[53]

What good, then, is work, Virgil asks, if all that awaits us are old age, illness, and death?[54] As an initial matter, he notes, there is the continuity of life itself. "Be sure new young are born, year after year," Virgil counsels the farmer.[55] In this way, nature replenishes itself, and loss is countered with gain. In our own children, too, we obtain a measure of immortality or at least make an investment in the continuity of life after we are gone. Fortunate the farmer, whose "children gather around him for his kisses."[56]

For the childless Virgil, however, the deeper answer is to be found in the tale of Orpheus and Eurydice with which he ends the *Georgics*. Eurydice, wife of the famed singer Orpheus, was bitten by a poisonous snake hiding in the tall grass along a riverbank. Inconsolable in his grief, Orpheus resolves to conquer death itself with his song. He descends into the underworld, playing his lyre and singing of his love: "the house of Death was spellbound by his music."[57] Even Cerberus, the three-headed guard dog of hell, forgets to bare his sets of fangs. With his song, Orpheus softens "the hearts no human prayers can cause to pity."[58] He fetches his Eurydice and, step by step, returns with her to the world of light. But, in the end, he falters.

Just as they were just about to emerge
Out into the light, suddenly, seized by love,
Bewildered into heedlessness, alas!
His purpose overcome, he turned, and looked
Back at Eurydice! And then and there
His labor was spilled and flowed away like water.
. . .
. . . like smoke
Disintegrating into air she was
Dispersed away and vanished from his eyes
And never saw him again, and he was left
Clutching at shadows, with so much still to say.[59]

Art cannot conquer death. And yet, in this beautiful myth, whose ending appears to be Virgil's unique invention, it comes very close, as close as humankind can ever do.

The farm of the *Georgics* is every bit as figurative as the shaded dell in the *Eclogues*. The adult Virgil was no more a farmer than he was a shepherd. Yet he somehow managed in his poetry to combine the *otium* (leisure for appreciation) of the pasture and the *labor improbus* (constant, grueling labor) of the farm. "The *Georgics*," classicist Adam Parry explained, "is ultimately about the life of man in this world, about a kind of art in living which can confront the absurdity and cruelty of both nature and civilization, and yet render our existence satisfactory and beautiful."[60] Through hard work and skill, through constant dedication and attention to detail, we can briefly impose a measure of order upon a chaotic and meaningless world. All that we experience can be transmuted into art. Poetry will not save us or those we love. But even "clutching at shadows" can give us purpose and beauty.

HOMER REDUX

In the *Eclogues*, Virgil was content to sing "a slender song" of shepherds and their loves. In the *Georgics*, he sang of farmers and their work and asked, rhetorically, "What need have I for a loftier song to sing?"[61] But the time had finally come for him to sing of kings and battles. Whether pressed by Augustus or impelled by his own artistic development, Virgil undertook to write the epic of Rome's founding. And, having used the Greek poets Theocritus and Hesiod as his first two models, he inevitably turned to Homer as his third.

"*Arma virumque cano*," he begins: "Arms and the man I sing."[62] He will sing of warfare and the human spirit both, combining the themes of the *Iliad* and the *Odyssey*. Yet he will do so in reverse order. For his hero, Aeneas, son of the goddess Venus and the Trojan Anchises, flees the destruction of Troy and spends seven long years wandering, as Odysseus did, among the islands and shores of the Mediterranean before finally landing in Italy where he must fight, not to destroy a city, but to lay the foundation for the future Roman Empire.

The explicit parallels with Homer are many. To name just a few: like Odysseus, Aeneas encounters the land of the Cyclops as well as Scylla and Charybdis on his voyages; he is driven by a storm into a foreign port, where he tells his tale to an enchanted court; and he descends into the underworld, where he encounters lost comrades and a lost parent and learns how to bring his journey to a close. Like

Achilles, he presides over funeral games; he is out of action when his camp is besieged; his goddess mother induces the smith-god, Vulcan, to prepare for him a set of armor and a fabulously emblazoned shield; and he wreaks a terrible revenge on the other side's greatest warrior, who has killed his dear friend. Smaller echoes also sound throughout the poem.

Yet the differences are even more significant. Virgil was not mimicking Homer. The homeric tradition had played itself out; Alexandrian epigones such as Apollonius of Rhodes had long since demonstrated that. Virgil was reenvisaging and revitalizing epic poetry to fit a very different world, as Dante would do 1,300 years later. In all its essentials, the *Aeneid* is a uniquely Roman poem just as Aeneas is a thoroughly Roman hero.

Achilles fought for *kleos* (personal honor), a heroic ideal that in the *Iliad* destroyed civilization and domestic life at Troy, as well as Achilles himself and so many of his comrades. Odysseus sought to leave war behind and regain his rightful place as husband, father, son, and king. His voyage in the *Odyssey* was one of reeducation and reconnection. Aeneas fights for a future civilization that he himself will never see and can only dimly imagine. His voyage schools him in the loss of the very ties that bind Odysseus: his home, his wife, his father, his attempt to find a new love, and even his innate humanity, which must give way before the higher fate to which he subordinates himself. Whereas personal assertion is the defining characteristic of Achilles and the retention of his personal identity through all buffetings is the defining characteristic of Odysseus (even when disguised as a beggar in his own house), Aeneas submits himself to an impersonal destiny that entails the loss of all he holds dear. The personal is given over to the grand historical destiny of Rome to be the most powerful state ever known to man.

Aeneas, in consequence, is deeper and more complex than either Achilles or Odysseus. He bears the burden of a distant future. But he also bears the burden—in memory and longing—of a past he must renounce. He is too melancholy and too lonely for Homer. But the world no longer needs homeric heroes. Caesar, Pompey, and Mark Antony all aspired to *kleos*, with disastrous and devastating results. The world needs a new sort of hero who will bring peace and stability to a violent and chaotic world.

The *Aeneid* is not an epic of Augustus. But it is an epic that casts Augustus in the light of history and myth, as the culmination of a process driven by fate and the gods. Aeneas is explicitly presented as Augustus's ancestor. In an important sense, Aeneas lives to make Augustus possible.

From that noble blood will arise a Trojan Caesar,
his empire bound by the Ocean, his glory by the stars.[63]

Yet what is remarkable in a national epic ostensibly celebrating Rome's founding and future greatness is the constant reminder of the human cost and the still-unanswered question whether it was worth so much suffering. Too many people were brutally slaughtered in the building of the empire, and even those who lived bore the scars of constant warfare. Virgil implicitly stresses the need for Rome under Augustus to redeem what went before or, if that is impossible, at least to retain the *Pax Romana* for as long as possible.

This ambivalence is embodied in the poem and in the character of Aeneas. "We hear two distinct voices in the *Aeneid*," Adam Parry writes, "a public voice of triumph, and a private voice of regret."[64] Virgil wrote an epic that could somehow satisfy Augustus and yet remain true to his own artistic sensibility. It is, as C. S. Lewis noted, an epic for grown-ups,[65] full of trade-offs and compromises, full of faint hopes, vivid regrets, and a pervasive melancholy that all the greatness of the Roman Empire cannot eradicate.

PIOUS AENEAS

We first meet Aeneas in the midst of a storm raging at sea, a storm that scatters his ships and threatens to drown him and all the men, women, and children he has brought from Troy. Aeneas cries out to the gods in both fear and accusation.

"Three, four times blest, my comrades
lucky to die beneath the soaring walls of Troy—
before their parents' eyes! If only I'd gone down
under your right hand—Diomedes, strongest Greek afield—
and poured out my life on the battlegrounds of Troy!"[66]

Aeneas longed for a hero's death at Troy. But the gods decreed he would escape that slaughter and found a new city on Italian soil.

Aeneas in book 2 provides a harrowing account of the night of Troy's fall. Amid the carnage and flames unleashed by the Greek warriors pouring forth from the wooden horse and then through the opened gates, Aeneas seizes his arms, rallies his men, and "fire[s] their hearts with the fury of despair."[67] He resolves to die in a now-hopeless cause, plunging into battle where the fighting is thickest. Yet three separate visions block him from such a fate. First, the dead Hector appears to him, "haggard with sorrow, . . . black with blood and grime,"[68] to tell him that Troy cannot be saved and that his duty now lies elsewhere. He must take the household gods of Troy and seek a new city for them. Second, his goddess mother, Venus, appears to him in all her glory and commands him not to contend with the gods intent on Troy's destruction but instead to look after his father, Anchises, his wife, Creusa, and his son, Ascanius, and with them to flee the city.

Following his mother's lead, Aeneas fights his way back to his house and gathers his family to escape. But Anchises will not leave "to drag his life out now and suffer exile."[69] He stands fast, and Aeneas again resolves to die with him, until omens from Jupiter convince Anchises to depart. Urging his father to hold the hearth gods, Aeneas takes Anchises upon his back and his son by the hand, and with Creusa following close behind they make their way from the city. But Greek troops are all about them, and they race through the dark streets, losing their way, until they reach the safety of the countryside. Creusa is no longer with them.

> Oh dear god, my wife, Creusa—
> torn from me by a brutal fate! What then,
> did she stop in her tracks or lose her way?
> Or exhausted, sink down to rest? Who knows?
> I never set my eyes on her again.[70]

Not alive, in any event. In a cruel twist on the myth of Orpheus and Eurydice, Aeneas's fault was his failure to look back. "I never looked back, she never crossed my mind," he admits,[71] while they fled the hell of Troy, overrun and in flames. Aeneas dons his armor yet again and, leaving his father and son hidden with other stragglers, goes back into Troy and retraces his route through the city. He finally encounters not Creusa but her stricken ghost—his third saving vision. She urges him to ease his grief, and prophesizes for him, after a lengthy exile, "a kingdom . . . to claim, and a queen to make your wife."[72] She was not destined to share his exile or his triumph, but at least she—"daughter of Dardanus that I am, the wife of Venus' son"[73]—would not be taken as the slave to some Greek warrior. "Hold dear the son we share, we love together," she urges him.[74] And then, like Eurydice, she dissolves into the empty air and leaves him to his tears.

> Three times I tried to fling my arms around her neck,
> three times I embraced—nothing . . . her phantom
> sifting through my fingers,
> light as wind, quick as a dream in flight.[75]

The scene echoes Achilles's attempt to embrace the ghost of Patroclus in the *Iliad* and that of Odysseus with his mother in the underworld, but it is more affecting than either. It is both unspeakably sad in its own right and a symbol of all that Aeneas has lost and will lose in pursuit of a fate he has not chosen for himself and that seems itself as elusive as Creusa's shade.

After leaving Troy with the remnants of his people, Aeneas knows nothing but exile and "blows . . . on land and sea from the gods above."[76] Even his honored father, Anchises—"my mainstay in every danger and defeat"[77]—dies on the journey. Jupiter, the king of the gods, has made clear his plans and intentions for Aeneas. But his wife, Juno, moves to thwart them at every twist and turn. She despises the Trojans for the judgment of Paris, which favored Venus's beauty over her own, and she fears the Romans for what they will do to her own favorite city, Carthage, in the years to come. She cannot stop Aeneas but harries him at every turn, including by convincing the god of the winds, Aeolus, to unleash their full fury on Aeneas's fleet as it nears Italy. And, in the second part of the poem, she herself will unleash Allecto, one of the three Furies, to stir up passionate war in Italy against the new arrivals.

There is no reason to think that Virgil believed in Jupiter and Juno as individual divinities. The Roman writers of the Augustan age were too sophisticated and cynical for that. But there is every reason to think that Virgil believed in a basic dichotomy between *fatum* and *furor*: between order and chaos, between reason and violence, between duty and unbridled passion. Aeneas lives with a foot in both realms and is constantly riven by their competing trajectories, as symbolized by Jupiter and Juno. Order, reason, and duty will ultimately prevail. Rome will be founded and, hence, it is fated to be. We cannot imagine it otherwise. Aeneas's actions are consequential enough to take on an aura of inevitability, and hence divine planning. But chaos, violence, and passion are never far removed, and constantly threaten to overwhelm him and his mission.

Aeneas is loyal to the gods, to his father, to his fellow Trojans, and, most of all, to the country he will found. His flight from Troy, his long wanderings, his renunciation of romantic love, and the war he will wage in Italy are all acts of piety, undertaken as the reluctant standard-bearer of a distant Rome. He must sacrifice the purely personal to his larger obligations. But that suppression merely intensifies his suffering. When seven of his ships, driven by the storm, find refuge on the shore of Africa, he does not know what happened to the rest of his fleet. But he "assumes a look of hope and keeps his anguish buried in his heart."[78] He encourages his men to summon their courage and dismiss grief and fear. "A joy it will be one day, perhaps, to remember even this," he urges,[79] though hardly believing it himself.

Aeneas, with his overpowering sense of duty and obligation, often seems to pale before the vividness of Juno's favorites, Dido and Turnus, as the angel Michael will pale before Satan in Milton's *Paradise Lost*. But Aeneas, too, has his moments of destructive, overriding fury. Indeed, he cannot succeed without them. The price of peace is war, and Aeneas must steel himself to war without making war an end in itself. Juno, in frustration with her inability to change what is fated, cries out: "If I cannot sway the heavens, I'll wake the powers of hell!"[80] Aeneas, too, must rely on the powers of the underworld for his strength and his steadfastness:

> As firm as a sturdy oak grown tough with age
> when the Northwinds blasting off the Alps compete,
> fighting left and right, to wrench it from the earth,
> and the winds scream, the trunk shudders, its leafy crest
> showers across the ground but it clings firm to its rock,
> its roots stretching as deep into the dark world below
> as its crown goes towering toward the gales of heaven—
> so firm the hero stands: buffeted left and right.[81]

Aeneas is a thoroughly modern hero, a man of internal conflicts and contradictions, more admirable than likeable. He is redeemed by the sorrow to which he clings, as he tried to cling to Creusa, and by the burden that he bears, as he bore his father and his household gods out of Troy. "This labor of love," he resolves, "will never wear me down."[82]

DIDO, QUEEN OF CARTHAGE

Aeneas and his followers, though widely dispersed during the storm that opens the poem, reunite at Carthage in North Africa. The city was founded and is ruled by Dido, who came there from Tyre after her beloved husband, Sychaeus, was murdered by her own brother in a power struggle. She too, then, is an exile, and she welcomes the Trojans openly, inviting them to settle there and share the kingdom as equal citizens.

Here, for the first time,
Aeneas dared to hope he had found some haven,
for all his hard straits, to trust in better days.[83]

Sitting in the royal court, with the young Ascanius by her side, Dido invites Aeneas to tell the story of the fall of Troy and his subsequent wanderings. He does so over the course of the next two books, ending with his father's death during the voyage and the storm that drove them to her shores. The scene is drawn directly from the *Odyssey*, in which Odysseus is invited to tell the tale of his rovings at the court of Phaeacia. Odysseus wins the admiration of his listeners and the heart of the young Princess Nausicaa, and he is invited to stay there and become her husband. But Odysseus longs for his true home and for the wife he has not seen for twenty years. Odysseus's departure is an expression of his own will, his indomitable sense of self. It will be otherwise with Aeneas.

Listening to and watching Aeneas, Dido, for the first time since the death of her husband, feels the stirrings of a "fresh, living love" in "a heart at rest for long— long numb to passion."[84] The spell cast upon her by Venus, seeking to ensure a safe welcome for her son, seems almost superfluous:

The man's courage, the sheer pride of his line,
they all come pressing home to her, over and over.
His looks, his words, they pierce her heart and cling—
no peace, no rest for her body, love will give her none.[85]

Dido nonetheless resolves to remain faithful to Sychaeus and suppress her wavering heart. She will not dishonor her love for the man who wed her first. But her sister, Anna, urges her not to resist this new passion, but instead to marry Aeneas and add the strength of the Trojan army to her own forces and make Carthage invincible. "These were the words that fanned her sister's fire, turned her doubts to hopes and dissolved her sense of shame."[86]

Dido is literally driven to frenzy by her love. She neglects her duties in Carthage and wanders the city streets like a wounded doe. In the evening, she hangs on Aeneas's words and then, "alone in the echoing hall, distraught, she flings herself on the couch that he left empty."[87] She cannot hold out for long, and indeed both Venus and Juno conspire in her downfall—the former, lest the Carthaginians turn on the Trojans, the latter, in a vain attempt to keep Aeneas from founding the kingdom of Italy, destined ultimately to destroy her favorite city.

During a hunt in the woods, Juno sends a cloudburst, and both Dido and Aeneas seek shelter in the same cave. There, as "lightning torches flare," they consummate their union.

> From now on, Dido cares no more
> for appearances, nor for her reputation, either.
> She no longer thinks to keep the affair a secret,
> no, she calls it a marriage,
> using the word to cloak her sense of guilt.[88]

Aeneas too luxuriates in their love. Wearing a cloak of Tyrian purple given to him by the queen, he lays the foundations for the city's fortifications. Rome is forgotten. Carthage has become his home; and Dido, all but his wife. Aeneas, for the first and only time in the poem, is happy.

But it cannot last. Jupiter sends his messenger, Mercury, to chide Aeneas for his delay. If the prospect of his own glorious destiny is not sufficient motivation, Mercury urges him to remember Ascanius, his son, who will one day rule Italy's realm. The god orders him to depart. Unsure how or when to approach Dido, stunned by the need to leave the land and the woman he loves, Aeneas orders his men to prepare the ships in secret while he waits for the right moment to tell her.

Dido, of course, is not deluded. She learns of the preparations and confronts the faithless Aeneas in a fury, accusing him of betraying her honor and then callously trying to steal away in silence. Aeneas is at his most human and vulnerable in his disjointed and halting response: he was going to tell her, he insists; he owes her so much; he will never regret his time with her; he never promised to marry her; everything is out of his hands. In the end, he can only shake his head in despair: *Italiam non sponte sequor* ("It is not by my wish that I make for Italy.").[89] Dido storms against him, but, although his heart is "shattered by his great love,"[90] he remains outwardly unmoved by her curses, tears, and prayers.

> He is deaf to all appeals. He won't relent.
> The Fates bar the way
> and heaven blocks his gentle, human ears.
> . . .
> He takes the full force
> of love and suffering deep in his great heart.
> His will stands unmoved. The falling tears are futile.[91]

Dido has a vast heap made of the arms, clothes, and other belongings Aeneas left behind in his haste to depart, topped by the bridal bed they shared together. She wants, she claims, to "obliterate every trace of the man."[92] As she watches the ships sail from the harbor, she casts her final curses down upon them: that Aeneas will die before his day and never enjoy his realm, that Carthage and Rome be locked in "endless war," and that an "avenger still unknown" (i.e., Hannibal) will bring fire and sword to the Italian homeland.[93]

Virgil captures Dido's unraveling in chilling and affecting detail:

> Dido,
> trembling, desperate now with the monstrous thing afoot—
> her bloodshot eyes rolling, quivering cheeks blotched
> and pale with imminent death—goes bursting through
> the doors to the inner courtyard, clambers in frenzy
> up the soaring pyre and unsheathes a sword, a Trojan sword
> she once sought as a gift, but not for such an end.[94]

After lying for a time on the bridal bed, she throws herself upon the sword. The departing Trojans see the fire from Dido's funeral pyre with grim foreboding, and sail on.

THE GOLDEN BOUGH

Hit with yet another storm, Aeneas and his followers take refuge on the coast of Sicily, where Acestes, of Trojan ancestry, rules. There, Aeneas fills the interlude with funeral games for Anchises. The games themselves seem an obligatory, if pale, imitation of those held for Patroclus in the *Iliad*. Even the same events are staged (though a boat race is substituted for the chariot race), with the same squabbles over prizes and preeminence, all graciously resolved by Aeneas qua Achilles.

But, while the men are busy with their contests, the women—"sick of struggling with the sea" and longing for a place to settle after seven years of exile—resolve to "burn these accursed ships to ashes."[95] They cast burning brands upon the decks, hoping the Trojans will be forced to stay in Sicily and build their walls there. Only a rainstorm sent by Jupiter limits the damage to four hulls lost. Aeneas himself, disheartened, wavers between staying and "chasing an Italy fading still."[96] In the dark night of his anguish, Anchises's spirit appears to him, vouchsafing him a vision of the glorious race he will found and the empire for which he will lay the cornerstone. Yet Aeneas must first, in the ultimate act of piety, descend into the underworld to seek his father's shade.

He embarks from Sicily with his best troops, leaving behind "the old men bent with age, the women sick of the sea," and "all those who elect to stay, who feel no need for glory."[97] They sail to Cumae, on the west coast of Italy above the Bay of Naples. There, in the cave of the Sibyl, the priestess of Apollo's oracle at Cumae, is the entrance to the underworld. The Sibyl prophesizes that Aeneas will soon reach his promised homeland but will rue the day: "Wars, horrendous wars, and the Tiber foaming with tides of blood, I see it all!"[98] Aeneas, who has borne more than his share of trials already, is undeterred and asks permission to visit his father in the underworld. The Sibyl coolly notes that the descent is easy, for the gates of Death stand wide open, "but to retrace your steps, to climb back to the upper air—there the struggle, there the labor lies."[99]

The Sibyl instructs Aeneas that, before he visits the Kingdom of the Dead, he must seek out the golden bough, sacred to Proserpina, queen of the underworld.

> "Hidden
> deep in a shady tree there grows a golden bough,
> its leaves and its hardy, sinewy stem all gold,
>
> . . .
>
> The whole grove covers it over, dusky valleys
> enfold it too, closing in around it. No one
> may pass below the secret places of earth before
> he plucks the fruit, the golden foliage of that tree.
>
> . . .
>
> Freely, easily,
> all by itself it comes away, if Fate calls you on.
> If not, no strength within you can overpower it,
> no iron blade, however hard, can tear it off."[100]

One scholar has called the golden bough "a symbol of wisdom and initiation";[101] another, "a symbol of splendor and lifelessness";[102] still another, a sign that the "power of life and death is a single reality."[103] Sir James Frazer named his monumental study of magic and religion *The Golden Bough*, as a marker of man's gradual progress from myth to science. All we can say about it for sure is that the golden bough enables Aeneas to visit the realm of the dead and yet return to the world of the living, as Orpheus (without his Eurydice), Theseus (with help from Hercules), and Odysseus did before him. For myself, I view the golden bough as a symbol of the power of art, which springs from life (as the bough grows on a living tree) but is not itself alive; which yields after much searching only to those who are called to it; and which allows one to explore the realm of the dead as well as the living and thereby achieve a form of immortality. Indeed, Virgil himself, in the voice of the Sibyl, invokes the gods of the dead as if they were the Muses of Homer: "lend me the right to tell what I have heard, lend your power to reveal the world immersed in the misty depths of earth."[104]

Led by twin doves sent by his goddess mother, Aeneas finds the hidden tree and tears away the golden bough. After presenting it to the Sibyl, he follows her into the underworld. Virgil's description of the underworld—including Tartarus (where punishments in keeping with their crimes are meted out to the wicked) and the Elysian Fields (where the blessed make their homes in shady groves and meadows washed with brooks)—is justly famous and must be read in its entirety. It exercised a profound influence on Dante, who chose Virgil as his initial guide to the Christian underworld and as the embodiment of pagan wisdom and virtue (which could take him only so far in his exploration of the divine plan).[105] For our purposes, three passages must be mentioned for, respectively, their elegiac beauty, their poignancy, and their importance to the overall narrative.

First, Aeneas must pass over the river Styx on the ferry of Charon. There the souls of the dead throng, waiting to cross:

> mothers and grown men and ghosts of great-souled heroes,
> their bodies stripped of life, and boys and unwed girls
> and sons laid on the pyre before their parents' eyes.
> As thick as leaves in autumn woods at the first frost
> that slip and float to earth, or dense as flocks of birds
> that wing from the heaving sea to shore when winter's chill
> drives them over the waves to landfalls drenched in sunlight.[106]

Charon's ferocity at the sight of a living man is quelled only by the presentation of the golden bough, and with his boat groaning under the unaccustomed weight, he carries Aeneas and the Sibyl across.

Second, in a separate Field of Mourning, where suicides and those consumed by cruel love abide, Aeneas encounters Dido with her wound still fresh. His worst fears confirmed, he speaks words of love and regret to her—words he could not find when she was still alive—and again urges that he left her against his will. He pleads in vain for some sign of reconciliation.

> Aeneas, with such appeals, with welling tears,
> tried to soothe her rage, her wild fiery glance.
> But she, her eyes fixed on the ground, turned away,
> her features no more moved by his pleas as he talked on
> than if she were set in stony flint or Parian marble rock.
> And at last she tears herself away, his enemy forever,
> fleeing back to the shadowed forests where Sychaeus,
> her husband long ago, answers all her anguish,
> meets her love with love.[107]

Finally, Aeneas reaches his father. He makes three futile attempts to embrace him, as he had with his wife, Creusa (whom, interestingly, he neither sees nor seeks in the underworld). Anchises cannot return his embrace, but he can show him the shadowy future that awaits. Aeneas will marry Lavinia, princess and sole heir of the kingdom of Latium, and in his old age will have a son, Silvius, who will mingle Trojan and Italian blood—"a king who fathers kings in turn, he founds our race that rules in Alba Longa"[108] (the city out of which Rome will evolve). Anchises shows him the spirits of future Roman heroes, cleansed of their prior earthly existence, their memories blank, who wait for life and their return to the world of men: Romulus (son of Mars and titular founder of Rome proper); the heroes of the republic, including noble Cato and the two Scipios who will conquer Carthage; Caesar and Pompey, who will bring civil war; and most importantly of all, Caesar Augustus, who will bring back the Age of Gold and extend the empire to the limits of the known earth.

The genius of the Roman people, Anchises explains, is precisely this: not to create but to rule.

> "Others, I have no doubt,
> will forge the bronze to breathe with suppler lines,
> draw from the block of marble features quick with life,
> plead their cases better, chart with their rods the stars
> that climb the sky and foretell the times they rise.
> But you, Roman, remember, rule with all your power
> the peoples of the earth—these will be your arts:
> to put your stamp on the works and ways of peace,
> to spare the defeated, break the proud in war."[109]

It is a curious concession by Rome's greatest poet, who hated war and valued art above all other things.

Having shown Aeneas this vision of glory yet to come, Anchises escorts him and the Sibyl to the two Gates of Sleep. Through one, made of horn, true shades may easily pass. Through the other, a gate of flawless, glistening ivory, "the dead send false dreams up toward the sky."[110] It is the ivory gate through which Aeneas and the Sibyl depart, which raises the question: in what sense is Rome's dream of glory a false one? Perhaps Virgil was not making such a concession to Rome's brutal exercise of power after all.

THE SHIELD OF AENEAS

Aeneas's *Odyssey* is at an end. His *Iliad* awaits. Virgil even feels called upon to reinvoke the Muses at the beginning of book 7: "A greater tide of events springs up before me now, I launch a greater labor."[111]

Aeneas and his troops finally sail into the Tiber and beach their boats in the kingdom of Latium. There, where the divine signs indicate that the long-wandering Trojans have reached their new home at last, they build a settlement with mounds and strong gates and ramparts. They prepare for war but seek peace. Aeneas dispatches envoys to the chief city of Laurentum, and they receive a friendly reception from King Latinus, who invites them to settle there. According to the omens, his daughter and sole heir, Lavinia, must not marry a Latin but instead a stranger from foreign shores, whose people will mingle their blood with the Latins and lift their name to the stars.[112] Latinus recognizes in Aeneas his destined son-in-law.

But Turnus, leader and mightiest warrior of the Rutulian tribe, had previously been promised Lavinia's hand. With the help of the queen—who desires Turnus for her son-in-law, and perhaps for more than her son-in-law—he stirs up hatred against the newcomers. A frenzy for war seizes the Latins, and they besiege their own king. Finding himself powerless to dissuade them, "he sealed himself in his house and dropped the reins of power."[113]

Turnus relishes the prospect of war; Aeneas abhors it, particularly since it will be in effect a civil war among those together destined to be citizens of a new Rome. It will be a war to bring peace, but a deadly war nonetheless. Aeneas deeply regrets this course but will not shrink from fighting.

"But, oh dear gods,
what slaughter threatens the poor Laurentine people!
What a price in bloodshed, Turnus, you will pay me soon!
How many shields and helmets and corpses of the brave
you'll churn beneath your tides, old Father Tiber!
All right then, you Rutulians,
beg for war! Break your pacts of peace!"[114]

In search of allies, Aeneas goes to visit King Evander, whose city is built upon the Palatine Hill of the future Rome. Evander and his people come from Arcadia in the Peloponnese, the quasi-mythical font of pastoral poetry. They share a common ancestry with the Trojans, through the Greeks who founded Ilium. Most important, they are already at war with the Latin people and welcome this new ally. Evander offers the Trojans four hundred horsemen, led by Pallas, his beloved son and sole heir, who he entrusts to Aeneas's care. The Etruscans—whose former king, Mezentius, expelled for his cruelty, has forged an alliance with the Rutulians—also make common cause with Aeneas.

Venus has her husband, Vulcan, god of the forge, make for Aeneas a complete set of armor and an emblazoned shield, as he did for Achilles. Unlike the shield of Achilles, however, with its juxtaposed, frozen-in-time scenes of war and peace, the shield of Aeneas shows the panoramic history of Rome, from the kings of Alba Longa through Romulus and Remus, all the way to the battle of Actium, at which Augustus Caesar devastated the combined forces of Mark Antony and Cleopatra and brought the long civil war to an end. When he takes up the shield, Aeneas is "lifting onto his shoulders now the fame and fates of all his children's children."[115]

While Aeneas is visiting and recruiting allies, the Italians attack the Trojan's camp. The Trojan defenders are hard-pressed, and Turnus fights with the ferocity of a homeric hero. At one point, he even breaks into the enclosure, but the gates close behind him and he must fight off the whole might of the Trojans before plunging into the Tiber and swimming to safety downstream.

Aeneas arrives in time to break the blockade. But young Pallas is quickly killed. While Aeneas is fighting elsewhere, Pallas boldly faces Turnus, a boy against a man. Pallas is felled by the spear of the stronger warrior, who exults over his body and strips from him a massive, engraved sword-belt. Turnus glories in the spoils that will soon lead to his own death: "How blind men's minds to their fate and what the future holds, how blind to limits when fortune lifts men high."[116]

It is now Aeneas's turn to assume the rage of Achilles. His Patroclus has been killed, and he will exact his revenge. Aeneas wreaks slaughter among the Rutulians, killing captain after captain, searching always for Turnus. But even as he kills, swiftly and brutally, Aeneas pities his victims. When he gravely wounds the former Etruscan king Mezentius, Mezentius's son Lausus leaps between them and harries Aeneas as his father is dragged to safety. Aeneas plunges his sword hilt-deep through the youth.

> Ah but then,
> when the son of Anchises saw his dying look,
> his face—that face so ashen, awesome in death—
> he groaned from his depths in pity, reached out his hand
> as this picture of love for a father pierced his heart,
> and said: "Forlorn young soldier, what can Aeneas,
> in all honor, give you to match your glory now?
> What gifts are worthy of such a noble spirit?
> Keep your armor that gave you so much joy.
> I give you back to your fathers' ash and shades
> if it offers any solace."[117]

Mezentius, horrified that Lausus met death to save his own life, throws himself at Aeneas, knowing he will die but asking only to "rest in the grave beside my son, in the comradeship of death."[118]

The Latins seek a truce to bury their dead, and Aeneas sends the body of Pallas, with a thousand mourners in train, back to Evander, "a father doomed to outlive his son."[119] Aeneas offers lasting peace to the Latins, a chance to live together in pacts of friendship on equal terms. He will fight Turnus, in man-to-man combat, with the winner to wed Lavinia. But the Rutulians, knowing that Turnus cannot win, break the pact and wound Aeneas with an arrow shot from their midst. They have simply delayed the inevitable and sent more brave warriors down to hell.

Juno is forbidden by Jupiter to intervene further in the fighting or to take any further steps to protect Turnus. But she exacts from Jupiter a promise that the Latins will retain their name, their language, and their ways.

> "Mingling in stock alone, the Trojans will subside.
> And I will add the rites and the forms of worship,
> and make them Latins all, who speak one Latin tongue."[120]

The final confrontation between Aeneas and Turnus is as anticlimactic as the duel between Achilles and Hector. A mere man is no match for the son of a god, particularly when his own gods have abandoned him. Aeneas sends a spear through Turnus's thigh and then stands over him, sword drawn. Turnus pleads with him in defeat and Aeneas wavers. But then he sees the sword-belt of Pallas draped across Turnus's shoulders.

> Aeneas,
> soon as his eyes drank in that plunder—keepsake
> of his own savage grief—flaring up in fury,
> terrible in his rage, he cries: "Decked in the spoils
> you stripped from one I loved—escape my clutches? Never—
> Pallas strikes his blow, Pallas sacrifices you now,
> makes you pay the price with your own guilty blood!"
> In the same breath, blazing with wrath he plants
> his iron sword hilt-deep in his enemy's heart.
> Turnus' limbs went limp in the chill of death.
> His life breath fled with a groan of outrage
> down to the shades below.[121]

THE PRICE OF EMPIRE

There is no reconciliation of enemies at the end of the *Aeneid*, nothing comparable to the human embrace of Achilles and Priam in the *Iliad*. Yet reconciliation of a sort would come in time. It is foretold by Jupiter in the first book of the poem that Aeneas will live only three short years after the death of Turnus. His son Ascanius will rule for thirty years, followed by three hundred for their descendants, the kings of Alba Longa. It is unclear where Silvius, Aeneas's son with Lavinia, fits here. Jupiter's chronology falls a bit short, moreover, since more than four hundred years passed between 1184, the accepted date in antiquity for the fall of Troy, and 753, the traditional date for the founding of Rome proper by Romulus, fathered by the war-god Mars with the daughter of an Alban king. Regardless, myth will gradually blend into history, and the Roman people will conquer the rest of Italy and most of the known world. And, after seemingly endless, bloody war, Caesar Augustus will finally usher in a time of relative peace. The *Pax Augusta* will become the *Pax Romana* and last for more than two hundred years.

But at what cost? That is a question constantly raised in the epic. One scholar suggests that "it is this perception of Roman history as a long Pyrrhic victory of the human spirit that makes Virgil his country's truest historian."[122] Yet that is not quite true. For there is a question that is also implicitly and perhaps even more urgently raised: what is the alternative? Constant violence, constant civil war, a recurring struggle for power and preeminence: these are the horrors through which Virgil and his compatriots lived and from which Caesar Augustus redeemed them.

In Homer, as Erich Auerbach famously explained, everything is foreground and uniformly illuminated.[123] In Virgil, the shadows predominate. Virgil sees little of the radiance Homer found in war. He sees suffering and chaos. That is why the last four books of the *Aeneid* seem more an obligation than a culmination. Turnus, magnificent in his self-assertion and focused on his own glory, whatever the human cost, is closer to a homeric hero than is Aeneas. But self-assertion has torn Rome apart. The world needs to move beyond that. The state must predominate over the individual; duty must take precedence over glory. Turnus, Dido, Troy—all must be sent "down to the shades below."

Again, this seems an odd message for a poet who valued the individual spirit above all else. Yet Virgil can have it both ways. The *Pax Romana* does not justify the suffering that preceded it. Yet neither does the latter undermine the former. Both simply are. Through art and poetry we can recapture and even sanctify pain, sorrow, and loss. "A joy it will be one day, perhaps, to remember even this," Aeneas told his harried followers. And the *Aeneid* is indeed a source of joy, as it remembers the tribulations that preceded peace.

Hermann Broch, in *The Death of Virgil*, paints an indelible picture of the dying Virgil at Brundisium, keeping the manuscript of the *Aeneid* close to his side, hoping to complete it but ready to destroy it for falling short of his aspirations. There is profound truth in this portrait. Fate called upon Virgil to pluck the golden bough, yet he died "clutching at shadows, with so much still to say."

CHAPTER 5

HORACE—
ODES TO A POET

[Horace's] great gift was to make the commonplace notable, even luminous, not to be discarded as part of the small change of existence.
—D. S. Carne-Ross[1]

Quintus Horatius Flaccus, known to us as Horace, was born in Venusia, a remote garrison town in southern Italy, on December 8 in the year 65 BCE. His father was a freedman and owned a small farm but eventually moved to Rome to ensure that his precocious son received the best-possible education. He worked there as a broker for auctioneers and accompanied Horace to classes. Horace, when not openly irreverent in his poetry, was often quietly ironic, but he was neither where his father was concerned. Even in the early satires, in which invective frequently overwhelmed other sentiments, Horace offered unqualified praise and respect for the man who dedicated himself wholeheartedly to his son's moral and intellectual development and who provided a steady example of old-fashioned virtue and moderation.[2]

When Horace was nineteen or twenty years old, he moved to Athens to complete his education. There he was recruited by Marcus Brutus, one of Caesar's assassins. He joined Brutus's republican forces and served as a staff officer at the battle of Philippi in 42. The triumvirate of Octavian, Mark Antony, and Lepidus won decisively, and Brutus committed suicide. Horace later disparaged his own role in the battle: "I ran away, leaving my shield, / And Mercury got me out of it, carrying me / In a cloud, in a panic, right through the enemy rage."[3] This humorous and self-deprecating account was certainly politic, but it may also have contained a germ of truth. Suetonius, in his *Life of Horace*,[4] describes the poet as short and fat, and the

137

poems themselves portray a man more dedicated to Dionysus and Venus than to Mars.

By the end of the civil war, Horace's father was dead, and the farm Horace inherited had been forfeited to the state. But the triumvirate declared a general amnesty, and Horace returned to Rome in 41. There, he somehow purchased a job as a clerk to the *quaestors* who handled the public treasury. He began to write and gradually attracted notice. Sponsored by Virgil, he was in 37 accepted into the circle of Maecenas, a longtime friend, confidant, and minister of Octavian. Maecenas was a generous and influential patron. Indeed, in 33 or thereabouts, he gave Horace a small estate located in modern Tivoli, a few miles from Rome. This "Sabine Farm," as Horace referred to it, became both his financial mainstay and his personal refuge. "This is what I prayed for," he wrote,

> a piece of land—not so very big,
> with a garden and, near the house, a spring that never fails,
> and a bit of wood to round it off. All this and more
> the gods have granted. So be it. I ask for nothing else,
> O son of Maia, except that you make these blessings last.[5]

Horace was deeply grateful for the patronage but also carefully guarded his independence. He even turned down a position as secretary to Octavian, who by that time had defeated the combined forces of Antony and Cleopatra at Actium and assumed the title Caesar Augustus. Augustus—often referred to simply as the *princeps*, or leading man—was remarkably tolerant and did not take offense at this rebuff. To the contrary, he commissioned poems from Horace for state occasions and even gently expressed the wish that he be included in the circle to which Horace directed his odes and epistles. Those requests Horace did not ignore, and he became a poet of public events as well as private moments.

But it is for the private moments that we most cherish Horace. The loveliness and security of the Sabine Farm—Edith Hamilton called it "the most famous farm in literature,"[6]—played a decisive and not just symbolic role in his poetic development. His bitter early satires and aggressive epodes mellowed into the lyric, wise, contented brilliance of the odes. Horace is perhaps most remembered today for the phrase *carpe diem*—"seize the day." It is an entire philosophy distilled into two words. But it was, in Horace's hands, a subtle philosophy nonetheless. For Horace, the gods played no role in human affairs, and there was no afterlife to atone for this one. He recognized and accepted man's limitations, both moral and mortal.

Indeed, more than any poet before or since, he delighted in the objects, events, and processes of everyday life, and we, as readers, take delight in his delight. "Poetry of the sort I write," he explained somewhat apologetically in an epistle to Augustus, "keeps itself . . . close to the level ground."[7]

Horace uninhibitedly celebrated the simple pleasures of country living, the diversity (and perversity) of human character, the sustaining warmth of friendship, and the fleeting but renewable joys of sex, food, and, most especially, wine. But his greatest pleasure was in poetry itself. "Everyone has his own way of enjoying himself," Horace wrote. "Mine is to put words into metre."[8] More, he sought to capture "the cadences and meter of living right."[9] Indeed, poetry itself was for Horace the highest form of living right because it was the only sure way to seize the day and make it eternal.

> My aim is to take familiar things and make
> Poetry of them, and do it in such a way
> That it looks as if it was easy as could be
> For anybody to do it (although he'd sweat
> And strain and work his head off, all in vain).
> Such is the power of judgment, of knowing what
> It means to put the elements together
> In just the right way; such is the power of making
> A perfectly wonderful thing out of nothing much.[10]

Even more than *carpe diem*, the two words most emblematic of Horace are *sparge rosas*, his injunction to "scatter roses."[11] For that is what he did. He scattered roses in his odes and made a perfectly wonderful thing out of ordinary human life.

SATIRES AND EPODES

Horace published his first book of ten satires in 35. He added eight more in 30. Satire, or *satura*, was a peculiarly Roman genre, which originated with Gaius Lucilius (ca. 168–102), whose thirty books have survived only in fragments. The fragments are sufficient to give us a sense of the distinguishing features of satire, which were a personal, autobiographical tone (though whether autobiographical in fact is of course a completely different and largely unanswerable question) and a trenchant analysis of all aspects of contemporary life. Lucilius's satires, like those of

Horace after him, embraced everything from political polemics, personal slanders, literary parodies, and travelogues, to moral instruction, love letters, and culinary advice. But they were principally used, as Italian critic Gian Biagio Conte explains, "as a tool of personal aggression, of mordant criticism."[12]

Horace himself recognized that his *Satires* were little more than elegantly metered prose,[13] in which he "present[ed] the truth with a laugh."[14] The morals he draws are relatively banal; his descriptions of contemporary Roman vices are where the interest and amusement lie. (Dante and Milton would also find that hell makes better copy than heaven.) In his first satire, Horace describes the envy, greed, and restlessness that render men chronically discontent with their occupations and, most of all, with their wealth. "'Nothing is enough,' they say, 'for you're only worth what you have.'"[15] Yet, Horace asks, "if a man lives within nature's limits, what matter whether he has a hundred or a thousand acres of ploughed land?"[16] We never focus on our actual needs. We never compare ourselves with those who have less but only with those whom we perceive to be ahead. As a result, we never know the happiness of a "guest who has had his fill."[17]

In the second satire, Horace takes a comic look at the "middle way" between opposing vices. He cautions against sex with married women and sex with whores as equally fraught with peril. Freedwomen and servants are the safest and most accessible. "I like sex to be there and easy to get. 'Not just yet,' 'But I need more money,' 'If my husband's away'— that kind of girl's for the Gauls."[18] Horace paints a crude but unforgettable picture of why his proposed course surpasses the alternative:

> No fear, while I'm fucking, that her husband will rush back to town,
> the door crash open, the dog bark, and the house resound
> with an awful din; that the woman, deathly white, will jump
> out of bed, her accomplice shriek, and we'll all be in terror—the maid
> for her legs, the guilty mistress for her dowry, and me for myself.
> I have to run off barefoot with my clothes undone, or else
> my cash or my arse or at least my respectability has had it.[19]

The *Satires* continue along these lines as Horace skewers our tendency to judge others harshly for minor foibles while ignoring our own glaring faults; attacks alike the snob, the social-climbing boor, and the false friend; deplores "the cruel compulsion to get to the top";[20] and laments the irrational variability of love:

There are always two troubles in love:
war and peace—things which change much as the weather.
They come and go by blind chance; so if anyone sweated
to give an account of their movements he'd make no better sense
than if he tried to go mad with the aid of rules and logic.[21]

Horace pleads that his outspoken jokes not offend. He criticizes only to instruct, he explains, but moralizing is more palatable when leavened with a sharp wit and a deft touch, and bad examples make more of an impression as a warning than good examples do as a spur.

In his penultimate satire, however, Horace himself is on the receiving end of moral instruction and doesn't much like it. His slave, Davus, seeks permission to report on a lecture by the Stoic philosopher Crispinus—a lecture the slave did not himself hear but about which he received an account from the hall porter who listened in at the door of the lecture room. On the basis of that derivative learning, Davus informs his master that he, Horace, is one of those people who "love their faults," flee from themselves, and observe virtue only when the opportunities for vice are absent. Davus explains that Horace, though putatively the master, is a fellow slave, a slave to money, power, and especially sex: "a cruel master is riding your soul, jabbing the spurs in your weary flanks."[22] Only the sage is truly free, Davus concludes, as Horace threatens to brain him with a stone. Horace, the dispenser of derivative wisdom, is hoist with his own petard. Yet, aside from mocking his own project, Horace has another point, which is that it is best to live within natural human limits, neither slave nor sage. Horace attacks excess without advocating the opposite extreme of Stoic restraint. He celebrates tolerance, moderation, contentment, the joys of friendship, and the pleasures of everyday life.

There is, however, very little that is moderate about the *Epodes*, seventeen short poems written between 41 and 30, and published in 29. They are modeled on the seventh-century Greek poet Archilochus, a master of invective. Horace begins, modestly enough, with a tribute to his "dear friend" and patron Maecenas, who has left to fight with Octavian at Actium. He adds a later poem to celebrate the subsequent victory (epode 9). Otherwise, though, the poems are aggressive in tone: comic, in his diatribe against garlic (epode 3); erotic, in his celebration of bisexual passion (epode 12); jealous, in decrying the falseness of love (epode 15); gruesome, in describing the torments of a young boy captured by a coven of witches (epode 5); vicious, in his attack on an ugly, old woman he blames for his impotence (epode 8); and outraged, in his lamentations that Rome has been cursed with civil war since Romulus murdered his brother, Remus:

> It is harsh Fate that drives
> the Romans, and the crime of fratricide
> since Remus' blameless lifeblood poured upon the ground—
> a curse to generations yet unborn.[23]

In a subsequent poem he notes that a new generation is now "ground down by civil wars, / and Rome is falling, ruined by the might of Rome."[24] What so many outsiders tried and failed to do, Rome is doing to itself.

These poems are far from the wise and genial Horace of the *Odes*. Perhaps, as some have suggested, the *Satires* and *Epodes* reflected the bitterness of his unsettled position after the first civil war. Or perhaps they were simply an aspect of his personality he had to express before he could transcend.

At least two of the *Epodes*, however, have a charm and gentle irony that foretell the later work. The second epode is a beautiful paean to country life and the simple pleasures of working the soil, free from the public and private business of Rome. Yet we learn in the last four lines that the speaker is a money lender, whose resolve to be a country man lasts all of two weeks: "he called in all his money on the Ides [the 13th or 15th]— / and on the Kalends [first day of the next month] now he tries to place it out again."[25] This is vintage Horace: there is both hypocrisy and sincerity in the longing for country life when in the city and vice versa. We are nothing if not inconstant.

Epode 13 responds to a fierce (metaphorical) storm with what will become a familiar refrain:

> let's seize
> the moment, friends, and while our knees are spry and while
> with decency we may, let's smooth away the frown of age.
> You there, bring wine pressed in the year of my Torquatus.
> Forget the rest; God will perhaps put all to rights again,
> a gentler time will come.[26]

THE LYRIC POET

That gentler time did come for Horace, and it is reflected in his greatest achievement, the first three books of *Odes*, which were published in 23. A fourth book, with fifteen more poems, was added in 13. Horace called them *Carmina* (songs), but they were rechristened *Odes* in the Renaissance. They were his attempt to equal in

Latin the great lyric poetry of ancient Greece from the second half of the seventh century through the first half of the fifth century. He more than succeeded, though only a tiny and mostly fragmentary sample of Greek lyric poetry is available to us for comparison. One commenter, David Armstrong, called the *Odes* "the most profoundly finished, variegated, and learned book in the whole of Roman poetry."[27] Another, Maurice Bowra, was more expansive: "the four books of the Odes, with their hundred and three short poems, cover a wider range of experience and present it in a more satisfying form than almost any other comparable book written by man."[28] Friedrich Nietzsche was equally enthusiastic: "To this day, no other poet has given me the same artistic delight that a Horatian ode gave me from the first."[29]

The guiding spirit of the *Odes* is captured in the famous Soracte ode, in book 1, arguably the greatest lyric poem ever written. There are several online recordings available that allow Latin-less readers to appreciate the flow and music of the verse.[30]

Vides ut alta stet nive candidum
Soracte, nec iam sustineant onus
silvae laborantes, geluque
flumina constiterint acuto.

Dissolve frigus ligna super foco
large reponens atque benignius
deprome quadrimum Sabina,
o Thaliarche, merum diota.

Permitte divis cetera, qui simul
stravere ventos aequore fervido
deproeliantis, nec cupressi
nec veteres agitantur orni.

Quid sit futurum cras fuge quaerere, et
quem Fors dierum cumque dabit lucro
appone, nec dulcis amores
sperne puer neque tu choreas,

donec virenti canities abest
morosa. Nunc et campus et areae
lenesque sub noctem susurri
composita repetantur hora,

nunc et latentis proditor intimo
gratus puellae risus ab angulo
pignusque dereptum lacertis
aut digito male pertinaci.[31]

This poem has been translated dozens of times, by John Dryden among others. Here is my own attempt at a translation:

See how Soracte stands clear and bright
under the thick snow, the trees
laboring to sustain their burden,
and the streams blocked by sharp ice.

Drive out the cold, Thaliarchus,
pile logs on the fire and pour generously
the four-year-old Sabine wine
from the twin-handled jug.

Leave everything else to the gods.
Once they calm the winds and raging seas,
neither the ancient ash trees
nor the sacred cypresses will be disturbed.

Don't ask what the future holds.
Set down as profit each day's chance.
Spurn neither love nor dancing,
while youthful bloom is far from fretful grey.

Now, seek out parks and squares at nightfall,
soft whispers at the appointed time.
Sweet laughter betrays the girl
hidden in the most intimate corner,
a pledge snatched from her arm
or faintly resisting finger.[32]

There is a famous story about this poem set in occupied Crete during World War II. A German general was captured by the Cretan resistance. Together with a British agent, Major Patrick Leigh Fermor, the partisans were fleeing with their captive through thick snow, across mountain passes, a German garrison in close pursuit. A brilliant dawn showed them Mount Ida across the valley, and the general murmured to himself:

> *Vides ut alta stet nive candidum*
> *Soracte . . .*

Fermor, who knew the poem by heart from his school days, recited the rest, picking up where the general trailed off:

> The general's blue eyes had swiveled away from the mountain-top to mine—and when I'd finished, after a long silence, he said: "Ach so, Herr Major!" It was very strange. As though, for a long moment, the war had ceased to exist. We had both drunk at the same fountains long before.[33]

A strange moment, indeed, and a sad one as well—a metaphor inside a metaphor—for the shared cultural heritage did nothing to soften, and indeed may have spurred, Nazi Germany's relentless and brutal efforts to create a new Roman empire with its Italian ally.

But we cannot blame Horace for that. To the contrary, Horace reminds us that we can weather such storms, as cypresses and old ash trees do, without forgetting the pleasures that life also has to offer. He urges his young host to pile wood on the warming fire, to be generous with the wine, to sit together in friendship, and to let tomorrow take care of itself. Those are the comforts of Horace's "morose old age," his frozen winter; but he has the perspective also to urge his young friend to seize youth and love while there is still time, as Horace himself once did and is fond of recalling.

We happen to possess the fragment from the Greek poet Alcaeus of Mytilene (born ca. 620) that must have served as Horace's model.

> Rain falls from Zeus, and out of the sky a great
> winter storm comes; the streams are frozen . . .
> [two lines missing]
> Defy the storm, lay wood upon
> the fire, mix the honey-sweet wine
> unstintingly, and about your temples
> place a headband of soft wool.[34]

It is hardly fair to compare a completed poem to a fragment, but certainly our admiration for Horace is only enhanced by considering the source of his inspiration.

He has made a poem that is uniquely his own and that beautifully combines the main themes of the *Odes*.

CARPE DIEM

Michel de Montaigne quotes from Horace 148 times in his complete *Essais*. Only one other Roman poet, Lucretius, is cited as much. This is hardly surprising. Horace and Lucretius, together, present a worldview highly conducive to Montaigne, who also lived through an age of violence, uncertainty, and civil strife and who sought, in the tower library of his private estate, to envision a life of tolerance and moderation, in which wisdom and pleasure were conjoined. The *simplex munditiis* (elegant simplicity) of Horace's verses was bound to appeal to Montaigne. Even more important, the two men had a similar project: to present to the world a highly personal and uninhibited self-portrait. Each projected a literary persona that, whether autobiographical or not, readers find endlessly intriguing and appealing. It would be hard to imagine better dinner-table company than the Montaigne of the *Essais* or the Horace of the *Odes*, though Samuel Johnson, another candidate for dinner, when told that "it appeared from Horace's writings that he was a cheerful, contented man," responded, "We have no reason to believe that. . . . Are we to think Pope was happy, because he says so in his writings? We see in his writings what he wished the state of his mind to appear."[35]

Horace was Boswell to his own Johnson and, as such, is notoriously hard to pin down. Like Montaigne, he was not afraid to contradict himself if fidelity to feeling so required, as it frequently did (and often within the same ode). But the state of mind that appears in the *Odes* is bracketed by three obvious yet elegantly simple propositions familiar to students of Epicurean and Stoic philosophy. Horace, of course, was not a philosopher; he was a poet. The great Horace scholar Steele Commager rightly reminds us that "an Ode's meaning, like that of any other poem, does not lie in a phrase or a paraphrase. It inheres in the sounds, the figures, the tone, the emotional coloring; in many cases, the logic is less important than the mood."[36] Yet there are common themes through the *Odes* that color the emotions and set the mood and that make us feel that there is some consistency in the persona presented in the *Odes*.

The first is that fortune is fickle and unpredictable. However powerful and secure we might feel, we are playthings of chance and circumstance. The rich man loses his wealth; the healthy man is wracked with disease; the favored politician finds himself banished; the traveler is caught in a sudden storm. The only real certainty is change. Horace has plenty of examples of the vagaries of fortune vividly before him: Pompey, Julius Caesar, Brutus, Mark Antony—each had a fall commensurate with his rise. "The lot of each of us," Horace writes in a favorite metaphor, "is in the shaking urn,"[37] and we have no idea how or when it will fall out. Indeed, we are never even afraid of the right things: "Nobody watches out for what he should / Watch out for," Horace explains, in a charming, comic ode on the "wretched rotten / Falling tree" that nearly came down on its master's head.[38]

> Nor should we seek to know what is in store:
> Don't be too eager to ask
> What the gods have in mind for us,
> What will become of you,
> What will become of me,
> . . .
> It's better not to know.[39]

What appears as a disaster may in fact prove a boon, and vice versa. Since we cannot know what to watch out for—since we never even fear the right things—ours hearts must be ready for anything. We should expect and prepare for reversals, hopeful in trouble and worried when things go well: "Be resolute when things are going against you, / But shorten sail when the fair wind blows too strong."[40] The same steady mind must, as Rudyard Kipling (a writer steeped in Horace) would later echo, "meet with Triumph and Disaster / And treat those two impostors just the same."[41]

The second proposition, related to the first, is that ambition and greed are self-destructive. Even if fortune happens to smile upon us, we will never be satisfied with what we have obtained. No position will be high enough or secure enough; no amount of money will seem sufficient once wealth becomes an end in itself.

> Peace isn't
> Something money or some high office can buy.
> They won't dispel the miseries the soul
> Is vulnerable to, the anxieties that hover
> Around your coffered ceiling.[42]

Indeed, far from bringing peace to an already-turbulent soul, a focus on getting and keeping will bring a host of fresh troubles in its wake. The more money, the more greed; the greater the greed, the greater the anxiety.

> Menace and Fear
> Are there in the seaside palace;
> Anxiety is on board the elegant yacht,
> For all its trimmings of brass; black Sorrow sits
> Behind the horseman as he rides his horse.[43]

The only way to obtain peace of soul and mind is to forswear ambition and disdain fortune. "That man alone is happy . . . who can gaze untempted / At all the heaped-up treasure of the world."[44]

The third proposition is that the time we have is short and fleeting.

> Youth and good looks go by pretty fast, after all,
> And we go on getting older. The pleasures of sex
> Get to be less and less than they used to be;
> And easy sleep's no longer so easily come by.
> Flowers don't bloom forever; and as for the moon,
> It never stays the same. The brightness dims.[45]

We can do nothing to slow life down or to evade its inevitable passing. Like the moon, our brightness quickly dims. Death stalks us from the moment we are born.

> Rich man or poor man, whatever, it doesn't matter.
> . . .
> Each one of us must leave the earth he loves
> And leave his home and leave his tender wife,
> And leave the trees he planted and took good care of.
> . . .
> Your heir will drink the choice Caecuban wine
> You did not know that you were saving for him
> When you locked it up securely in your cellar.
> The wine he spills is priceless, it doesn't matter.[46]

These reflections are not a cause for despair but an injunction to take pleasure in what remains. The unpredictability of fortune, the hollowness of what most of us strive for, and the brevity of life lead Horace to "accept the gift of pleasure when it's given."[47] To be sure, a certain melancholy pervades Horace's work—as it does Lucretius's and Virgil's—but so does a determination to relish and intensify the joys of the moment.

> Let the heart rejoice in whatever it has right now;
> Don't worry about whatever might come in the future;
> Turn it aside with a smile. There's no such thing
> As absolute guaranteed bliss.[48]

David Ferry translates *carpe diem, quam minimum credula postero*, which appears at the end of ode 1.11, as "hold on to the day." This may seem a quibble with an otherwise fine translation, but Horace's point is that we can*not* hold the day. The day will pass regardless, so we must *seize* it and wring from it what fleeting pleasure we can. We can *pluck* each day as if it were a flower of priceless beauty and fragrance: "let there be roses, / Let there be lilies, and long-live blossom-of-parsley."[49] Moreover, Ferry leaves out the last four words, which I would translate as "put as little faith as possible in tomorrow." Whether we spend our days in sorrow or in holiday pleasure, the same fate awaits us all. So we might as well choose holiday pleasure, "while youth, / And circumstance, and the black threads of the [Fates] / Suffer this to be so."[50] As he advised his young friend in the Soracte ode: "Set down as profit each day's chance." Even old age has its consolations. In Donald Frame's memorable translation of ode 1.31, quoted in Latin by Montaigne:

> Grant me but health, Latona's son,
> And to enjoy the wealth I've won,
> And honored age, with mind entire
> And not unsolaced by the lyre.[51]

There is little angst in Horace. No great passion either, except for poetry. His is a "gay and sociable wisdom," as Montaigne explained.[52] Horace is determined to be content with and to make the most of his lot. He does not envy the rich and powerful. Because he asks for little, he is a greater master of wealth than those who long for more.[53] He enjoys the good things, without being dependent on them, and he weathers his storms without forgetting the pleasures of life. Horace seeks the *aurea mediocritas* (golden mean): "That man does best / Who chooses the middle way."[54] Horace is moderate even in his moderation. On suitable occasions he would "strike a blow for folly"[55] and "keep the torches lighted until dawn."[56] And he has a genuine fascination with extravagant emotions. There is a constant tension in his poems between restraint and excess.

For the most part, though, Horace's pantheon of pleasures is not extreme. They can be divided roughly into four categories of increasing importance. The first is pleasures of table and hearth. Meals are occasions for friends to gather and converse. The quality of the food is less important than the company; indeed, Horace mocks the tendency of the wealthy to make a display of exotic offerings. Yet he does not disdain fine food when it is available. (The banquet of life is a favorite metaphor, driven by a genuine affection for the food.) Music, too, is welcome. In the ode "To His Lyre," he calls it the "medicine of sorrows," "gladly heard at Jupiter's table itself."[57] But Horace is particularly eloquent on the subject of wine, which helps us to put aside for a time the cares and anxiety of life.[58] He paints an indelible portrait of the man who likes "his cup of wine, / Taking his ease in the busiest time of the day, / Under the shady boughs of the green arbutus / Or near the secret source of some murmuring brook."[59] Mostly, though, he advocates the conviviality of drinking in company. In his ode "To a Jar of Massic Wine," he writes:

> Your gentle discipline encourages
> The dull to be less dull than usual,
>
> . . .
>
> You bring back hope to the despairing heart
> And you give courage to the poor man . . .
>
> . . .
>
> Bacchus attends thee, and Venus, if she's willing,
> And torchlight, and the Graces dancing together,
> Until the moment the returning sun
> Puts all the stars to flight, and the party's over.[60]

As the reference to "Venus, if she's willing" indicates, love and sex come next. Venus is a powerful, indeed overwhelming, force, particularly for the young. She drives them to acts of madness and despair, as well as great joy:

> You terrify mothers terrified for their sons,
> And fathers terrified for their sons' money,
> And young brides terrified lest their young husbands never
> Come home tonight, spellbound in your power.[61]

Such passion may be irrational, but it is an essential aspect of life, and sex one of its most intense pleasures. Horace writes of his love for "Glycera's body, / Smoother than shining marble is shining and smooth, / And with her way of behaving, so wanton and pleasing, / And with the bold lubricious look on her face, / That makes you lose your footing to look at her."[62] But even the Horace of the *Satires* and the *Epodes* seemed more to play at passion than truly to feel it. His list of conquests was almost whimsical, and the despair he occasionally purported to feel was more literary than genuine. However pleased he may be with its physical aspect, Horace is frankly amused by the violent vagaries of love.

In ode 1.13, Horace notes his jealousy when a former love, Lydia, praises her current lover. But his agony at the visible marks of their passion is mock heroic and, in its extremity, a dig at the literary tradition of love poems from Sappho to Catullus and Propertius. In this, Horace anticipates Ovid. But the ode has a lovely, quiet ending as Horace reminds Lydia that

> Those lovers are happy and more than happy who
> Are peacefully bound together in amity.
> Love will not part such lovers until death parts them.[63]

Similarly, in ode 1.5, he imagines that his successor with Pyrrha is young and slender and perfumed. Yet his jealousy is not excited. The ardent, hapless youth who urges himself upon the self-contained Pyrrha—her hair done up, like Horace's *Odes*, *simplex munditiis*—has no conception of the tears to come. He is like a new sailor setting out on a beautiful calm ocean, "not knowing at all how quickly the wind can change."[64] But tempests will come regardless and so, too, Pyrrha will betray him, and her moods will be altered by dark winds. Horace regards the young man with a certain nostalgic humor and fond detachment. Horace himself claims to have foresworn the sea: "I have hung up my sea-soaked garment" in the temple of the gods as an offering for his release.[65]

The Horace of the *Odes* has evolved in his conception of love. "It's right to be foolish when the time is right," he notes.[66] But sexual passion becomes ridiculous as one ages, and even sad. "Cupid scorns the old,"[67] and Horace has had enough.

> Not long ago I was
> A not inglorious soldier,
> But now upon this wall,
>
> . . .
>
> I place these weapons and

This lyre no longer fit
For use in the wars of love.
Here I offer the torch,
The crowbar and the bow,
Siege weapons used
Against those closed-up doors.[68]

One can no more rely upon the putative Horace of this ode than the Horace who threw away his shield at Philippi, or the Horace whose litany of past loves (male and female) could fill an index. But perhaps his relief at being released from the yoke of passion is genuine, if wistful. Certainly, he proposed a new, detached perspective, noting that in the house of death it will no longer matter—what mattered so deeply in life—who loved whom.[69] He invites Phyllis to be "the last of my loves; there will be no others," and suggests only that she learn a new song to sing to him and alleviate sorrow.[70] Old age has different comforts, and yet the loss of youthful passion is not unmourned.

But why, Ligurinus, why,
Every once in a while
Do my eyes fill up with tears?
Why sometimes when I'm talking
Do I suddenly fall silent?
I hold you fast, sometimes,
Sometimes, at night, in a dream,
Or I follow you as you flee
Across the Campus Martius,
. . .
Or as you are lost among
The bewildering waves of the river.[71]

The third category of pleasure—one that has only augmented with age—is friendship. In ode 4.11, as we saw, Horace proposes that his love for Phyllis resolve itself into a comfortable and companionable friendship. We will discuss the poems on friendship in the context of patronage, for his greatest friendship was with his patron, Maecenas.

The fourth, and by far the most important, category was poetry. Horace values above all things "going my own way, wandering in my learned / Well-considered folly."[72] Indeed, in his very first ode he provides a litany of the frantic pursuits of men—to be Olympic victors, holders of high office, wealthy farmers, traders on the open sea, soldiers, hunters, even drinkers—and somehow conveys "with genial ease," as scholar David West puts it, "the lunacy in men's activities."[73] But Horace considers himself "set apart from other men":

> What links *me* to the gods is that I study
> To wear the ivy wreath that poets wear.[74]

If he can succeed in *that* endeavor, "then my exalted head will knock against the stars."[75]

We will discuss below Horace's views on *ars poetica*, the art of poetry. But here, let us focus on the poet's life, which Horace considers the highest and most satisfying type of existence. The man who can find the right words for things and put those words into meter knows himself and the world. Only the poet, through discipline and active pursuit of the good, "make[s] a proper use of the gifts / The gods have given."[76] Only the poet truly seizes the day and renders it immortal. Horace is ironic and elusive throughout much of the *Odes*. But there is no mistaking the claims he makes for his accomplishment when he completed the third book:

> Today I have finished a work outlasting bronze
> And the pyramids of ancient royal kings.
> The North Wind raging cannot scatter it
> Nor can the rain obliterate this work,
> Nor can the years, nor can the ages passing.
> Some part of me will live and not be given
> Over into the hands of the death goddess.
> I will live on forever, kept ever young
> By the praise in times to come for what I have done.[77]

PATRONAGE

When he finished the first three books of the *Odes* in 23, Horace renounced lyric poetry for a time in favor of more extended letters in verse dealing with philosophy, patronage, politics, and the art of poetry, among other topics.

> I'm giving up my verses and all
> Other foolishness of the sort, and now
> Devote myself entirely to the study
> Of what is genuine and right for me,
> Storing up what I learn for the sake of the future.[78]

The first twenty of these epistles were published in the year 20. In 17, Horace was commissioned to write the *Carmen Saeculare*, a hymn to celebrate the reign of Augustus. A second book of epistles, consisting of three much longer poems, including the famous *Ars Poetica*, was published in 14, and the fourth and final book of odes in 13.

These later writings are much more conscious of the role of the individual as part of a social and political community. The earlier focus on transient personal fulfillment is not abandoned but placed within a broader, more enduring context. While Horace was writing the first three books of the *Odes*, the fear of renewed civil war and social unrest was still strong. But gradually, Rome and its territories settled into a *Pax Augusta* or *Pax Romana* that was to last hundreds of years and provide a measure of stability and security for Roman citizens and those subject states willing to submit to Roman rule.

The *Epistles* place much more emphasis on philosophy than on hedonistic pleasures. Horace was not a systematic thinker—he presents a mishmash of Stoic, Epicurean, and Skeptical doctrines—but he was thoughtful and borrowed from each school what seemed to him most pertinent to his life, while leavening the whole with humor. The wisdom of philosophy, he wrote to his friend and patron, Maecenas, makes a man free, beautiful, and sane, "unless, of course, he's got a bad toothache."[79]

Maecenas had need of such counsel. In 23, his brother-in-law Varro was arrested and executed for plotting against Augustus. Though Maecenas himself was not implicated, he was politically marginalized and potentially in danger from that point on. Yet Horace continued to recognize his debt to Maecenas and reaffirmed his loyalty and friendship in the first epistle.

> Maecenas, you were the first to be named in the first
> Poem I ever wrote and you'll be the first
> To be named in the last I'm ever going to write.[80]

Horace wrote some of his finest and most moving tributes to Maecenas during these years, in the context of an otherwise dry-eyed account of the Roman tradition of *amicitia*, under which a rich or influential man gathers an entourage to dine with him, visit his country house, accompany him to the Forum, and otherwise dance attendance in exchange for material benefits conferred.

Horace is well aware of the dangers of such a relationship for both parties. "Flatterers and true friends resemble each other / No more than whores and wives," he notes,[81] and undeserved praise has as bad effect on the recipient as it does on the one offering the praise. Cultivating powerful friends is sweet only to those who haven't tried it.[82] You must accommodate your patron in many wishes, even if you would rather write a poem than go hunting or join a communal meal.

Yet Horace professes no bad conscience about being the recipient of Maecenas's generosity to artists: "command us to write poems," he cheerfully enjoins, "and forbid us to be poor."[83] Horace is happy to receive such benefits. "I don't go in for praising the poor man's lot," he explains, "just as I've finished off an excellent dinner."[84] He distinguishes himself from "the fickle whores and hangers-on of power," who drain the wine-jars of a rich man and then abandon him when trouble comes.[85] It is possible for a man to be patronized and praise and please the mighty "with his integrity intact."[86]

> It makes a difference whether
> A gift is accepted with modesty and decorum
> Or grabbed at rapaciously. The style is what counts.[87]

There are many different types of service, and benefits can be conferred on both sides. In this equation, Horace more than holds his own with the gift poems he bestows upon and dedicates to Maecenas. "It is poetry I can give, and I know its worth."[88] He professes to meet Maecenas as at least an equal, as someone valued and cherished for his own merits. "Certainly I have every intention of being / Deserving of all your kindnesses to me," he explains.[89] "But see if I wouldn't cheerfully return / All of the gifts you generously have given" if necessary to preserve his independence,[90] an independence somewhat ironically symbolized by the Sabine Farm, which was itself a gift from Maecenas.

Yet Horace professes deep affection and genuine friendship for his patron. The circle about Maecenas was clearly a substitute for the family Horace did not have. Maecenas, on his deathbed, enjoined the emperor, "Be mindful of Horatius Flaccus as of myself."[91] Horace himself had earlier indicated that he had no intention of surviving Maecenas, whose "friendship is the thing / My life most glories in":

That fatal day would be
The ruin of us both.
This oath is not sworn falsely:
You and I will go together,
We will go together, Maecenas,
I following your lead,
Whenever that day comes,
Companions ready to go.[92]

Sincere or not at the time it was written, Horace was true to his promise. Maecenas died in October of the year 8, and Horace followed him, through natural causes, the next month.

POLITICS

Horace kept Augustus at arm's length during his early years as a poet. As he explained in an ode to Agrippa, Caesar Augustus's top military commander,

Self-knowledge and the Muse of peaceful things
Prohibit me from dimming with my verses
Your glory and the glory of great Caesar.
. . .
It falls to me to make up easygoing
Songs about such battlefields as parties,
Epic encounters between young men and women.[93]

This ode is a standard *recusatio*, in which the poet insists that his powers are too small properly to deal with grander subjects. (The Greek poet Callimachus originated the recusatio as a tongue-in-cheek justification for his refusal to write epic poetry, which he considered a moribund genre.) Here, it is a form of praise (noting the grandeur of the deeds) and also a refusal to praise (as beyond the scope of the poet's powers), which is a very convenient excuse and seems to have satisfied or at least appeased Augustus for a number of years.

But Horace did not altogether shun political topics. He repeatedly deplored the violence and the crimes of civil war: "What field is there that isn't fertilized / With Roman blood, where Roman graves bear witness / To the impiety of Romans fighting Romans?"[94] He also wrote a remarkable and courageous ode after the death of Cleopatra. He began by condemning her as a "besotted queen" who planned "the death and destruction of the empire."[95] He then celebrated the destruction of her fleet at Actium and appeared to praise the vigorous manner in which Caesar chased her down, cornered her in Egypt, and sought to bring her back to Rome a prisoner. Yet the mood of the poem suddenly changes to one of admiration for her fierce nobility and quiet dignity in death, refusing to be paraded in chains before a Roman mob:

> Bravely, as if unmoved, she looked upon
> The ruins of her palace; bravely reached out,
> And touched the poison snakes, and picked them up,
> And handled them, and held them to her so
> Her heart might drink its fill of their black venom.
> In truth—no abject woman she—she scorned
> In triumph to be brought in galleys unqueened
> Across the seas to Rome to be a show.[96]

Augustus could hardly have been pleased with this tribute to his former enemy, with its implication that Augustus had hounded her "the way a hawk / Chases a frightened dove."[97] Certainly, it is a rare instance in the *Odes* when Horace drops his distancing irony and enters movingly into the thoughts and feelings of Cleopatra in her final moments. Perhaps Brutus's defeat and subsequent suicide at Philippi were still vivid in his mind.

But Horace gradually reconciled himself to the Augustan consolidation of power. "No longer will I fear a civil war," he wrote, "nor other cause of violent bloody death. / Caesar is in command of all the earth."[98] He wrote a series of Roman odes, the first six odes of book 3, in which he celebrates the discipline, the piety, the austerity, and the patriotism that contributed to Rome's greatness. The odes were in keeping with Augustus's program to counter lax contemporary attitudes on sex, greed, luxury, and religion.

One of these odes in particular warrants mention, in which Horace cites the example of Regulus, whose troops were captured and held in Carthage. He was sent back to Rome on a safe conduct by the Carthaginians to offer their return in exchange for peace. But when he arrived, he argued vigorously against the shame and debilitating effect of accepting such an offer. Roman soldiers should know that if they allow themselves to be captured, they can expect no ransom and will be "left—to die if they must—in the enemy camp."[99] The story was already familiar to all Romans.

The magnificence of the ode lies in the simple, powerful language of its conclusion, and the vision of Regulus pushing his way through the crowd of family and friends toward his solitary fate, driven by nothing more than his sense of honor and duty.

> It is said that Regulus shunned his wife's embraces
> And the kisses of his weeping little children,
> As if he had no right to them, and stood,
> Eyes gazing fixed upon the ground, as waiting
> For the wavering Roman Fathers in their Senate
> To come to understand his argument.
> And then—oh yes, he knew that torture and death
> Were ready for him when he went back to Carthage,
> As he had promised—Regulus shouldered his way
> Through the protesting crowd of friends and relations,
> Looking as if he had just completed a case
> In court or some other tedious legal chore,
> And was off for a weekend at his place in the country.[100]

By the time of the fourth book of odes and the second book of epistles, Horace was prepared to praise Augustus more or less unqualifiedly for keeping Rome safe, improving her laws, and reestablishing the virtues of an earlier age. He even notes that, whereas Romulus and other Roman heroes were worshipped as gods after their deaths, Augustus properly receives such "early-ripened honors" in his lifetime.[101] Yet Horace is not so slavish as this hagiography might suggest. For in the very same epistle he quickly shifts his focus to the overriding importance of poetry in shaping the mind and character of a people. Rome may have conquered Greece and the rest of the Mediterranean world, but Greece schooled Rome in what truly matters.

> Captive Greece took its Roman captor captive,
> Invading uncouth Latium with its arts.[102]

And in the fourth book of odes, Horace notes expressly that the immortality of heroes (and hence, by implication, Augustus) is due entirely to the poets.

> Heroes have lived before Agamemnon lived,
> But all of them are lost somewhere in the night,
> Unwept, unknown, unless they had a poet
> To tell what was their story.[103]

Human life is fleeting. Power is precarious. Augustus, too, could be lost, unwept, and unknown but for the power of poetry to make him immortal.

ARS POETICA

The *Ars Poetica* is, after Aristotle's *Poetics*, the most sustained and thoughtful work of literary criticism in antiquity. Unlike Aristotle's *Poetics*, however, it is also a delight to read—witty, knowledgeable, confident, wise, and thoroughly practical.

> I'll teach what it is to write, what fosters a poet
> And makes him what he is; what's right; what's wrong;
> What paths he ought or ought not to set out on.[104]

Horace presents a nine-point plan for aspiring poets and playwrights who must master their craft. First, he offers what is surely the oldest and soundest advice for any poet: "he should write / Out of himself and out of what he knows."[105] The poet needs a thorough background knowledge of literature, philosophy, and history. And if he is to write, say, about generals or statesmen or farmers, he must understand military strategy, politics, and agriculture. Whatever his topic, he must master it. Yet books are not enough. The poet must learn directly from life the manners and the voices of his time; he must understand, without being corrupted by, the pettiness of most men's everyday pursuit of money and power.[106] All his experience must be filtered through the lens of, and focused on, art:

> The man who does this will find he doesn't have trouble
> Thinking of what to say and in what order.[107]

Second, "be sure to be careful to pick / Material that you're strong enough to handle."[108] Whether you write short love poems or biting satires or vast epics, the choice must be driven by a proper estimation of your own powers. Virgil, of course, went from pastoral to didactic to epic poetry as his powers expanded. In each case, he was ready for the challenge and able to master and even reinvent the genre.

Third, the principal virtue of a poem or play is coherence, having the pieces fit together, with nothing superfluous.[109] Thus, a poet should either work within existing conventions or, if he tries something new, be sure it is consistent and functions as a unit: "whatever the work is supposed to be, / Let it be true to itself, essentially simple."[110]

Fourth, the poet must choose the meter appropriate to the genre. "Homer first showed us how the verse should move / That tells the deeds of kings and sorrows of war."[111] Epic poetry should follow the same hexameter meter. Elegiac poetry has its own proper meter, presented in couplets with lines of uneven length (hexameter and pentameter), "as spoken brokenhearted."[112] Plays properly use iambic meter (short/long or unstressed/stressed) "because its urgent alternating rhythm / Propels the energies of the dialogue / And drives the action forward and wins out over / The coughs and whispers of the customers."[113] Horace's *Odes*, it should be noted, employ a wide variety of meters, which shows that the true poet must know his tools and choose the right one for each occasion.

Fifth, and relatedly, language should be chosen with the greatest care. The words must act upon the soul of the listener so that he will respond as the poet intends. "Men smile if the language smiles; / They weep if the language truly weeps."[114] Old and tired words should be given a new context so that they appear fresh and striking. And the poet must not shrink from coining new words to fit the sense he wishes to convey and to enrich our language; for language is a living instrument, in which some words fade away like falling leaves in a forest and new ones bloom and take their place. Horace stressed the importance of what Flaubert would call *le mot juste*, the exact right word for the situation. The poet's duty is to give our common nature just the right words to reveal itself in shared experience.

> For Nature has made us such that we're in a sense
> Ready for all that happens, expressive creatures;
> She gives us cause for joy, and cause for sorrow,
> She humbles us down to the ground, oppressed with trouble,
> And she gives us the tongue with which to tell how it is.[115]

Sixth, Horace urges poets not to start their poems in a pompous way, advertising more than they can deliver. It was well enough for Homer and Virgil to start grandly. They were up to it. But the homeric imitators who begin—"I sing of the famous war and Priam's fate"—are bound to disappoint. "The mountain labored and brought forth a mouse," as Horace sardonically explains.[116] Yet, like Homer, a poet should start *in medias res*,[117] in the middle of things, and strip the story to its essentials, as Aristotle too advised. There should be no superfluous details. If you want to write about Diomedes, Horace counsels, don't start with his uncle; or if about Helen, don't begin in the womb.[118] The true poet "goes right to the point and carries the reader / Into the midst of things, as if known already."[119]

Whatever does not make the story shine must be left out so that the poem is an integral whole. Similarly, in theater, choose carefully what should be described and what shown. As a general rule, playgoers are more moved by what they see than by what they hear. But some actions, as the ancient Greeks knew, are too revolting to be enacted on stage, such as Medea killing her own children or Atreus cooking a meal of human flesh, or so incredible as to invoke laughter if portrayed directly, such as Procne being turned into a bird or Cadmus into a snake.[120] He also advises against bringing gods onto the stage to resolve the action "unless the crisis is really up to it,"[121] which it rarely is.

Seventh, Horace urges the poet to be true to human nature and a careful observer of how people really behave at the different stages of their lives. Horace here describes the ages of man: the toddler learning to walk and playing with his mates; the beardless youth who shuns his tutor in favor of horses and hounds; the grown man single-mindedly pursuing money and influence; and the old man:

> In everything he does, cold, timid, slow,
> Fearful of the future, afraid to die,
> Difficult, querulous, disparaging the young
> While full of praise for the days of his own lost youth.[122]

This passage clearly influenced Shakespeare, who had Jacques elaborate with such wit and brilliance upon the seven ages of man in *As You Like It*.

Eighth, it is the poet's duty to instruct as well as to delight. "Dare to be wise," Horace enjoins.[123] The young prefer only what gives pleasure, but the old will reject any work that doesn't impart wisdom. The true poet should satisfy them both. Despite the love of philosophy displayed in his *Epistles*, Horace unsurprisingly suggests that we learn more from Homer than from the philosophers "and learn it more clearly, about / The good and bad of things, what's helpful to know, / What isn't."[124] The poet is the true legislator of reality,[125] who teaches us "the proper names of things."[126] Without poetry, "we're nothing but ciphers, born only to eat and drink."[127] Since his very first ode, Horace has insisted that the poet is more important to Roman life than is the trader, the politician, or the general: "What links *me* to the gods is that I study / To wear the ivy wreath that poets wear."

Ninth, the poet must polish, polish again, and polish some more. "My songs are made laboriously and slow," Horace explains.[128] The poet should never rest trying to "find exactly the proper words / To calibrate to the cadences and meter / Of the Latin lyre,"[129] and put the elements together in precisely the right way.

Consistent perfection is impossible, especially in a long poem. Even Homer nods, Horace reluctantly notes in a famous phrase (*dormitat Homerus*).[130] But constant revision and self-criticism are crucial means of approaching the ideal.

> He who desires to write a legitimate poem
> Will be an honest critic of what he does.
> He won't be afraid, if some expression doesn't
> Seem right, if it lacks the appropriate weight or luster,
> Or if it's wrong for the tone of the passage it's part of,
> To take it away, although it's reluctant to go
> And struggles to keep the place it felt enshrined in.
> . . .
> He'll prune back whatever is overgrown, smooth out
> Whatever is rough, get rid of whatever weakness
> Inhibits power; he'll make it look like child's play,
> Although, in fact, he tortures himself to do so.[131]

This self-torture separates the true poet from the amateur. People who know nothing about how to sail a ship or perform an operation would shrink from doing so. "But skilled or unskilled we all feel free to write poems."[132] And perhaps there is little harm in that if writing makes them happy and "happily reverential of themselves."[133] But, whereas even a mediocre lawyer can perform some useful functions, a mediocre poet "has nothing / Of any value to bring to men or gods."[134] Art requires a rare combination of natural talent and relentless work: "Each has to depend on the other, and so together / They do the work as friends."[135] Horace mock laments that he cannot be an easygoing, contented hack, oblivious to his own faults, "rather than be / Grinding my teeth to endure my own self-knowledge."[136] Yet the poet will seek out honest criticism from others as well as from himself. It is no act of friendship to praise "lifeless verses, / Or harsh or graceless verses" where an editor's heavy pen is warranted.[137] These are "serious matters," not "little things" that should give way to delicacy for the author's feelings.[138]

Following these precepts, modern poets can match and even surpass their older models. Horace decries the tendency to equate ancient with worthy and modern with worthless. Poems are not better simply with age, like wine,[139] and "old writers sometimes / Sound very old-fashioned, sometimes rather clumsy, / And in stretches flat and boring."[140] If the Greeks had spurned new works as Romans are wont to do, he notes, nothing would have been preserved to grow old and become revered, and we would have nothing to read.[141]

DEATH

Horace died on November 27, 8 BCE. He had been preparing for that day his entire life. A consciousness of death pervades the *Odes* and the *Epistles*. Death is the ultimate argument against the pursuit of wealth and power or any other activity that distracts us from wringing the most out of each passing day. "Treat every new day as the last you're going to have," he wrote, "then welcome the next as unexpectedly granted."[142] Horace had finally worn out his welcome.

Indeed, particularly in his later years, with dear friends gone and his powers fading, Horace struck more resonantly the somber note that had always lurked in his poems: "We're nothing but dust, we're nothing but shadows," he lamented.[143] He wrote, on the death of Virgil, that certain things must simply be endured, "and by endurance what can never be changed / Will be at last made easier in the heart."[144] His late epistles emphasized kindness, forgiveness, a steadfast mind, and a mellowing of the spirit:

> The years as they go by take everything with them,
> One thing after another; they've taken away
> Laughter, and revelry, and love from me, and now
> They want to take poetry.[145]

But the passing years could never take poetry from Horace, for poetry conquers death. Nor could they take away the fact that he had lived, in his poems, as intensely as anyone has ever done. In the famous translation by John Dryden, Horace had earned that right to say:

> Happy the man, and happy he alone,
> He, who can call today his own;
> He who, secure within, can say,
> "To-morrow do thy worst, for I have lived today;
> Be fair or foul, or rain, or shine,
> The joys I have possessed, in spite of fate, are mine;
> Not heaven itself upon the past has power,
> But what has been, has been, and I have had my hour."[146]

CHAPTER 6

OVID—
POET OF LOVE AND CHANGE

Publius Ovidius Naso was born on March 20, 43 BCE, in the city of Sulmona, about ninety miles east and slightly north of Rome. As he recounts in *Tristia*—his "laments" written in exile—he came from an ancient and well-off family. He and his brother, who was exactly one year older, were sent to Rome at an early age to be educated by the best teachers. Both were groomed for senatorial careers. His brother had a knack for law and rhetoric. Ovid's own taste was for poetry. His father chided him repeatedly: "Why study such useless subjects? / Even Homer left no inheritance."[1] But whenever Ovid sought to write prose, he notes, poetry intruded, and his words spontaneously formed themselves into verse.

Ovid's brother died unexpectedly at the age of twenty. Ovid himself went on to hold minor posts on the senatorial ladder but lost any inclination he once might have had for public life and claimed he could not bear "the stress of ambition."[2] He was also wealthy enough for a life of cultivated leisure. He joined the literary circle of Messalla Corvinus, who, like the more famous Maecenas, was a high official, sometime author, and full-time patron of the arts. Ovid became enchanted with the great poets of his day, especially Tibullus and Propertius, writers of love elegies. He listened to Horace sing his odes to the accompaniment of the lyre. "Virgil I only saw," he notes wistfully.[3]

Ovid began reciting his own love poems in public and quickly developed a reputation. He published five books of elegies, the *Amores*, in 20, at the age of twenty-three. Later, he discarded and revised many of these youthful efforts for a shorter edition in three books, published around 1 CE, which is the edition that has survived. With the early deaths of Tibullus (ca. 19) and Propertius (ca. 16), and the passing of Virgil (in 19) and Horace (in 8), Ovid became the most famous poet of his day. Indeed, his great epic, *Metamorphoses*, arguably exercised a more wide-spread (if not deeper) influence on artists and poets for the next 1,800 years than any other Roman poem, including *On the Nature of Things*, the *Aeneid*, and the *Odes* of Horace. He was a favorite of Shakespeare.

Ovid's poetic sensibility was very different from that of Lucretius, Virgil, and Horace. He was twelve at the time of Actium, and thus came of age after the civil wars that devastated Rome. The urgency, the sense of vulnerability, and the seriousness of purpose that anchor the poetry of his great predecessors are missing. In their place Ovid offers an elegant, witty, highly literary, at times decadent and at times frivolous body of work, but one that is alive to psychological nuance and the changing panorama of human life in contemporary Rome. Ovid covers many of the same topics and themes as Horace: love, sex, friendship, politics, art, and language. But he does so with an almost-whimsical detachment that is very different from the gentle yet somehow earnest irony of Horace. Horace's poems were often about the critical role of poetry in human life. Ovid plays riffs on the poetic and mythical tradition. His vast and varied output is held together by a sheer delight in language, in change, and in flouting moral, artistic, and even political conventions. The last of these tendencies finally landed him in serious trouble.

In 8 CE, at the height of his powers, Ovid was banished by Augustus to the remote and barren outpost of Tomis, on the Black Sea, in what is now Romania. It was a cruel fate for this most urbane and sophisticated of poets who loved Rome, the Latin language, and cultivated company. The barbarian inhabitants of Tomis did not even speak Latin, and native bowmen occasionally launched poison arrows over the primitive wooden stockade. Sometimes Ovid himself had to help man the battlements to prevent the fortifications from being overrun. And in winter, Ovid notes, the hair on his body froze and wine was served in chopped-off blocks. Ovid retained his possessions and citizenship and forged a literary life of sorts—"writing a poem you can read to no one," he noted, "is like dancing in the dark"[4]—but was never allowed to return to Rome, even after the death of Augustus. There in Tomis—even as he wrote plaintive but futile verse letters seeking some measure of forgiveness and, if not a recall to Rome, at least a less harsh place of banishment—Ovid took the measure of his accomplishments. He recognized both the greatness and the limitations of his work. "Which I was it triumphed?" he asked, seeking the source of his widespread fame: "True poet or fashion's pander?"[5] There is no doubt which way Ovid himself would have answered that question. And there should be no doubt today—despite his neglect during the Romantic period when sincere outpourings of searing passion were valued above all things—that Ovid stands among the ranks of true poets.

AMORES

Ovid had three wives. The first, whom he married when he was only sixteen, he later dismissed as "both worthless and useless,"[6] and the marriage ended quickly in divorce (which was both common and easily obtained in ancient Rome). Some speculate that she (and her infidelities) was part of the inspiration behind his love elegies and was "the girl to whom I gave / the pseudonym of 'Corinna.'"[7] But there is no direct evidence for such an equation, however intriguing. The second marriage—to "a bride you could not find fault with"[8]—was happier, but also brief. She apparently died, perhaps in childbirth, for she was "not destined / to warm my bed for long."[9] Regardless, a daughter survived to present Ovid with two grandchildren (by different husbands) at an early age. Ovid married a third and last time—"the partner who's grown old with me, who's learnt to shoulder / the burden of living as an exile's wife."[10] It is unclear whether she spent the entire time of Ovid's exile in Rome working for her husband's return or, when that proved fruitless, finally joined him in Tomis.

In either event, Ovid had ample experience of love even within the bounds of matrimony. The persona he presents in the *Amores*, however, is a more rakish figure, bedding not only his "Corinna," but a whole succession of other women, married and unmarried, shy and bold, sophisticated and naive, noble and common, short and tall, old and young. "My sex-life runs the entire / Mythological gamut," he boasts. "There's a vast cross-section / Of desirable beauties in Rome—*and I want them all!*"[11]

One cannot rely on the *Amores* for autobiographical accuracy. Indeed, Ovid himself later dismissed any such connection.

> My morals, believe me, are quite distinct from my verses—
> a respectable life-style, a flirtatious Muse—
> and the larger part of my writings is mendacious, fictive,
> assumes the licence its author denies himself.[12]

But this disclaimer is not wholly convincing. He wrote it from exile after he had been banished, at least in part, for his libertine verses and presumptively libertine ways. Ovid thus had a strong interest in trying to rehabilitate his reputation with the regime. And yet his disclaimer—that he was following a poetic convention, not reporting on serial liaisons—could possibly be true. Indeed, it would be a delicious and uniquely Ovidian irony if the author of the *Amores* turned out to be rather a prude in his private life.

Be that as it may, Ovid was completing a tradition of Roman love poetry that began at least with Catullus, whose enthrallment to "Lesbia" (the pseudonym he adopted for Clodia, the sister of Clodius Pulcher) was mentioned in the chapter on Cicero. Catullus used a variety of meters in his poems. The love elegy proper began with Cornelius Gallus (ca. 70–26), a close friend of Virgil and successful general who, after too much self-promotion, lost favor with Augustus and killed himself in 26. Almost nothing of his poetry survives, but we do know that in his poems to "Lycoris" he adapted to Latin the elegiac couplet—a dactylic (long or stressed syllable followed by two short or unstressed syllables) hexameter line followed by a dactylic pentameter line—that became standard for love poetry through Ovid.

Albius Tibullus (ca. 55–ca. 19), an older friend of Ovid, infuses a strong pastoral element into his love elegies. He imagines an idyllic setting among tall fruit trees and young vines, lying by the hearth fire with his Delia while storms rage outside. But the impoverished poet cannot compete with a wealthier rival, and by the tenth poem Delia is lost to him along with his dreams of rural bliss. Yet Tibullus finds substitutes. Three poems tell of his love for Marathus, a handsome youth. Another, more fiery mistress, Nemesis, became his muse in a second book of elegies. The countryside is now a last refuge for a man tormented by cruel love and an unfaithful mistress, yet held in bondage by trustful hope. Tibullus develops many of the motifs that became standard in love elegies: he writes a poem addressing his mistress's door, now bolted against him; he complains that she deceives him with the very tricks he taught her; and he declares himself her willing slave—"I will never shrink from chains and lashes!"[13]

Sextus Propertius (ca. 48–ca. 16) brings his elegies to an even higher pitch. He is wholly absorbed by his passion for "Cynthia," a high-style courtesan. Propertius professes indifference to politics, military service, civic virtue, and contemporary mores. He is not just a willing slave to Cynthia; he revels in his own degradation at her hands:

> My fate is neither to love another nor break with *her*:
> Cynthia was first and Cynthia shall be last.[14]

Propertius provides a richer picture of his Cynthia—"red-gold hair, long hands, big build"[15]—and her vagaries than his predecessors. His poems are full of the contradictions of love: he is devoted to her, he detests her; he rejoices in their passion, he rails at her indifference; he will make her jealous, he has eyes for no one else; he will leave her, he is bound to her; he seeks revenge, he seeks reconciliation.

Contemporary metaphors are inadequate, and so Propertius constantly resorts to mythological parallels. His Cynthia is Ariadne, she is Andromeda, she is blessed by Venus and Minerva, "she moves like / Juno, fit sibling for Jove himself."[16] As for Propertius himself, he notes what great Achilles went through in his passion for Briseis and concludes: it is "no wonder love can triumph over me!"[17]

There is already an element of self-mockery in Propertius. His love elegies are so highly wrought as to approach the comic. Ovid's genius was to recognize that there was nowhere else to go with the genre and boldly to cross that line. After Gallus, Tibullus, and Propertius, Ovid explains, "I was next, the fourth in line."[18] His "Corinna" replaces Delia and Cynthia and all the other dactylic love interests. Ovid abides by the conventions of the love elegy: the highly personal, putatively autobiographical account of the experience of love without limits, of love that gives meaning to life; the devoted, impoverished poet who would make his mistress immortal in verse; the infidelities, the rage, and the despair that mark the demise of love. Yet the conventions are plainly just that—conventions to be playfully exploited for myriad purposes.

Ovid does not even attempt to appear sincere, yet his poems recall André Gide's remark: "One cannot both be sincere and seem so."[19] He is ironic and detached, using multiple poses to give us multiple perspectives on the experience of love. The reader doesn't really believe in the "I" of the poet or his Corinna. Ovid's devotion is not to a mistress but to the love elegy itself as a literary genre. Yet, somehow, in his lighter treatment Ovid gives a more rounded and realistic picture of the experience of love than any of his elegiac predecessors. He holds it up like a prism and views all of its many surfaces. What Ovid offers us, as he himself explains, is an "anatomy of desire."[20] Whether or not that anatomy is autobiographical is beside the point; it is both funny and poignantly true to life.

Ovid starts with "Arms, warfare, violence . . ."—his intention was to write an epic in hexameter verse. But Cupid "lopped off one foot from each alternate line."[21] He grows exalted in the opening line; the second always brings him down. Ovid writes elegiac couplets against his will. He is not even in love. The meter comes first, the love interest second. He is adopting a literary form and a literary convention that require a beloved. Once he decides to "let my verse rise with six stresses, drop to five on the downbeat,"[22] he is dutifully on fire. Love in the flesh, in the form of Corinna, will not even make an appearance until the fifth poem, though, admittedly, a more dramatic appearance would be hard to find.

In the second poem, Ovid concludes that he must be in love only because he shows all the signs of love: insomnia, a "heart skewered by shafts of desire, the raging / Beast, passion, out at prowl in my breast."[23] He fancifully portrays himself as a prisoner marching in Cupid's triumph "with Conscience, hands bound behind her, and Modesty, and all Love's / Other enemies, whipped into line."[24] In the next, he professes himself hooked by "this girl," but fails to identify her and practices his pleas before Venus instead. He makes the conventional disclaimers—he has neither wealth nor position to recommend himself. But he does have poetic genius, which will link their names with the gods forever. He also claims "unswerving fidelity" and "morals above suspicion."[25] "I'm no sexual circus-rider," he insists,[26] though, in the next book, as already noted, he will boast that his "sex-life runs the entire / Mythological gamut." Apparently he served a quick apprenticeship, or perhaps his unswerving fidelity is to love itself rather than to the particular, though still unnamed, woman to whom he finally addresses the fourth poem.

It turns out that she is married, and she and her husband are both to be present at a dinner party. The poet writhes with jealousy and urges her to deny her husband kisses and begrudge him any endearments. The two lovers must communicate by "nods and eye-talk," sending stealthy messages to one another. "I shall speak whole silent volumes with one raised eyebrow, / Words will spring from my fingers, words traced in wine."[27] He urges her to nudge his foot while she passes, to use secret signals (a touch to her cheek, a turn of her ring), to leave her wine goblet so that he can drink from the place touched by her lips, and to stick to the middle of the crowd when she departs so that he can find a chance to touch her. It is a lovely and amusing poem that builds the erotic tension for what is to come in the next one. But it also forms a deliberate contrast with the fifth poem of book 2, in which the same situation (with him now as escort) is turned against him and he complains of

> Those eyebrow-signals, those eloquent nods,
> . . . little messages traced on the table
> By your finger, in wine; the remarks
> Loaded with hidden meaning, the code-words given
> A private significance.[28]

In the fifth poem of book 1, the mood suddenly changes. There is nothing frivolous or abstract in this poem of sultry sensuality. The poet is in his room on a hot afternoon taking a siesta, one shutter closed, the other partially open to allow a slanting light. Suddenly, Corinna is before him, "long hair tumbled about her / Soft white throat, a rustle of summer skirts."[29] They tussle playfully until she stands naked before him, and he praises her faultless body in detail, then clasps her to him.

The scene is realistic and vividly erotic. There is nothing archly literary about it. If Ovid is merely ringing changes on the experience of love, he has sounded here a true and powerful note.

He follows it with a drunken, early-morning plea to the porter guarding Corinna's door. The poet, returning from a party, threatens, cajoles, flatters, and pleads, all to no avail. The door stays resolutely shut.[30] He cannot reenact the prior scene in reverse, stealing in upon his sleeping mistress. Nor, one feels, would he be welcome if he did. The situation is comic and yet again realistic, this time uncomfortably so.

Ovid reports on a fight in which he went mad and assaulted his mistress. He self-mockingly invokes mythic parallels—such as Ajax slaughtering the sheep he thought were his fellow Greeks—and promises himself a triumph for heroically defeating a girl. He tries to make light of her injuries—which consist of some scratches and a hairdo in disarray—and his own self-proclaimed misdemeanor. Yet there is also genuine remorse and shame in the poem: "her silent, frozen expression still condemned me, her speechless / Tears proclaimed my guilt."[31] He beautifully captures both the overblown nature of the lovers' quarrel and the ways in which our own characters can suddenly become foreign to us and our behavior inexplicable.

The quick changes in perspective and experience continue throughout the first book. He rails against a procuress who advises Corinna on how to attract and secure the affections of a rich young nobleman.[32] Yet he himself urges any would-be lover to follow the model of a soldier and lay siege to his girl as a soldier lays siege to a city. "Night patrols and eluding sentries are games both soldiers / And lovers need to learn."[33] He chides his mistress for nagging him for presents and spoiling the generous innocence of love. He will give freely of trust and devotion, and will make verses his gift. But if she wants presents, she must (as the procuress advised) dun the rich.[34] He juxtaposes poems on a writing tablet, which he praises as the perfect go-between to fix their private assignations,[35] and then condemns on its return as "that damned obstructive / Tablet, its coffinwood frame / And *no*-saying wax."[36]

There are moments of lyric intensity, as when he bids the dawn delay.

> Now, if ever, I love to lie in my mistress's tender
> Embrace, feel her close by my side,
> At this cool hour of deep sleep, with liquid bird-song
> Tremulous in the air.[37]

But there are also poems on the grittier aspects of love, especially in the later books. He consoles his mistress on the loss of her hair from too many rinses and dyes.[38]

He offers tender concern, but cannot suppress recrimination, when she secretly has an abortion that leaves her in danger of losing her life. "It was me by whom she conceived," he notes, "or at least, I assume so: / I often jump to conclusions."[39] He even writes of his own impotence on one embarrassing occasion with another woman, alternately boasting of his past virility ("she made me perform / Nine times, no less") and decrying this present "humiliating / Blow to my masculine pride."[40]

The later books also introduce the poet as playful libertine. He now claims that he dropped epic poetry because it leaves women cold; the wanton frivolities of love poems are a better tool of seduction.

> I'll get nowhere with swift-footed
> Achilles, or with either of Atreus' sons.
> Old what's-his-name wasting twenty years on war and travel,
> Poor Hector dragged in the dust—
> No good. But lavish fine words on some young girl's profile
> And sooner or later she'll tender herself as the fee.[41]

The "unswerving fidelity" professed in the early poems is "whirled away / Like a skiff in a current,"[42] and he embarks on serial conquests worthy of a Don Juan. "Virility feeds on sex," he notes, and "is boosted by practice."[43] He even writes of the pleasures of group sex: "If one girl can drain my powers / Fair enough—but if she can't, I'll take two. / I can stand the strain."[44]

Love has become a game. Corinna is still his mistress, but her bedding is now an occasion for boasts. "Corinna is here, in my arms, / Despite the united efforts of husband, door, and porter / (That unholy trinity) to keep her secure."[45] Unlike a general, moreover, he does not have to share the glory for his bloodless conquests; he triumphs on his own—commander, cavalry, infantry, and standard-bearer all in one. He even writes a poem chiding the consort of his "latest eye-ravisher" for *failing* to guard her and hence depriving him of the logistical challenges that sharpen desire.[46] We covet what is forbidden. "Illicit passion—like it / Or not— is sweeter."[47] In another poem, though, he acknowledges that guarding one's wife or mistress will do no good unless she is truly chaste: "no watchdog can stopper desire."[48] Besides, he rather blandly notes, "it's so provincial / To object to adulterous wives—a deplorable lack / Of that *ton* for which Rome is famous."[49]

He angrily rejects Corinna's suggestion that he has been sleeping with her maid.

What?
Proposition a maid so devoted to her mistress?
Not likely. She'd turn me down—and blab.
By Venus and the bow of her winged offspring,
I protest my innocence![50]

Yet the very next poem is written to the maid herself and queries how Corinna could have known that they were having sex. In his denial to Corinna, he was simply following the advice he gives to other women, which is never to admit their infidelities.

My principles aren't based on exclusive possession,
But they *do* require some attempt
To cover one's tracks.[51]

The true lover is an expert on self-deception and will deny even the evidence of his own senses. "Your case may / Be weak—but then so is your judge!"[52] A woman's skill at deception, her intermittent rebuffs, and her volatile moods are all part of the mix that secures and enhances love.

Yet none of this—his own serial infidelities, his sophisticated embrace of open relationships, his devil-may-care pose toward false oaths and broken promises—keeps the poet from bemoaning Corinna's faithlessness or complaining that she has mistreated him. He even laments that her embraces are "*so* much better / Than the ones I taught her."[53] The lover, in his rapidly changing moods, is all contradictions and turbulence. "My capricious heart's a cockpit for conflicting emotions, / Love versus hate—but love, I think, will win."[54] He renounces Corinna yet cannot renounce her. Love is an "exquisite hell,"[55] and he expects "to expire in Love's duel."[56] There is plenty of time to rest in the grave.

But even if the author is not exhausted, he recognizes that the love elegy has run its course, and he finally bids farewell to "unheroic elegiacs."[57] Just as Virgil brought the pastoral to an end for at least a millennium, so too there was nowhere to go with the love elegy after Ovid mined its remarkably rich vein of comedy and pathos, of the absurd and the all too real.

HEROIDES

In the *Heroides* (heroines), Ovid moves from contemporary Rome to the realm of mythology; from the man's perspective to that of the woman; and from love elegies to letters in verse. But his fundamental approach is the same. Ovid still eschews the epic style in favor of an exploration of human emotion, particularly in extreme situations of love and loss. His heroines are taken from the epic and tragic traditions, but Ovid has given them a new and very human voice. Their letters to absent lovers and husbands are full of passionate entreaties, bitter accusations, and heartfelt laments, colored by their individual strengths and weaknesses and the particular yet somehow universal situations in which they find themselves. Like Euripides, Ovid reenvisions the heroic corpus in more realistic terms. He gives us flesh-and-blood women.

A number of the letters are from abandoned lovers. Hypsipyle, queen of Lemnos, entertained Jason and his Argonauts on their voyage in search of the Golden Fleece. The women of Lemnos had killed all their men folk and therefore welcomed the Argonauts with open arms and hopes for a new generation. Hypsipyle bore Jason's twins and believed his promise to return, but soon learned that he had married the barbarian princess Medea who, with her magic, helped him to outwit her father and capture the Golden Fleece. Yet Medea's magic will be no proof against Jason casting her out in turn. Ariadne, who enabled Theseus to defeat the Minotaur on her native Crete, writes on the isolated island of Naxos from which Theseus stole away while she slept. Phyllis, a princess in Thrace, rescued the Greek captain Demophoon on his return from Troy and gave of herself and her kingdom. Dido was an even more famous host of the Trojan Aeneas who was driven by fate to be false to his pledges.

Hypsipyle writes in anger of the false tears shed by Jason on his departure. She prayed for his safety and made "innocent vows that now I must observe,"[58] since he is in fact safe, although with another woman. "This makes me sick; my heart seethes with rage and love mixed in me."[59] In keeping with the queen who ordered all the men of the island to be murdered, she curses Jason and particularly his new love, hoping (as will be the case) that "she also one day [will] lose both her husband and her children" and "wander always an exile."[60] Medea, in turn, is a model of vicious self-justification and unrestrained evil. She claims it was "girlish innocence" that led her to betray her father and dismember her brother to make good their escape.[61] She is enraged not just at what she has lost (throne, country, home, and husband) but at the thought that Jason and his new wife will laugh at her foreign ways and her "eagerness to trust."[62] She will wreak a horrible revenge, killing her own children as well as Jason's betrothed.

> My wrath labours to bear all my threats.
> I will not hesitate to follow
> wherever this anger leads, you can be sure.
> I will loathe the revenge I take but
> now I hate myself because I was concerned
> for the good of a faithless husband.
> Let that be in the care of the god who prods me;
> I do not know for certain what is in my soul.[63]

Compared to these two, the other abandoned lovers are far more sympathetic. Phyllis does not lament that she aided Demophoon or even that she loved him, but only that she was so foolishly credulous. Indeed, even now she scans the sea for a sail like an ancient Madame Butterfly and nurtures a small hope in her heart that reason tells her is absurd. Her strongest reproach is that "my trust deserved consideration," and her mild and largely correct prediction is that his betrayal "will be the only thing remembered of you."[64] Otherwise, she blames herself. Ariadne laments not the loss of Theseus but her utter isolation on Naxos, where she must die unwept, unmourned, and unburied. Dido, queen of Carthage, cannot quite bring herself to believe that Aeneas would choose more wandering and hardship, in search of an elusive homeland in Italy, when she has already proffered to him a kingdom and herself. She recognizes that she cannot move his heart because the gods have decreed it otherwise, and yet she pleads with him nonetheless. Dido and Phyllis took their own lives. Only Ariadne, who in most traditions is rescued and married by the god Bacchus and becomes herself a goddess, has a happier fate. Yet there is no hint of that future in her letter.

Some of the writers are wives awaiting their husbands' return. The most famous, Penelope, has waited first through ten years of the Trojan War and then through another ten years of wanderings for the return of her lord, Ulysses. She does not view the events of either decade as a heroic adventure; she reduces them to the level of her personal loss: "all of Troy and Priam himself are not worth the price I've paid for victory."[65] Other Greek warriors have returned; their wives give thanks and "marvel in silence" as their men tell of "fate and the conquest of Troy."[66] She cannot understand what has caused her own husband's delay and is alternately concerned for his safety and worried (justifiably) that he is detained by other lovers. We know from Homer, of course, that Ulysses spent an entire year with Circe and even more time with the nymph Calypso, though we also know that Penelope's complaint that perhaps he chooses to stay away is not true; no man fought harder to return to hearth, and home, and wife. Yet one sympathizes with Penelope and her "endless nights and days spent working like a poor widow at my tedious loom."[67] There is something heroic in the sheer fact of her endurance, particularly against the insistent pleas of her many suitors: "I have been your wife and yours I shall remain."[68] As John Milton would write, "They also serve who only stand and wait."[69] And there is something deeply touching in her lament that her best years have been spent alone and in her fear that Ulysses will find her greatly changed.

> Just remember, I was a young girl when you left;
> if you came at once you would find an old woman.[70]

Laodamia is consumed with love and longing for her husband, Protesilaus, another Greek captain at Troy. She even envies the Trojan wife who, with the enemy so near to hand, can buckle her husband's armor in the morning and send him off with kisses and prayers for his safety:

> When he is back again with her, she will take
> his shield from his body, his helmet
> from his head and then at last she will welcome
> his weary flesh to her warm embrace.[71]

Yet, unbeknownst to her, Protesilaus was the first Greek warrior to jump from his ship and onto Trojan soil and (pursuant to a prophecy) the first to die, as well. When she learned of his death, Laodamia grieved with such passion that the god of the underworld allowed Protesilaus to return to her for three hours, at the end of which she killed herself in order not to be parted from him again.

Contrasted with these lawful wives is the slave girl, Briseis, who sparked the quarrel around which the *Iliad* is composed. Briseis was the daughter of a king allied with the Trojans. When the Greeks sacked her city and killed her father, her husband, and her brothers, she was awarded as a prize to Achilles. Agamemnon, leader of the Greek forces, seized her in turn when he was compelled to return his own prize, Chryseis, to her father, a priest of Apollo. With Achilles in high dudgeon, sulking in his tent, the Trojans had the advantage in battle and drove the Greeks back to their ships. But emissaries from Agamemnon, offering to return Briseis along with many other gifts, failed to move Achilles. Briseis's letter is written after the emissaries' return. Its interest lies in the psychology of the princess turned slave. Achilles has become all to her:

> Though I lost so many dear to me
> my loss was eased by loving you as brother,
> as my husband, and as my master.[72]

She upbraids him for letting her go so easily and then for failing to accept her back, even with a dowry of extravagant gifts. She imperiously mocks him for lounging on the couch, with his lyre and other slave girls to console him. He should fight and win glory by destroying his Trojan enemies. Yet, even though she claims to know that he will eventually marry another, she is terrified by his threats to depart without her and wishes only to remain in his service and identify herself with his deeds. It is a chilling and wrenching plea by a character who, in the *Iliad*, is given no voice and is largely a pawn of greater forces.

Two more of these remarkable letters warrant mention. Phaedra, the sister of Ariadne, now wife of Theseus, writes to seduce her stepson Hippolytus. In Euripides's play, Phaedra is ashamed of her incestuous passion, which is betrayed by an intermeddling nurse. Here, she is a modern Roman matron who dismisses the usual taboos as "silly words" and claims that "such virtue was out of date in Saturn's reign and it died in the next age when Jove decreed that virtue was pleasure."[73] Indeed, she notes that being under the same roof will simply make their dalliance so much easier: "no austere husband's gate will need unbolting," no guard need be evaded, no one will question his presence, and "even on my couch you will be safe."[74] Ovid's Phaedra would be perfectly at home in the realm of his love elegies.

Finally, Sappho writes of her failed September–May romance with Phaon. Sappho is the only historical character in the *Heroides*. She ran a girls' school on the island of Lesbos circa 600 and wrote exquisite lyric poems to the young women who were also her lovers. But a heterosexual passion for (the likely fictional) Phaon has changed everything.

> Atthis no longer brings joy to my eyes as
> she did once. Nor do I find pleasure
> in the hundred others I have loved in shame.
> Yours is now the love these maids once had.
> Your face, the beauty that astonished my eyes.[75]

Yet Phaon, first entranced by the genius of the older poet, has tired of her and slipped away without any farewell words, tears, or kisses. Sappho's delicate feelings for women, captured with such nuance in her poems, have been overwhelmed in this tidal wave of new emotions, and she can no longer write.

> I wish that eloquence were mine now, but grief
> kills my art and woe stops my genius.
> The gift of song I enjoyed will not answer
> my call; lyre and plectrum are silent.[76]

With neither love nor poetry to sustain her, only death remains.

Ovid published the first fifteen letters in the year 15. A second set of three paired letters (Paris/Helen; Leander/Hero; Acontius/Cydippe) was published around 4 to 8 CE, shortly before his exile. The paired letters are particularly interesting in their displays of self-deception and misdirection. Helen expresses outrage at Paris's importunities and yet, even as she rejects his every suggestion, manifests her coquetry and her willingness to yield to him in the end—a willingness that will lead to the Trojan War. Hero, while expressing her concern for Leander's safety in swimming across the Hellespont to meet her in secret, also shows her impatience that foul weather keeps him from her—an impatience that will result in both of their deaths. And Cydippe, who has been tricked by Acontius into an involuntary oath to marry him, while refuting all of his arguments with the skill of an accomplished lawyer, makes clear that she prefers Acontius to the suitor chosen by her father.

The *Heroides* can only make us regret even more the loss of the one tragedy written by Ovid: his *Medea* was much praised in antiquity, but only a few lines have survived. Still, in these letters, we have the tragic speeches of his would-be heroines; speeches of love and loss, of courage and despair, of endurance and lament.

ARS AMATORIA

The first two books of *Ars Amatoria* (*Art of Love*) were published between 1 BCE and 1 CE. A third book followed a short time later, along with *Remedia Amoris* (*Cures for Love*) and a bizarre (but mercifully brief and unfinished) piece, *On Facial Treatment for Ladies*. These are all didactic poems in the tradition of Hesiod's *Works and Days*, Lucretius's *On the Nature of Things*, and Virgil's *Georgics*. Ovid, of course, uses the didactic tradition (as he used the elegiac tradition) to very different effect. Indeed, the incongruity is even greater here. Hesiod, Lucretius, and Virgil were each, in their own way, deeply concerned with the question of how to live and sincerely sought to provide both practical guidance and moral instruction.

Ovid is concerned solely with the question of how to seduce women (or, in the third book, how women can seduce men), and, though his guidance may at times be practical, his only instruction on morality is either to ignore it or to manipulate it to one's advantage. The disconnect between the didactic style and the lubricious content is, of course, the source of its humor. Ovid is intent on demonstrating that poetry is not bound by traditional forms and solemn conventions and does not serve as the handmaid of morality. He also appears intent on following the Virgilian path from short poems through the didactic to a new type of epic. The *Art of Love* is his way station on the road to the *Metamorphoses*. Yet it is also a stop worth making in its own right.

The narrator starts out like a carnival barker, hawking his tried-and-true technique: "results are guaranteed!"[77] He claims to be "Love's preceptor," who has practiced what he now preaches.[78] "My poem," he assures us, "will deal in truth."[79] The clear implication is that Virgil's *Georgics*, his closest stylistic model to which the poem makes constant allusions, is beautiful and lofty bunk. Virgil was never a farmer in his maturity, and the small farm life of which he writes was mostly a fiction by his day. But Ovid is himself a lover and will tell us what is actually worth knowing and applying in the modern Roman world.

The narrator purports to be cynical, practical, and shrewd, like the procuress he condemned in the *Amores*.[80] Unlike the procuress, however, he is also a pompous fool who regularly calls up mythical parallels for his petty seductions, which has a reductive effect on the former, rather than exalting the latter. As Sara Mack notes in her monograph on Ovid, the narrator of the *Art of Love* "is a comic figure whose tone becomes inappropriately more sober and reflective as his message becomes more outrageous."[81] We cannot rely on this narrator, who has no moral qualms and promotes lying and trickery. We can only enjoy his antics, which are usually funny and insightful (they would not be funny unless they were also insightful) and offensive (ditto), but in a number of instances go too far to be anything but repulsive. In that respect, reading the *Art of Love* is rather like watching *National Lampoon's Animal House*.

The instruction manual is divided into three parts: first, how to find a woman; second, how to win her; and, third, how to keep her. Finding a woman is easy as long as you know the richest hunting grounds. The law courts are good, where people mingle easily, but the theater is better, where the spectators come to see and to be seen. Indeed, courtship at spectacles is a long Roman tradition, dating back to the kidnapping of the Sabine women as "marriage-bed plunder."[82] The races are also excellent, since you can sit in close proximity, engage in casual chat, and perform small services to ingratiate yourself.

> Banquets, too, give you an *entrée*, offer
> More to the palate than wine:
> There flushed Love has often clasped the horns of reclining
> Bacchus in a seductive embrace.[83]

Once you set your sights on a particular woman, fortune favors the bold. Remember that "every single / Girl can be caught" if you set the right traps.[84] Women may be better at camouflaging their desires, but they love illicit passion as much as men do.[85] Indeed, the narrator explains, woman's lust "far / Outstrips ours in keenness and frenzy."[86] Even if she turns you down at first, she will enjoy being propositioned.

A key first step is to corrupt the lady's maid with promises, prayers, and gifts. Get her to introduce your name or your letters when her mistress is in "a receptive, seducible mood" or perhaps miffed by a rival and eager for revenge.[87] The question arises whether one should also bed the maid. Perhaps, if her figure appeals, but the rule should be "mistress first, maid second. Never *begin* your wooing / With the lady's companion."[88]

A second injunction is not to give presents to your would-be mistress on spec. Otherwise, she will have fleeced you at no loss to herself.

> *This the task, this the labour*, to win her
> Gift-free: she'll continue to give
> Lest she lose what she's given already.[89]

But for this you will need the writer's and the advocate's arts: persuasive letters and "familiar yet coaxing words."[90] Persistence is the key: "Troy fell late, / But fall it did."[91] Gaze deep in her eyes, flatter her, wipe away tears, and sigh with longing.

> You must play the lover,
> Ape heartache with words, use every subtle device
> To compel her belief. It's not hard—what woman doesn't believe she's
> A natural object for love . . .[92]

Promises should be proffered without compunction or any intent of fulfilling them. Invoke the gods in their support. They will not punish forsworn lovers. You are just following the example of Jupiter himself. Where women are concerned, good faith, not deception, should make you blush.

> They're cheats, so cheat *them*: . . . let them
> Fall into the traps they've set themselves.[93]

And no bashfulness. Take your kisses and more, regardless of her protests. In the ultimate male delusional fantasy, the narrator counsels:

> It's all right to use force—force of *that* sort goes down well with
> The girls: what in fact they love to yield
> They'd often rather have stolen. Rough seduction
> Delights them, the audacity of near-rape
> Is a compliment—so the girl who *could* have been forced, yet somehow
> Got away unscathed, may feign delight, but in fact
> Feels sadly let down.[94]

Yet, since women differ one from another, flexibility is key. A man must adjust his wooing to the character and mood of his beloved. He should, like Proteus, change shapes as the occasion demands—a thousand devices to win a thousand hearts.[95]

Keeping a mistress once gained is largely a matter of not acting like a spouse. Cultivate the art of conversation (since physical beauty will fade); be constantly attentive; yield to her moods, whims, and opinions; choose presents with care (but not great expense); praise her liberally; and "use proximate virtues to camouflage each fault."[96] Most important:

> Keep clear of all quarrels, sharp-tongued recriminations—
> Love's sensitive, needs to be fed
> With gentle words. Leave nagging to wives and husbands.[97]

Get her used to your constant presence; absent yourself only when you are sure to be missed: "a field improves when fallow, / Parched soil soaks up the rain."[98]

Be discrete in your own intrigues (even if caught, deny, deny, deny), while tolerant of, and ostensibly blind to, hers. The former, he notes, is easy; the latter is much more difficult, but patience will triumph in the end. Yet if love seems to wane, then publish your affairs. "Get her anxious about you, reheat her tepid passions."[99]

You want to be the one "without whom, / Try as she will, she cannot live!"[100] Ovid concludes his advice to men with the surprisingly modern admonition that sexual pleasure should be equal and as far as possible simultaneous:

> ... take care not to cram on sail and outrace your mistress,
> Or let *her* overtake *you*; both should pass
> The winning-post neck and neck—that's the height of pleasure,
> When man and woman lie knocked out at once.[101]

Thus, Ovid ends his second book and the originally planned scope of the *Art of Love*. Yet he later added a third book to advise women on how to disguise flaws of figure, face, and temper in order to present themselves to their best advantage. "Where does art not enter?" he asks rhetorically,[102] as he revisits from the opposite perspective all the ways, *mutatis mutandis*, that one sex can attract and hold another. He even advises on the proper time to arrive at a party—late, after the lamps are lit, both because delay raises anticipation and because "soft lights and shadows will mask your faults."[103] Again, he ends with sex, urging women to insist on equal pleasure, but if they can't achieve that then at least (like the famous deli scene from *When Harry Met Sally*) fake it convincingly: "Thrash about in a frenzy, roll your eyes, / Let your cries and gasping breath suggest what pleasure / You're getting."[104]

There is little here of love or romance. Conquest and pleasure are everything. Yet behind the cynical humor and the libertine creed, there is also a Horatian undercurrent of sadness and loss.

> Have fun while you can, in your salad days; the years glide
> Past like a moving stream,
> And the water that's gone can never be recovered,
> The lost hour never returns.[105]

METAMORPHOSES

Ovid's masterpiece was written between 2 and 8 CE and was unfinished (or at least, like Virgil's *Aeneid*, without its final polish) at the time of his exile. It is an epic poem in fifteen books, and yet like no epic poem (or any other poem) before it. The work both encapsulates and transcends existing poetic boundaries. It realizes, on a vastly greater scale, what Virginia Woolf would later attempt in *Orlando*: a history, a synthesis, a parody, and a startling reenvisioning of the literary tradition to date.

There is no single, coherent tale. There is no transparent, omniscient narrator. The *Metamorphoses* is a compendium of loosely, often artificially, joined myths and stories, with elements of cosmology, philosophy, and history mixed in. It sweeps "from the world's beginning to the present day."[106] Yet the chronology is anything but strict. The poem deliberately meanders at times. So, too, does the narrator—intrusive and chatty at one moment and wholly absent the next, as tales are embedded within tales like Russian dolls, and one or another character becomes in turn the teller.

Ovid's narrative drive, eye for telling details, and comic brilliance make him compulsively readable. Unsurprisingly, the *Metamorphoses* became the definitive repository of the Greek and Roman myths about gods and heroes that so influenced Petrarch, Boccaccio, Shakespeare, and later writers. Yet the irony is that myth did not have for Ovid the resonance it had even for Virgil, who didn't believe a word of it but still invested it with cosmic symbolism. For Ovid, as Gian Biagio Conte explained, myth is but "an ornament of daily life, a decorative backdrop,"[107] like a Fragonard wall panel. Euripides mocked and brought down to earth myths that still mattered to his predecessor, Sophocles. There is no similar rebellion in Ovid, who maintains an amused, ironic detachment from the myths that he uses as occasions for telling stories and exploring human character.

These varied stories are unified, paradoxically, by the theme of change. Change is the law of the universe—Ovid even includes a speech by the philosopher Pythagoras about the transmigration of souls to give the point humorous theoretical heft—and the characters in the myth are variously changed into animals, birds, trees, and even rivers. Their loss of humanity is sometimes a symbolic punishment and sometimes a welcome relief from unbearable sorrow. Ambiguity and deception are inherent in an ever-shifting array of shapes and perspectives. But underlying most of the tales is love, in all its humanity and inhumanity. Ovid has really not strayed from the preoccupation of all his previous poems. To quote Brooks Otis, Ovid "took the one thing that was to him emotionally real—the love that unites or destroys men and women—and made an epic of it."[108]

GENESIS

The poem begins with the creation of the universe out of shapeless chaos. "Some god (or kinder nature)" separated night from day, earth from sky, and land from sea.[109] The primal heap of disconnected elements was given shape by "this creator god" who arranged "that every region of the world / should have its own distinctive forms of life."[110] Into this world

> now man was born,
> either because the framer of all things,
> . . .
> created man out of his own divine
> substance—or else because Prometheus
> took up a clod (so lately broken off
> from lofty aether that it still contained
> some elements in common with its kin),
> and mixing it with water, molded it
> into the shape of gods, who govern all.[111]

The parallels to the Hebrew Bible are striking. Man, made in god's image, even began in a golden, Eden-like era in which the earth "gave / of herself freely, providing all essentials,"[112] and man had no need of laws or weapons. But man steadily descended through ages of silver and bronze to one of iron, in which "modesty, fidelity, / and truth departed; in their absence, came / fraud, guile, deceit, the use of violence, / and shameful lusting after acquisitions."[113] Jupiter sends a flood to wipe out all but a single man and woman, both blameless and devout, who then repopulate the world.

Yet Ovid's own intent is anything but devout. His gods—who gather on Mount Olympus to decide man's fate—are a delicious parody of Augustan politics. They are the squabbling Senate, and Jove is their Caesar. The greater gods live in an exclusive enclave in their hillside palaces, while the more "plebian gods" reside below, in other sections of town. "If I were permitted to speak freely," Ovid notes, "I would not hesitate to call this enclave / the Palatine of heaven's ruling class."[114] Thus, the equation is made at the outset, not of Augustus to Jove, but of Jove to Augustus. Man is not made in the image of god. The gods are made in the image of men, with all their fraud, guile, deceit, and use of violence.

LUSTFUL GODS

This equation of gods and men is hardly flattering to men. The gods take what they want without compunction or remorse. The beautiful Io is enshrouded in mist and raped by Jove, who then turns her into a heifer to hide his offense from a jealous Juno. Juno harries the poor cow across the world before finally relenting and allowing her to resume her human shape in Egypt, where she is worshipped as a god.[115] With Europa, it is Jove himself who assumes the shape of a beautiful, tame bull, enticing the innocent girl to climb upon his back and bearing her across the seas, "her garments streaming in the wind behind her."[116] Callisto, a follower of Diana, pledged to virginity, is ravished by Jove while hunting in the forest and then, when she becomes pregnant, is cast out by Diana and her company. After she gives birth to Arcas, she is turned by Juno into a bear; the huntress becomes the hunted and is about to be killed by a spear thrust from her own son, when Jove turns them both into adjacent constellations in the sky. Juno, further enflamed to see her husband's mistress gleaming among the stars, ensures that the bear constellation will never dip into the waters of the sea.[117]

Not all the gods are so successful in their pursuits. Daphne, daughter of a river god, flees from Apollo in a beautiful but disturbing passage:

> he accelerates,
> and runs as swiftly as a Gallic hound
> chasing a rabbit through an open field;
> the one seeks shelter and the other, prey—
> he clings to her, is just about to spring,
> with his long muzzle straining at her heels,
> while she, not knowing whether she's been caught,
> in one swift burst, eludes those snapping jaws,
> no longer the anticipated feast;
> so he in hope and she in terror race.[118]

Finally, her strength fading, Daphne prays to her father and is turned into a laurel tree, which becomes sacred to Apollo and forever green.

ALL-TOO-HUMAN HEROES

The heroes of ancient mythology fare no better than the gods in Ovid's pages. They are relentlessly debunked and yet their stories still shine with interest. Often their major exploits—Perseus's slaying of Medusa, Jason's recovery of the Golden Fleece, Theseus's battle with the Minotaur, and the Twelve Labors of Hercules—are glossed over in favor of incidental events that reveal their human weaknesses. Perseus banters with Andromeda and negotiates a dowry with her parents before finally deigning to rescue her from a sea monster. When a battle sparked by her other suitors breaks out at the wedding ceremony, and he is in danger of being overwhelmed, he coolly pulls out Medusa's head and literally petrifies his adversaries.

Jason, Theseus, and others gather at Calydon to rescue the city from a huge and savage boar sent by the goddess Diana to avenge a perceived slight in offerings. But their parts in the famous hunt are anything but heroic. Theseus keeps a careful distance—"For heroes are permitted / to do their acts of valor from afar," he explains,[119] as he casts his heavy spear with great fanfare, only to have it catch on a nearby tree branch. Jason with his errant throw manages to pin one of the hunting dogs "by its privates to the ground."[120] And Nestor, destined to fame in the Trojan War, uses his own spear to pole vault himself into a nearby oak, "from whose convenient branches he look[s] down / in safety at the enemy below."[121] A young girl, Atalanta outshines and embarrasses the men by at least wounding the boar with an arrow before Meleager closes in for the kill. But when Meleager—enchanted by her beauty—offers Atalanta the pelt and head as spoils, the others protest and attempt to seize the gifts, provoking mayhem worse than that caused by the boar.

Hercules is conspicuous by his absence from the tale told by Nestor—in an interlude of the Trojan War—of the Lapiths from Thessaly and the centaurs, who were invited to a wedding and, after consuming copious quantities of wine, tried to abduct the bride. Ovid through Nestor presents a mock epic battle that abounds in vivid descriptions of gory wounds and parodies such homeric standards as the hero picking up and hurling a great rock that could not be lifted by any two lesser, modern men.

> "It happened that an antique mixing bowl,
> engraved elaborately, stood nearby;
> though it was large, Theseus was larger,
> and so the greathearted hero hoisted it
> and smashed it into his opponent's face;

bits of his brain, gobbets of gore and wine
came vomiting from mouth and wound alike,
as he crashed backward on the blood-soaked sands."[122]

As a screenplay, Nestor's account would be worthy of Sam Peckinpah. But when he finishes, Tlepolemus, son of Hercules, protests that his father was left out of the account despite his key role in defeating the centaurs. Nestor defends his narrative prerogative to exclude the deeds of Hercules on the grounds that Hercules was a savage brute who sacked Nestor's city and killed his brothers. Personal agenda trumps narrative fidelity.

The actual fighting of the Trojan War is largely by-passed in favor of such stories. Indeed, the most extensive coverage is given to the debate between Ajax and Ulysses over who has the greater right to the armor of Achilles. Ajax, slow of wit and heavy of thought, relies on his traditional heroic virtues: he never shirks from combat and has never been defeated, not even by Hector, whom he faced alone when no one else would do so. But stolid Ajax is no match for glib Ulysses, who reminds the men of his constant feats of cleverness. When Achilles's mother, foreseeing his death at Troy, disguised him as a woman, it was Ulysses who saw through the disguise and inspired Achilles with martial valor. It was Ulysses who convinced Agamemnon to put aside parental feeling and sacrifice his daughter to ensure favorable winds. And it is Ulysses who will bring back Philoctetes and his bow (without which Troy cannot be conquered) and who will devise the ultimate plan for the city's fall. The modern man of wiles and stratagems wins out over the ancient virtues of Ajax, who kills himself in anger and humiliation.

OVERREACHING MORTALS

More interesting than the classical heroes are the men and women who strive beyond their mortal limitations and are punished by gods who will brook no challenge or perceived affront. Sometimes their crime is inadvertent, as when the hunter Actaeon stumbles upon the pool where Diana is bathing (naked) and surprises her. He is turned into a stag and ripped to pieces by his own hounds. Sometimes the crime is merely obtuseness, as when King Pentheus refuses to acknowledge the divinity of Bacchus and is torn apart by a group of bacchant revelers that includes his own mother. Yet sometimes it is quite deliberate, as when Niobe claims that she—with her beauty, her riches, and her seven sons and seven daughters—is beyond the reach of Fortune and should be worshipped in place of the goddess

Latona, mother of Apollo and Diana. Apollo kills her seven sons, and her husband kills himself, "putting one end to sorrow and to life."[123] Yet still she boasts of her seven remaining daughters, each of whom then dies in turn.

> Now bereft,
> she sits, surrounded by the lifeless bodies
> of her sons, her daughters, and her husband,
> she sits there stilly, rigid in her grief:
> not a hair upon her head stirs in the breeze,
> her face is colorless, and her eyes fixed,
> and in this image of her nothing lives;
> her tongue is stone, frozen to her palate,
> her veins no longer move; she cannot turn
> her head nor raise her hand nor move a foot;
> her viscera are stone; and yet Niobe wept.[124]

Others, too, strive to be godlike. Phaëthon, the sun god's child with a mortal woman, exacts from his father a promise to grant him one wish and then insists upon driving the chariot that bears the sun across the daytime sky. The task is beyond his strength and his years, but he foolishly insists, and, when he loses control of the winged horses and the sun threatens to scorch the earth, he is struck from the chariot by a thunderbolt from Jove. Semele, tricked by Juno, demands that her lover, Jove, reveal himself in his full glory and is incinerated on the spot, though not before Jove rescues the fetus of Bacchus from her womb and sews it into his own thigh, where it will remain until it comes to term. Saddest of all is young Icarus, whose ingenious father, Daedalus, devised wings made of feathers and wax for them to escape their exile in Crete. Intoxicated by the power and freedom of flight, Icarus flew too close to the sun, which melted the wax, and he plunged to his death into the sea. Daedalus "saw the feathers on the waves / and cursed his arts."[125]

Artists rarely fare well in Ovid's pages. They pay a heavy price—as Ovid himself soon would—for their achievements. Arachne is turned into a spider for defeating Minerva in a weaving contest. The nine daughters of Pierus are changed into magpies after vying with the Muses. And Marsyas, the satyr, has the skin stripped from his body for challenging Apollo with his flute. The punishment of Orpheus was his inability to conquer death with his song, but, after being stoned to death by a coven of scorned Maenads, he at least is reunited with his lost Eurydice in the underworld:

> Here now they walk together, side by side,
> or now he follows as she goes before,
> or he precedes, and she goes after him;
> and now there is no longer any danger
> when Orpheus looks on Eurydice.[126]

Pygmalion may be the only truly rewarded artist in the poem. Put off by the defects in living women, he creates an idealized ivory statue and then falls in love with his own creation, which is brought to life by Venus: "she felt his kisses, / and timidly blushing, she opened her eyes to the sunlight, / and at the same time, first looked on her lover and heaven!"[127] The goddess herself attended their wedding.

HUMAN LOVE

Pygmalion notwithstanding, neither art nor love can conquer death. But each can make life worthwhile and offer immortality of a sort. The lovers in the *Metamorphoses*, like the artists, are largely doomed, and yet their stories are among the most beautiful in the poem. The parent-crossed lovers, Pyramus and Thisbe—whose "fire burned more hotly, being hidden"[128]—manage to communicate through a chink in the garden wall. Their story (or at least the presentation of it by a group of rustic tradesmen) would be fondly parodied in *A Midsummer Night's Dream*, but in Ovid's hands the two painfully young and painfully earnest lovers reach an apotheosis of sorts. Kept apart in life, they join one another in death. Their mingled blood dyes the mulberry bush forever red and "their blent ashes share a single urn."[129]

Ceyx and Alcyone share a mature, but no less powerful, conjugal love. When Ceyx departs by sea to consult the oracle at Delphi, Alcyone is filled with foreboding and pleads to accompany him. Wishing to spare her the hardship and danger, Ceyx departs with promises of a prompt return "if the Fates permit."[130] Instead, the Fates send a gale, whose effect on the small ship is so vividly and dramatically described that no one can doubt Ovid's ability to write in an epic style should he choose. The boat is shattered, and Ceyx clings vainly to flotsam, uncertain even which way to swim:

> he prayed that he might float where she would find him,
> and that his lifeless corpse could be entombed
> by her devoted hands. And while he swam,

as often as the waves allowed him breath,
he murmured Alcyone's name to them
and to himself.[131]

Alerted in a dream that her husband has drowned, Alcyone tears her hair, her face, her garments: "Alcyone is no one any more," she cries: "she died with Ceyx! No consolation, please!"[132] She throws herself from a cliff overlooking the sea but is turned into a halcyon, and skimming the whitecaps she reaches the silent corpse of her husband, embracing him with her wings, kissing him with her hard beak. They are both transformed, and as birds "their love and conjugal vows remain in force."[133] They mate and rear their young in winter on a nest that floats upon the water—*halcyon days* in which the winds are still and they find peace and happiness together.

Baucis and Philemon have an even happier ending. This loving old couple, cheerful in their poverty, once entertained Jupiter and Mercury, who visited them in disguise. "A thousand doors were bolted fast against them,"[134] but Baucis and Philemon welcomed the travelers to their humble hut, bathed them, warmed them by the fire, and prepared such a feast as their modest circumstances allowed. When the visitors revealed themselves and offered the couple whatever they wanted, their request was prompt and mutual:

> " We ask to be allowed to guard your temple
> as its priests, and, since we have lived together
> so many years in harmony, we ask
> that the same hour take us both together,
> and that I should not live to see her tomb
> nor she survive to bury me in mine."[135]

They spend their remaining years quietly together until they are simultaneously transformed into trees, standing side by side, sharing a single trunk, with their limbs intertwined.

It may seem ironic that the author of the *Art of Love* should celebrate steadfast, conjugal love above all other things. Yet the power of such love, in youth, in maturity, and in old age, to join and heal—in a world that is uncertain and dangerous and ever changing—is one of the few constants in the *Metamorphoses*. So, too, however, is the opposite: the power of love thwarted and perverted to separate and destroy, as in the appalling rage of Medea that leads her to murder her own children in revenge against Jason; or the brutal rape and mutilation of Philomela by Tereus, and the equally savage revenge exacted by Procne—her sister and his wife.

What is astonishing, though, is Ovid's ability to portray even pathological aspects of love with understanding and sympathy, if not approval. Byblis loves her own brother. At first, she does not recognize her passion, and then she attempts to suppress it; but, gradually, it overcomes all resistance, and she rationalizes it sufficiently to attempt a written confession: "She starts and stops. Sets down—and then condemns. / Adds and deletes. Doubts; finds fault with; approves. / She throws the tablet down, then picks it up!"[136] On finally receiving the tablet, her brother is horrified and spurns her. But Byblis, realizing that she cannot undo what she has done, continues to press her suit until her brother flees the country and she sets off in pursuit. Frenzied, exhausted, and in despair, Byblis finally collapses upon the earth, where she is consumed by her own tears and turns into a flowing spring.[137]

Myrrha is somewhat more successful, if you can call it that, in her love for her father. Led to him under cover of darkness by an old nurse in whom she confides, she conceives a child. But when her father discovers the imposture, she is forced to flee his rage. She is ultimately transformed into a tree, with warm drops of myrrh spilling from her trunk. Even so, she gives birth to a boy, through a fissure in the tree, and he becomes Adonis, beloved of Venus.[138]

Even transgender mysteries are treated with kindness by Ovid: the mother of Iphis (a girl) pretends she is a boy and raises her as a boy, fooling Iphis's father. Only the ever-indispensable old nurse knows the truth. By the time Iphis is betrothed to Ianthe, she/he is in a crisis of gender identity: "Iphis . . . loves / with hopeless desperation, which increases / in strict proportion to its hopelessness, / and burns—a maiden—for another maid!"[139] Nature has made her a girl, but perhaps, she thinks, human art can make her a boy:

> "If every form of ingenuity
> were gathered here from all around the world,
> if Daedalus flew back on waxen wings,
> what could he do? Could all his learned arts
> transform me from a girl into a boy?"[140]

Hormone treatments and sex-change operations are far in the future, but a visit to the temple of Isis has the same effect, and Iphis departs therefrom "with longer strides, / darker complexion, and with greater force, / a keener countenance, . . . and with more vigor than a woman has."[141]

Only Narcissus perverts love so completely as to allow no connection with another being. After spurning all others, Narcissus falls in love with his own reflection in a pool, and despairing of any fulfillment for his love, is transformed into a beautiful but solitary flower.

THE AUGUSTAN APOTHEOSIS

In the final two books of the *Metamorphoses*, Ovid travels with Aeneas from Troy to Rome and then quickly skims over Roman history from Romulus through the assassination of Julius Caesar to the triumph of Caesar Augustus, master of the known world. Ovid's epic history "from the world's beginning to the present day" is now complete. Indeed, all history is complete. It has reached its goal and its fulfillment in the person of Augustus, who has given the world peace and the rule of law:

> late be that day and not in our time
> when he, Augustus, ruler of the world,
> departs from it, and rises to the stars,
> and absent, is attentive to our prayers.[142]

There is a tacked-on quality to this ending, as if Ovid already knew of the emperor's anger and was trying to make amends through belated praise and a show of Roman patriotism. In the proem, he notes that the gods have not only inspired his undertaking but "changed [it] as well."[143] Perhaps this sudden upsurge of piety is the change he means.

But Ovid is no Virgil, and a careful reader detects a strong undercurrent of satire. Ovid deflates even as he seems to extol. Ovid makes use of Virgil as a scene-setter for the stories he wishes to emphasize. But he wisely does not attempt to compete with him head-to-head, just as he did not attempt to compete with Homer in what he chose to emphasize about the Trojan War. Ovid is always interested in the humor and pathos of the personal, not the divine march of history. As Brooks Otis has written, "Virgil . . . enters into his readers' and characters' feelings in order to enhance the majesty of his epic and Roman theme, to suggest the symbolic relevance of even the most incredible scenes. Ovid, instead, exhibits all the incongruities and absurdities, all the unpalatable truth, behind the epic décor."[144] For Ovid, entering into his readers' and characters' feelings is an end in itself.

Just before suggesting that the Augustan empire is the end of history, Ovid interjects a lengthy speech by the Greek philosopher and mathematician Pythagoras, who preached vegetarianism and metempsychosis and the inevitability of change. The speech is a parody of philosophy but contains a doctrinal paradox that underwrites and unifies the entire poem: everything changes but nothing is destroyed.

> "Nothing persists without changing its outward appearance,
> for Nature is always engaged in acts of renewal,
> creating new forms everywhere out of the old ones;
> nothing in all the cosmos can perish, believe me,
> but takes on a different shape; and what we call birth is
> when something first changes out of its former condition,
> and what we call death is when its identity ceases;
> things may perhaps be translated hither and thither;
> nevertheless, they stay constant in their sum total."[145]

The only constant is metamorphosis. Not even empires endure. As one nation gains in strength, another collapses. It happened to Troy, Mycenae, Athens, Sparta, and Thebes; and it will happen to Rome. The apotheosis of Augustus, Ovid makes clear, is just another great wave trumpeting its own immortality before it crashes upon the sands of time and is absorbed back into the massive, undifferentiating ocean. Ovid's true focus is on the personal, not the epic, and in his countless stories of individuals "every moment's occasion is a renewal."[146]

POEMS IN EXILE

Ovid was banished to Tomis in 8 CE. The reasons for this *relegatio*—which allowed Ovid to retain his citizenship and possessions—have remained obscure. The official explanation was the immorality of his *Ars Amatoria*, published about eight years earlier. Given contemporary Roman morals—and, indeed, those of the emperor himself—the claim invites skepticism. But the emperor was trying to set a new public tone and had already banished his daughter and granddaughter (both named Julia) for rampant promiscuity. So there may have been something to the charge.

Regardless, there was a deeper cause, which Ovid would only refer to as an "error" on his part.[147] Recent scholars have suggested that Ovid was at least aware of, and did not disclose, even if he did not participate in, a plot to ensure a "Julian succession" by the emperor's grandson, Agrippa Postumus.[148] This may have been the true reason for the banishment of Augustus's granddaughter and the later assassination of Agrippa. It is sadly ironic if Ovid, who was relentlessly apolitical in his work, suffered so greatly for a political indiscretion.

He wrote many poems and letters in verse from exile. Most of them are full of apologies, exaggerated praise for the emperor, and pleas for a return to Rome or at least a closer, more civilized place of exile. All were in vain. Even after the death of the emperor in 14 CE, Ovid was not allowed to return by his successor, Tiberius (which is understandable if Ovid was implicated, however tangentially, in a conspiracy to put Agrippa on the throne). He died in Tomis in 17 or 18 CE. His poems in exile make for painful (and repetitive) reading, but they still show flashes of humor and genius, his distinctive voice, and even a bit of final, proud, well-justified defiance:

> They've stripped me of all they could take,
> yet my talent remains my joy, my constant companion:
> over *this*, Caesar could have no rights. . . .
>
> . . .
>
> . . . *I shall be read.*[149]

CHAPTER 7

SENECA AS TRAGEDIAN

S eneca is known today, if he is known at all, primarily as a Stoic philosopher. His treatises and dialogues and, even more, his letters, make a compelling case for the Stoic virtues of courage and endurance. Seneca himself had need of those virtues. He lived during a period of intense violence and uncertainty under a succession of emperors who, when not actively psychotic, were certainly willful, unpredictable, and vicious. Seneca's mentoring letters to the ambitious young Lucilius—written in rural retirement shortly before Seneca was ordered by Nero to commit suicide—are models of ripe, quiet wisdom and direct forerunners of the *Essais* of Montaigne and Rilke's *Letters to a Young Poet.*

Yet Seneca was nothing if not complicated. He amassed an enormous fortune as tutor and then minister to Nero and wrote exculpatory speeches for the emperor, including one justifying Nero's murder of his mother, Agrippina. Seneca also wrote a series of tragedies whose "bombastic extravagance" and "passionate yet artificial rhetoric"[1] seemed to belie his Stoic philosophy. Those tragedies are never performed and are rarely read today. Scholars study them, it seems, largely to heap scorn upon them. Yet, in a famous 1927 essay, T. S. Eliot plausibly claimed that "no author exercised a wider or deeper influence upon the Elizabethan mind or upon the Elizabethan form of tragedy than did Seneca."[2] Renaissance drama is heavily based on his heightened style, his melodramatic plots, and his larger-than-life characters. Without Seneca's bombast, Eliot suggested, "we should not have had *King Lear.*"[3] Nor, we might add, should we have had *Macbeth* without Seneca's dark, violent moral vision.

The ten tragedies attributed to Seneca (only seven of which are both complete and reliably from his hand) are all that we possess of Roman drama. Only fragments remain from others, some of whom (like Ennius, Pacuvius, and Accius) were more celebrated in antiquity. We do have Greek versions for six of Seneca's seven plays. Yet scholars have tried in vain to trace influences and borrowings. These are not poor imitations of the Greek originals. Seneca borrowed existing plots but used them to very different effect. Indeed, dramatic action is wholly secondary in these plays, and, though they are far more explicitly gruesome than their Greek predecessors, the plays have a static feel to them.

Seneca constructs set-piece arias for his characters, in which they lay bare the battles taking place within their souls and within the universe at large. Seneca's violent imagery, intense moral feeling, and heightened declamatory rhetoric are all directed to showing the ways in which *logos* (reason) is perverted and engulfed by passion. The poetic language is accordingly intensified to (and sometimes beyond) the breaking point. And yet, both the aspirations and the perils of the human soul are articulated with a grandeur unsurpassed until Shakespeare. As Dana Gioia explains in the finest contemporary essay on Seneca, these are "lyric tragedies," grand operas sustained only by the music inherent in poetry and the human condition.[4]

What interests Seneca are not the vagaries of individual fortunes but the existence and progress of evil, a palpable force that infects and destroys the souls of men and women who are not steeled against it.[5] The dramas are highly philosophical and yet powerfully theatrical and often deeply moving. The fact that the same author could so profoundly influence the development of Italian opera, the formal, classical tragedies of Racine and Corneille, and the stormy, messier dramas of Elizabethan England is nothing short of astonishing.

Even Christians in the Middle Ages were eager to embrace Seneca as one of their own because he envisioned a universe ordered by a divine hand. But Seneca's god is distant and indifferent, and it is wholly man's business to bring his life into harmony with nature and to make himself, through an act of will and re-creation, impervious to the chances of fate. As Eliot rightly points out, that vision is more compatible with Nietzsche than with Christianity.[6]

Yet Seneca, for all his unsurpassed influence on later writers, is uniquely a Roman author. "In his plays," noted Edith Hamilton, "the tendencies of Roman thought and feeling stand out in a form so heightened that they are unmistakable."[7] Hamilton did not think Seneca was of the first rank; nor did Eliot, who acknowledged his flaws even while insisting upon his virtues. But they considered his plays worthy of close study in their own right, and in that they were surely correct. We must read Seneca afresh, as a Roman author with a profoundly devastating yet bleakly inspiring view of the universe.

LIFE AND TIMES

Lucius Annaeus Seneca was born circa 4 BCE in Cordoba, Spain, the second of three sons from a wealthy, equestrian family. Seneca's ancestors were Roman, but exactly when his family emigrated to Spain is unclear. His father, who lived into his nineties and is now commonly referred to as Seneca the Elder, wrote influential treatises on rhetoric, the master art for young students being groomed for a public career in law and politics.

Unsurprisingly, Seneca himself was intended for just such a public career. He was educated at Rome in rhetoric and Stoic philosophy. From 26 to 31 CE,[8] however, he lived in Egypt with an uncle serving there as prefect. Apparently, his father hoped that the dry climate would improve Seneca's poor health. He suffered from various ills—possibly asthma or even tuberculosis—throughout his life. Seneca said that, at one point, he held back from suicide only out of consideration for his father.

Seneca returned to Rome in 31. He rose rapidly as a public figure; too rapidly, it appears. He managed to incite Caligula's jealousy for his speaking ability and was saved from execution only by the intervention of friends. Caligula disparaged him as a "mere text-book orator" and, rather more cleverly, as "sand without lime."[9] Wisely, Seneca retired temporarily to private life in 39, a pattern he would follow on two more occasions.

Seneca returned to prominence during the reign of the emperor Claudius. But he was banished in 41 for alleged adultery with Julia Livilla, sister of the emperor Caligula. The charge appears to have been false and was prompted by Claudius's domineering young wife, Messalina, who thought Seneca somehow posed a threat to her stuttering, palsied husband. This time, he was relegated to the rugged mountains and barren civilization of Corsica for eight years. Both his wife and son died in Rome while he was in exile. While there, he wrote "consolations" on the brevity of life and the uncertainty of fortune. He probably also wrote a number of his tragedies during this period.

What one of Claudius's wives took away, another restored. Seneca was recalled in 49 by Agrippina to be the tutor to Nero, her son from an earlier marriage, who was then twelve. Seneca himself married again, and his union with Pompeia Paulina was long lasting, happy, and fulfilling. His relationship with Nero was also fulfilling but less happy and not so long lasting. In 54, Agrippina hastened Nero's succession by feeding Claudius poisoned mushrooms. Nero was now emperor, and Seneca, along with Sextus Afranius Burrus, head of the Praetorian Guard, were his most trusted advisors. There followed five years of good, moderate government in which Nero's more vicious instincts were redirected into relatively harmless, private pleasures, while Seneca wrote his public speeches, maintained good relations with the Senate, and guided the affairs of the empire in relative peace and prosperity.

Nero eventually grew tired of such restraint, and Seneca was increasingly compromised by the emperor's behavior. Yet he remained in his post and grew fabulously wealthy in the emperor's favor. According to Tacitus, Seneca's mansions and gardens outshone even those of the emperor himself.[10] He also made time for literary, scientific, and philosophical pursuits. Seneca even dispatched a team to investigate the sources of the Nile.

But after Nero killed his mother in 59, he grew increasingly erratic and unmanageable. Favor-currying intimates filled Nero's ears with slander about his longtime advisors. By 62, Burrus was dead, allegedly murdered with poisoned cough syrup.[11] Seneca attempted to withdraw to private life and even gave up his wealth in an effort to placate the emperor. At first Nero refused, but in 64 Seneca was allowed to go to the countryside and live as a philosophic recluse, where he wrote his famous letters to Lucilius. But that retirement was precarious at best.

In April 65 (one year after the Great Fire of Rome), a conspiracy to kill Nero and replace him with Gaius Calpurnius Piso was uncovered. Rightly or wrongly, Seneca was implicated. A widespread purge followed, and Nero ordered Seneca to commit suicide, along with both of his brothers and his nephew, the young poet Lucan. The death was a lengthy and painful affair described in Tacitus.[12] Seneca opened his veins, but his "aged body, lean from austere living, released the blood too slowly."[13] He then took poison and, finally, suffocated himself in a steam bath, all the while (according to Tacitus) dictating a new philosophical treatise. Seneca's wife, Paulina, wanted to die with him but was ordered by Nero to survive, which she did, though only for a short time. Before he died, "Seneca embraced his wife and, with a tenderness very different from his philosophical imperturbability, entreated her to moderate and set a term to her grief."[14]

Nero himself was driven to suicide in 68, bringing to an end the line of Julio-Claudian emperors that began with Julius Caesar. Seneca lived during the reigns of all five of Caesar's increasingly dubious successors: Augustus, Tiberius, Caligula, Claudius, and Nero. He figures in Suetonius's biographies of Caligula, Claudius, and Nero, as well as in the *Annals* of Tacitus and the *Roman History* of the Greek historian Cassius Dio. Seneca wrote extensive (some would say interminable) dialogues, essays, and treatises on philosophy, psychology, and science. Only a few of these are still worth reading. He also wrote a highly curious satire about the deification of Claudius called the *Apocolocyntosis*, or pumpkinification, in which Claudius vainly attempts to obtain admission to Olympus. The play is a modest revenge for eight years of exile and is endearing only for the way in which Seneca mocks his own high-tragic style.

But the tragedies and the letters belong in every library. In them, a man of the greatest rhetorical and intellectual power tries to articulate and affirm enduring human values and the fundamental decency that can and must survive the iron grip of fate and the violent passions that so often make a misery and a mockery of our lives.

SENECA AND STOIC DOCTRINE

Stoicism as a philosophical school began when Zeno (ca. 334–ca. 262), from the town of Citium on Cyprus, taught in the covered colonnade or porch (*stoa*) that bordered one side of the marketplace below the Acropolis in Athens. Zeno's teachings were later systematized and developed by Chrysippus (ca. 279–ca. 206) in hundreds of treatises. Although little of his work survives, Chrysippus exercised a profound influence on Roman Stoics such as Cicero, Seneca, and Marcus Aurelius.

The Stoics grouped their studies under three main headings: logic, physics, and ethics. *Logos* (broader than our logic) dealt with language, speech, and rational thought. *Physis* (broader than our physics) covered all of nature, including all living things. And *areté* or virtue (broader than our puritan focus on moral behavior) was the art of living and what it means to be an excellent human being.

Despite their differences, these three areas of study were conceived as internally connected ways of approaching the same basic subject. In the Stoic view of the universe, *physis* is informed by *logos*, and man's highest calling is to live a life in accordance with natural reason. The Stoics saw nature as imbued with *pneuma* or soul (an active, self-generating principle) and as thoroughly rational. Nature is divine; indeed, nature and god are one and the same, a highly pantheistic view that would later influence Spinoza, Kant, and Einstein, among others.

The Stoics, like the Epicureans (up to a point), believed in strict universal causation. What we see as chance is simply ignorance of the natural laws that determine events. Unlike the Epicureans, however, who were convinced of the utter indifference and senselessness of the deterministic clash of atoms in the void, the Stoics viewed events teleologically, as divine providence unfolding through time. The

Stoics thought that everything that happens is directed by a divine plan. Natural law is god's law. Even though we humans cannot fully grasp the divine plan, we can accept that everything is divinely determined and that this is, accordingly, the best of all possible worlds.

There are two fundamental problems with such a position, problems that have plagued every faith that includes belief in a good and all-powerful god. First, bad things happen to good people. Monism cannot account for evil, and divine providence has trouble explaining the purpose behind natural disasters and other seemingly random events that destroy lives and blight hopes. Second, if everything is determined, then how do we account for human autonomy and morality (which seems to depend on the ability to choose between good and bad actions)?

The Stoics dealt with the first problem rather as the Hebrew Bible did. Natural disasters, plagues, and other unfortunate events are part of a broader universal plan that we cannot understand and, like Job, should not presume to question. If only we could grasp the perfection of the whole, we would find that each such event has its place. To quote the eighteenth-century English poet Alexander Pope, whose Christianity was strongly influenced by Stoic doctrine: "All discord, harmony not understood, all partial evil, universal good."[15] A lovely sentiment, but perhaps a small comfort for those living amid discord and evil.

As for the second problem, the Stoics attempted to distinguish between external factors (which are causally determined) and our internal responses to those factors (which are not). Man, alone among all living creatures, has the capacity through speech and thought to understand his circumstances and to make conscious choices. That means that only man has the capacity for evil as well as for good. Yet the bad actions of bad men do not change the perfect overall design of nature or disrupt the divine plan. This is something of a paradox, never fully resolved then or since. But it does make sense that only man is a moral agent, because only man has a choice between good and bad actions. Virtue needs vice in the sense that virtue would not exist without its opposite and without the ability to choose between them.

In Stoic philosophy, nature is inherently rational and divinely ordered. Considered as a whole, it is perfect. Man is not, but aspires to that condition. He aspires, in the Stoic's somewhat-elusive but still-compelling trope, to live in harmony with nature. That is to say, he aspires to live in accordance with *logos* by accepting divine providence and natural law. Moral progress is measured by the extent to which our desires and feelings and actions correspond to right reason, by the extent to which we value what should be valued and disdain what has no value. Somewhat circularly, virtue for the Stoics simply is knowledge of what is to be valued and what is to be disdained. And that knowledge of the good, once obtained, is unshakeable. Following Socrates and Plato, the Stoic moral system has no room for failure of will (*acrasia*). We act wrongly only because we value wrongly and hence engage our emotions wrongly. Emotions are judgments, and passions gone astray are errors of judgment, false beliefs about what is important.

All that is necessary for *eudaimonia* (happiness; well-being) is virtue. External goods such as health, wealth, power, political freedom, romantic relationships, friends, children, and even life itself have no intrinsic worth. That is not to say they cannot be preferred to their opposites; indeed, a rational man will generally prefer their presence to their absence. But the ideal Stoic sage does not mourn their passing. He cultivates *autarkeia* (self-sufficiency) and *apatheia* (indifference). He bears all misfortunes with equanimity, including poverty, torture, imprisonment, the death of loved ones, and even his own death, for he accepts that whatever happens is part of the divine plan. To protest against loss is to defy providence. External goods are not just irrelevant to the good life but often inimical to it by engaging the passions in a nonrational manner. Virtue alone is good, and virtue alone is necessary for happiness. Without it, we are in a boat with no keel. We are swept this way and that by irrelevancies; we are consumed by our desires and passions (as are so many of the characters in Seneca's tragedies).

This is a very hard doctrine, wholly antithetical to Aristotle's conception of *eudaimonia* as necessarily requiring not just virtue but also a measure of external goods. Aristotle, anticipating Zeno, contended that anyone who suggests that a person who is being tortured or has fallen into great misfortunes is still *eudaimōn* (happy) is "either intentionally or unintentionally talking nonsense."[16] More recently, Martha Nussbaum has also condemned the "radical detachment of the Stoic sage."[17] The ideal Stoic—who looks impassively even upon the death of his children—is a monster of self-sufficiency, indifferent to all that matters to us as human beings and all that connects us with one another.

Seneca wrestled with precisely this problem. He tried in his writings to humanize the Stoic sage, to make him less cold and hard, more connected to his fellow human beings and more accepting of emotional dependency. Seneca is not a strict adherent to Stoic doctrine. He is pragmatic and open to thinkers from a variety of traditions, including Epicureanism, the Platonic Academy, and the Peripatetic tradition derived from Aristotle. He softens the Stoic ideal to accommodate our attachment to others and to the world. Fortitude, self-reliance, and serenity are still essential virtues, while passion, dependence, and an overvaluation of externals remain fundamental vices. But the overall picture he presents is of a basically good man trying to reconcile a supposedly beneficent providence with the often-brutal realities of Roman life and to cherish the attachments and comforts of life without becoming a prisoner to them. Wisdom can never be fully attained, but we can move on the path toward it.

LETTERS FROM A STOIC

Seneca wrote extensive treatises, dialogues, and essays. T. S. Eliot dismissed them as "that extraordinarily dull and uninteresting body of Seneca's prose."[18] More charitably and pithily, the literary historian Donald Russell has chided Seneca's "incontinent ingenuity."[19] Seneca has a highly epigrammatic style, in which the order of the sentences is less important than the crystallized thought expressed in each. He will often make the same point over and over again, each time stated in a slightly different way, as if searching for the perfect formulation, but never discarding those on the way. As the first-century critic Quintilian explained, "There is in Seneca much with which one can agree, much even to admire; but his work requires selection; one could wish that he had done the selecting himself."[20] Indeed, selections from Seneca's prose works have been widespread since antiquity. He was heavily and mercifully anthologized. Seneca should have been, like Nietzsche, an aphorist.

But these concerns do not apply to his *Letters*, written probably in 62 and 63, during his final retirement. They bear reading and rereading in their entirety. In them, the elderly philosopher—stripped of all his worldly goods and facing likely death at the hands of a hostile and increasingly debased emperor—imparts wisdom to Lucilius, his young friend and mentee. These letters are highly personal reflections on individual conscience, moral growth, and the small victories one can win on the path toward virtue and wisdom. Seneca now shows impatience with dogma and logical "quibbles that would be shameful and discreditable even among persons occupying themselves with law reports."[21] "Language . . . which devotes its attention to truth," he noted, "ought to be plain and unadorned."[22] He will not countenance irrelevancies when there is a soul to remake in the image of god and so little time left to complete his task.

Seneca's first injunction for moral and spiritual growth is the importance of both leisure and solitude to allow time for reflection. We need space in which to pursue the good without undue distractions. We accordingly must retire into ourselves and spend time in our own company. "The mind . . . should be called daily to account for itself," hiding nothing, passing over nothing.[23] The only proper form of wisdom is to know what is worth pursuing and what is not, what is essential and what is not, what is honorable and what is not. "Even the beginnings of wisdom make life bearable."[24] Seek counsel among the great writers and thinkers of the past, drawing lasting nourishment from them. They will never send you away or allow you to leave empty-handed. Pick out a particularly intriguing thought and meditate upon it; make it your own. The seeds of virtue are inside each of us and need only the right stimulus.

Yet Seneca also recognizes our inherent need for others. Self-sufficient though the wise man may be, he still desires family and friends. "No one can lead a happy life if he thinks only of himself and turns everything to his own purposes. You should live for the other person if you wish to live for yourself."[25] Our attachments to others are fragile but should be cherished all the more for that. Sounding neither self-sufficient nor indifferent, Seneca writes, "Seize the pleasures your children bring, let them in turn take enjoyment in you, and drink the cup of happiness dry without delay."[26] You must trust your friends as you would trust yourself. Think hard before admitting a friend, but once you have chosen hold nothing back. Share your heart and your soul. Otherwise, it is just "a business deal, looking to the likely consequences, with advantage as its goal."[27]

Seneca is also accepting of wealth, fame, and power, up to a point. "No one has condemned wisdom to poverty,"[28] writes the man whose wealth once rivaled Nero's own. Who could deny, he asks (as if Zeno and Chrysippus did not deny), that "even the things we call 'indifferent' possess some inherent value, and that some are more to be prized than others?"[29] Worldly goods are "borrowed ornaments."[30] But there is nothing inherently wrong with them. Indeed, the only virtue of poverty is not to be bowed down by it, whereas wealth allows an array of virtues, such as moderation, generosity, and diligence. But we should look with suspicion on the snares of good fortune, which bind us to the world and engage our hopes and fears, our greed and avarice. We don't own our wealth if our wealth owns us.

All such gifts will be taken from us in the end. We must prepare for and face the blows of chance and circumstance. "No man is crushed by misfortune unless he has first been deceived by prosperity."[31] There are many conditions we cannot change; we can only face them with a noble spirit. The reality of any misfortune is never as bad as we imagine it to be. Indeed, we need adversity to hone our strength and to develop our powers of endurance. We suffer the pain of toil and loss so that we may acquire strength. In hardship, we learn our true capacities. "Nature's wants are small, while those of opinion are limitless."[32] The things that are most important belong to no man. They are common property.

He who does not think that what he has is ample is unhappy, however wealthy. "It is in no man's power to have whatever he wants; but he has it in his power not to wish for what he hasn't got, and cheerfully make the most of the things that do come his way."[33] The wise man is content with what he has. In the end, we must "seek riches, not from Fortune, but from ourselves."[34] We can depend on nothing other than a good character as a guarantor of happiness. "The man who looks for the morrow without worrying over it knows a peaceful independence and a happiness beyond all others. Whoever has said 'I have lived' receives a windfall every day he gets up in the morning."[35]

The failure to accept fate, by contrast, arouses the passions. Anger, in particular, is a form of madness. It is more evil than envy since it actively wishes to harm another. "Anger has brought grief to a father, divorce to a husband, hatred to a magistrate, defeat to a candidate. It is worse than riotous living, as that derives pleasure from its own enjoyment, but anger from another's pain."[36] Such strong emotions derive from erroneous judgments about what is important. We succumb to false gods and let the world undermine our serenity. Our hopes and plans are inevitably thwarted in countless ways, and we react with anger against another person, a job, our luck, ourselves. Such anger is a form of poison that infects and corrupts our whole being. "Devotion to what is right is simple, devotion to what is wrong is complex and admits of infinite variations."[37] Only right reason can put our souls at rest and allow us to maintain our focus on the majesty and sublimity of everyday life. Expectation forfeits today for tomorrow, yet tomorrow may never come.

If we knew the measure of our days, we would dole them out preciously. But, as we do not know, and the end could come at any time, we should be even more careful. Death is what makes life so precious. We journey each day toward death, and the longer we journey, the shorter the distance yet to travel. Live each day as if it were your last, Seneca enjoins: "maybe it isn't, but it's not so far away from it."[38] Life is short and fleeting, but it is long enough to put our souls in order. Do not delay your time of leisure and contemplation. We must not wait to the end of our lives to learn how to live. "Only those who find time for philosophy are at leisure."[39]

Indeed, the only truly free man is a slave to philosophy. No other study "dispels fear, roots out desire or reins in passion."[40] Life may be a gift from god, but living well is the gift of philosophy.[41] Instead of a "mind in suspense,"[42] the philosopher focuses on the present and accepts what comes. He banishes anxiety and restlessness. For this task, doctrine is less important than character. Plato, Aristotle, and other philosophers "derived more from Socrates' character than from his words."[43] We should keep such examples constantly before our minds. Being a philosopher is not a matter of subtle theories; "truth lies open to everyone."[44] Nor does it mean standing out from the crowd in outward appearance or living in conspicuous poverty. It is an inward transformation: "your merits should not be outward facing."[45]

We are in a frail bark on a violent sea—a favorite metaphor that Seneca would invoke often in his plays. All we can do is face the storm with tranquility and courage—"let Fate find us ready and eager."[46] We must even prepare for the deaths of those we love and give up grief as promptly as we can. Extravagant mourning is often a substitute for neglect in life, whereas our recollections of departed loved ones should be mellow and sweet. "For when I had them with me it was with the feeling that I was going to lose them, and now that I have lost them I keep the feeling that I have them with me still."[47] The Stoic sage, in Seneca's book, is not immune to grief (indeed, he is more somber and melancholy than otherwise), but he is still accepting of providence and the losses it imposes on us: "we live among things that are destined to perish."[48] By giving in to unhappiness and anguish, we allow them to take root and grow. In a very modern insight, Seneca notes that "the pain felt by an unhappy mind becomes an unhealthy pleasure."[49]

When death finally comes for us, let it find us ready for that as well. Death is not to be feared. There is no difference between our state before birth and after death. "You didn't exist and you won't exist—you've no concern with either period."[50] We cannot extend our moment with either prayers or tears. Every journey has an end. All we can do is make the journey, as well as its ending, a good one. Indeed, death itself can be a form of freedom. "No one has power over us when death is within our own power,"[51] wrote the philosopher who, condemned by Nero, will die by his own hand.

Seneca does not himself claim to be a perfect example of Stoic virtue. He suffers from the same diseases as other men. "Demand of me, not that I should be equal to the best," Seneca asks, "but that I should be better than the wicked: I am satisfied if each day I make some reduction in the number of my vices and find fault with my mistakes."[52] He is determined to inch forward, as best he can, on a road that leads to the gods, believing that nothing is good unless it is honorable and that nothing bad can happen to a good man.[53] "I shall take my leave, having shown to all that I have loved a good conscience and noble aspirations, and that by no action of mine has any man's freedom been impaired, least of all my own."[54]

THE PLAYS

There are ten tragedies in the traditional Senecan corpus. But *The Phoenician Women*—an apparent amalgam of Euripides's play of the same name and Sophocles's *Oedipus at Colonus*—survives only in fragments. *Octavia* (the only play not drawn from mythology) is unlikely to be authentic, since Seneca himself appears as a character, and the play rather accurately anticipates Nero's death, which took place three years after Seneca's own. Scholars also question the authenticity of *A Cloak for Hercules*, loosely modeled on Sophocles's *The Women of Trachis*. The play is overly long—almost twice the length of most of the others—but if not by Seneca, then it was composed (or augmented) by a poet highly attuned to Seneca's matter and manner.

That leaves seven complete and uncontested plays, all with Greek (and in some cases also Roman) counterparts: *The Madness of Hercules*, based on Euripides's *Heracles*; *The Trojan Women*, based on two of Euripides's plays, *The Trojan Women* and *Hecuba*; *Medea*, based on Euripides's play and possibly Ovid's lost tragedy of the same name; *Phaedra*, based on Euripides's *Hippolytus* and Ovid's *Heroides*; *Oedipus*, based on Sophocles's *Oedipus Rex*; *Agamemnon*, based on the first play in Aeschylus's *Oresteia*; and *Thyestes*, based on lost plays of Sophocles, Euripides, and Varius.

There is no accepted or acceptable chronology of these plays. There is no evidence when or even if they were ever staged. Some scholars suggest they were intended only for private recitals or were simply meant to be read. The dramas are powerfully theatrical, even if not to our taste today. Given Seneca's wealth and prominence, he could undoubtedly have arranged for their performance. On the other hand, the implicit criticism of empires and emperors in several of the plays might have made private circulation a wiser option.

Seneca's plays are melodramatic, often gruesome, invariably violent, and sometimes extravagant to the point of absurdity. In other words, they are a rather accurate reflection of the time in which he lived. The plays are not just blood and bombast, however. They are bounded in a strict intellectual and moral framework, in much the way Dante's *Divine Comedy* will be. The plays are Stoic in conception and execution, and part of their interest lies in how "philosophy and drama are fused."[55] Yet it is Seneca's peculiar brand of Stoicism that governs here. The traditional Stoics believed in a rational world order imposed by divine providence. Some critics claim to discern such providence in the plays,[56] just as they find a message of Christian redemption in *King Lear*. But it is hard to see any cosmic beneficence in either place, and none of Seneca's characters appears to experience it. When good confronts evil in these plays, evil generally triumphs in a universe that is, if not godless, decidedly indifferent to human suffering and moral worth. The only virtues are fragile human ones, and, though they can be maintained with courage, they are generally swamped in a rising tide of evil.

What we see over and over again in the plays are the destructive effects of passion (anger, greed, the lust for power, violent love, a thirst for revenge) on human life and reason. C. J. Herington, in a classic essay, delineates three critical stages in Seneca's dramas: the gathering cloud of evil, the defeat of reason by passion, and the explosion of evil and its devastating human consequences.[57] A quiet, dignified humanity—generally given voice by the chorus—forms the individual's only bulwark in a hostile, alien world, and it seems a very fragile bulwark indeed in these plays. Seneca combines Sophocles's emphasis on human isolation amid cosmic indifference with Euripides's desire to give poetic, declamatory expression to the conflicting internal forces warring for the soul. But there is none of the sense we find in Aeschylus of human progress within a divine scheme of justice. There may be a measure of redemption to be found in human endurance and human connection. But no god inhabits the bleak Senecan landscape, any more than the barren, windswept heath of *King Lear*. If, as medieval thinkers believed, Seneca was preparing the way for a Christian vision, he contributed the darkness, not the light.

WAR AND DEATH: *THE TROJAN WOMEN*

Seneca's play begins as does that of Euripides. The women of Troy are gathered together on the shore. The ruins of their city still smolder in the background as they await their future slavery at the hands of the Greeks. Euripides presented his play of the same name on the eve of the Sicilian expedition as a reminder of the brutality of war and a plea against an attempted conquest that would bring only misery to the conquered and unexpungeable guilt to the conqueror. (What neither Euripides nor the blindly ambitious Athenians knew was that the roles would be reversed, and the expedition would fail dismally, leading eventually to the fall of Athens itself.) Seneca writes during the height of the Roman Empire, which maintained its stranglehold on the known world through iron discipline and indiscriminate slaughter. (What neither Seneca nor the Roman people knew was that Rome, too, would be sacked and its empire shattered. The interlude would be longer, but the result would be even worse, and both plays inevitably must be viewed in that hindsight.)

Hecuba, former queen, widow of Priam, and mother of the slain Hector, opens the play with standard Stoic reflections on the unreliability of fortune. There is a certain artificiality in this speech, but the setting and the poetry lend it both nobility and power.

> Whoever believes in wealth, power, the state,
> those fragile toys of man's contrivance, whoever
> puts his trust in such things and does not fear
> the whimsical gods, let him look upon me,
> and this, behind me—all that remains of Troy.
> Never did we imagine the ground we stood on
> could give way, shudder, gape open, and swallow
> all we had and were.[58]

She describes the death of Priam, who had his throat cut by Achilles's son, Pyrrhus, as he prayed at the altar and "honored gods who seem to have no care left for any of us."[59] At least he is better off than they, for he will never feel the conquerors' yoke around his neck. Indeed, worse is yet to come for the captives. In terrible symmetry, just as Iphigenia, daughter of the Greek leader Agamemnon, was murdered ten years earlier to ensure favorable winds for the expeditionary force, so, too, the death of a young virgin of Troy is required to obtain favorable winds home. The Greek prophet Calchas claims that Achilles's spirit demands such tribute. Achilles, of course, had been the pretended groom who lured Iphigenia to Aulis. Polyxena, the sole remaining child of Hecuba, is told by Helen that she will marry Pyrrhus. Another mock marriage will end in death.

Even Agamemnon is appalled by this senseless murder and urges the Greeks to give way.

> Troy cannot
> be built again, or all those dead brought back.
> But those who have survived, let them alone . . .
> Let there be an end of bloodshed, a hope
> among mankind of decent pity.[60]

It is a false hope. All decency is cast down and ignored. When Agamemnon appeals to a higher law of mercy and shame, Pyrrhus dismisses him with words that echo those of the Athenian envoys in the Melian Dialogue of Thucydides:[61] "Having the right, we are in the right!"[62]

Not only will Polyxena be sacrificed, but Hector's three-year-old son, Astyanax, is to be carried up to the rampart and cast upon the rocks below. Ulysses brushes aside Andromache's efforts to hide her son. In her despair, she is unable even to call upon the gods "in whose compassion I believe no longer."[63] The only truth is grief, and the only consolation for the women of Troy is that they can share that grief with one another. "That we are not alone is a comfort as voices of dirges and moaning merge to become one voice."[64]

> This is the world,
> brutal and cruel, that Troy tried to withstand.
> Cruelty wins in the end. Our little clearings
> of civilization may seem real, but mindless
> wilderness always lurks, may take its time,
> but in the end overwhelms all our pretensions
> to decency. We revert to beastliness.[65]

There are no limits to human cruelty. Our "little clearings of civilization" may delight awhile, but they will be overwhelmed in the end. Evil will conquer. The darkness of the wilderness will overtake even Rome, in all its grandeur.

The chorus meditates upon death and finds no hope there either:

> A man's breath on the winter air
> is a ghostlike puff, and disappears
> to mingle with other gasses and vapors.
> Can all those sunsets, all those dawns
> simply stop and come to nothing?[66]

The answer of the play is yes. Nothing remains after a body is burned upon the funeral pyre. Hades is just a story for children. All those sunsets, all those dawns amount to nothing. The play ends as the Trojan women are carried off to servitude.

There is no redemption to be found here, except possibly in the courage of those who seek to maintain the little clearings of civilization and provide "a hope among mankind of decent pity." There is also the courage of those who simply endure: "With tears and time, we are able to bear almost impossible burdens."[67] But there is no higher order; there are no merciful gods in whom to find solace. Nature is utterly indifferent to evil.

THE LUST FOR POWER: *THYESTES*

The musicologist Joseph Kerman famously dismissed Puccini's *Tosca* as a "shabby little shocker."[68] The same might be said, with more justice, of Seneca's *Thyestes*. Nothing survives from the lost plays of Sophocles and Euripides by that name. Given the conventions of Greek theater, however, it is hard to imagine that they were anywhere near as explicitly and revoltingly gruesome as Seneca's version.

Thyestes deals with but one incident in the long and sorry history of the House of Atreus, which ruled in the territory of Argos in the Peloponnese.[69] From Tantalus through Pelops, to Atreus and his sons Agamemnon and Menelaus, down to the matricide of Orestes, the House of Atreus was marred by one grisly crime after another and provided endless fodder for tragic drama.

It is clear, however, that Seneca is more concerned with the House of Caesar and the Julio-Claudian line of emperors that would end with Nero. It would be very surprising if this play was ever performed publicly. Seneca confronts as directly as possible the corruption, the evil, and the delusions of godhood that accompany absolute power. If the action of the play seems exaggerated, recall that Nero obtained the throne when his mother, Agrippina, poisoned her husband, Claudius, and Nero in turn murdered Claudius's son, Britannicus. Later, when he tired of her meddling, Nero had Agrippina murdered, with express instructions that she be stabbed in the womb. He also kicked to death his own pregnant wife, Poppea (of whom he was apparently genuinely fond), when she complained that he had stayed away all day at the races. Caligula, the heir of Tiberius, was, if anything, worse: having impregnated his sister, he cut the fetus from her womb and attempted to devour it, in imitation of the god Kronos, who sought to prevent the birth of Zeus, the son who would overthrow him. Atreus could be Nero or Caligula when he proclaims, "No god remains, but only myself, my pure will imposing itself on the world."[70] Power—and the thirst to assert, defend, and avenge affronts to that power—has literally driven him mad.

The play opens with the ghost of Tantalus, the first in this line of hereditary kings. Beginning a revenge drama with a ghost would be only one of the Senecan devices mimicked by Shakespeare and other Renaissance dramatists. Here, however, the appearance of Tantalus has nothing to do with the plot itself. He merely serves as a foil for Fury to explain that this succession of emperors began in evil and that there will be "competition among your issue to exceed one another in guilt," and their "passions know neither bounds nor shame."[71] Indeed, as Atreus later notes, if his sons do not already know evil, "the throne, itself, would teach them."[72]

Tantalus's two sons, Atreus and Thyestes, contested for the kingship. They murdered their half-brother, Chrysippus. According to an oracle, the possessor of a ram with a golden fleece would rule in Argos. Atreus had just such a ram secreted in a meadow surrounded by high stone walls. But his wife, Aerope, was having an affair with Thyestes. She enabled Thyestes to snatch the ram and claim the kingship. Atreus was exiled. Eventually, however, the omens from the gods were so adverse (the sun moved backward in the sky and set in the east) that Atreus was recalled as king, and Thyestes was banished.

Having since learned of Aerope's adultery, and after brooding ceaselessly upon his own betrayal and disgrace, Atreus resolves to "dare something atrocious, spectacular, so bloody, and altogether beastly that my own brother will be driven to envy, even as he suffers its dire effects."[73] Atreus angrily rejects calls for moderation and piety. Echoing Nero and Caligula, he contends that a ruler need recognize no such restraints. "The point of being a king is exactly this: that whatever the people cannot praise in your actions, they have to endure. . . . Let them suffer whatever they must and, first of all, me."[74]

Atreus pretends to propose reconciliation to Thyestes and invites him to return home. Thyestes is both suspicious and reluctant but agrees for the sake of his three sons. Atreus ostentatiously hugs his brother and his nephews and offers to share the throne with Thyestes. The chorus, taken in by the apparent reconciliation of the brothers, declares, "It does us good to see that it can happen, restoring our faith in human kindness."[75]

That faith does not last long. In what is, if not the longest, certainly the most explicit messenger speech in all of ancient tragedy, the breathless bearer of bad tidings describes in exquisite detail how Atreus brought his three nephews to the altar in an ancient grove, deep within the palace complex, to offer sacrifices to the gods. Atreus slaughtered each of the boys in turn with his sword. But the horror did not end there:

> Atreus sliced them open,
> tore out their quivering vitals, the little hearts
> twitching with life's last spark. Then, like a butcher,
> he hacked the limbs from the trunks, cracked their bones,
> and stripped off the flesh he fixed on cooking spits
> and set on the fire to turn and drip.[76]

He fried their livers and boiled their organs, and served a splendid feast to his brother, Thyestes. As the now-enlightened chorus notes, "The world is sick, mad and sick, that such vile things can happen."[77]

There is no redeeming message in this play. "There ought to be limits to wickedness,"[78] the chorus notes, but clearly there are none. "The sun should flee from the sky," and the sky itself shrink from such profanation,[79] but the sun continues its course across the blue heavens.

> There are no gods! The earth lies there, like a
> lump of stupid rock. And the gods have all gone away,
> leaving us here abandoned, like little children
> suddenly orphaned. We call out, and our voices
> echo in emptiness and mock our grief.[80]

The cycle of violence will continue. In his search for an instrument of vengeance, Thyestes will father another son, Aegisthus, by coupling with his own daughter. (Seneca's *Agamemnon* opens with the ghost of Thyestes howling for revenge by his son.) Aegisthus will in turn seduce Clytemnestra, while her husband, Agamemnon, is off at Troy (having sacrificed their daughter Iphigenia to ensure a swift voyage). Together, Aegisthus and Clytemnestra will murder Agamemnon in his bath when he returns, only to be murdered in their turn by Iphigenia's brother, Orestes. Aeschylus made use of this cycle to describe the progress from personal vengeance toward a system of justice under the guidance of a beneficent Zeus. No such divine order is present in Seneca.

> There's nothing there. Nothing but black space,
> in which case we must worship night and cold,
> and learn to love death and adore corruption.[81]

The only hope for man, and it is a slender one indeed, is to live simply, far from power, subduing his own baser nature through "hard campaigns he has fought alone in the small hours."[82] "The real riches," Thyestes notes, "are those of the soul, the talent to take the small satisfactions that come to hand."[83] But, of course, he said that before he was confronted with the heads of his sons and the wrenching knowledge that he had consumed their flesh and their innards.

UNBRIDLED PASSION: *PHAEDRA* AND *MEDEA*

Both Euripides and Ovid told the story of Phaedra, whose love for her own stepson led to the death of both. In Euripides, that love is forced upon Phaedra by Aphrodite, and her actions are driven largely by a sense of shame and a fear of dishonor. In Ovid, she is a wanton sophisticate who sees nothing amiss in a dalliance with her conveniently at hand stepson. Seneca has neither the dramatic tension of Euripides nor the playfulness of Ovid. His Phaedra is a case study in the insidious and corrosive effects of passion.

Phaedra is the daughter of Pasiphaë and King Minos of Crete. The god Poseidon (Neptune in Roman mythology), in response to some unknown affront, inspired Pasiphaë with love for a beautiful, white bull. She contrived to consummate her passion and gave birth to a creature, half bull and half man, the Minotaur, kept in a labyrinth deep within the bowels of the palace at Knossos. Athens was compelled periodically to send seven boys and seven girls as tribute to Crete, where they were devoured by the Minotaur. Theseus, the legendary hero of Athens—son of King Aegeus and Poseidon, both of whom lay with his mother on the same night—volunteered to join their numbers. With the help of another of King Minos's daughters, Ariadne, and a ball of string, Theseus managed to kill the Minotaur, find his way out of the labyrinth, and flee in a ship with the other youths and with Ariadne (whom he soon abandoned on the isle of Naxos).

Theseus subsequently abducted and married the Amazon queen Hippolyta, and they had a son, Hippolytus. After Hippolyta's death, Theseus married Phaedra, as part of a trade pact with Crete. But Phaedra detests Theseus. Her eyes instead feast upon the beautiful, chaste, young hunter, Hippolytus. In most respects, Hippolytus should be a Stoic hero. He shuns the corrupt life of the city, with its cruelty, envy, and lust. "All civilization—which everyone seems so proud of—is bathed in blood, rivers of blood from piteous, countless wounded."[84] He prefers a simple life with his fellow huntsmen, a life in harmony with nature. Sounding like an ancient Thoreau, he states, "I hunt in the woods for a better idea of what life may be like."[85] "It's virtue I chase, and decency I hunt."[86] Yet Hippolytus is still not a wholly admirable character. He is a fastidious prig whose asexuality and militant purity debar him from sympathy with basic human feelings. He is impoverished in his self-sufficiency.

Phaedra has no such immunity to the pain of human love. "A sickness grows in my soul, and its heat fevers my blood."[87] She is restless, exhausted, and haunted. She longs for death. She longs for life. Most of all, she longs for Hippolytus.

My skin tingles with shame
and delight, and I am ashamed of that delight,
but nevertheless—or all the more—delighted.[88]

Her nurse (the indispensable confidant from Euripides through Shakespeare) explains to her in perfect Stoic fashion that passions "are merely errors of judgment, lapses of taste, and failures of character."[89] She must extirpate them at the first sign lest they grow too strong and consume her:

These first subversive inklings you must stamp out
like small sparks struck from a flint, for the fire,
once it has caught and touched the heart's dry tinder,
can run wild and destroy you.[90]

But Phaedra has no wish to be well, and hence such advice is useless. "I know what's good and what's bad," Phaedra explains,[91] but she doesn't really want to corral her emotion, much less drive it out. Love can degrade our humanity and make us bestial. But it also, as the nurse herself vainly explains to Hippolytus, provides "a deeper connection" and a "sense . . . of the real business of living and dying."[92] Like her mother before her, Phaedra is drawn by forces she cannot and will not resist. She will seek fulfillment.

Inevitably, Hippolytus repulses her. She faints; he flees in his chariot, feeling polluted. To mask the truth, the nurse cries out that Hippolytus attempted to rape his stepmother. Phaedra confirms this story to Theseus, who calls upon his father Neptune for vengeance. In another instance of terrible symmetry and obvious symbolism, a bull from the sea charges Hippolytus, driving his horses to a frenzy. As described by a messenger, Hippolytus loses control, is thrown, dragged, trampled, and ripped to pieces. A distraught Phaedra confesses her lie and throws herself upon a sword.

Passion may be a form of madness, but without it we are incomplete, without it we miss out on "the real business of living and dying." Seneca, the tragic playwright, has no resolution to offer for this paradox. As a Stoic philosopher, he does not believe, with Aristotle, that it is possible to love the right person in the right way at the right time.[93] Passion, once introduced, becomes all-consuming and, when threatened, leads to violence and destruction. Yet the alternative is a cold indifference that is more like death than life.

This paradox is intensified even further in *Medea*. Indeed, Phaedra pales as a character in comparison to Medea, the ultimate tragic diva, who, in her fury, rains death and destruction on those about her. In a magnificent opening aria, Medea, like Mozart's Queen of the Night, invokes the forces of darkness and chaos and calls down curses on Jason, to whom she has given everything, including two sons, and who now proposes to abandon her.

> I pray to Chaos itself, to endless night,
> to the dark lord and lady of death, and you,
> the Furies, nightmare doyennes of writhing hair
> and smoking torches, be present now and hear me.[94]

But, in *The Magic Flute*, the forces of darkness are ultimately repulsed. In *Medea*, they are horribly triumphant. Medea herself is horribly triumphant.

Love and hatred, she notes, are just two aspects of the same passion. The more one loves, the more capacity one has to hate.

> Life matters, or else it does not.
> If it does, then one must fight, risk everything,
> even disturb the balance and order we see
> in the cold heavens. And if not, then we risk
> nothing.[95]

If life matters, if we truly attach ourselves to others, then breaking that attachment will give rise to pain and anger and fury, and the greater the attachment, the greater the emotional consequences of its dissolution. Trivial attachments may be suppressed, Medea notes, but deeper ones must be expressed.

Through love we give others power over us. That is true even for the otherwise-calculating Jason. He may no longer love Medea. He may not even love the beautiful, young, politically connected Creusa for whom he plans to leave Medea. But he loves his sons and is therefore vulnerable. "This is the tender place where I shall wound him," vows Medea.[96] She kills Jason's fiancée and would-be father-in-law. But her true vengeance lies in killing the two sons whom she bore for Jason. In doing so, she wounds herself as well. But her hatred is boundless: "I reject such business as measure, limit, proportion, counting."[97]

It is only because life matters that tragedy exists. If there are gods, they are as distant, as orderly, and as undisturbed as the constellations overhead. But we are human, and our potential for suffering, as well as our potential to inflict suffering, knows no bounds.

THE IRON GRIP OF FATE: *OEDIPUS* AND *THE MADNESS OF HERCULES*

The story of Oedipus should be highly congenial to a Stoic. It is a drama of a man's vain efforts to escape his fate. We experience the free will of Oedipus as he seeks to uncover the causes of the pestilence wracking his city and its people. His internal responses to external circumstances are not determined; they are a reflection of his character. And yet, the oracle is fulfilled. Oedipus himself is the cause of the plague because he inadvertently killed his own father and married his mother, actions he fled his apparent homeland to avoid and thereby brought to pass. His claim to self-knowledge—"Better than the gods know me, I know myself"[98]—proves empty. Creon, having braved the underworld and sought help from the shades, has a darker view: "For you no way is open but your fate."[99] But the chorus, which in Seneca often articulates the fundamental truths at work in the plays, is slightly more nuanced.

> Through narrow channels our lives move:
> our first day singles out our last.
> No god can cause events to swerve
> which, meshed in motives, roll along;
> each life proceeds untouched by prayer.[100]

Fate propels us. To fate we must yield. Prayers are unavailing, since even the gods, if they exist, cannot swerve events. And yet our motives still mesh with events within these narrow channels, granting us a measure of moral freedom. Oedipus's "crimes"—if we can call them that—were all inadvertent. But his acceptance of the sins of his humanity provides a measure of redemption for himself and his city. He blinds himself in expiation and goes into voluntary exile to spare his people further grief.

> Go offer hope to those resigned to die;
> the pestilence leaves Thebes along with me.
> Destructive Fates and sickness' trembling fear,
> wasting, black plague, dementia—come here,
> be my companions! All to me are dear.[101]

Oedipus is not Christ—the differences are more striking than the parallels—and the redemption he offers contains no element of the divine. But because of him, because of his sacrifice, "a gentler spirit animates the sky."[102] Through his efforts, he has somewhat ameliorated human suffering.

Hercules attempts such a transformation on an even grander scale. He wants to impose universal peace by warring with all the evils of the world.

> I have subdued the earth and pacified
> The swelling seas. Even the underworld
> Has felt my force. Now only heaven stands
> As the last labor worthy of my aim.[103]

Yet Hercules's hubris is a form of madness. Juno, the queen of heaven, despises the bastard son of Jupiter, this living reminder of her husband's infidelities and her own shame. She cannot defeat him openly, but she can propel him to destroy himself, unleashing his own violence against those he loves. Hercules, believing them enemies, is led to kill his wife and children in the most brutal fashion.

In a sense, Hercules is no more responsible for his crimes than is Oedipus. But when his sanity is restored, he too must expiate his guilt. Convinced that self-destruction would be too soft a recompense, he goes into exile, at war with nature and himself, never to know peace except in death, when Jupiter will gather him among the stars.

The Stoic moral intoned by the chorus is altogether too facile for this play:

> Let others seek far-reaching glory,
> Salute the crowd from triumph's car,
> Gain immortality in story,
> Be deified in shining star.
>
> But grant me just one quiet acre,
> A humble cottage far from trouble,
> To live out my allotted span,
> Though great cities fall to rubble.[104]

Seneca himself, in his capacity as Nero's minister, sought to prevent great cities from falling to rubble. And his tragedies depend on the willingness of characters to extend beyond moderation and restraint toward a form of far-reaching glory. Such efforts inevitably end in disaster. But if "life matters," if engagement with the world and with others is critical to our fulfillment as human beings, then the alternative advocated by doctrinaire Stoicism is a form of death in life and a betrayal of our deepest selves.

Seneca's great courage as a poet and a philosopher was to explore without disguising this chasm between reason and emotion. If emotion inevitably overwhelms reason, but emotion can only be extirpated at a cost too great to pay, then there is no bridge between the orderly but indifferent heavens and the violent chaos of the world. As Medea explains,

> Horror, we know, is real. The rest is a dream,
> pretense, or a children's story we cannot
> quite abandon.[105]

And yet the Stoic hero can accept, endure, and seek to lessen the suffering of his fellows. He is not as cold and indifferent as the stars or the gods.

CHAPTER 8

PLUTARCH AND THE INVENTION OF BIOGRAPHY

In Plutarch we have a kind of living repository of the wisdom of the Greeks and . . . the Romans.

—Ian Kidd, introduction to
Plutarch: Essays, trans. Robin Waterfield[1]

L. Mestrius Plutarchus (as he was known in Latin) was born in the town of Chaeronea in western Boeotia in 46 CE, during the reign of the emperor Claudius. Plutarch came from a wealthy and socially prominent family of local distinction. He traveled to Egypt and Asia Minor and served on a diplomatic mission to Rome that apparently kept him there for a period of years.

Yet Plutarch passed most of his life in the narrow geographic region centered on Chaeronea, extending sixty miles to Athens in the southeast and twenty-five miles northwest to Delphi. Athens was his shrine of learning; Delphi, of religion. In his maturity, Plutarch was a priest at Delphi, and (though he disdained superstition) he took seriously his religion and his religious duties. He studied rhetoric and philosophy as a youth in Athens. Later, he taught there and became an honorary citizen. As Plutarch noted in the preface to his life of Demosthenes, happiness and virtue are consistent with life in a small, obscure town. But to write history one must have access to a city of note where learning is valued and books of all sorts, in many languages, are gathered.

Despite the draw of these two more significant centers, Plutarch kept his home in Chaeronea. "As to myself," he wrote, "I live in a little town, and I choose to live there, lest it should become still less."[2] Plutarch served in a number of administrative posts in Chaeronea, from the relatively exalted (*archon*) to the menial (measuring and surveying). Yet he did not distinguish between the two extremes. "The meaner the office you sustain may be, the greater is the compliment that you pay to the public."[3] For the most part, though, he passed his life quietly as a scholar and a family man. Plutarch was devoted to his wife, Timoxena, and together they had as many as seven children (four sons and three daughters). The early loss of one daughter and two sons affected them both deeply.

Though Plutarch chose to confine his life geographically, his writings ranged over the entire Roman and Greek world and extended through the centuries. Plutarch did his mature work during the largely peaceful and prosperous reigns of Nerva, Trajan, and Hadrian. He was honored by the latter two of these emperors and was named a citizen of Rome.

But, as a Greek, Plutarch wrote in Greek. He even lamented his poor grasp of Latin. "Having had no leisure, while I was in Rome and other parts of Italy, to exercise myself in the Roman language, on account of public business and of those who came to be instructed by me in philosophy," he explained, "it was very late, and in the decline of my age, before I applied myself to the reading of Latin authors."[4] Even then, he noted, he did not have the leisure and degree of practice needed to master and fully appreciate the beauties of the language.

It is unclear, therefore, how familiar he was with the works of his major Roman contemporaries: Tacitus, Pliny the Younger, and the poets Martial and Juvenal. Epictetus, the Greek slave turned Stoic philosopher, was also active during this period. Plutarch himself wrote constantly, and there was little that did not interest him and engage his intellect. More than seventy of his dialogues, essays, and lectures survive, gathered together under the somewhat-misleading heading of *Moralia*. They occupy sixteen volumes in the Loeb Classical Library edition. Together, they provide a vivid picture of the intellectual currents in the age of *imperium* between Nero and Hadrian.

But Plutarch's major work was his *Parallel Lives*. He began writing them in 96, pairing a Greek military or political figure with a Roman counterpart, and then adding a short comparison of the two to make up a book. Twenty-two such sets have survived (including a double set dealing, on the Roman end, with the Gracchi brothers). It is a measure of Plutarch's immediate popularity and widespread distribution that only one book is missing from what we know he wrote, along with a few of the comparisons. Some isolated individual lives are also extant, probably parts of another series, and are generally published together with the *Parallel Lives*.

Plutarch found both joy and instruction in writing the *Lives*. "It was for the sake of others that I first commenced writing biographies," he explained, "but I find myself proceeding and attaching myself to it for my own; the virtues of these great men serving me as a sort of looking-glass, in which I may see how to adjust and adorn my own life."[5] Philosophically, Plutarch was a Platonist rather than a Stoic or an Epicurean, but he shared with the latter two a pragmatic bent and a practical application of theory to everyday life and behavior. For Plutarch, the study of philosophy, history, and even poetry are of value only insofar as they contribute to excellence and improve character.

The premise of the *Lives* is that we can learn more by meditation upon concrete examples, both good and bad, than by abstract teachings. Plutarch's *Moralia* are full of arguments; his *Lives* are full of illustrations. A catalogue of deeds and their motivations is an essential part of the analysis of character, which is revealed in actions, public and private, consequential and trivial. Plutarch is a master of the psychologically revealing (and highly entertaining) anecdote. He is a storyteller to rival Herodotus: vivid, engaging, and insightful. But first and foremost he is a moralist: he entertains in order to instruct.

The *Lives* are the product of widespread research. Plutarch's accumulation of facts and anecdotes is an invaluable repository for historians. But there was little direct documentation available to Plutarch, particularly for his earliest lives. Even for those closer in time, he necessarily relied on hearsay and memory. Moreover, like Herodotus (though with more awareness), he is happy to repeat stories that seem particularly apt, even if they are chronologically impossible.

> That Solon should discourse with Croesus, some think not agreeable with chronology; but I cannot reject so famous and well-attested a narrative, and, what is more, so agreeable to Solon's temper, and so worthy his wisdom and greatness of mind, because, forsooth, it does not agree with some chronological canons, which thousands have endeavoured to regulate, and yet, to this day, could never bring their differing opinions to any agreement.[6]

In this, however, Plutarch differs very little from modern biographers, even brilliant and serious ones such as Edmund Morris, who cannot resist delightful anecdotes of dubious authenticity.[7]

Although Plutarch is not always reliable as a historian, the *Lives* do function as a military and political history of Greece and Rome. In addition to offering both instruction and entertainment, Plutarch wants to remind his readers that the Greeks (and particularly the Athenians, who account for most of the Greek lives) were once as preeminent as the Romans had become. Greece may have been marginalized by the rise of Rome, but Rome can still be weighed, measured, and evaluated according to Greek metrics. Yet Plutarch does not focus directly on the Greek poets, playwrights, and philosophers who so plainly towered above their Roman counterparts. More audaciously, through an evaluation of Greek and Roman military and political figures, he seeks to demonstrate that, in character, prowess, and success, the Greeks were every bit the equals of their Roman counterparts. As one scholar, Timothy Duff, explains, the *Parallel Lives* are "documents of a Greek reaction to Roman power, a Greek attempt to absorb Roman history into the orbit of Greek values and Greek historiographical tradition."[8] Another, Robert Lamberton, rightly finds in Plutarch a "conciliatory vision of a dynamic, ahistorical equilibrium between Athens and Rome."[9]

Plutarch died in the reign of Hadrian, circa 120, when the Roman Empire had reached its apogee of size, power, wealth, and good government. (It would fall to Edward Gibbon, 1,700 years later, to write the story of its decline.) More than anyone else, Plutarch shaped our knowledge and popular perception of classical Greece and Rome. He makes the ancients real to us; he invites us into their consciousness and their lives. Indeed, he so quickly became canonical as almost to obscure the originality of his enterprise. A modern reader is thoroughly comfortable with his easy, engaging, and highly personal style, as well as with his blending of the public and the private, of historic events and intimate moments.

Plutarch was popular throughout the Middle Ages but gained increasing steam during the Renaissance with a renowned translation into French by Jacques Amyot. Montaigne was among Plutarch's avid readers and quoted him freely. Thomas North, in turn, translated the French edition into English in 1579. Shakespeare, Ben Jonson, Francis Bacon, and many others read Plutarch in this form, and we owe the Roman plays of Shakespeare—*Coriolanus, Julius Caesar*, and *Antony and Cleopatra*—to Plutarch's inherently dramatic vision, his narrative skill, his focus on character and motive, and his unerring eye for key details that bring a character to life.

The poet John Dryden wrote the preface for a new translation of Plutarch published between 1684 and 1688 under the title *Lives of the Noble Grecians and Romans*. It was in this translation that Plutarch exercised a profound influence on our Founding Fathers in his account of the fall of the republic and the rise of tyranny. And it was this translation that was read by generations of British schoolboys. The so-called Dryden translation, with revisions, is still the most popular one today and is used here.

What we owe to Plutarch is the entire genre of modern biography, from celebrity bios full of gossip to the heavy tomes of scholars. We live in an age of great biographies (of Teddy Roosevelt, Henry James, Fyodor Dostoevsky, Winston Churchill, and James Joyce, to name just a few), and it is a format shaped largely by Plutarch.

THE BIOGRAPHER'S ART

In prefaces to several of the parallel lives, Plutarch explains why he writes biographies and how he chooses his subjects. We possess an innate love of inquiry and observation, he notes in the life of Pericles, which should not be expended on "objects unworthy of attention."[10] If we waste our time and pains over things of little or no value, we show ourselves to be negligent and indifferent to what is good. We should not only employ our curiosity and comprehension but be improved by it. We can learn from biography, as Thucydides thought we could learn from history, but only if we study "such [characters] as are excellent in themselves" and worthy of our emulation.[11] Following the lives of great men can help to shape the minds and characters of the readers: "virtue, by the bare statement of its actions, can so affect men's minds as to create at once both admiration of the things done and desire to imitate the doers of them."[12] Any display of moral virtue inspires an impulse to practice. This is accomplished, however, not by open preaching and the drawing of explicit moral lessons; rather, "the statement of the fact creates a moral purpose which we form."[13]

This is a very interesting and highly Aristotelian thought: we learn excellence not through precepts but through "the statement of the fact" and a natural inclination toward imitation. This conception leads to the basic pattern of a Plutarch biography, which became the standard pattern of modern biographies. Plutarch describes the family background and circumstances into which his subject was born. He sketches his childhood and education, followed by his entry into public life. Then, Plutarch details the key moments of his career, followed by his death and posthumous reputation. Through this "statement of the fact" we come to know intimately another human being and why he behaved as he did.

As previously noted, Plutarch said he began writing the *Lives* for others but continued for his own benefit. Writing the biography of another person, he noted in the preface of his life of Timoleon, "can be compared to nothing but daily living and associating together."[14] If that person is of great character and excellence, then there is no more effective means to one's own moral improvement than such daily association. "The virtues of these great men [serve] me as a sort of looking-glass," he explains, "in which I may see how to adjust and adorn my own life." He habituates himself to the company of the best and worthiest characters, and derives thereby not only pleasure but also benefit. The reader, albeit at further remove, echoes that experience through the vividness of the dialogues and the anecdotes, which makes the subjects seem like living contemporaries.

Plutarch focuses his attention on public men—soldiers and statesmen of active virtue, not philosophers or sages. Military prowess predominates as a measure of greatness, and the *Lives* often seem to degenerate (to the delight, once, of Victorian schoolboys) into a numbing series of battles. His heroes are bathed in the blood of conquered peoples, and he laments the onset of civil war largely because that energy could have been used to defeat barbarian nations and add to the scope and security of the empire. In his own time of relative peace and stability, it is hard at first to see how Plutarch, a quiet scholar and family man of "happy and calm temper,"[15] can emulate the lives of these warrior heroes. Yet Plutarch is primarily interested in the formation of character and the way that character manifests itself in action. Military and political crises are the most intense crucibles of character. And, for Plutarch, we achieve our highest excellence as citizens. He accordingly celebrates public success and the characteristics that lead to it. But Plutarch does not focus on public virtue to the exclusion of private virtue. Nor does he see a gap between the two. Accordingly, he describes not only public moments of stress but also moments when his subjects are not in the public eye as perhaps even more revealing of character.

In his most famous passage on the art of biography, in the life of Alexander the Great, he explains,

> It must be borne in mind that my design is not to write histories, but lives. And the most glorious exploits do not always furnish us with the clearest discoveries of virtue or vice in men; sometimes a matter of less moment, an expression or a jest, informs us better of their characters and inclinations, than the most famous sieges, the greatest armaments, or the bloodiest battles. . . . I must be allowed to give my more particular attention to the marks and indications of the souls of men, and while I endeavour by these to portray their lives, may be free to leave more weighty matters and great battles to be treated of by others.[16]

Though his quarry is virtue, Plutarch does not shy from vice. Following Plato (and anticipating Shakespeare), he believes that "great natures produce great vices as well as virtues."[17] Aristotle's doctrine of the mean may well be advisable. But, in great natures, moderation is unlikely, and practical reason may well be overwhelmed by ambition, avarice, anger, and lust. We can learn by studying such negative examples. Just as medicine must analyze disease to promote health—and music discord, to produce harmony—so too those who would achieve virtue must contemplate injustice and wickedness. Inexperience of evil is not mere innocence, but rather "simpleness and ignorance of what all men who live aright should know."[18] Accordingly, Plutarch will introduce negative examples not "to amuse and divert my readers," but because "we shall be all the more zealous and more emulous to read, observe, and imitate the better lives, if we are not left in ignorance of the blameworthy and the bad."[19] Montaigne, a close student of Plutarch, would later note that he always found the repulsive force of bad examples more instructive than the attractions of good ones.[20]

Yet Plutarch deals in individuals, not types. So his moral judgments are necessarily more subtle than you would find in simple morality tales. As an initial matter, they are largely implicit (in "the statement of the fact") rather than explicit. Plutarch also recognizes that no man's life is blameless. We carry a mixture of good and bad traits; indeed, our bad traits are sometimes just our good traits carried to extremes. Great natures and great events place issues of morality and character in stark relief. But moral dilemmas do not always have an easy resolution. And judging men who are greater than ourselves requires a thoughtful response, not blind imitation or condemnation. The *Lives* are an invitation to Socratic self-examination for reader and author alike: Why does he act in this manner? How did he achieve greatness? Are his actions morally correct? What can we learn from them? How can we improve our own actions?

Plutarch, moreover, is inclined to emphasize the good traits of his subjects rather than the bad traits. He is far from censorious. Even Antony, his primary "bad example," has an inherent greatness. In presenting a written account of a person's character and habits, as in painting a portrait, we should be true to life and not leave out the inevitable imperfections. We should not, Plutarch notes in his life of Cimon, "abuse his memory with a false and counterfeit narration."[21] But neither should we stress faults over virtues. Plutarch's innate humanity looks to the best traits of character and interprets any flaws and failings in their light.

> Since it is hard, or indeed perhaps impossible, to show the life of a man wholly free from blemish, in all that is excellent we must follow truth exactly, and give it fully; any lapses or faults that occur, through human passions or political necessi-

ties, we may regard rather as the shortcomings of some particular virtue, than as the natural effects of vice; and may be content without introducing them, curiously and officiously, into our narrative, if it be but out of tenderness to the weakness of nature, which has never succeeded in producing any human character so perfect in virtue as to be pure from all admixture and open to no criticism.[22]

FOUNDERS AND LAWGIVERS

Plutarch aspires to "exact history," in which evidence is submitted to "the purifying processes of Reason."[23] He recognizes, however, that the further back in time his work extends, the harder it will be to attain such a goal. Just as a map maker marks the end of the known world and then speculates about the deserts and monsters, the bogs and frozen seas beyond those limits, so must he provide a warning of fable "after passing through those periods which probable reasoning can reach to and real history find a footing in."[24]

It is in this spirit that Plutarch ventures upon a comparison of the lives of Theseus and Romulus, the legendary founders of Athens and Rome, respectively. This comparison is critical to his attempt to equate Athens with Rome and the Greek world generally with the Roman one. "I found none so fit as him that peopled the beautiful and far-famed city of Athens," Plutarch explains, "to be set in opposition with the father of the invincible and renowned city of Rome."[25] Plutarch adds Sparta to the scales, and a few select heroes from Thebes, Macedonia, and elsewhere. But the bulk of his Greek lives will come from Athens during the period from her founding through the repulsion of the Persians, the growth of her empire, and her ultimate defeat in the Peloponnesian War and consequent marginalization as a military and political power.

Plutarch draws numerous parallels between Theseus and Romulus. Both were reputed to be sons of gods: Theseus of Neptune and Romulus of Mars. Both were the primal kings of cities destined for greatness. (Theseus, unlike Romulus, was not technically the founder of Athens, but he was generally regarded as its father and the font of its greatness.) Both were guilty of the abduction of women: Theseus of a series that included Ariadne, Hippolyta, and even Helen as a young girl, whose beauty was famous long before the Trojan War; Romulus of the Sabine women. Both were guilty of rash and unreasonable anger: Theseus in cursing his son, Hippolytus, and Romulus in the murder of his brother, Remus. And both died under suspicious circumstances.

Plutarch also notes the differences. Theseus could have lived quietly in retirement and never have gone to Athens, but he sought out great deeds in ridding Greece of numerous oppressors, and he volunteered to go to Crete with the young boys and virgins marked for sacrifice to the Minotaur. Romulus, by contrast, "attempted great enterprises out of mere necessity."[26] He and his brother revolted and killed the tyrant Amulius only because Amulius posed a threat to them. Romulus, however, rose to greatness from a more humble position, as a servant and apparent son of a swine-herd. Romulus was also more calculating and careful: the rape of the Sabine women was designed to build the strength of Rome. Romulus had a genius for incorporating conquered peoples, making them citizens rather than subjects of Rome. Theseus's serial marriages, by contrast, were the result of impulse and caused wars and division that did not add to the power of Athens. Both men, Plutarch concluded, were indifferent kings; one was too lax, the other too strict. Theseus erred in the direction of popularity; Romulus leaned toward tyranny, and, indeed, Plutarch suggests that the myth of Romulus's apotheosis was devised by unhappy patricians to cover up his murder.

This last point is of great interest because it highlights Plutarch's complicated treatment of the divine in human affairs. Plutarch disdains superstition, but he does not (with the Epicureans) believe that the gods are divorced from and indifferent to human life. His work is full of supernatural signs—dreams, omens, portents, and oracles. He believes in them, but not necessarily in man's ability to grasp their significance. The truth behind appearance is ever elusive. Thus, while he acknowledges that the myth of Rome's founding by the sons of Mars is perhaps overly dramatic, he cautions that "it would not wholly be disbelieved, if men would remember what a poet fortune sometimes shows herself, and consider that the Roman power would hardly have reached so high a pitch without a divinely ordered origin, attended with great and extraordinary circumstances."[27] Yet, at the same time, he dismisses the story that the two abandoned infants were suckled by a she-wolf, explaining that Latins used the word *lupae* for loose women as well as for wolves. And he flatly rejects the account of Romulus's being carried bodily up to heaven. "Though altogether to disown a divine nature in human virtue were impious and base," he explains, "so again, to mix heaven with earth is ridiculous."[28] Plutarch is a confirmed Platonist who believes that what is divine in man is separate from the body. The bodies of good men may not be sent to heaven, but their souls may go through a process of cleansing and sanctification that frees them "from all that pertains to mortality and sense" and elevates them into gods.[29]

Some of Plutarch's parallels are illuminating; others are more perfunctory or even strained. The individual lives are generally more interesting than the explicit comparisons drawn between them. But the juxtaposition is always worth noting if only because it reveals so deeply Plutarch's pro-Greek bias. He regularly favors his Greek heroes over his Roman ones, and where the latter stand out, as they must sometimes do, he often attributes their moral superiority to the benefits of a solid education in the Greek classics, an education that has molded their souls and softened their ferocity.

The influence of Greek thought on Roman heroes is particularly notable among the lawgivers featured by Plutarch. He starts with Lycurgus, who established Sparta's oligarchic constitution in the eighth century BCE. Plutarch offers an indelible portrait of the religious rituals, rigorous training, frugal existence, and well-honed discipline that made Sparta a model of stability for centuries. The last attainment in the art of government, he notes, is "to inspire men with a willingness to obey,"[30] and all of Lycurgus's innovations were devised with that end in mind.

To Lycurgus, Plutarch compares Numa Pompilius, the second king of Rome who succeeded Romulus circa 715 BCE. Numa was of Sabine origin. He lived a quiet and studious life in the country and was not implicated in Romulus's death. Numa was Spartan in his habits: incorruptible, austere, and highly religious. His high reputation for excellence, and a desire to solidify the Sabine alliance, made him a natural choice for the kingship. But the same qualities of character that were most commended made him reluctant to accept. It would be "madness," he said, for one "who needs nothing, and is satisfied with everything," to quit his accustomed life for a position to which he is unfitted by training and temperament.[31] In the end, however, his sense of duty prevailed over his love of retirement.

Numa, Plutarch approvingly notes, gave a decidedly Spartan cast to his laws, and many of Rome's most important religious and political institutions are attributed to him. His first act, however, was to disband the personal bodyguard established by Romulus, "saying that he would not distrust those who put confidence in him; nor rule over a people that distrusted him."[32] Numa established the position of Pontifex Maximus (chief priest), built temples, and founded orders of priests and priestesses. He focused on the divine to such an extent that he "once, when a message was brought to him that 'Enemies are approaching,' answered with a smile, 'And I am sacrificing.'"[33] This anecdote echoes a famous incident in Herodotus, in which the Spartans could not come to help the Athenians fight the Persians at Marathon because they were in the midst of a religious festival.

In comparing Numa with Lycurgus, Plutarch rather astonishingly suggests that Numa was "the more humane and *Greek-like* legislator."[34] The implicit criticism of

Lycurgus based on the brutal oppression of the helots seems justified. But Plutarch clearly believes that justice and humanity are inherently "Greek-like," and, to the extent that Romans embody such traits, it reflects their Greek heritage.

Otherwise, Plutarch favors Lycurgus over Numa on grounds equally surprising. He criticizes Numa for being too democratic and cultivating an open society, in which men, within general constraints to avoid harm to others, could fashion their lives and devote their energies as they saw fit. While suppressing military rapacity, Numa "allow[ed] free scope to every other means of obtaining wealth," did not try to do away with inequalities of wealth, and took no precautions against the avarice that was "the real seed and first beginning of all the great and extensive evils of after-times."[35] Clearly, Plutarch preferred the rigid egalitarianism and communal conformity in Sparta. He also notes that Lycurgus drew up exact rules for the education, discipline, and association of children, including their meals, exercises, and sports. Numa, however, left such matters to be decided by the parents and even softened the rigors of family law. As a result, Plutarch explains, Lycurgus gave to his laws a permanence and stability that Numa could not match. Numa lived more than eighty years, and, "during the whole reign of Numa, there was neither war, nor sedition, nor innovation in the state, nor any envy or ill-will to his person, nor plot or conspiracy from views of ambition."[36] But the peace and goodwill he hoped to instill lasted only through his lifetime.

Plutarch takes a more favorable view of Publius Valerius Publicola, known as "Poplicola," or "friend of the people." Poplicola participated with Brutus in the overthrow of the monarchy in 509 BCE and served with him as one of the first two consuls. He uncovered and disrupted an internal plot to overthrow the government and restore the Tarquins. The conspirators, who included two sons of Brutus, were executed by agreement of both consuls. When Brutus died a short time later at the battle of Silva Arsia, Poplicola delivered the first funeral oration in his honor, something that would become as cherished a Roman tradition as the first "triumph," in which Poplicola paraded into Rome in a four-horse chariot, displaying the prisoners and spoils of his victory over the Tarquins and their Tuscan allies.

The people began to grumble, however, when Poplicola failed to replace Brutus and thus served as sole consul, and built himself a grand house overlooking the Forum to which he descended accompanied by *lictors* with all the rods and axes. They claimed he was imitating Tarquin, whose demolished kingly mansion had been no less grand and whose power had been no less absolute. Fortunately, Plutarch notes, Poplicola "showed how well it were for men in power and great offices to have ears that give admittance to truth before flattery."[37] Learning that he had displeased the people, Poplicola sent workers in the night to demolish his house and took a modest lodging with friends. He also parted with the rods and axes whenever he entered the assembly as a symbol of his subservience to the people. Yet, Plutarch notes approvingly, these were mere gestures, for "whatever he detracted from his authority he added to his real power," to which the people submitted with satisfaction.[38]

Poplicola used that power to lay the lasting foundations of a republican government. He made it possible for any citizen to seek the consulship, not just the patricians (though that right would not be exercised successfully for generations, until "new men" such as Marius and Cicero came to power). He provided the people with a right of appeal from all judgments of the consuls. He expanded the membership of the Senate, and he appointed *quaestors*, separate from the consuls, to control the treasury. He eliminated taxes for the poorer citizens. And, most interesting of all, he made it lawful without trial to kill any man who aspired to tyranny. The descendant of his friend and former colleague Brutus would later claim this justification for the murder of Caesar.

Plutarch compares Poplicola favorably to Solon, the famed Athenian lawmaker, who thoroughly overhauled the harsh laws of his predecessor, Draco, which appointed death for almost all offenses (hence, our word *draconian*). Solon, confronting a dramatic disparity in wealth that led to civil unrest and saw many Athenians remitted as slaves for their inability to repay money they owed, canceled all debts and prohibited using the person as security for loans. At the same time, he resisted calls to redistribute property—a middle ground that pleased neither class completely, although it certainly benefited those individuals (including, apparently, some friends of Solon) who had recently purchased land on credit and thus retained the land though the debt was canceled.

Despite his reforms, Plutarch notes, Solon was unable to prevent a subsequent tyranny by Pisistratus, even though he foresaw just such a danger. But Poplicola, who died in 503 BCE, laid more effective precautions against monarchy. The republic he established lasted more than 350 years and greatly influenced our own founders. Indeed, the series of essays written in 1787–1788 by Alexander Hamilton, James Madison, and John Jay advocating adoption of the US Constitution—essays that were later collected as the *Federalist Papers*—were all published under the name "Publius," in honor of Poplicola and his critical role in ensuring the success of the Roman Republic.

DEFENDERS AND CONQUERORS

Ancient Rome, like modern Israel, was surrounded by enemies and under attack from the day of its founding. Inevitably, therefore, many of Plutarch's lives focus on the generals who steadily and inexorably transformed a besieged village into the most powerful empire the world had known. Rome was in thrall to the military men who brought it security and rapidly increasing wealth. But the affections of the people sometimes proved fickle. For even where power did not lead to willfulness and arrogance in the possessor, it caused envy and resentment in others. This is a stock theme in Plutarch, repeated over and over again.

Plutarch sets the stage with the story of Themistocles, the Greek hero of Salamis who was later banished by the Athenians. While still a young man, his father took him to the seashore and showed him the discarded hulks of galleys on the beach. This is how the people behave toward their leaders, he explained, when they have no further use for them. Themistocles, like Miltiades (the hero of Marathon) and Aristides (whose nickname, "the Just," did not prevent and indeed may have helped provoke his own banishment), learned the lesson too late.

The Romans were neither better nor worse than the Athenians in this regard. Marcus Furius Camillus (ca. 446–365 BCE) did more than anyone else to conquer and pacify the Latin tribes of the central Italian peninsula. He was chosen dictator on multiple occasions to deal with these regional conflicts and repeatedly won great victories. But, because he did not bring in enough plunder, he was prosecuted and likely would have faced a large fine. His friends offered to pay the fine, but Camillus resolved in anger to leave the city instead with his wife and children. Like Achilles, he publicly prayed that Rome would soon repent for dishonoring its greatest warrior. Like Achilles, his prayer was soon answered. Unlike Achilles, however, he responded immediately to his city's call. When the Gauls sacked Rome in 390 BCE, the patricians besieged on the fortified Capitol sent word to Camillus, appointing him dictator once again. He immediately gathered troops and drove off the Gauls. He then—when the people would not allow him to lay down the dictatorship—oversaw the rebuilding of the city. On his death he was mourned as "the second founder of Rome."

Coriolanus had an even rockier relationship with the people of Rome. As the eponymous protagonist in Shakespeare's play, Coriolanus briefly became an icon for some American conservatives in the 1980s for his high merit, his uncompromising integrity, and his unwillingness to pander to the masses. But Plutarch (and

likely Shakespeare) had a darker assessment of his "overbearing, haughty, and imperious temper."[39] "While the force and vigour of his soul, and a persevering constancy in all he undertook, led him successfully into many noble achievements,"
Plutarch notes, "by indulging the vehemence of his passion, and through an obsti-
nate reluctance to yield or accommodate his humours and sentiments to those of
a people about him," he rendered himself unfit for life in a republic.[40] Coriolanus
disdained any effort to gain favor and, indeed, actively opposed those who would
make concessions to the people. Yet he still expected to be elected consul and bitterly resented his defeat, though, as Plutarch notes, "he who least likes courting
favour, ought also least to think of resenting neglect."[41] Ultimately, Coriolanus was
banished despite his military victories and sought refuge with Rome's then-greatest
enemy, the Volscians. He led a Volscian army to the very gates of Rome and was
only dissuaded from attacking and likely sacking the city by the intervention of his
mother and his wife.

The changing favors of the Roman people played out in high relief during the
Second Punic War, when Hannibal invaded the peninsula. After a Roman army of
thirty thousand was ambushed and cut to pieces at the battle of Lake Trasimene in
June 217 BCE, Fabius Maximus (ca. 280–203 BCE), who had cautioned against
the engagement, was appointed dictator. He sought to contain Hannibal, to wear
him out and exhaust his resources, while avoiding any major battle. This strategy of
attrition kept Rome safe but proved unpopular. Only Hannibal, Plutarch claims,
discerned Fabius's skill and understood his tactics. At Rome, Fabius was derisively
nicknamed Cunctator (or Delayer). His friends urged him to adopt a more aggressive approach to stave off criticism, but he steadfastly refused.

> "I should be more faint-hearted than they make me, if, through fear of idle
> reproaches, I should abandon my own convictions. It is no inglorious thing to
> have fear for the safety of our country, but to be turned from one's course by men's
> opinions, by blame, and by misrepresentation, shows a man unfit to hold an office
> such as this, which, by such conduct, he makes the slaves of those whose errors it
> is his business to control."[42]

The Roman people remained unimpressed. They gave co-command of the
army to Marcus Minucius, a fire-breathing political enemy of Fabius, who insisted
on having half the army under his direct control. Against the advice of Fabius,
Minucius moved quickly to confront Hannibal. He, too, was lured into a trap
from which he and his men had to be rescued by Fabius. Minucius then yielded

his command to Fabius and acknowledged his superior wisdom. But the Roman people did not. When Fabius laid down his dictatorship, the two new consuls again followed a policy of aggressive confrontation. Despite what should have been an overwhelming advantage in numbers, they were routed at the battle of Cannae in August 216 BCE. As many as seventy thousand Romans were killed.

Suddenly, "Cunctator" became an epithet of distinction. What before the Roman people had disparaged as failings were now seen as supreme virtues: "his slowness in words and actions, the effect of a true prudence; his want of rapidity and his sluggishness, as constancy and firmness."[43] And what they condemned as fear, and even cowardice, was rebranded as an almost-superhuman wisdom. Yet Fabius was as tranquil and unmoved by the praise as he had been by the blame. Plutarch compares him to the Athenian statesman Pericles, in the soundness of his judgment and his ability to stand firm against the tide of opinion and advice. George Washington would be dubbed the "American Fabius" for his conduct of a war of attrition that finally persuaded the British to give the colonies their freedom.

Yet, as the war dragged on, Fabius was again paired as co-commander with a man of action, Marcus Claudius Marcellus (ca. 268–208 BCE), who, in a battle with the Gauls, had gained the most prestigious military recognition a Roman general could earn, the *spolia opima* (or "ultimate spoils"), for killing the opposing general in hand-to-hand combat. Marcellus had also laid siege to and sacked Syracuse as part of the Roman conquest of Sicily. He was a bold and creative general. Hannibal said he feared "Marcellus when he was in motion and Fabius when he sat still."[44] But Hannibal lured Marcellus to disaster at Venusia. Yet again, Fabius was left to pick up the pieces and patiently thwart Hannibal's designs. In the end, Hannibal was recalled when Scipio attacked Carthage, a venture the ever-cautious Fabius opposed and whose successful conclusion he did not live to see. After that victory, the primary threat to the Roman Republic would come from within, though not in the Social War with Italian allies seeking greater rights or even in the slave rebellion led by Spartacus. The republic was destroyed by her greatest sons.

THE MEN WHO WOULD BE KING

In his life of Themistocles, Plutarch suggests that "the wildest colts make the best horses, if they only get properly trained and broken in."[45] He knows that greatness has an inherent capacity for evil as well as for good. But Plutarch possesses a deep faith in education (by which he invariably means a study of the Greek classics and particularly the philosophers) to tip the balance toward virtue and liberality. "Education and study, and the favours of the muses," he writes in the life of Coriolanus, "confer no greater benefit on those that seek them than these humanising and civilising lessons, which teach our natural qualities to submit to the limitations prescribed by reason, and to avoid the wildness of extremes."[46] Coriolanus failed in those lessons. He reined in neither his self-willed ambition nor his anger and resentment and would have destroyed the republic but for a sudden access of shame and piety when confronted by his mother and his wife.

Neither shame nor piety would stop others. From the perspective of Roman history, the most valuable portion of the *Lives* contains the portraits of those individuals from the Gracchi through Mark Antony, whose enormous talents and strong, often-appealing, and always-compelling personalities led to the destruction of the Roman Republic and the loss of political freedom. With so many other nations already conquered, their tremendous energies and ambitions were turned inward, and their thirst for power could not be quenched within the limitations of the republic. Our focus will not be on repeating the history of the fall of the republic but on how Plutarch reveals the characters of its major figures. While not disregarding broader social and political forces, Plutarch is perhaps the primary exponent of the role of the individual in shaping historical events.

THE GRACCHI

Plutarch suggests that Tiberius and Gaius Gracchus had "a genius to virtue beyond all other Romans, which was improved also by a generous education."[47] But their efforts on behalf of the poor and powerless fanned fires of discord that they could not control. Their mother, Cornelia, was the daughter of Scipio Africanus, who defeated Hannibal at the battle of Zama in 202 BCE. When her husband died, she preferred to remain a widow, refusing even an offer of marriage from King Ptolemy of Egypt, and alone raised her daughter and two sons (all that survived of the twelve children she had borne). She laid upon the boys an injunction to be first among the Romans and frequently upbraided them "that the Romans as yet rather called her the daughter of Scipio, than the mother of the Gracchi."[48]

The boys were a study in contrasts. Tiberius (163–133 BCE) was nine years older than his brother, Gaius (154–121 BCE). (Plutarch laments this age gap as "one of the principal causes of the failure of their enterprises" because they could not exercise their power together and support one another.[49]) Tiberius was gentle and reasonable, where Gaius was impetuous and passionate. His oratory was calm and relied on soft persuasion, where Gaius was heated and inclined toward the bombastic; so much so, indeed, that Gaius employed a servant to strike a soft note on a pipe whenever his voice grew shrill and threatened to break with anger, so that Gaius might check his vehemence. Where Tiberius was frugal and austere, Gaius inclined toward delicacies and the latest fashions.

Yet they were alike in aligning with the dispossessed (whether from innate conviction, as Plutarch suggests, or as the surest way to make their mark in a Rome already dominated by patricians, as Cicero more cynically contended). When Tiberius was elected Tribune of the People, he argued vehemently for a distribution of public land, particularly to former soldiers who, "having no houses or settlements of their own," fought and died "to maintain the luxury and the wealth of other men."[50] But his fellow tribune, Octavius, with the support of the Senate, blocked his every effort. Finally, Tiberius gave way to his frustration and had Octavius forcibly removed in order to pass the highly popular law. His victory was short-lived. Tiberius was killed in a brawl instigated by the richer members of the Senate, who did not even allow him a proper burial, but had his body thrown into the Tiber River.

Gaius laid low and bided his time. He studied eloquence and excelled in the army. But when he, too, was finally elected tribune, he embarked on an even more ambitious program designed to improve the lot of ordinary Romans and check the power of the Senate. He passed laws that redistributed land; gave free clothing to soldiers (instead of docking their pay for it); extended the franchise to all Italians; lowered the price of corn; and eliminated the Senate's monopoly on judges in the courts of justice. He also began an extensive road-building program, employing the Roman genius for engineering to fashion the roads straight and level—building bridges, filling gullies, and making cuts as needed—and marking the miles with stones. Plutarch says that Gaius "was invested with a sort of a kingly power."[51] But that did not prevent him, too, from being assassinated. The people erected a statute of Cornelia and labeled it simply, "Cornelia, the mother of the Gracchi."

Marius and Sulla

After the death of the Gracchi, ambitious politicians had to choose sides. They were either *populares* (who appealed to the lower classes with plans to redistribute power, land, and other resources of the rapidly growing empire) or *optimates* (who defended the privileges of wealth and nobility). Gaius Marius (157–86 BCE) quickly became the champion of the former; Lucius Cornelius Sulla[52] (ca. 138–78 BCE) of the latter. But each man was, in fact, a party of one, promoting his own advancement and forging alliances out of convenience rather than conviction.

It is clear from the outset that Plutarch had a poor opinion of Gaius Marius: "He is said never to have either studied Greek, or to have use of that language in any matter of consequence; thinking it ridiculous to bestow time in that learning, the teachers of which were little better than slaves."[53] His origins, moreover, were obscure; his father was a day laborer, and Marius enlisted as a common soldier. Yet Marius so distinguished himself in war that he won quick advancement and even married into the distinguished Caesar family—his wife, Julia, was the aunt of Julius Caesar. Marius won the affections of his soldiers by sharing their food, their labor, and their hardships. He also deftly maneuvered to steal the glory from Metellus, his commanding officer in Africa, convincing the Roman people that he alone would bring the war against Jugurtha, the formidable king of Numidia, to a quick and successful conclusion. He was elected consul an unprecedented (and completely unlawful) seven times.

Plutarch's opinion of Sulla was little better: he was vain, self-indulgent, licentious, and by turns fawning and imperious. Sulla was initially a younger protégé of Marius, serving him as *quaestor* in his first consulship and traveling with him to Africa. There, Sulla so arranged matters that Jugurtha, who had been defeated and sought refuge with his unreliable father-in-law, was handed over to him rather than to Marius. Sulla thus "deprived [Marius] of the glory of the action as he had done Metellus."[54] Marius was incensed when Sulla had a signet ring made showing him receiving the prisoner. "So slight and childish," Plutarch notes, "were the first occasions and motives of that enmity between them, which, passing afterwards through a long course of civil bloodshed and incurable divisions to find its end in tyranny, and the confusion of the whole state."[55]

Their enmity was interrupted for a time, first by the threat of the Teutones and the Cimbri from beyond the Rhine, and then by the Social War. But, when the aging Marius tried to displace Sulla in command of the troops bound to deal with Mithridates in Parthia (ancient Persia), open civil war broke out. Sulla twice led his army into Rome; the first time, Marius fled but returned with savage reprisals once Sulla was gone to fight Mithridates. The second time, Marius (barely into his seventh consulship) had the good fortune to die of illness before Sulla arrived and "fill[ed] the city with executions."[56] Some were proscribed for political reasons and some out of private enmity, but many were condemned simply because they had money coveted by Sulla and his friends. As one unfortunate victim who found himself on the list bemoaned, "Woe is me, my Alban farm has informed against me."[57]

Marius had initiated various popular reforms, which Sulla more than reversed. Sulla laid down his own self-proclaimed dictatorship, restored the republic, and retired to the country before his death. But the legacy of both men was the example of their unlawful seizure and exercise of absolute power. Pompey and Caesar would soon reenact their struggles with more lasting and even more deadly consequences.

POMPEY AND CAESAR

"So inconsiderable a thing is fortune in respect of human nature," Plutarch writes, "and so insufficient to give content to a covetous mind," that Gnaeus Pompeius Magnus (106–48 BCE) and Gaius Julius Caesar (100–44 BCE) "thought the whole Roman empire not sufficient to contain them, though they were but two."[58] Each man wrought his own destruction and the destruction of the republic rather than settle for second place.

Plutarch plainly prefers Pompey as the more dignified and honorable of the two. Pompey started as a protégé of Sulla and served in Gaul with singular success. He also cleared out pockets of resistance in Africa and Spain, where exiled men of note who had escaped the proscriptions sought refuge and gathered forces. While in Africa, he reconquered Numidia. While in Spain, he suppressed disorder. After the death of Sulla, he helped protect the republic from others trying to seize power and restored the full powers of the tribuneship.

Many citizens were concerned that Pompey would himself march his army into Rome, but he did not. He triumphed and then discharged his soldiers. Indeed, with a fine eye for showmanship, he went further. It was the custom for knights (the class to which Pompey belonged since, though he was now consul, he had never been a senator) to lead their horses into the marketplace and give an account of their service—the commanders under whom they fought and the places and actions where they served—to the censors. Pompey led his horse with the others, and, when the censors demanded of him whether he had served the full time prescribed by law, loudly answered, "Yes, I have served all, and all under myself as general."[59] The people answered him with tumultuous applause and cries of delight as they accompanied him home.

Pompey retired after his consulship, but the people still had need of him.

Pirates were rampant in the Mediterranean, strangling commerce and causing shortages at Rome. Even "men of wealth and noble birth and superior abilities" joined their ranks as if it were a respectable occupation (rather like the law today).[60] Pompey was granted "absolute power and authority in all the seas within the pillars of Hercules, and in the adjacent mainland for the space of four hundred furlongs from the sea."[61] That pretty much encompassed the entire Roman Empire. The senators resisted such a grant of authority, but the people insisted. After careful preparation, Pompey cleared the sea of pirates within three months. Rather than put his captives to death, he spread them throughout the empire and gave them gainful employment tilling the land.

The people, in response, gave him even greater authority to deal with outbreaks in Asia. "Pompey, in his absence, was made lord of almost all that power which Sulla only obtained by force of arms, after a conquest of the very city itself."[62] Yet, after further successes, he again disbanded his army. A few previous consuls had triumphed three times, but only Pompey did so over each of the three divisions of the world: Africa, Europe, and Asia. He had better have died then, Plutarch suggests, at the height of his glory, for no good fortune is unmixed with evil, and the very greatness of Pompey's power led to his overthrow and destroyed his reputation.

Pompey's principal problem was that he was oblivious to the threat posed by Caesar. Caesar had earned the enmity of Sulla because of his relationship with Marius. He barely escaped the proscriptions. Yet he showed his mettle early. Still a youth, he was captured by pirates. While chiding them for asking too little in ransom, he also promised that he would capture and crucify them once he was freed. He was true to his word. On reading a history of Alexander the Great, he shed tears to think that he was already the age at which Alexander had conquered so many nations. At Rome, Caesar preferred to revive the broken faction of Marius and make it his own rather than play a lesser role among the successors of Sulla. Passing through a small, miserable barbarian village in the Alps, one of his lieutenants laughingly wondered whether the people there contended among themselves for power and canvassed for votes. "For my part," Caesar responded, "I had rather be the first man among these fellows, than the second man in Rome."[63]

Caesar was lavish in his expenditures in favor of the populace even before he could afford them. Despite amassing large debts for what many thought an uncertain return, Plutarch notes that, in fact, he purchased "what was of the greatest value at an inconsiderable rate."[64] Yet the key for Caesar was his military genius. Caesar enjoyed remarkable and brutal success in Gaul and Britain. His troops killed perhaps a million people—out of a population of three million—in pacifying Gaul alone. Caesar overcame a natural weakness of body through vigorous exertions. He exposed himself to every danger and shared every hardship and won the absolute loyalty of his troops. All the wealth he accumulated he used not for his own luxury but as a "public fund" for the benefit of his soldiers and the people of Rome.[65]

Pompey, grown complacent, was oblivious to Caesar's growing influence and subversive designs. He even married Caesar's daughter, Julia, to whom he was devoted. Cicero, as usual, was more insightful and "detected the ambition for absolute power" behind the disguise of affability.[66] Pompey willingly entered into the First Triumvirate with Caesar and Crassus, and even connived in Cicero's banishment. Ultimately, he had Cicero recalled, but it was too late. "For it was not the quarrel between Pompey and Caesar, as most men imagine, which was the origin of the civil wars, but their union, their conspiring together at first to subvert the aristocracy, and so quarrelling afterwards between themselves."[67] The death of Julia broke the ties between the two men, revealing them as marks not of friendship but of convenience. The death of Crassus in Parthia made an open break inevitable as each vied for supreme power.

Yet Pompey was still slow to respond. When Caesar crossed the Rubicon "in a sort of passion, casting aside calculation, and abandoning himself to what might come,"[68] Pompey was unprepared and foolishly fled to Greece. Caesar became the master of Rome and all Italy without shedding a drop of blood.

Even so, Pompey and the champions of the republic who joined him might, indeed should, have won. They completely controlled the seas, and their forces outnumbered Caesar's on land by at least two to one. Moreover, Caesar was ill-supplied. Pompey knew that the best strategy was one of attrition that avoided a set battle. Yet Pompey, "who never could bear reproach, or resist the expectations of his friends," was no Fabius and "thus . . . forsook his own prudent resolution to follow their vain hopes and desires."[69] The result was the mismanaged battle of Pharsalus, which "lost in one hour all that glory and power which [Pompey] had been getting in so many wars and bloody battles."[70] It is accordingly Caesar whom Plutarch pairs with Alexander the Great, not Pompey.

Yet Plutarch pauses, as the troops are ranged against one another on the field, to lament "to what a pass private ambition and emulation had brought the empire. Common arms, and kindred ranks drawn up under the selfsame standards, the whole flower and strength of the same single city here meeting in collision with itself, offered plain proof how blind and how mad a thing human nature is when once possessed with any passion."[71] After Pharsalus, Caesar mopped up the remaining opposition in Africa and Spain. He was not just merciful but generous to his former opponents and ruled with some mildness. Yet he outraged sensibilities by holding a triumph for victory over his own countrymen. "It did not look well to lead a procession in celebration of the calamities of his country, and to rejoice in those things for which no other apology could be made either to gods or men than their being absolutely necessary."[72] Moreover, even being named dictator for life by a people weary of civil war did not content him. Caesar would be king, and that ambition sealed his fate.

Plutarch's epithet on Caesar is harsh: "That empire and power which he had pursued through the whole course of his life with so much hazard, he did at last with much difficulty compass, but reaped no other fruits from it than the empty name and invidious glory."[73] Shakespeare's Mark Antony echoes these sentiments as he stands over the newly dead Caesar:

> O mighty Caesar! Dost thou lie so low?
> Are all thy conquests, glories, triumphs, spoils,
> Shrunk to this little measure?[74]

Yet Plutarch rather mildly concludes that, though the republicans were on his side, no one could say whether Pompey would have used his victory better than Caesar.

ANTONY AND CLEOPATRA

We will not linger over the mixture of high tragedy and opera buffa that is the life of Antony. It is one of the most entertaining in all of Plutarch and vividly illustrates his point that greatness corrupted has a boundless capacity for mischief. Antony was a handsome, generous, and brilliant general who inspired absolute loyalty among his troops. But he was also lazy, arrogant, and debauched, and he had an intense desire to be first and most powerful. It was a desire he almost realized following the assassination of Caesar (of which, Plutarch suggests, he had advance knowledge and yet said nothing). Only the cold, calculating manipulations of Caesar's nephew and heir, the young Octavian, thwarted his ambition.

Plutarch, however, contends that Antony was undone mostly by the fury of his passion for Cleopatra. She was not remarkably beautiful, "but the contact of her presence, if you lived with her, was irresistible; the attraction of her person, joining with the charm of her conversation, and the character that attended all she said or did, was something bewitching."[75] Antony ignored his marriage to Octavian's half-sister, Octavia, and lived a life of extravagance and pleasure in Alexandria. When the critical break with Octavian finally came, Antony even brought Cleopatra with him and, at her behest, fought at sea with her large, slow-moving Egyptian vessels rather than on land, where he had an advantage. With the battle still undecided, Cleopatra fled with sixty ships, and Antony, incredibly, abandoned those fighting and dying for him and set off after her in a galley. Thus was lost the sea battle at Actium. The leaderless troops on shore sued for clemency from Octavian. Antony and Cleopatra would soon be dead, Antony by his own hand. Cleopatra, who had experimented with poisons and snake bites on condemned criminals in search of a speedy and painless death, chose the bite of an asp to escape being led through the streets of Rome in the triumph of Octavian (soon to become Caesar Augustus, first of the emperors).

Shakespeare invested the lovers with tragic grandeur. Yet he also captured their histrionic sordidness. All the elements are already present in Plutarch.

REPUBLICAN HEROES

The death of Antony and Cleopatra is the chronological high-water mark of the parallel lives. Plutarch wrote a separate, unpaired series on the Roman emperors from Augustus to Vitellius; unfortunately, only two of those lives, and those among the least significant—Galba and Otho, who together reigned but ten months—survive. For the imperial period, we must look to Tacitus and Suetonius.

Although the Roman half of the *Lives* is heavily focused on the collapse of the republic, it is clear that Plutarch most admired those who lived and died in support of political freedom and autonomy. His lives of Cato the Younger, Cicero, and Brutus had a profound impact on our own founders. All three men were, of course, close students of Greek philosophy, the touchstone for Plutarch of a civilized mind and proper training in virtue. Yet each had the defects of his qualities, and Plutarch does not allow admiration to dull his biographer's eye for such details.

The death of Cato the Younger at Utica may be the most affecting passage in all of Plutarch. Like his ancestor, Cato the Censor, Marcus Porcius Cato showed from his earliest days "an inflexible temper, unmoved by any passion, and firm in everything."[76] He repulsed flattery and defied intimidation with equal vigor. He was straightforward and rough in his speech, yet possessed a certain natural grace that commanded attention. Despite his love of philosophy, Cato viewed service to the state as "the proper business of an honest man."[77] His reputation for honesty was proverbial and his commitment to justice so unstinting as to cause considerable resentment. "There is no virtue," Plutarch notes, "the honour and credit for which procures a man more odium than that of justice."[78]

Yet Cato's inflexibility made political compromise well nigh impossible. He opposed Pompey and Caesar alike, thereby pushing them into alliance and never reflecting that Pompey's faults might be less than those of Caesar. As Plutarch notes, "Cato's virtue looked like a kind of ecstasy of contention in the cause of what was good and just."[79] He did finally join forces with Pompey, after Caesar grabbed power. After Pompey's defeat, he continued to rally the republican forces in North Africa. But, when it became clear those efforts would fail, Cato refused to be beholden to a tyrant for clemency. As a proper Stoic, he believed that "the good man only is free."[80] After reading twice through the *Phaedrus*, Plato's dialogue on the death of Socrates, Cato stabbed himself with his sword. Because of a wound to his hand suffered at Pharsalus, the pressure he could exert was limited and he did not die immediately. But, when his friends and relations tried to minister to him, he repelled their efforts, tore open his wound, and pulled out his own bowels. Upon hearing of this, Caesar remarked, "Cato, I grudge you your death, as you have grudged me the preservation of your life."[81] If Cato had been willing to accept clemency and bide his time, he might have been an invaluable ally of Cicero and Brutus after the death of Caesar. But then he would not have been Cato.

Cicero, aside from his weak constitution and lack of physical courage, also miscarried. He let his hatred of Antony blind him to the threat of Octavian, who had no interest in promoting freedom and who willingly sacrificed Cicero, his most important supporter, to a convenient alliance with Antony that dashed republican hopes.

Marcus Brutus was perhaps the most complicated of the three. He was reputed to be a direct descendant of the Brutus who drove out the last of the Roman kings. As such, he bore the burden of republican expectations, though Plutarch suggests he may in fact have been Caesar's illegitimate son, since Caesar had a passionate affair with Brutus's mother, Servilia, in exactly the right time frame.[82] Whether Brutus himself had any such suspicions is unclear. Plutarch tells us that Brutus had a gentle nature and "a temper exactly framed for virtue,"[83] and that even his enemies acknowledged he entered into the plot to assassinate Caesar "out of a sense of the glory and the apparent justice of the action" unmixed with private envy or malice.[84] In his *Julius Caesar*, Shakespeare follows Plutarch exactly, even down to the "lean and hungry look" he gives to Cassius[85] and the ideals of honor that motivate a deeply conflicted but "most noble Brutus,"[86] who "did love Caesar when I struck him,"[87] and who asks, almost plaintively, "Did not great Julius bleed for justice's sake?"[88]

But Brutus made two fatal mistakes. First, he spared the life of Antony, insisting that it would be unjust to kill him and that, once the tyrant Caesar fell, they could convince Antony to join with them in restoring the liberty of their country. Second, he allowed Antony to speak at a public funeral for Caesar, at which his body and his wounds were displayed, and to read aloud Caesar's will, in which he gave a large sum to every citizen and left his extensive gardens to the benefit of the public. Antony—whose speech is famously reimagined by Shakespeare—so inflamed the people that Brutus and the other assassins fled the city, and Antony set up "a kind of monarchy for himself,"[89] before he was driven out by the imprecations of Cicero and the wiles of Octavian. Yet Antony soon joined with Octavian and Lepidus in the Second Triumvirate, which destroyed the republican forces gathered at Philippi in Macedonia. Brutus threw himself on his sword, noting that he was happier than those who had overcome him, for he had fought for freedom and glory, while "they had destroyed the just and the good, and usurped a power to which they had no right."[90] Shakespeare's Brutus voices the same sentiments:

> My heart doth joy ...
> I shall have glory by this losing day
> More than Octavius and Mark Antony
> By this vile conquest shall attain unto.[91]

More than anyone, Plutarch preserved the memory of the Roman Republic and its greatest figures. It was more than fitting, then, that the Romans erected a statue to the sage of Chaeronea, as he was known in the Middle Ages. The inscription was translated by Dryden:

> Chaeronean Plutarch, to thy deathless praise
> Does martial Rome this grateful statue raise,
> Because both Greece and she thy fame have shared,
> (Their heroes written, and their lives compared).
> But thou thyself couldst never write thy own;
> Their lives have parallels, but thine has none.[92]

CHAPTER 9

TACITUS AND THE ROMAN HISTORIANS

O f all the Roman historians, only Livy and Tacitus belong on the same shelf with Herodotus and Thucydides. It is tempting to draw parallels between the two pairs. Livy, like Herodotus, focuses on the personal in history and is a master of the entertaining (if occasionally suspect) anecdote. Tacitus, like Thucydides, disdains romance and offers a penetrating analysis of the causes and consequences of political events. Both Tacitus and Thucydides—by way of tribute and differentiation—begin their histories where their great predecessors leave off.

But it would be a mistake not to view each writer on his own terms. Livy's sweeping, 142-book history of Rome, from its small-village origins to its mastery of the known world, has no true models. Tacitus's more intensive treatment of the Julio-Claudian emperors and the chaos that followed them transcends the lessons of all earlier historians, both Greek and Roman. Tacitus does not offer us the charming digressions of Herodotus, the heroic tales of Livy, or even the international realpolitik of Thucydides. What he offers instead, in his memorably trenchant style, is an insider's knowledge of the principate that combines psychological acumen and a fierce moral vision of the corrosive influence of absolute power—the loss of individual and political freedom, the rise of informers and sycophants, and the debasement of public discourse in an atmosphere of repression and fear.

Tacitus's *Annals* covers the period from the death of Augustus in 14 CE to the death of Nero in 68. His *Histories* (which was written first) starts amid the chaos and civil wars of 69—the "year of four emperors"—and extends to the death of the tyrant Domitian in 96. This entire period is noted for its ambition, treachery, greed, and debauchery, and it finds its natural historian in the dour, acerbic Tacitus. Indeed, Tacitus (along with his lesser contemporary Suetonius) is largely responsible for our contemporary impressions of the series of emperors during this eighty-two-year stretch. Gibbon, who was steeped in Tacitus, shared his judgment of this period.

> The dark unrelenting Tiberius, the furious Caligula, the stupid Claudius, the profligate and cruel Nero, the beastly Vitellius, and the timid inhuman Domitian are condemned to everlasting infamy. During fourscore years (excepting only the short and doubtful respite of Vespasian's reign), Rome groaned beneath an unremitting tyranny, which exterminated the ancient families of the republic, and was fatal to almost every virtue and every talent that arose in that unhappy period.[1]

Tacitus presents his facts with remarkable accuracy. Around those facts he weaves a relentlessly dark interpretation of characters and motives, while exposing the realities of power behind the facades of public life and language. His prose is never dispassionate. Yet his political views, to the extent we can discern them, are complicated. He recognizes the chaos of the late republic and the inevitability of the autocracy to prevent civil war and concentrate power over the armies and the sprawling empire. But he condemns its excesses and the paranoia and slavishness it engenders. Moderation is perhaps his most cherished virtue. Within a moderate autocracy he wants to retain a vibrant Senate (of which he was a member) and other republican forms, as well as the freedom to speak and to write without fear of reprisal. Augustus managed something of the sort. Even better was Trajan. But Tacitus, who was not constituted to celebrate happy times, writes about the period in between.

Despite his dark vision, Tacitus steadfastly maintains that it is possible, if rare, to be a good man under bad emperors. Individual citizens can, within the limits imposed by tyranny, work for the benefit of the state both militarily and in civic affairs, while avoiding excessive servility and excessive ambition. Tacitus admits that he failed to strike that balance in his own political life under Domitian. But he makes amends in his writing. For Tacitus, history is an exercise in freedom and honesty and courage, with a fundamentally moral purpose: "It is a special duty of history to see that virtues are not left unrecorded, and also that fear of disgrace in posterity attends iniquitous words and actions."[2] A crucial part of the historian's task, then, is to assign praise and blame, to extol where he can and condemn where he must. Tyrants may control the present, but they cannot control how they will be portrayed by historians. In the end, it is Tacitus who judges the emperors and those who serve them, not the other way around.

PREDECESSORS

Tacitus had four predecessors whose works have survived sufficiently to give us a full appreciation of their varied gifts and divergent approaches to the study of history. Only the last of these was a historian of genius, but Tacitus found elements in each worthy of imitation.

POLYBIUS (CA. 200–CA. 118 BCE)

Since the Romans inherited the writing of history from the Greeks, as conscious models, it is only fitting, if still ironic, that the first surviving historian of ancient Rome was a Greek writing in Greek. Polybius was from the town of Megalopolis in the southern Peloponnese. When the Romans finally shattered the power of Macedonia at Pydna in 168, they demanded hostages from members of the Achaean League, a loose confederation of Greek city-states that had offered limited support to Perseus, the last of the Antigonid kings who ruled over Macedonia following the death of Alexander the Great. Polybius was among those hostages and was detained in Rome for sixteen years. There, he was befriended by the family of Scipio Aemilianus, whose adoptive grandfather had defeated the Carthaginians at the battle of Zama in 202 and who himself would complete the destruction of Carthage in 146. Even after his release in 152, Polybius returned the following year to accompany the younger Scipio on campaigns in Spain and North Africa. He joined Scipio again for the Third Punic War and was present at the eradication of Carthage.

Polybius wrote his history to explain to his fellow Greeks "by what means and under what system of government the Romans succeeded in less than fifty-three years in bringing under their rule almost the whole of the inhabited world, an achievement which is without parallel in human history."[3] After considerable table setting, he focuses on the period from 220 (shortly before the Second Punic War) to 167, after Rome had conquered Macedonia and effectively ended Greek independence. Polybius has little interest in Rome's conquest and consolidation of Italy. He is concerned with the period in which Roman history became world history, from Rome's first forays into Sicily to its domination of the entire Mediterranean.

> Now in earlier times the world's history had consisted, so to speak, of a series of unrelated episodes, the origins and results of each being as widely separated as their localities, but from this point onwards history becomes an organic whole:

the affairs of Italy and of Africa are connected with those of Asia and of Greece, and all events bear a relationship and contribute to a single end.[4]

Polybius wrote forty books of his "universal history," but only the first five are still complete. Much of the sixth also survives, as well as fragments from a number of others. The centerpiece of what remains is his account of the Second Punic War, which ended before his birth but was heavily documented and still allowed for eyewitness testimony. Despite his host ties to Rome, Polybius lays claim to objectivity. Loyalty to friends and love of country are important virtues, he notes. "But once a man takes up the role of the historian he must discard all considerations of this kind."[5] He should praise his enemies and find fault with friends as appropriate, for "if history is deprived of the truth, we are left with nothing but an idle, unprofitable tale."[6]

Whether Polybius succeeded in this pose of objectivity is questionable. His history is told very much from the Roman perspective. But his reflections on the purpose of history and the role of the historian are of lasting interest. Polybius emphatically condemns, as too emotional and too lax with the truth, history that attempts to mimic epic poetry and tragedy. The purpose of history is not to arouse pity or enlist sympathy through graphically reimagined scenes: women clinging to one another; noble speeches by rival commanders on the eve of battle; the tears and lamentations of those led away into captivity. The historian's task is not to thrill or charm but "to record with fidelity what actually happened and was said, however commonplace this may be."[7] The tragic poet aims at temporary effects, whereas the historian seeks permanent lessons in a straightforward (purposefully dry) presentation of the facts.

Polybius aims at what he calls "pragmatic history," which seeks to instruct and not just to entertain. Inspired by Thucydides, he strives to provide causal explanations for political and military events. His history is analytic rather than personality driven. For Polybius, "the best education for the situations of actual life consists of the experience we acquire from the study of serious history."[8] We can learn from the errors of others without the bitter experience of personal failure. But if the study of history is proper training for a political career, so, too, a political career is ideal training for a historian. History cannot be written in the library alone. It requires judgment and experience to discern true causes behind partisan dissembling and the surface chaos of events, and to understand the dual role of *tyche* (both chance and fate) in the changing fortunes of men and cities.

Polybius believes that history reflects inevitable cycles of growth and decline, which it is the historian's business to trace and explain. Previous empires—Persian, Greek, Macedonian—came into being, flourished for a time, and were then conquered in turn. Rome has now absorbed all of those earlier domains and more. It is already the greatest empire the world has ever known.

Polybius attributes the astonishing growth of Roman hegemony to three factors. First, the spirit of the Roman people was rendered indomitable through the constant celebration of courage and patriotic self-sacrifice. Once they have decided to accomplish something, the Roman people feel bound to carry it through and will stop at nothing because they believe that nothing is impossible for them.[9] The same spirit animated the Spartans and the troops of Alexander the Great. Sometimes it results in disasters, but more often in dramatic and unlikely successes.

Second, the strict discipline and organization of the military and the refinement of training and tactics made the Roman legions well-nigh invincible against lesser opponents (which almost everyone but Hannibal proved to be). Polybius offers a careful study of the structure of the army and the selection and training of its soldiers as well as military equipment and tactical formations.

Third—and most important because the first two factors are dependent upon it—the Roman constitution provided a stability and balance that allowed Rome to surmount or at least suspend for a time the cycles of history. "Every kind of state," Polybius argues, "is liable to decline from two sources, the one being external and the other due to its own internal evolution. For the first we cannot lay down any fixed principle, but the second pursues a regular sequence."[10] Polybius follows Aristotle in noting that pure forms of government inevitably decay into their corrupt counterparts. Kingship becomes tyranny, which is displaced by a coalition of the best (aristocracy), which degenerates into oligarchy, which becomes insufferable and is overthrown by democracy, which degenerates into mob rule until, eventually, a single strong leader again emerges. "Such is the cycle of political revolution, the law of nature according to which constitutions change, are transformed, and finally revert to their original form."[11] This will happen to any "simple" constitution founded on a single principle. Each form of government has an inbred vice, a natural evolution leading to its decay.

But the Romans, through "many struggles and difficulties,"[12] developed a balanced constitution in which all three forms of government are represented. Polybius carefully describes the elements of kingship (the consuls), aristocracy (the Senate), and democracy (the popular assembly), and the intricate relations among them. The power of each element is constrained and counterbalanced by the others, so that no single element either withers or dominates. The result, he claims, "is a union which is strong enough to withstand all emergencies, so that it is impossible to find a better form of constitution than this."[13] In this respect, Polybius, more directly than Aristotle, influenced our founders' views on the importance of the separation of powers and a system of checks and balances.

Despite his admiration for the Roman constitution, implicit in Polybius are both a prediction and a warning. Decline can come from external and internal causes. The former are unpredictable, as rival states or barbarian tribes wax in power, as disease or natural disaster devastates a commonwealth. But it is the internal constitution that has allowed Rome "to withstand all emergencies." Should an imbalance in the powers of the state occur, Rome will be susceptible to decline from the same external forces it has hitherto held in check.

CAESAR (100–44 BCE)

For Caesar, politics was not training for the writing of history; the writing of history was itself a political act. His two books, *The Gallic Wars* and *The Civil Wars*, were works of self-promotion and self-justification, in which he refers to himself always in the third person. Like modern presidential memoirs, the books disguise failures, magnify (and take credit for) any successes, and portray ruthless ambition as patriotism and a necessary response to the evils of other men. Yet these books were written, not in the quiet of retirement, but in the midst of campaigns. They were drafted close to the events in question, and the style is vigorous, direct, clear, and concise. Although they must be read skeptically, they are still read both for their intrinsic interest and as unique contemporary accounts. Caesar's seven books on the Gallic Wars (an eighth is from another hand) provide a crucial portrait of a surprisingly urbanized and civilized Gaul in the period from 58 to 52, and follow Caesar's dubious forays into Germany and Britain. As one might expect, the descriptions of battles and tactics are excellent, though the brutality and slaughter are recounted so casually that it takes effort for the reader to focus on the human cost of Roman plunder. His three books on the civil wars cover 49–48 and end magnificently with the battle of Pharsalus and the death of Pompey. Caesar's particular brief in this work is to demonstrate that he was forced to march on Rome to save the empire from the intransigence of the Senate and the machinations of Pompey. There is no anguished crossing of the Rubicon in Caesar's own account.

SALLUST (86–CA. 35 BCE)

Sallust produced his two famous monographs, *Catiline's War* and *The Jugurthine War*, after he retired from public life. In the proem to *Catiline's War*, he writes that, as a young man, he was swept up by an enthusiasm for politics until he realized what it actually entailed.

> For instead of propriety, self-denial and [manly virtue], it was daring, bribery and avarice which were thriving; and, even though my mind rejected those things, unaccustomed as it was to wicked practices, nevertheless amidst such great faults my youthful weakness was corrupted and gripped by ambition; and, although I disagreed with the wicked behaviour of others, nonetheless my desire for honours afflicted me with the same reputation and resentment as it did the rest.[14]

Ultimately, he claims, he freed himself from "the many miseries and dangers" of a political life and voluntarily retired to the country to write about episodes in Roman history that seemed particularly worthy of recollection.[15] In this corrupt era, he suggests, one may more properly find glory in words than in deeds; without the former, the latter would fade from memory, and the lessons of history would be lost forever.[16] He was, moreover, uniquely qualified to draw such lessons because his "mind was free from hope, dread and political partisanship."[17]

It is a pretty proem. It is also, as we know from other sources, complete nonsense. Sallust was in fact justly driven from public life. He began well enough, serving as *quaestor* and later as Tribune of the People. But he was expelled from the Senate by the censors for uncertain reasons. He rebounded in the service of Caesar, returned to the Senate, and even became a governor in Africa, where he enriched himself so shamelessly that, upon his return in 45, he faced prosecution for corruption and extortion. A well-placed bribe (probably to Caesar himself) allowed Sallust to retire to a villa so fabulous and ostentatious that it became a future home of emperors. There, he poured his bitterness into his writings and somehow managed to escape the proscriptions that followed the assassination of Caesar and the formation of the Second Triumvirate.

All that said, Sallust's two monographs are still of interest, and not just for his tightly structured and highly compressed writing or his break with the "annalist" tradition, which progressed by consular years, in favor of a topical focus. Sallust's great theme, echoed by so many later writers, is the contrast between Rome's past greatness and its present decline. He constantly emphasizes the corruption of modern times by extolling the virtues of ancient Rome. In his own version of *The Greatest Generation*, Sallust writes of a golden age in which citizens competed in virtue and were pious, loyal to their friends, daring in war, and just in times of peace. All that changed, he suggests, after the defeat of Carthage left Rome without a serious external threat. Ever-growing riches made Rome soft; avarice "taught men haughtiness, cruelty, to neglect the gods, to regard everything as for sale."[18] The growing gap between rich and poor and the intransigence and greed of the elite doomed the republic to civil strife.

Jugurtha was able to prolong his defiance of Roman rule in North Africa by the assumption, which sadly proved true, that almost anyone and everyone of influence in Rome could be bought. Catiline was able to launch his attempted seizure of the government because he gathered together the dispossessed, the indolent, the depraved, and the many young men without prospects by promising them a share of the spoils. In the end, both Jugurtha and Catiline failed. Jugurtha was cornered by Marius and betrayed to Sulla, two men who would precipitate their own civil war. For dramatic effect, Sallust probably exaggerated the threat Catiline posed to the republic; Cicero, who was consul at the time, had done the same for reasons of self-aggrandizement. Catiline saw his support collapse when word of the plot leaked out and some of his leading supporters were arrested. Indeed, the most dramatic incident in Sallust's account is not the attempted coup itself but the debate between Caesar and Cato on the fate of these conspirators, with the former pleading for clemency and the latter, successfully, for a swift execution. Sallust calls Caesar and Cato the two men of his time most notable for the ancient Roman virtues, "yet differing [in] behaviour."[19] Their ultimate clash would end the republic, an end Sallust considered inevitable in light of the greed and corruption of the times, vices he both shared and deplored.

Livy (ca. 59 BCE–ca. 17 CE)

As a historian, Livy could not be more different from Sallust. Where Sallust wrote from personal political experience, Livy was a full-time scholar who never held public office. Where Sallust was topical, Livy was annalistic. Where Sallust was concise, Livy was expansive. Where Sallust was epigrammatic, Livy's prose was known for its *lactea ubertas* ("milky richness").[20] Where Sallust was analytic, Livy was emotive. Where Sallust was bitter and cynical, Livy was sentimental and idealistic.

Yet both men shared the same view of Rome's past greatness and current moral decline. In Sallust, the abstract references to Rome's golden age were largely a device to criticize the present. But, in Livy, Rome's past is fully envisioned and alive. The reader feels his immense pride in the Roman virtues that led a small, besieged village to become the greatest power in history, as well as his disgust with the current corruption, which he saw as a betrayal of that past. In "the dark dawning of our modern day," Livy courageously wrote in the preface to his life's work, "we can neither endure our vices nor face the remedies needed to cure them."[21] The vices—especially greed, ambition, and luxury—had led to almost-constant civil war, from Marius through Antony. But, instead of curing those vices, Rome's answer to civil war was a single strong man and a republic in name only.

Livy was born and died in Padua. But he spent most of his life among the libraries and archives of Rome. He started his *History of Rome* at the age of thirty, shortly before Augustus became emperor. Though Livy himself benefited from the *Pax Romana* declared by Augustus and the remarkable intellectual freedom the emperor allowed (to all but Ovid, at least), he never reconciled himself to the present. "I shall find antiquity a rewarding study," he explained, "if only because, while I am absorbed in it, I shall be able to turn my eyes from the troubles which for so long have tormented the modern world, and to write without any of that over-anxious consideration which may well plague a writer on contemporary life, even if it does not lead him to conceal the truth."[22] Livy worked on his history for more than forty years. Apparently, he had hoped to bring it down to the death of Augustus in 14 CE. He fell short of that goal, but Tacitus, in tribute to his greatest predecessor, made that the starting point of his own *Annals*.

At his death in 17 CE, Livy had written 142 books, covering the eight centuries from Rome's founding to the death of Augustus's stepson, Drusus, in 9 BCE. The books were grouped into pentads, and seven of those units survived. Books 1–5 cover the early history of Rome down to the Gallic invasion, which Livy puts at 390; books 6–10 cover the initial stages of the conquest of Italy from 389 to 293; books 21–30 cover the Second Punic War (otherwise known as the War with Hannibal), 218–201; and books 31–45 describe the conquest of the eastern Mediterranean, including Macedonia, Greece, and Syria, 200–167. The four volumes of the Penguin edition comprise about two thousand pages. The complete work would have been eight thousand. Books 11–20 and from 46 on have all been lost.

As the numbers indicate, Livy added more and more detail as the years advanced and the archive material multiplied. His first five books sped through more than 450 years. His ten books on the Second Punic War managed only eighteen. In the preface to book 31, Livy wrote that he felt like someone who had started close to shore in the shallow water and was steadily advancing into an ever deeper, fathomless sea. His words resonate for any writer with an absurdly ambitious project. "The task undertaken seemed to grow less with the completion of each of the early stages; now, in anticipation, it seems almost to increase as I proceed."[23]

Livy called the Second Punic War "the most memorable war in history," in part because the two rivals were at the peak of their power, each with enormous resources, and in part because "the final issue hung so much in doubt that the eventual victors came nearer to destruction than their adversaries."[24] Certainly, Livy's dramatic description of Hannibal's march over the Alps, elephants in tow, is one of the most memorable historical vignettes ever written. So, too, is the story of Hannibal's remarkable successes as he swept down into a panic-stricken Italy and cut to pieces army after army sent against him. *Hannibal ad portus* ("Hannibal is at the gates"), they cried in Rome,[25] though, inexplicably, Hannibal never pressed his luck that far.

But it is for the early years of Rome that Livy is most remembered and read today. He writes of "good citizens and noble deeds"[26] and celebrates the constellation of virtues—patriotism, courage, loyalty, self-sacrifice, piety, and austerity—that was the foundation of Rome's greatness. Livy acknowledged that his account of Rome's earliest days had "more of the charm of poetry than of a sound historical record."[27] Some might say that was true of his entire work. Certainly Livy, like Herodotus before him and Plutarch after him, rarely lets the facts interfere with a good story.

But the basic historical framework into which Livy incorporates his stories is in most respects a sound one. He simply viewed history as a very different endeavor from Thucydides or Polybius or Sallust. For Livy, history is fundamentally moral and imaginative rather than pragmatic and analytic; it provides a series of "examples and warnings; fine things to take as models, base things, rotten through and through, to avoid."[28] Livy focused on character, and episodes that revealed character and taught a moral lesson. As a younger contemporary of Virgil and Horace, Livy was imbued with their romanticism and their tendency to view events in personal and emotional terms.

In Livy, even the many battles in the conquest of Italy, the Punic Wars, and the eastern Mediterranean are treated more as background for the conflict of personalities than as a tactical matching of armies. Livy is not very precise on geography. (To this I can personally attest, having tried to duplicate Hannibal's route across the Alps, albeit without elephants.) He includes little analysis of social conditions, military equipment, or tactics. He is equally uninterested in partisan politics and ideological clashes except insofar as they reflect moral decline. His speeches do not, as in Thucydides, articulate motives and help reveal the underlying causes of events; they reveal character, for it is character that is most important to Livy.

Livy is the historian as dramatist. His great work is a theater in which colorful characters and strong personalities strut upon the stage. But it is not to be denigrated on that account. To the contrary, Livy's imaginative reconstruction of history is more compelling than anything that preceded him. The wonderful stories of Rome's early heroes in the introduction to this volume are all from Livy. They live in his pages. He is also brilliant in capturing the shifting moods of peoples and crowds. As classicist Betty Radice notes, "He can make us feel what it is like to suffer a long siege, to lie on a battlefield wounded and dying, to be trapped in a panic-stricken crowd, and to face action cold and wet and hungry. All his great battle-accounts are memorable for some individual reaction or mass emotion."[29]

Like Virgil, Livy created a myth of Rome's early years. But, unlike Virgil, it is a myth no less solidly grounded in history than that offered by Polybius or Sallust or any other ancient historian. It is simply more compelling. Livy created our persisting vision of ancient Rome and the uncompromising discipline and moral rectitude essential to building the new state. Moreover, he wove into his story of Rome's steady expansion two powerful explanatory themes. The first was Rome's inclusiveness. Rome turned conquests into accretions and assimilations as citizenship was extended throughout the empire. Thus, wars of conquest increased rather than diminished the power of Rome. Second, and even more important for Livy, was the increasing development of the rule of law. A focus on laws that govern all men may seem at odds with Livy's celebration of great individuals. But it is the rule of law that guarantees personal freedom and provides both the opportunity for and the public value of individual acts of heroism. The evolving Roman constitution is therefore the key component in Livy's compelling vision of "a free nation, governed by annually elected officers of state and subject not to the caprice of individual men, but to the overriding authority of law."[30] Yet a constitution, in the end, is only as strong as the commitment of the citizens who uphold it. According to Livy—and it is hard to dispute him on this point—moral decay ultimately cost the Romans their constitution and their freedom.

LIFE AND EARLY WORKS

Great as these earlier historians were, they were but a prelude to Publius Cornelius Tacitus, who was born circa 56 CE in Gaul to a family of equestrian rank. He studied rhetoric in Rome along with his friend Pliny the Younger. There, in 77, he married the daughter of Julius Agricola, who was a consul and military hero. Tacitus started his own career around the same time with minor posts under Vespasian, the first of the three Flavian emperors. Vespasian's son Titus made Tacitus *quaestor* in 81, and he thus became a senator. But his real success came under Domitian, Titus's brother (and perhaps his murderer), who was emperor from 81 to 96. Tacitus served Domitian as *praetor* and was then a senior provincial official, or possibly in command of a legion, from 89 to 93. Tacitus was nominated to the consulship, which he served in 97 despite Domitian's assassination the previous year. After his consulship, Tacitus began to write history. In 112, under Trajan, Tacitus was proconsul in the "province" of Asia (embracing all of modern Turkey). But, otherwise, he took advantage of the intellectual freedom restored under Trajan. He probably died in 117, the same year as the emperor.

Tacitus's first book, *Agricola*, paid tribute to his father-in-law, who had died in 93. Tacitus notes that, in past times, he would have given a funeral oration for Agricola, celebrating his deeds and character. But, not only was he absent from Rome at the time, Domitian would not in any event have permitted it. Thus, *Agricola* pays a belated debt to an obviously loved and respected father-in-law. "Many of the men of old will be buried in oblivion, inglorious and unknown," Tacitus confidently notes. "Agricola's story has been told for posterity and he will survive."[31]

The book also begins to pay a debt of another kind. Tacitus clearly hated Domitian despite (and because of) his prior patronage. He paints the portrait of a paranoid tyrant who suppressed free speech, was jealous of any distinction among his subjects, and, we know from Suetonius, demanded that he be addressed as *dominus et deus* (master and god). In his final years, Domitian launched a reign of terror. Tacitus rejoices that "Agricola did not live to see the senate-house under siege, the senate hedged in by armed men, the killing of so many consulars in that same act of butchery, so many most noble women forced into exile or flight."[32]

Tacitus's experience under Domitian would color the way he looked at the entire line of emperors. He recognized the need for order and centralized power to prevent civil war. But he feared the corruption of that power, the suppression of individual freedom, and the disregard of republican formalities that preserved at least the fiction of political participation. He decries the many years that were stolen from his contemporaries' lives by oppression. "Just as the former age witnessed an extreme in freedom, so we have experienced the depths of servitude, deprived by espionage even of the intercourse of speaking and listening to one another. We should have lost our memories as well as our voices, were it as easy to forget as to be silent."[33]

Unlike Sallust, who minimized his own misconduct, Tacitus is frank about his complicity and that of other senators in Domitian's savage totalitarianism. Domitian deliberately forced such complicity to humble the Senate and to break any spirited opposition. Some resisted at first. "But soon we ourselves led Helvidius to prison, the faces of Mauricus and Rusticus put us to shame, we were stained by Senecio's innocent blood."[34] Domitian punished even those who, without actively resisting, showed signs of shock and disgust at this purge. Their very facial expressions had to be suppressed. Yet Tacitus suggests, somewhat self-servingly, that duty and discretion serve the commonwealth better than futile resistance and a self-dramatizing death. He contends that "there can be great men even under bad emperors."[35] One of the purposes of his book is to demonstrate that Agricola was such a man (and perhaps to suggest that Tacitus himself is another).

Agricola served as governor of Britain, following his consulship in 77. Caesar had made only a limited foray into Britain: "He can be considered to have pointed it out, not handed it over, to future generations," Tacitus notes.[36] Claudius greatly expanded the original beachhead. But it was left to Agricola to bring Britain fully under Roman rule. "Agricola handed over to his successor a province peaceful and secure."[37] Tacitus laments that Rome did not retain its control over the island and that Agricola was rewarded for his success by the emperor's jealous resentment, which Agricola evaded only by living with great discretion in retirement.

Agricola contains the earliest surviving history of Britain, covering the period from 55 to 83. Holinshed's *Chronicles of England, Scotland, and Ireland*, which provided material for Shakespeare, made liberal use of Tacitus. Even current readers can enjoy Tacitus's comments on the weather—"The climate is miserable, with frequent rain and mists. But extreme cold is not found there"[38]—and the ethnography and topography of what Shakespeare would call "this blessed plot, this earth, this realm, this England."[39]

But, mostly, Tacitus deals with the hard fighting necessary to quell a fiercely proud people. The British do not readily yield their freedom, and Tacitus clearly admires the heroic, if ultimately futile, resistance of the warrior-queen Boudicca and the Caledonian leader Calgacus. Tacitus gives the latter the most famous eve-of-battle speech before Shakespeare's Henry V at Agincourt, as Calgacus urges his people to cast off their enslavement and face the Romans with a united front.

> "It is no use trying to escape their arrogance by submission or good behaviour. They have pillaged the world: when the land has nothing left for men who ravage everything, they scour the sea. If an enemy is rich, they are greedy, if he is poor,

they crave glory. Neither East nor West can sate their appetite. They are the only people on earth to covet wealth and poverty with equal craving. They plunder, they butcher, they ravish, and call it by the lying name of 'empire.' They make a desert and call it 'peace.'"[40]

The moving nature of this speech is doubly ironic in light of Tacitus's insistence that discretion is better than an ostentatious death and that Agricola's conquest of Britain was the noble action of a great man. Tacitus was frequently ambivalent.

That ambivalence is equally reflected in *Germany*, a more explicit work of ethnography, covering topics such as German topography and natural resources, arms and military tactics, religion, government, housing, clothing, and marital customs, as well as providing a breakdown of the individual tribal groups. Here, Tacitus's purpose is to offer both a warning and an example. The Germans are a warrior people, primitive but uncorrupted, who pose a serious threat to a Rome grown soft through luxury and license. In words that would be twisted and embraced by the Nazis, he writes,

> I myself accept the view of those who judge that the peoples of Germany have never been contaminated by intermarriage with other nations and that the race remains unique, pure, and unlike any other. As a result, their physical appearance too, if one may generalize about so large a population, is always the same: fierce blue eyes, red hair, and large bodies.[41]

Tacitus's praise is qualified, for he also notes the Germans' idleness and drunkenness, as well as their propensity for violence. Yet he does strongly approve of their strict marriage code and "sheltered chastity," which is untempted by lewd public shows, lascivious banquets, and clandestine letters. In a shot at love elegists and satirists, from Ovid's day to his own, he snarls, "No one there laughs about vice, nor is seducing and being seduced called 'modern.'"[42]

THE HISTORIES

"The story I now commence," Tacitus writes, "is rich in vicissitudes, grim with warfare, torn by civil strife, a tale of horror even during times of peace. Four emperors slain by the sword. Three civil wars: often entwined with these, an even larger number of foreign wars."[43] Following the death of Nero in 68, the Praetorian

Guard favored the aspirations of Galba, an aging commander of armies in Spain. He marched to Rome to become the new emperor without any real opposition, but lasted only seven months. Galba was inherently stingy and old-fashioned and failed to adjust to the new reality that the armies, not their commanders, ruled Rome. Bounties promised in his name were not forthcoming, and the guard realized that it stood to benefit more from war than from peace. The people, too, were unimpressed with the bent and wrinkled Galba after the youthful, attractive Nero. Galba simply did not look like their idea of an emperor.

The guard quickly settled instead on the extravagant young Otho, once an intimate of Nero until Otho's beautiful wife, Poppea, caught the emperor's eye and convinced him to send her husband off to a remote post. Otho had marched with and sworn allegiance to Galba. But his bitterness when Galba adopted Piso as his successor overrode any oath. Galba and Piso were too surprised and disorganized to put up a fight, and the people of Rome found the sudden civil war at their doorsteps more entertaining than otherwise. Galba and Piso were both readily and brutally slain on January 15, in the year 69.

Yet Otho fared even worse. A separate civil war (knowledge of which had been suppressed by Galba) was already brewing in Germany, where several legions declared their support for Vitellius. Otho mustered his troops and sought to confront the rebels north of the River Po. Inexplicably, however, Otho himself remained behind with a considerable reserve force, while his impetuous brother Titianus pressed forward to Bedriacum, where he was defeated and his surviving troops quickly switched allegiance to Vitellius. Otho still had ample forces to contest the ultimate outcome, but he declined to put more Roman soldiers at risk simply to preserve his own life and ambitions. One battle was enough to decide the issue, he said, as he retired to his tent, where he stabbed himself on April 16. As Malcolm would say of Cawdor (echoing a line from the *Annals*), "Nothing in his life / Became him like the leaving it."[44]

The same could not be said of Vitellius. Tacitus describes his well-appointed and disciplined army parading into Rome and concludes, "It was a noble spectacle, an army worthy of a better emperor."[45] The troops in the eastern provinces under Titus Flavius Vespasianus were planning Vitellius's destruction before he ever took the throne. Yet Vespasian was cautious and built his power base slowly, making sure to secure Syria, Egypt (with its critical grain supplies), and Judea (which was then in rebellion). As Tacitus explains, Vespasian "realized that it would be a critical day for him when he committed his sixty summers and his two youthful sons to the chances of war. In his private ambitions a man may feel his way and rely less or more on fortune according as he feels inclined; but when one covets a throne there is no middle way between the zenith of success and headlong ruin."[46]

Vespasian's own march on Rome was conducted by proxy. While he remained in Egypt, his forces won a decisive victory, ironically, at Bedriacum, where Vitellius had defeated Otho and for the same reason: Vitellius divided rather than fully committed his forces. Vitellius toyed with abdication in exchange for the promise of a safe, well-endowed retreat. But he was paralyzed by the growing disaster. He and his followers indulged in what Tacitus calls "the last consolations that the conquered can enjoy."[47] They destroyed what they could not defend. They fouled the streets and houses of Rome with their own and their enemies' blood. In the course of the fighting, the Capitol—the symbol of the empire and Rome's endurance even against the Gauls—was burned to the ground, "brought utterly to ruin by the mad folly of rival emperors!"[48] A cowering Vitellius was dragged through the streets, where he was mocked, abused, and finally slaughtered. The date was December 20, 69, and the year of four emperors and three civil wars was finally coming to a close.

It is indeed a grim and brutal, though thoroughly gripping, tale that occupies the first three books of the *Histories*: three civil wars and three dead emperors. Even worse, notes Tacitus, Italy was treated by rival forces, not as their native land, but as a foreign shore. "They burnt, ravaged, plundered, with results all the more horrible since no precautions had been taken against danger."[49] The armies were uncontrolled because they themselves controlled events. Their generals did not dare try to curb their excesses, which were rendered all the more odious by examples of courage and dignity shown by the besieged citizens. Thus, a Ligurian woman refused even under torture to reveal the whereabouts of her son, whom the soldiers believed she had hidden, along with her money. She continually pointed to her womb, saying, "He hides here," and neither torture nor death could change "that resolute and noble answer."[50]

By the beginning of the fourth book, the Flavian dynasty had begun. Vespasian would rule from 69 to 79, followed briefly by his son Titus and then by his other son, Domitian, who terrorized the Senate until he was murdered by acclamation in 96. But the relative stability in rulers during this period was not reflected in the empire itself. "The death of Vitellius had ended the war," Tacitus notes, "without inaugurating the peace."[51] Not only were the remaining Vitellians hunted down in an atmosphere of riot and disorder, but there was still frequent insubordination among the armies, and the Germans and Gauls, encouraged by the chaos at Rome, revolted. Their Batavian leader, Civilis, united disparate tribes and posed a serious threat to Roman hegemony. Book 4 is mainly occupied with the close run but ultimately successful efforts to suppress that rebellion.

Unfortunately, those four books, and part of 5 (dealing with the Jewish War), are all that remain of the twelve written by Tacitus. His account of the Flavian dynasty and, in particular, the disastrous reign of Domitian has been lost. At the outset of his work, Tacitus writes, "I cannot deny that I owe the launching of my career to Vespasian, or that I was advanced by Titus and still further promoted by Domitian; but those who lay claim to unbiased accuracy must speak of no man with either hatred or affection."[52] This claim to unbiased accuracy is inherently suspect given the bitter hatred of Domitian already displayed in *Agricola*. But his authoritative insider's account of all three regimes would be invaluable. Tacitus, though he always had strong opinions, was rarely inaccurate.

Indeed, Tacitus is among the greatest historians precisely because he combines an accurate portrayal of events with an acute, if dark, interpretation of individual and group motivations. His psychological acumen and relentlessly pessimistic view of human nature corrupted by power (whether bowing to it or exercising it) give his writing a moral authority that has rarely, if ever, been equaled. Philosophers, in the abstract, decry greed, ambition, fear, and the human penchant for violence. Tacitus shows their corrosive effects and the disaster they wreak upon the commonwealth. Moreover, his highly condensed, mordant prose—a prose that has rightly been compared to the greatest Latin poetry—conveys his judgments with the force of hammer blows. It is evident even in translation that Tacitus is a master of the telling epigram:

- "If a man had no enemies, he was ruined by his friends."[53]
- "Galba's affability . . . halved the risk of crime and doubled the reward."[54]
- "The public was always ready to hear and believe any news, provided it was bad."[55]
- Otho "played the slave to gain a throne."[56]
- "As so often happens in disasters, the best course always seemed the one for which it was now too late."[57]
- "They heaped insults on Galba . . . and covered Otho's hand with kisses, their extravagance in inverse proportion to their sincerity."[58]
- "The universal view was that [Galba] had the qualifications to be a ruler—if only he had not ruled."[59]
- Otho and Vitellius "accused each other of lechery and crime—here neither lied."[60]
- "The Emperor had, indeed, formed a habit of regarding wholesome advice

as unpleasant, and listening only to what was agreeable—and ultimately fatal."[61]

- "The Gauls were enemies today because their yoke was easy: when they had been stripped and plundered they would be friends."[62]
- "[Civilis and his] nephew hated each other with all the aggravated bitterness of near relatives."[63]

Tacitus, of course, has far more to offer than incisive sarcasm. His overriding theme is the disastrous effects of tyranny on ruler and ruled alike. Whether the decline of morals precipitated the loss of individual and political freedom or vice versa is a moot point. The darkness has gathered regardless. Under an absolute monarchy, loyalty, courage, forthrightness, and patriotism are guarantors of personal disaster; servility, dissimulation, and well-timed treachery become the new virtues. The Senate, the army, and the Roman people all lost their traditional moorings as the principate itself became increasingly degenerate. The result was the horrific series of civil wars described in the *Histories*. In his last work, the *Annals*, Tacitus goes back in time to the death of Augustus and chronicles the steady erosion of Roman values under the Julio-Claudian line of emperors that led to such a pass.

THE *ANNALS*

The first two words of the *Annals* are *Urbem Romam* ("the city of Rome"). That is Tacitus's subject: the city that was the seat of the empire. He focuses narrowly on the personal and political machinations that govern the relations among the emperor, his potential successors, the Senate, the Praetorian Guard, and the broader populace of Rome. Even his accounts of foreign wars and other upheavals are framed from the perspective of Rome.

Tacitus sums up 142 books of Livy in a single, condensed paragraph, noting Rome's transition from kingship to republican freedom, through transient dictatorships to the age of Augustus, who "brought a world exhausted from civil dissension under his authority, with the title of 'First Citizen.'"[64] Tacitus feels no need to retread this ground, already well covered by "famous authors."[65] And, even though Livy never brought his work up to the death of Augustus, as he had planned, Augustus preserved enough individual freedom that the Roman historical tradition continued under and accurately recorded his rule. But the histories of later emperors were distorted by fear while they reigned, and by hostility after their deaths. Tacitus, accordingly, plans to start his own history with the final days of Augustus and pledges to cover the subsequent four emperors, from Tiberius through Nero, *sine ira et studio* ("without rancor or bias"). Without bias, perhaps (unless one counts the hatred of tyranny as a bias), but there is ample rancor in Tacitus's biting portraits of Tiberius and his ill-chosen successors.

Tacitus wrote eighteen books of the *Annals*, divided into three hexades. The first six books cover Tiberius; the second six, Caligula and Claudius; and the last hexade, Nero. We possess books 1 through 6 (though much of 5 is missing) from one manuscript, and part of 11 followed by books 12–15 and part of 16 from another. The rest is lost, including the years 29–31, during the reign of Tiberius (r. 14–37); all of Caligula (r. 37–41); the first six years of Claudius (r. 41–54); and the last two years of Nero (r. 54–68).

We do, however, have Suetonius's *Lives of the Caesars* to fill in the missing material. Suetonius (ca. 70–ca. 130), a younger contemporary, devotes a book each to Julius Caesar, Augustus Caesar, and each of the four remaining Julio-Claudian emperors. The remainder of his work overlaps with Tacitus's *Histories*, covering the first three emperors from 69, followed by the three Flavians. But Suetonius is a biographer, not a historian of the period. His aims and his sensibility could not be more different from those of Tacitus. Suetonius is more entertaining than profound, more amused than somber. Many have dismissed Suetonius as a purveyor of gossip and sordid details—an early *People* magazine. Even Gian Biagio Conte, an otherwise-impeccable critic, sniffs, "Wherever readers have retained an interest in the bizarre excesses of absolute power and in the mixture of the significant, the banal, and the salacious, Suetonius has continued to be read."[66] But Suetonius cannot be blamed because he is not Tacitus. He was not interested in political issues such as the relations between emperor and Senate. He focused on the personal life of the principate, as well as such practical details as temples built and roads constructed. Suetonius accumulates factoids that are both fascinating and invaluable, even though he makes no attempt to present a coherent interpretation of the motives and personalities of the emperors he studies, much less to formulate the sort of moral judgments that Tacitus pronounces with such authority. Tacitus is more satisfying, but Suetonius is still indispensable.

The contrast between the two shows in their respective portraits of Tiberius, the Claudian stepson of Augustus, who was compelled to marry Augustus's promiscuous daughter, Julia, and was later adopted by Augustus. Suetonius, like Tacitus, notes that Tiberius was "close-fisted to the point of miserliness," had a "savage and dour character," and was a "filthy old man" with disgusting sexual habits that Suetonius records in detail.[67] Tiberius had no paternal feelings either for his son, Drusus, or his nephew and adopted son, Germanicus (who was the grandson of Mark Antony and Augustus's sister, Octavia, and hence the grand-nephew of Augustus). Suetonius even cites the rumor (accepted by Tacitus) that Tiberius arranged for Germanicus to be poisoned. Tiberius, especially in his later years, was a man who lived in fear and visited terror on others.

But Tiberius does not inhabit the pages of Suetonius as he does those of Tacitus. In Tacitus, Tiberius is a psychologically complex whole, a brooding, duplicitous, paranoid monster. He only became emperor because all the more-likely candidates died, except Agrippa Postumus, Augustus's sole remaining grandson, who appears to have been mentally unstable and was banished to the island of Planasia in the Tuscan archipelago. According to Tacitus, Tiberius and his mother, Livia, had Agrippa Postumus assassinated as soon as Augustus expired.

Tiberius had an excellent military record and was a competent administrator. But the principate brought his worst qualities—"resentment, hypocritical behaviour and covert depravity"[68]—to the fore and gave them free rein. From the first days, he played coy with the Senate and pretended to shun imperial power and disdain sycophancy, even as he consolidated his hold on the government and kept careful track of those who failed to pay him sufficient homage. Drusus and Germanicus each were dispatched to put down mutinies sparked by the change in emperors and the prospect that civil unrest might bring profit or at least concessions to the army. Tacitus presents a memorable scene (later copied by Shakespeare for *Henry V*) in which Germanicus disguises himself as a common soldier and, on the eve of battle, mingles with the troops by the fires to gauge their mood and test their resolve. Yet Tiberius was jealous of any distinction shown to Germanicus and, when Germanicus's popularity soared, sent him off to deal with upheavals in Asia. There, Tiberius enlisted Gnaeus Piso, the governor of Syria, to undermine Germanicus and ultimately poison him. Piso, brought to trial in Rome, either killed himself (or was killed by order of Tiberius) before he could expose Tiberius's role in the plot.

What Tacitus most blames Tiberius for, however, was the ever-increasing number of informers, "a class of men devised for the destruction of society."[69] With his mixture of paranoia and credulity, Tiberius was easily manipulated into festering hatred for those who allegedly slighted him or the principate. No one was safe as each man rushed to condemn others, either in self-defense or in self-promotion. Executions, forced suicides, and banishments multiplied. "Never had the city known greater tension and panic, with people tight-lipped even with their closest relatives. They avoided meetings and conversations, and the ears of friend and stranger alike. Even mute and lifeless objects—roofs and walls—were eyed with suspicion" because they might conceal an informant.[70] One woman was put to death merely for weeping at the execution of her son. Ordinary human feelings and interactions were suppressed or destroyed by the power of fear.[71] Even informants died in their turn—perhaps the only time that Tiberius's actions met with popular approval—as the emperor tired of their influence or was led to suspect their loyalty.

Tacitus apologizes for "presenting a series of cruel orders, endless accusations, faithless friendships, and calamities befalling innocent people, with the causes of their ruin being always the same—for I am faced with a tedious abundance of recurrent material."[72] He notes that writers on earlier times could, to the delight of their readers, "recount the history of mighty wars, the storming of cities, or the defeat and capture of kings."[73] But his own work was "restricted and without glory," for the empire was at peace "or only weakly challenged," and the emperor had no interest in extending its boundaries.[74] More fundamentally, the political focus had changed. Arguments in the assembly, the election of consuls, the deliberations of the Senate—all such activities were now subordinate to the will of one man. Everything depended not on the balanced Roman constitution or the rule of law but on the psychology of a single individual and its devastating effects on the populace at large.

Integrity is dangerous in an absolutist state; participating in the corruption of morals is far safer, though itself not immune from harm. Yet, even under such a regime, Tacitus continues to ask (plainly thinking of his own service under Domitian) whether it is possible "to trim a path between downright obstinacy and degrading sycophancy, a path free from favour-seeking and danger alike."[75] Showy resistance is futile; it helps neither the individual nor the state. Yet succumbing to moral degradation and servility is equally untenable. At best, Tacitus suggests, one can serve the state competently, nurture a quiet conscience, and bide one's time. He writes of a historian, one Cremutius, who offended the emperor by presenting a favorable account of Cassius and Brutus and was forced to end his life by starvation. His books were ordered burned but in fact survived by being hidden and later republished. "This makes one all the more inclined to laugh at the stupidity of those who believe that the memories of succeeding generations can be stifled by power in the present day," Tacitus writes. They succeed "only in bringing shame on themselves and glory on their victims."[76]

No one exercised a longer and more insidious sway on the emperor than Lucius

Aelius Sejanus, head of the Praetorian Guard. With a "blend of sycophancy and arrogance," he insinuated himself increasingly into Tiberius's confidence, making him "feel relaxed and off his guard only with him."[77] Sejanus seduced Livilla, the sister of Germanicus, who was married to Tiberius's natural son, Drusus. Together, they poisoned Drusus. After encouraging Tiberius to retire to Capri, where he would be proof against importunities and safe from any threats, and then strictly controlling access to him, Sejanus began acting as the de facto emperor. But even that was not sufficient for his ambitions. He wanted to clear the path of more legitimate contenders. So Sejanus convinced Tiberius to do away with two of the three sons of Germanicus, along with their mother, Agrippina, the granddaughter of Augustus. When Sejanus sought permission to marry Livilla and enter the royal family, however, Tiberius finally woke up to the threat he posed. The relevant pages of book 5, unfortunately, are lost. But, according to Suetonius, Tiberius summoned Sejanus to Capri on the pretext of further advancement and had him murdered along the way.

Tiberius stayed on Capri for eleven years. He had no male children or grandchildren of his own left. Only one male child survived from his nephew and adopted son, Germanicus, and that was Gaius Caesar, nicknamed Caligula ("little boots") for his time spent with the army as a child. Tacitus explains that Caligula "concealed a monstrous personality beneath a deceitful veneer of moderation, and had uttered not a word at his mother's condemnation or his brothers' ruin."[78] Provided his road to power was shortened, nothing else mattered. Yet he was the only heir the increasingly debauched and broken Tiberius had left. (Claudius, the younger brother of Germanicus and, hence, Tiberius's nephew, was considered too odd and infirm for public office, a perception that probably saved his life.) Tiberius had only a brief opportunity to regret his choice. He fell, for some hours, into unconsciousness on Capri and was thought dead. Caligula already was assuming his role as the new emperor when Tiberius revived and called for food. Without hesitation, Caligula smothered the old man.

In a letter to the Senate written shortly before his death, Tiberius complained of his constant torments. Tacitus suggests that Tiberius was tortured by his own villainy. "If the minds of tyrants were opened up, gashes and wounds would become visible, since the soul is torn apart by cruelty, lust, and evil designs, no less than the body is torn by beatings."[79] That is precisely what Tacitus himself did in the *Annals*. He opened up the mind of the tyrant Tiberius and revealed to us a soul torn apart by cruelty, lust, and evil designs. As Shakespeare did with Richard III, Tacitus made Tiberius the villain he has always been in the judgment of history.

Caligula himself would die four years later in a conspiracy between the Senate and the Praetorian Guard. Books 7 through 10 of the *Annals* and the first part of 11 are all lost, so we rely on Suetonius for our most intimate knowledge of Caligula's vicious brutality and indiscriminate debauchery. After they dispatched Caligula, members of the guard found his terrified uncle, Claudius, hiding behind some curtains in the palace and declared him emperor. This unlikely turn of events caused Tacitus to remark, "Personally, the more I consider recent or earlier history, the more I find myself face to face with the farcical nature of all human affairs. For in terms of reputation, hopes, and respect, everyone was more likely to succeed to power than the man whom fortune was keeping under cover as the future emperor."[80] Clearly, Tacitus was no believer in the predetermined, Hegelian march of history. Man is subject to chance and circumstance, often in ways so unexpected and bizarre as to make a mockery of his careful plans and expectations.

The surviving manuscript of the second half of the *Annals* picks up in book 11 midway through the reign of Claudius, which ran from 41 to 54. Tacitus reports some notable achievements: Claudius boldly expanded the grant of citizenship to conquered peoples outside of Italy and engaged in the conquest of Britain. Mostly, though, Tacitus portrays him as a hapless and passive creature, manipulated by his wives. His third wife, Messalina, engaged in flagrant adultery and, quite bizarrely, went through a formal marriage ceremony with her paramour while Claudius was absent from Rome. The hitherto oblivious or complacent Claudius was finally coaxed into outrage, yet even so he vacillated, thinking of his wife's bedchamber and the two children they had together. His concerned friends chose to take his ambiguous remarks as a condemnation and had Messalina quickly run through with a sword before she could reconcile with Claudius.

Claudius learned little from the experience. He was next seduced by and married his niece Julia Agrippina, a daughter of Germanicus and the sister of Caligula. A special order of the Senate was required to legitimate the incest. Agrippina, too, took lovers. She also murdered rivals who incited her jealousy. Most remarkably, however, she convinced Claudius to betroth his daughter Octavia to her son, Nero, and then to adopt Nero and give him precedence even over Claudius's natural son, Britannicus. When Claudius began to regret these steps, and Agrippina was threatened with the same end as Messalina, she fed Claudius "a particularly succulent mushroom" smeared with poison.[81] She then expertly managed the Senate, the guard, and the populace to have Nero presented as the new emperor at the age of seventeen. Britannicus did not even last to his fourteenth birthday before he was poisoned in turn.

We have already discussed the reign of Nero in the introduction and in the chapter on Seneca. Among the highlights of Tacitus's account are Nero's increasing (and, in Tacitus's eyes, degrading) insistence on composing verses and appearing on stage to sing and play the lyre, while his soldiers compelled a wildly enthusiastic response from the audience and the judges duly awarded him first prize. More darkly, Tacitus describes Nero's steady slide into all manner of cruelty and depravity after he murdered first his mother and later Burrus and Seneca, his two steady advisors who had tried to channel his excesses in ways least harmful to the state. Nero gruesomely disposed of his first wife, Octavia (the daughter of Claudius), in favor of Poppea (who, Tacitus notes, "had to her credit everything but decency"[82]), yet he also went through a formal "marriage" ceremony with another man, in which Nero played the bride and wore a veil. Tacitus also includes a dramatic account of the Great Fire of 64 and the widespread death and destruction it caused, and reports (without endorsing) the rumor that, during the fire, "Nero had appeared on his private stage and sung about the destruction of Troy, drawing a comparison between the sorrows of the present and the disasters of old."[83]

Tacitus is most compelling on the formation of the Pisonian conspiracy that followed the Great Fire, on the vacillations and happenstance that led to its disclosure, and on the grim revenge taken by Nero against the participants and other objects of his hatred (such as Seneca) whom he claimed, on little evidence, were participants. Seneca's nephew Lucan, the great poet of the battle of Pharsalus, who had been forbidden by a jealous Nero from any publication or performance of his poetry, apparently was a conspirator. Tacitus claims that Lucan readily gave up his own mother and other names in a fruitless bid for clemency. Yet he died well, reciting some of his own lines that described a wounded soldier similarly bleeding to death. Others also died bravely, including a freedwoman, Epicharis, who, despite her knowledge of the details and participants, withstood torture and then killed herself rather than implicate persons to whom she was unrelated and even a stranger. So, too, did Seneca, as we have seen, though Tacitus's account is a bit arch, noting that Seneca's final words to his friends "had the air of a public address"[84] and that, when it took too long for him to bleed out, "he summoned his scribes and dictated a long work to them."[85]

Tacitus is more sympathetic to the very different death of the comic novelist Petronius, "a man of educated extravagance" and once Nero's *arbiter elegantiae*.[86] Ordered to commit suicide, Petronius opened his veins but then alternately bandaged and reopened them through the course of an evening with friends in which he chatted amiably, reciting light poetry and playful verses, while offering "nothing on the immortality of the soul or the tenets of philosophers" or other serious matters "that would win him glory for his resolve."[87] During dinner, he simply dropped off as if he were falling asleep. And in his will, instead of trying to placate the emperor with a bequest, "he itemized in writing the emperor's depravities, naming the male prostitutes and women involved, and describing all their novel sexual acts, and sent it to Nero under seal. He then broke his signet ring to prevent its later use for manufacturing danger."[88]

In *Agricola*, Tacitus had disparaged a defiant death as doing no good either to the commonwealth or to the individual. By the end of the *Annals*, however, he was more receptive to a death not sought but endured with courage and grace. Sometimes, he recognized, that is the only course for a good man under a bad emperor. It was not a course Tacitus himself took under Domitian, but that is very much to our benefit, for he was able to blend his political experience, his powerful intellect, and his punishing wit into what has plausibly been called the "greatest of all Roman prose works."[89]

The sort of engaged history written by Tacitus has gone out of fashion, or at least has gone underground. Academic history is now expected to be dispassionate and dry. Tacitus was neither. Unlike earlier historians of Rome, Tacitus had no great faith in the mixed constitution or the rule of law.[90] He recognized that neither was a bulwark against a concentration of too much power in a single person. His protest against totalitarianism has a special significance to us after the horrors of Stalinist Russia and the dark oppression of the Eastern Bloc. But even more important is his broader understanding of the individual in relation to society and how he or she is shaped and too often distorted by the political regime. We gravitate to power and are warped by it into sycophancy and even crime. Only the rarest among us trim a path between degradation and despair. Tacitus was among the rarest and the finest.

CHAPTER 10

THE EMPEROR
AND THE SLAVE

No man is free who is not master of himself.
—Epictetus, fragment 35

Along with the *Letters* of Seneca, the greatest surviving works of Stoic thought are the *Discourses* of Epictetus and the *Meditations* of Marcus Aurelius. Epictetus was a slave. Marcus reigned as emperor for almost twenty years. There was no greater gulf in the Roman world than that between the supreme power of the emperor and the utter powerlessness of the slave, whose life and death were within the absolute control of another. Yet it was Epictetus the slave who exercised a profound influence over Marcus the emperor.

Epictetus wrote, "That man is free who lives as he wishes; who can be neither compelled, nor hindered, nor constrained; whose impulses are unimpeded, who attains his desires and does not fall into what he wants to avoid."[1] That description seems to fit perfectly an emperor whose every wish bore the force of command. And it is plainly inapposite for a slave, who is constantly compelled, hindered, and constrained; who can neither live as he wishes nor avoid what he fears. Yet Marcus would be the first to acknowledge that Epictetus was the freer man.

The slave, Epictetus notes, longs to be free. Then I will be happy, he says. I will meet others as equals; I will bow to no one; I will go where I please, when I want, and associate with those I choose.[2] But as soon as that freedom is achieved, he finds he must flatter others for a meal or toil in degrading jobs, always longing for what is out of reach. He has handed himself over to be a slave again in all but name.[3] We all cajole ourselves in similar ways—if only I held high office, or had a lot of money, or were a military leader; then, I would be free and happy. Yet that is an illusion. If we

271

fix our desires on externals—power, money, honor, sex—we forfeit control over our happiness to others. Even a slave can be free within the sphere of his choice. Even an emperor is not free if governed by externals; he is simply "a slave in a purple-bordered robe."[4]

The central tenet of Epictetus's philosophy is that we must distinguish between those things within our control and those outside our control. Within our control are our value judgments, desires, and volitions. Outside our control are all the things that men lust after in this life but that depend on chance and circumstance. The Stoic finds his resources and his happiness within himself and directs his wishes accordingly. With regard to everything else, he says with Socrates, "If god so pleases, so be it."[5]

Friedrich Nietzsche would one day write of the radical revaluation of values effected by Christianity, in which the Christian virtues of love and meekness displaced the ancient homeric virtues of honor and prowess. Nietzsche called this "the slave revolt in morality,"[6] and traced its origins to the *ressentiment* of the masses, who sought to stigmatize and disparage those they could not directly overcome.

Epictetus was one of Nietzsche's heroes of the spirit. Yet Nietzsche seems utterly to have missed the fact that Christian doctrine had its most conspicuous origins in Stoicism and, in particular, in the work of Epictetus, who argued that we can never be free until we learn to limit our desires to the sphere of matters within our control; until, that is, we disdain worldly success, are masters of our own spirit, and calmly, even joyfully, accept what lies outside our power to change.

Marcus Aurelius had more worldly power than any man of his day; perhaps more than any single man has had since his day. Yet even he could not prevent plague, war, and intrigue from ravaging the empire and darkening his days. His sphere of control over externals might seem broader than that of a slave, but it was not different in kind. The philosophy of Epictetus—with its radical inversion of the concepts of freedom and slavery—captured the heart of this beleaguered emperor, just as Christianity would later capture the heart of the emperor Constantine, though for very different reasons. Constantine thought the Christian god was leading him to victory over his enemies. Marcus recognized that the greatest enemy of each of us is within and that our constant daily battle is to vanquish vain desires and forlorn hopes in order to achieve peace and tranquility and a new form of freedom and joy in accepting divine providence and serving our fellow men.

EPICTETUS

Epictetus was born into slavery circa 55 in the province of Phrygia, which is now part of modern Turkey. Apparently, brutal treatment by a master left him lame and in poor health. Somehow he ended up in Rome as the property of Epaphroditus, himself a freedman and secretary to the emperor Nero. There, Epictetus was permitted to attend the lectures of Musonius Rufus, a well-known Stoic teacher. He was subsequently freed by Epaphroditus and began teaching philosophy in his own right.

In 89 (or, in some accounts, 95), the emperor Domitian banished all philosophers from Rome. Epictetus went to Nicopolis, the "city of victory" founded by Octavian in Epirus, near where the battle of Actium was fought. It was a natural stopping point between Attic Greece and Italy, and students from both Athens and Rome came to study with Epictetus. He chose to stay there even after the death of Domitian in 96.

Epictetus, like his model, Socrates, left no writings of his own. Fortunately, and also like Socrates, an admiring student made a record of his teachings. Arrian would later serve as consul and a military commander. He was also a historian, whose *Anabasis of Alexander*, completed in 140, is still read today. Most important, though, are the eight books of *Discourses* he prepared from his early days as a student of Epictetus. Four of those books have survived, along with the *Enchiridion*, or *Handbook*, which is a collection of maxims drawn by Arrian from the *Discourses*. Arrian was no Plato, but that is perhaps an advantage since we do not have to separate his own views from those of his teacher. Arrian explains his methodology in a short preface to the *Discourses*.

> I tried to note down whatever I heard him say, so far as possible in his own words, to preserve reminders for myself in future days of his cast of mind, and frankness of speech. These are, then, as you would expect, the kind of discourses that one person would address to another as the moment demands, and not such as he would compose formally for people to read in the future.[7]

The *Discourses* is not an exact stenographic record but rather a compressed depiction of the teacher in action that seeks to be as accurate as possible.

Epictetus lived very simply in Nicopolis. He did not marry until old age, when he decided to adopt an infant who was to be abandoned by his parents and allowed to die, and he took a wife to help him. He was a contemporary of Plutarch and

Tacitus. He was befriended by the emperor Hadrian, who stopped in Nicopolis to hear him teach. Despite a legacy of slavery, ill health, modest means, and exile, Epictetus was able to rise above his circumstances, to achieve tranquility, and to act with integrity. He was a beloved and sought-after teacher in large part because he embodied the doctrines that he taught. Epictetus died in Nicopolis circa 135, when Marcus was still fourteen.

CHOOSING FREEDOM

Epictetus shares another key trait with Socrates: both men believe that to study philosophy is to learn how to live. Philosophy is useless if it does not transform your life for the better. The theoretical aspects of philosophy may provide guidance and support. But they are not an end in themselves and indeed may become a distraction from or, worse, a substitute for true progress. "Never look for your work in one place and your progress in another," Epictetus counsels a student who was proud of his detailed exegesis of the Stoic philosopher Chrysippus.[8] Lecturing on logic and rhetoric does not make a sophist into a philosopher. Reading books and traveling to attend lectures does not make one a student of philosophy. "Do you think you can behave as you do, yet be a philosopher?" he asks. To make progress as a philosopher is, first and foremost, to make progress in virtue. All else—ambition, wealth, honors, even scholarship—must be set aside as, at most, distant seconds. "Philosophy does not promise to secure anything external for man."[9] Indeed, the philosopher will invariably come off worse than others in everyday affairs. But he will nonetheless be a better and happier person; "elevated, free, unrestrained, unhindered, faithful, self-respecting."[10] That is the promise made by Epictetus in the *Discourses*.

The claim that philosophy can or should change your life is ignored and even disparaged in most modern philosophy departments. From students, it generally meets with either skepticism or enthusiastic acknowledgment before they return their focus to their careers and their social lives. But Epictetus actually delivers the goods. He explains how this transformation is possible and how, even without expecting perfection, each of us can make progress toward this ideal. We can reject the ideal. We can decide that we prefer to focus our energies on coming off better than others in the external marks of success. But Epictetus will not let us pretend to master Stoicism simply as an academic discipline. Stoicism is a way of living, not just a set of doctrines. We either change or we do not. The choice is up to us.

Epictetus explains that choice in the most important passage in his work, chosen by Arrian to open the *Handbook*.

> Some things are up to us and others are not. Up to us are opinion, impulse, desire, aversion, and, in a word, whatever is our own action. Not up to us are body, property, reputation, office, and, in a word, whatever is not our own action. The things that are up to us are by nature free, unhindered and unimpeded; but those that are not up to us are weak, servile, subject to hindrance, and not our own. Remember, then, that if you suppose what is naturally enslaved to be free, and what is not your own to be your own, you will be hampered, you will lament, you will be disturbed, and you will find fault with both gods and men. But if you suppose only what is your own to be your own, and what is not your own not to be your own (as is indeed the case), no one will ever coerce you, no one will hinder you, you will find fault with no one, you will accuse no one, you will not do a single thing against your will, you will have no enemy, and no one will harm you because no harm can affect you.[11]

Unsurprisingly, the former slave is focused on freedom and lack of restraint. The words *free* and *freedom* appear repeatedly throughout the *Discourses*. But freedom for Epictetus is achieved not through the satisfaction of desire but through the suppression of desire for things that lie outside our control. Greatness of soul and a noble spirit are within our control; a large estate, a high position, and an active sex life are not. We might take steps to try to obtain these externals. We might work hard and maneuver and even act dishonorably in their service. But, ultimately, the fulfillment of all such desires depends on others to whom we have voluntarily enslaved ourselves. "Who is your master?" asks Epictetus. "He who has authority over any of the things that you strive to acquire, or want to avoid."[12] "Whoever, then, wants to be free, let him neither want anything, nor avoid anything, that depends on others; otherwise, he must necessarily be a slave."[13]

The claim that philosophy can break the hidden chains that bind us is already familiar from Plato's allegory of the cave. Plato likens all of us to prisoners in a cave, with necks and legs fettered, who confuse mere images and shadows for reality. The philosopher is the one who can break those chains and transcend the everyday existence that so captivates others. But, for Plato, this ascension out of the cave and into the light requires detailed philosophical knowledge of (and belief in) a realm of eternal and immutable forms that show us the true structure of the world. Epictetus has no such metaphysical designs, and his philosopher requires no such esoteric knowledge.

For Epictetus, the arena of freedom is within our own souls. Epictetus develops a complex moral psychology to explain the exact nature and scope of this freedom, which we will discuss below. The point to emphasize here, however, is disarmingly simple: we don't control events; we control only how we react and respond to events. Let's take a specific example from daily life—one not available to Epictetus but of the sort that peppers the *Discourses*. Many of us drive to work. The commute may be short or long, crowded or untrammeled. We may have options as to the route or the precise timing. But, otherwise, the traffic is not within our control, nor are the habits—good and bad—of other drivers. Given these external constraints, we have two choices. We can fume and fret over every delay and seek every possible advantage (however illusory) through sharp lane changes, sudden accelerations, and blasts from the horn. Or we can accept that the traffic conditions, once we are on the road, are not within our control and not worth the anguish and aggravation they so readily occasion. If you choose the former course, "you will be hampered, you will lament, you will be disturbed, and you will find fault with both gods and men." But if you choose the latter course, Epictetus tells us, you will find a new freedom and inner peace and will not expend psychic energy blaming others. The traffic is what it is. The only thing within your control is how you react to it and whether you let it disturb and upset you and turn you into a person you do not wish to be. If you do, then you have handed over control of your inner self to others; you have allowed them, through your reactions, to hijack your soul.

The particular example is deliberately banal, in contrast to the metaphorical flights of Plato. But it can be extended to almost any activity in life, from the trivial to the most serious. The important thing to recognize is how difficult it is to follow Epictetus's advice even in the smallest matters, how difficult it is to obtain mastery over our own reactions to events. But if we do not do so, Epictetus explains, we will live in constant fear, anxiety, pain, and distress because we cannot control those events. That is not freedom but slavery. "What, then, is to be done?" he asks. "To make the best of what is in our power, and take the rest as it naturally happens."[14]

Epictetus gives the example of the philosopher Agrippinus who, when told he was being tried before the Senate, went off to exercise and have a bath. When told afterward that he was condemned to exile, he responded simply, "Well, then, let us go to Aricia, and eat our meal there."[15] Like Agrippinus, we must cultivate an ability to endure and to accept and thereby transcend all that happens. Sickness impedes the body; lameness, the leg. But neither need impede our ability to choose how to respond to such eventualities. Every impediment is an impediment to something else, not to our true selves. If it lies outside the sphere of choice, it is not an evil;

it is simply a fact, and we can choose how we respond to that fact. Even a tyrant with absolute power cannot break a spirit that is constantly prepared to reply, "It is nothing to me."[16]

> Thus, when the tyrant says to anyone, "I will chain your leg," he who values his leg, cries out, "No, have mercy," while he who sets the value on his own will and choice, says: "If you think it to your greater advantage to do so, chain it." — "What! Do you not care?" — "No; I do not care." — "I will show you that I am master." — "You? How could you be? Zeus has set me free. . . . You are master of my carcass. Take it."[17]

Most of us expect all benefit and harm to come from externals. Even Aristotle treated some externals (friends, family, health, and honor) as integral parts of the good life. He therefore acknowledged that our happiness is to a considerable extent hostage to fortune. But Epictetus admits no such fragility. He treats all external goods, however natural, as matters of indifference. Happiness is not to be found in the body, in wealth, or in high office; it is found only within, in a well-ordered mind that is impervious to fortune. Epictetus makes a limited concession to Aristotle: we may treat external goods as if someone were scattering nuts and figs. If one falls in your lap, "pick it up and eat it; for one can value even a fig as far as that."[18] But we cannot let our desires attach themselves to such fortuities, for "the only way to freedom is to despise things that are not up to us."[19]

It is a hard, even impossible, doctrine. It also seems wholly negative, as if all that was truly good in life was to avoid stress, fear, pain, envy, and longing; as if dependence on the goodwill and affection of others was the worst form of slavery, rather than a natural and desirable acknowledgement of our humanity. Epictetus, the former slave, may have been willing to give up all desire for externals: "I for my part yield up all the rest," he explains. "It suffices me, if I become able to pass my life free from hindrance and distress, and to hold up my head in the face of events like a free man, and to look up to heaven as the friend of god, fearing nothing that can happen."[20] But should that really be enough for the rest of us? Is freedom from distress and hindrance the same as happiness? Is that really the highest form of human flourishing? Epictetus himself seeks to answer these questions in his account of moral psychology and of the extent to which, driven by duty and affection, we should commit ourselves to others. But, in exploring his answers, we should keep in mind the force of his injunction (echoing the New Testament) that if we always seek happiness outside ourselves, we will never be able to find it. "For you seek it where it is not, and neglect to seek it where it is."[21]

MORAL PSYCHOLOGY

For Epictetus, the autonomous self has three components: judgment, desire/aversion, and volition or choice. It is in the proper functioning of each of these components and the harmony among them that freedom, integrity, and happiness are to be found. But the most important of the three is judgment, for from proper judgments flow correct desires and choices.

We are constantly bombarded with impressions—we see a beautiful person and are filled with lust; we observe luxury and covet it; we are struck by the trappings of high office and are fired with ambition; we are threatened or constrained and experience fear. But Epictetus is careful to distinguish the impression itself from the reaction we have to it. The former is a fact; the latter contains a value judgment. We are disturbed not by things themselves but by our judgments about things, by our assignment of good and evil to various impressions. We need to break this seemingly automatic connection—in which impressions trigger reactions—and interpose reason between them. We can thereby withhold our assent from the reactions that certain impressions typically engender in us. The impressions themselves are involuntary and not subject to our wishes. But acts of approval or assent "are voluntary and involve human judgment."[22]

Our reasoning faculty allows us to make proper use of impressions, to distinguish between appropriate objects of desire and fear and inappropriate objects. The key first step is not to let impressions carry us away but to gain time for the application of judgment. The goal is to withdraw our "conception of good and evil from things that are not up to us, and [place] it only in those that are."[23] That is where education plays its part. We must extirpate errors of judgment as we would tumors from the body. If we are depressed or irritated by certain events, it is because of our own judgment that these events appear depressing or irritating. If we withhold that judgment, then the depression and irritation disappear. We cannot blame anyone else for the evils that befall us; only our own judgment. "What is by nature free, cannot be disturbed or hindered by anything but itself. But it is a man's own judgments that disturb him."[24]

Once we form proper judgments, desire/aversion and volition fall into place. We no longer fear what is not within our control because we recognize that it is not an evil. And we no longer covet what is outside our control because we recognize that it is not a good. As a consequence, we will no longer have vain desires or make wrong choices. We choose the peace and tranquility of our souls over attempts to control external events. Epictetus accepts the Socratic presumption that to know the good is to do the good. As long as our judgments about good and evil are sound, we will neither desire nor fear, neither choose nor avoid, what is outside our control and therefore indifferent to our well-being.

Epictetus recognizes, however, that we will not truly form proper value judgments through abstract reasoning alone. We need to engage our desires and choices from the outset. Part of forming proper judgments is to "discover a source of goodness that is purely internal, independent of outward contingencies, yet capable of generating both personal happiness and integrity."[25] In other words, we have to recognize that desire and choice find their fulfillment in autonomy from external events. "If you ask me what is the good of man, I can only reply to you that it consists in a certain disposition of our choice."[26] By letting go of what lies outside our control, we find happiness, serenity, and an untroubled mind. Within ourselves we have all that we need to live a good life.

This is not a wholly self-centered project, however. For in the process of realizing the good life for ourselves, we will also treat others with justice and affection. Epictetus recognizes that there is a "natural fellowship of rational beings."[27] As members of that fellowship we have obligations to one another. We have an innate moral sense of the respect and consideration that we owe to other people. As long as that innate moral sense is not distorted by desire for, or aversion to, externals, we will naturally fulfill it. Justice and happiness are not conflicting goals. They coalesce in the freedom, tranquility, and stability that reveal a proper attitude toward those things outside our control. A. A. Long, the premiere authority on Hellenistic philosophy, notes that "Epictetus' fundamental claim is that any allocation of unconditional value to external contingencies or possibilities is both an abrogation of self-respect (esteeming indifferent things above one's rationality and internal goodness) and a certain recipe for lack of integrity in one's behaviour towards other people."[28] How we treat others is not an external state of affairs outside our control but a fundamental aspect of our personal identity and volition.[29]

This connection between our essential selves and others is even stronger in the case of our more intimate human relationships (husband-wife, parent-child, siblings, friends). These relationships are, by nature, marked with affection and loyalty. "I should not be unfeeling like a statue," Epictetus notes, "but should preserve my natural and acquired relations as a man who honours the gods, as a son, as a brother, as a father, as a citizen."[30] Again, although the Stoic sage treats externals with indifference, he does not view his relationships with others as externals, but rather as fundamental aspects of his own humanity. And these relationships may engender positive emotions of love, joy, gratitude, and affection.

The problem, of course, is that such relationships can also engender negative emotions of sorrow, loss, and despair. Our loved ones may suffer setbacks and sorrows of their own in which we necessarily share. Or we may lose them altogether to separation or death. Epictetus would nonetheless ask us to retain our own equilibrium by remembering two things. First, the good of those we love is the same as the good of ourselves; it lies within a well-ordered soul, not in the acquisition of external goods. Thus, a failure of those we love to obtain high office or riches or other marks of success is no more properly an occasion of fear and sorrow than our own failure to do so. What matters is a spirit that is free and a soul that is ordered and tranquil. Externals are no more within the control of those we love than they are within our own control, and should be objects of neither desire nor aversion.

Second, we are asked to maintain a "stark appreciation of the vulnerability of what one loves."[31] We can and should cherish those we love while we have them, but we must meet their passing with fortitude and acceptance. That is one of Stoicism's harshest lessons: "no good man laments, nor sighs, nor groans."[32] Epictetus asks us to treat those we love as a precious gift we may be asked to restore. We should do so without complaint, thankful for the time they have spent with us. The physical well-being of others is as much outside our control as our own. Death is not an evil; it is simply a fact we can face with courage or without. Either way, the result is the same.

PROVIDENCE

Epictetus is aided in this philosophy of acceptance by his views on divine providence. According to Stoic doctrine generally, and Epictetus in particular, the universe is governed by an all-wise, all-good divinity. All that happens is by design. Accordingly, we must not only reconcile ourselves to the will of god; we must affirmatively embrace that will and make it our own. We must accept that there is a broader plan of which we can see only a part. Our job is to accept the fact that everything happens for a reason even if that reason is elusive.

Epictetus goes even further by noting that we ourselves partake of the divine. We share our bodies with animals but our minds with god; our identity as humans, what elevates us above the beasts, lies in our minds. God is within you, he cautions, "you are a fragment of god."[33] Accordingly, "to be of one mind with god," to accept and embrace all that is, is to be pure and beautiful in the presence of god.[34] "In a word," he counsels, "have no will but the will of god."[35]

Divine providence does not necessarily mean determinism, however. A belief in divine providence, in Epictetus's view, is consistent with personal freedom; indeed, it is essential to realize that freedom. To be free, unhindered, and unconstrained is to be one with the will of god. We are on a ship in a storm. Piloting the ship is the helmsman's concern. All we can do is look to ourselves—to our judgments, desires, and impulses. That is the realm in which we are autonomous. "I do what I can, and that alone. I drown without fear, without crying out, or accusing god, but as one who knows that what is born must likewise die."[36] We adapt, we accept, and we strive to understand. The rest we leave to god.

For the modern reader, the question inevitably arises whether this belief in providence is essential to Stoicism. The answer is yes, and no. Some Stoics, and even Epictetus, speak as if god and nature were one. Thus arises that most elusive of Stoic ideas: "a way of life in harmony with nature."[37] If god equals nature, if the divinity is immanent rather than transcendent, then much of the religious overlay of Stoicism simply disappears. The Stoic god becomes the god of Spinoza and Einstein, which is to say not at all like the god of Christianity, Judaism, or Islam. God becomes a trope for the preternatural mystery, beauty, wonder, and order of the natural world. At the same time, the acceptance of divine providence becomes a different sort of trope for the Stoic's refusal to lament or blame anyone for present circumstances, for his reliance on his own resources of mind and spirit to meet all eventualities.

The central doctrine Epictetus wishes to convey is that we must live in the present. We cannot change the past. It is outside our control. There is no profit to be found in discontent with what one has and what has been granted by fortune. We must overcome negative emotions of regret, blame, anger, anxiety, and fear. All such backward-looking emotions depend on false value judgments and are a waste of life. The Stoic accepts the past and thus also the present to which the past has led; it is what it is. He also embraces whatever is to come that is outside his control. "Do not ask things to happen as you wish, but wish them to happen as they do happen, and your life will go smoothly."[38] The irreducible core of human thought and will—what Epictetus calls the god within—can remain impervious to circumstance. We have reason to understand the world and to guide our judgments and desires. The right doctrines and constant vigilance can make us better able to cope with the vicissitudes of human life. Progress in Stoicism is "learning to will that things should happen as they do,"[39] and not to expend psychic energy wishing they were otherwise.

Henry James advised that we take Epictetus "as we take all things in these critical days, eclectically."[40] For those who find talk of divine providence and the god within problematic, the essential teaching of Stoicism can be readily restated. Friedrich Nietzsche, who was decidedly not a religious thinker (though he thought very hard indeed *about* religion), expressed the core Stoic thought at a somewhat fever pitch (since he had no faith in providence or a benign nature). "My formula for greatness in a human being is *amor fati*: that one wants nothing to be different, not forward, not backward, not in all eternity. Not merely bear what is necessary, still less conceal it—all idealism is mendaciousness in the face of what is necessary—but *love* it."[41]

THE INVINCIBLE MAN

If you embrace whatever happens, then your equanimity cannot be disturbed. The Stoic sage is therefore immune to the buffeting of fate. "Who, then, is the invincible man?" asks Epictetus. "He whom nothing outside the sphere of choice can disconcert."[42] Epictetus recognizes that we can only approximate that ideal to a greater or lesser degree. Yet even small steps in the right direction will make us freer, happier, safer, and more fulfilled.

Epictetus accordingly advises that we undertake spiritual exercises, training our desires/aversions and volitions the same way we would train our bodies to keep them healthy and in shape. We should practice in little things and then proceed to greater ones. "I have lost my cloak. Yes, because you had a cloak."[43] If we develop the right responses on minor occasions, then we will build up proper habits of judgment that stand up to more severe tests. Long training and practice will make considered assent, correct desire, and appropriate impulse a matter of habit. Anger and lust are not only present evils; they strengthen bad habits. But if we defer our response to such impressions until we can gain mastery over them, until our better judgment has time to kick in, then we will grow our strength and resolve.

Before undertaking this training, however, Epictetus asks us to consider what it means to make such a commitment. Otherwise, we will be like children who play one moment at being an Olympic athlete and another at being a gladiator. "First tell yourself what sort of man you want to be; then act accordingly in all you do."[44] Philosophy requires vigilance and training at every hour of the day. The philosopher must not only get the better of his desires; he must be prepared to be scorned and laughed at and come off worse in office, in honor, in the courts: in short, in everything that matters most to others. We cannot have it both ways. Devotion to externals is the path of turmoil, disappointment, and mental disturbance. But if we cultivate our ruling faculty through the proper exercise of judgment—distinguishing that which is within our control from that which is outside it—then we can shed those negative emotions. "That was how Socrates became the man he was, by heeding nothing but his reason in all that he encountered. And even if you are not yet a Socrates, you should live as one who does indeed wish to be a Socrates."[45]

Whatever happens to you, ask yourself what resources of endurance and self-control you have for dealing with it. Treat it as a test and an opportunity. "If you meet with anything that is burdensome or sweet, or glorious or inglorious, remember that now is the time of the contest, and the Olympic games have arrived, and that you cannot defer things any longer, and that it rests on a single day and a single action whether your progress is lost or maintained."[46] Having a bad neighbor can train one to be good-tempered and fair-minded or the opposite. Poverty, sickness, lack of office—all these things can be treated as personal disasters or as opportunities to face fortune with equanimity. Now is the time to choose.

Epictetus asks us to prepare ourselves for such choices through a process of negative visualization.[47] Keep the prospect of death and loss always before your mind, he advises. Then nothing will seem terrible to you. Paradoxically, if we regularly remind ourselves of the frailty of our attachments, we not only prepare ourselves for the possibility of loss, but we learn to cherish what we have. Our natural human tendency is to fantasize about the things we want, as if they would make us happy, rather than to focus on all the reasons that happiness already is within our grasp. If we fully enjoy the blessings we already possess, we will also be better able to endure their passing. Conversely, in arming ourselves against negative emotions, we will fill our lives with positive emotions of joy, wonder, and contentment.

Free yourself from slavery to externals, withhold your assent from things outside your control, embrace fate, build your powers of endurance and self-control, visualize the inevitability of loss and yet find joy in the present. "These are the things that philosophers ought to study," Epictetus advises; "it is these that they should write about each day; and it is in these that they should exercise themselves."[48] That is precisely the task Epictetus's greatest pupil undertook for himself.

MARCUS AURELIUS

Marcus was born in Rome on April 26 in the year 121, to Marcus Annius Verus. On his father's death, the three-year-old Marcus was adopted by his paternal grandfather. He was educated in Rome by private tutors, studying rhetoric, the Greek classics, and Stoic philosophy. His earnest but noble demeanor attracted favorable attention from the emperor Hadrian. The emperor died in 138, when Marcus was seventeen. Hadrian chose as his successor Titus Aurelius Antoninus, known to posterity as Antoninus Pius. But Hadrian also directed Antoninus to adopt Marcus, who became known thereafter as Marcus Aurelius. Antoninus was married to Marcus's aunt, and Marcus married his cousin Faustina, the daughter of Antoninus, in 145. Marcus himself became emperor in 161. He enlisted Lucius Verus, who had also been adopted by Antoninus, as coemperor. It proved a poor and unnecessary decision. Verus was a weak and unreliable partner in running the empire. When he died in 169, Marcus continued on as sole emperor.

Marcus was not physically strong, but he was hard working and conscientious. He needed every ounce of his energy and determination, for the empire was beset by wars and natural disasters from the moment of his ascension to the moment of his death. This succession of trials began in 161 with the flooding of the Tiber and a devastating earthquake at Cyzicus in what is now modern Turkey. The following year brought war with the Parthians (in ancient Persia), which lasted until 165. The war was successfully concluded, but the returning troops carried with them a devastating plague that, by some estimates, killed five million people and greatly weakened the army. German tribes north of the Danube chose 167 to revolt, and pacifying those tribes, along with a related revolt in Gaul, consumed the rest of Marcus's reign. He also had to contend with a short-lived effort by one of his commanders in Asia to have himself declared emperor in Marcus's stead.

Marcus died of disease on campaign near the Danube on March 17, 180. He and Faustina had numerous children, perhaps as many as thirteen. But, of the boys, only Commodus survived, and he may not have been Marcus's natural son. Although Marcus expressed sincere love for Faustina ("I must thank heaven for such a wife as mine, so submissive, so loving, and so artless"[49]), persistent rumors marked her as serially unfaithful. Unfortunately, Marcus did not determine succession by adoption. Instead, he allowed Commodus to succeed him, and even made him coemperor in 177. It was a terrible choice, for Commodus became a despised tyrant on the order of Domitian. Marcus, the last of the so-called five good emperors, either showed poor judgment in this regard or allowed paternal affection to override it. Yet he himself was perhaps the finest emperor of all. As Gibbon notes, Marcus "was severe to himself, indulgent to the imperfection of others, just and beneficent to all mankind."[50] The judgment pronounced by Gibbon on Marcus and his adoptive father still stands: "Their united reigns are possibly the only period of history in which the happiness of a great people was the sole object of government."[51]

The *Meditations* was written in the last years of Marcus's life, while on campaign against the German tribes. It was not intended for publication but consisted simply of philosophical exercises jotted down for his own improvement. The title and even the grouping into twelve books were likely the work of a later editor. Marcus wrote in Greek, which spared him having to find suitable Latin counterparts to the philosophical vocabulary of Epictetus and other Greek philosophers. His work survived in a single manuscript, probably rescued from destruction by a loyal servant. Though heavily influenced by Epictetus and other predecessors, Marcus put his own stamp on Stoicism. There is more humility and less pride in his writing; he is not quite as militantly self-sufficient as other Stoics and is more willing to emphasize his own weaknesses and faults. There is also greater concern with the welfare and happiness of others and a stronger emphasis on duty and justice. Finally, he takes a more overtly religious attitude even than Epictetus and, as such, forms a natural bridge to Christianity. Marcus contended that we are bound together by an all-pervading love of god and one another. Henry James, in contemplating the equestrian statue of Marcus at Rome, noted, "One may call it singular that in the capital of Christendom the portrait most suggestive of a Christian conscience is that of a pagan emperor."[52] He could as easily have made the same remark about the conscience portrayed in the *Meditations*.

"IT LIES WITH ME"

In sonnet 111, Shakespeare will write, "My nature is subdued / To what it works in, like the dyer's hand."[53] That insight already animates the *Meditations*. "Your mind will be like its habitual thoughts," Marcus writes, "for the soul becomes dyed with the colour of its thoughts."[54] Through a series of spiritual exercises and exhortations, he seeks to infuse his soul with Stoic virtue.

The *Meditations* is not a journal or an autobiography in any traditional sense. Aside from book 1, Marcus rarely mentions incidents from his own life. Yet he engages in a form of self-scrutiny that is as open and honest as anything that will be found in Augustine and Montaigne. Marcus is converting his innermost being to Stoicism through maxims and precepts, through examples of great virtue, and, most of all, through visualizations that place human life and concerns within a cosmic perspective.

The rules of life on which Marcus rings changes are few but fundamental: "a pious acceptance of the day's happenings, a just dealing towards the day's associates, and a scrupulous attention to the day's impressions."[55] These three rules operate within a coherent intellectual structure, yet Marcus eschews the logical and metaphysical arguments that occupied earlier Stoic thinkers. His only goal is to reform and improve his character. He counsels himself to be content with small steps in the direction of virtue and self-control, for even modest progress in such matters is no trifle.

Marcus accordingly returns to these same three injunctions, in new formulations, throughout the *Meditations*. They correspond to the three disciplines of Epictetus—assent and judgment; desire and aversion; inclination and action—and determine our relationship to reason, to providence, and to other people. First, we must actively exercise our judgment on impressions rather than allow them to exercise control over us. We must "look things in the face and know them for what they are."[56] Second, we must limit our desires and aversions to those things within our control and otherwise accept "a destiny [we] cannot control."[57] Third, we must purify our intentions and always act with justice toward our fellow humans. The good man "seeks only to be just in his doings and charitable in his ways."[58]

These "three disciplines of life"—the discipline of assent; the discipline of desire; and the discipline of action[59]—correspond roughly to the traditional Roman virtues but with a Stoic (and decidedly proto-Christian) twist. Prudence and the love of truth require us to exercise our judgment and withhold our assent from impressions that embody false values. Self-control and courage allow us to limit our desires and not just to accept but to embrace our fate. Justice is grounded not only in correct actions but also in love for our fellows.

The man who practices and lives these three disciplines will be wise, moderate, pious, and loving in all things. Most important, he will live freely and fully in the present. Neither the past nor the future should concern us.[60] The former is already gone; the latter lies with providence; both are indifferent. Yet we constantly abandon the present to lament the past or anticipate the future. Any such focus is a waste of life, a waste of the infinite blessing that is the present moment.

In the present moment, everything that matters lies within our own power. If we expel from our minds all consideration of externals, then we have control over our judgments, our desires, and our intentions. We have become free. That is the choice we face at every moment. If it is not the truth, don't think it. If it is not within your control, don't covet it. If it is not the right thing to do, don't will it.[61] It is up to you! At the end of the day, Marcus tells us, it really is that simple. "A new life lies within your grasp."[62]

"HOW TRANSIENT AND TRIVIAL IS ALL MORTAL LIFE"

One of Marcus's most important thought exercises is to deromanticize impressions and therefore break their reflexive hold upon us. We infuse things with false value judgments. If we strip those judgments away—if we deliberately withhold our assent from the idealization of externals—we can train ourselves to see without sentiment or illusion. "Reflections of this kind go to the bottom of things, penetrating into them and exposing their real nature."[63] Meat, however well dressed, is just the carcass of an animal; wine is grape juice fermented with yeast; fancy purple robes are sheep's wool stained with the blood of a shellfish; sex is the friction of members and ejaculation of fluid. Mortal life is "transient and trivial" in its passage from a drop of semen to a handful of ashes.[64] In death, the greatest emperor and the lowest slave meet with the same process of physical corruption and decay. Even a posthumous reputation is "no more than empty sound and reiteration."[65] In short, everything men set their hearts upon "is banal in experience, fleeting in duration, sordid in content; in all respects the same today as generations now dead and buried have found it to be."[66]

Like Hamlet, then, Marcus pronounces "all the uses of this world" to be "weary, stale, flat, and unprofitable."[67] But Marcus's contempt for things mortal is deliberate. It is calculated as a device for educating and training the spirit. Commentators frequently diagnose Marcus as a forebear of the melancholy Dane. R. B. Rutherford notes "the unique note of unhappiness and disillusionment that permeates the *Meditations*."[68] D. A. Rees concludes that "Marcus, with all his devotion to duty, inhabits a sad and colourless world."[69] But Pierre Hadot rightly argues that we cannot draw inferences about the personality of the real Marcus from the somewhat-stylized exercises he conducts. "Generally speaking, we can say that Marcus' seemingly pessimistic declarations are not expressions of his disgust or disillusion at the spectacle of life; rather, they are a *means* he employs in order to change his way of evaluating the events and objects which go to make up human existence."[70]

Marcus is engaged in an effort of philosophical imagination. As with Plato's journey out of the cave, he strives to view nature as a whole, in all its immensity and eternity, a perspective that necessarily renders human concerns flat and fleeting. "Let your mind constantly dwell on all time and all being," he urges, "and thus learn that each separate thing is but as a grain of sand in comparison with being, and as a single screw's-turn in comparison with time."[71] Without such perspective, we fall into "the folly of those who weary their days in much business, but lack any aim on which their whole effort, nay, their whole thought, is focused."[72] When Marcus says, "I can think of nothing that is worth prizing highly or pursuing seriously,"[73] he is not expressing a personal revelation but a universal and philosophical one.

Paradoxically, moreover, it is in recognizing the transience and triviality of traditional human concerns that we discover both beauty and meaning in all that exists. Just as the laws of nature provide the organizing principle of the universe, reason provides the organizing principle of our lives and actions. By ridding ourselves of false values, we find freedom as part of a greater whole, and we escape "the myriad enmities, suspicions, animosities, and conflicts that are now vanished with the dust and ashes of the men who knew them."[74] Marcus's vaunted "pessimism" is just a way station on the path to a fuller appreciation of the blessings that we, as humans, inherently possess. The shedding of false values allows us, for the first time, to value things truly and to experience the deepest joy in our submission to providence and our dedication to others.

"THE GOD WITHIN"

Marcus reinforces his belief in providence with a logical dichotomy. Either Epicurus is right or the Stoics are right. "Either the world is a mere hotchpotch of random cohesions and dispersions, or else it is a unity of order and providence."[75] Yet, Marcus notes, our response to either picture should be the same. We cannot reprimand a chance array of atoms any more than we should impeach providence.[76] In either eventuality, we must use our reason to distinguish those things within our power from those which lie outside it. The basic moral teaching is the same; we can will our conformity with circumstance. We can limit our assent to things that are true and our desires to things within our control. Even if the universe is aimless, we need not be aimless as well.[77]

Thus, even if Epicurus were right about the universe, Marcus contends, the

Stoic response to that universe would still be correct. But that shows that Epicurus was wrong, since the Stoic response demonstrates that reason and order can prevail over chance and chaos. Our ability to maintain an internal order implies a broader order and rationality in the cosmos. "Can there be some measure of order subsisting in yourself, and at the same time disorder in the greater whole?" Marcus asks,[78] and not just rhetorically. He believes we have a direct apprehension of divine providence in the workings of our own souls.

At the very least, Marcus assumes such providence as a working hypothesis. "Let my first conviction be that I am part of a whole which is under Nature's governance."[79] This is not quite Pascal's wager, in which Pascal proposes to act *as if* god exists because the benefits of being right on such a question (eternal beatitude) are so great, whereas the costs (living a pious and upright life and eschewing "those poisonous pleasures, glory and luxury") are as nothing.[80] But it is close. Marcus is making a choice that he recognizes is not logically compelled yet feels right to him because of his own experience of divine order.

Marcus views the universe "as one living organism, with a single substance and a single soul."[81] This is what allows him to move from acceptance to joy. He is willing not just to endure what fate and nature bring but to embrace them fully, to greet them with joy and love. "Whatever happens, happens rightly."[82] We cannot view the good in purely personal terms. We need a broader perspective. "For all things are born to change and pass away and perish, that others in their turn may come to be."[83] Even death is natural and inevitable and to be neither feared nor deplored. Our own deaths have little importance from a cosmic perspective.

> Flux and change are forever renewing the fabric of the universe, just as the ceaseless sweep of time is forever renewing the face of eternity. In such a running river, where there is no firm foothold, what is there for a man to value among all the many things that are racing past him? It would be like setting the affections on some sparrow flitting by, which in the selfsame moment is lost to sight.[84]

We must fix our affections instead on the intelligent force that governs all. It does not matter whether we call this force Nature, Zeus, Fate, God, Providence, or, more abstractly, the immanence of the divine in nature. The crucial point is to recognize that we are part of something larger than ourselves that gives our lives meaning and allows us to share in the purpose and order—"the intricate tapestry"—of the whole.[85]

Marcus's views on providence necessarily include a reverence for the self; not self-absorption or even self-approval, but rather recognition that one carries the divine within oneself and must respect and nurture it. We are a small piece of the World-Nature, partaking of the same reason and order that governs the whole. As such, we can find both an untroubled retreat and an entrée to the universe within our own souls. A well-ordered spirit has all it needs for happiness. "To quarrel with circumstances is always a rebellion against Nature,"[86] and hence a rebellion against "the god within you."[87]

> To be a philosopher is to keep unsullied and unscathed the divine spirit within him, so that it may transcend all pleasure and all pain, take nothing in hand without purpose and nothing falsely or with dissimulation, depend not on another's actions or inactions, accept each and every dispensation as coming from the same source as itself.[88]

"JUST IN HIS DOINGS AND CHARITABLE IN HIS WAYS"

The god within each of us is, of course, within others as well. Thus, Marcus's second conviction is the existence of a natural bond of kinship among men insofar as we all partake of the divine. These intertwined convictions—divine providence and the brotherhood of man—are the two premises of his life. From them he derives a litany of virtues that he praises throughout the *Meditations*: courtesy, piety, serenity, generosity, simplicity, love, duty, justice, industriousness, charity, kindliness, and unselfconscious dignity.[89] These same virtues would largely become those of Christianity as well.

It is unsurprising, therefore, that Marcus emphasizes both public service and private charity throughout his book. His Stoicism is not a fortress of the self but a Stoicism of duty and obligation, and even love. He acknowledges that service to others is fraught with difficulties. If you maintain your integrity and trustworthiness and sense of shame, you are unlikely to obtain high office or extensive power. Moreover, you cannot expect your efforts to meet with gratitude or just dealing in return. We must be charitable "even with the false and unjust," he claims.[90] We must love others without getting caught up in what *they* love. A man's worth is no greater than the things he values, the things he cares about and strives to bring to fruition. We realize our true natures through justice and love.

Although our good actions will meet with obstacles, nothing external can prevent us from acting justly. Moral good is measured by the purity of our intentions. As Immanuel Kant would later argue, it is the good will that animates actions, rather than the consequences of those actions, that counts from a moral point of view. If the consequences fall short of the intentions, as they inevitably will, we simply adjust and persevere. The only thing that matters is that you play your part well, not how you are rewarded for your efforts or how the audience responds. Moreover, you will be rewarded because service to the human community brings joy as an unexpected by-product.[91] Love underlies all natural processes, and if we act with love we touch upon the divine.[92] "Life is short," Marcus warns, "and this earthly existence has but a single fruit to yield—holiness within and selfless action without."[93]

The *Meditations* is a remarkable document. We follow Marcus as he examines himself, criticizes himself, and exhorts himself, tentatively and experimentally at first, but with more confidence and conviction as he learns how to think and how to live. As Pierre Hadot notes,

> We feel a quite particular emotion as we catch a person in the process of doing what we are all trying to do: to give a meaning to our life, to strive to live in a state of perfect awareness and to give each of life's instants its full value. To be sure, Marcus is talking to himself, but we still get the impression that he is talking to each one of us as well.[94]

Marcus Aurelius was the last great writer of pagan antiquity. With his death began the long decline and fall of the empire chronicled in such matchless prose by Gibbon. Marcus was not a Christian, and there is no indication that he read the gospels and other writings of the still-fledgling sect. Yet he is a key transitional figure in the seismic shift from the ancient world to the Christian Middle Ages. As many scholars have remarked, although the *Meditations* is still rooted in classical thought, much in it "reads like . . . a direct echo of the New Testament."[95] Marcus reflects the changing zeitgeist that heralded a radical conversion of the human spirit. It is with the New Testament and the origins of Christianity, accordingly, that I hope to begin my exploration of the medieval search for wisdom.

ACKNOWLEDGMENTS

I have not tried to document every source for the ideas in this book. But my extensive debt to generations of classical scholars and translators will be obvious to those in the field. I have tried to list the books and articles on which I most relied, as well as those from which general readers would most benefit, in the section on "Suggestions for Further Reading." I also cite there in full the excellent translations of Robert Fagles, David Ferry, Dana Gioia, Michael Grant, Peter Green, Robin Hard, R. E. Latham, Charles Martin, Betty Radice, Niall Rudd, David Slavitt, Maxwell Staniforth, E. F. Watling, David West, and others, from which the quotations in the text are derived.

I was helped by many readers of individual chapters in draft form, among them, Harry Kellogg, Peter Kellogg, Marissa Miller, and Aaron Panner. Dana Gioia, John Lachs, and Richard Saller read the finished manuscript and provided generous comments in support. Dean Saller also made a number of helpful suggestions and corrections.

Darrin Leverette scrupulously polished the entire manuscript, checking the cites, the facts, and the prose. His intelligence, attention to detail, willingness to track down obscure sources, and sensitivity to the nuances of language were all indispensable. So, too, was the work of Bernadette Murphy and my longtime assistant, Marilyn Williams, in proofing the manuscript and putting it in final form.

I was fortunate once again to have Jade Zora Scibilia as my editor at Prometheus Books. She improved the writing, sharpened the ideas, and saved me from many errors. She was also a delight to work with.

As always, my greatest thanks go to my wife, Lucy, and to my three children—Baird, Cole, and Camille—who supported and encouraged me throughout the writing of this book.

CHRONOLOGY

Assassination of Julius Caesar	44
Second Triumvirate	43–33
Ovid	43–17/18 CE
Battle of Philippi	42
Treaty of Brundisium	40
Battle of Actium	31
Augustus	r. 27–14 CE
Seneca	4 BCE–65 CE
Tiberius	r. 14–37
Pliny the Elder	23–79
Petronius	ca. 27–66
Crucifixion of Jesus	ca. 36
Caligula	r. 37–41
Lucan	39–65
Martial	ca. 40–ca. 103
Claudius	r. 41–54
Plutarch	46–ca. 120
Nero	r. 54–68
Epictetus	55–ca. 135
Juvenal	ca. 55–ca. 130
Tacitus	ca. 56–ca. 117
Pliny the Younger	61–ca. 112
Great Fire of Rome	64
Year of Four Emperors	69
Vespasian	r. 69–79
Suetonius	ca. 70–ca. 130
Completion of the Coliseum	80
Domitian	r. 81–96
Nerva	r. 96–98
Trajan	r. 98–117
Hadrian	r. 117–138
Antoninus Pius	r. 138–161
Marcus Aurelius	121–180; r. 161–180
Diocletian	r. 284–305
Great Persecution of Christians	303–313
Constantine	r. 312–337
Ammianus Marcellinus	ca. 330–395

SUGGESTIONS FOR FURTHER READING

INTRODUCTION

We are blessed with an abundance of ancient historians of Rome. Their works are discussed in chapter 9 and are listed in the corresponding section below. A modern reader interested in Rome could do no better than to start with Livy, Tacitus, Plutarch, and Suetonius.

Three "modern" histories of Rome still tower over all competitors: Edward Gibbon's *Decline and Fall of the Roman Empire* (completed in 1787) covers the period from the end of the first century CE through the fall of the Eastern Empire in the fifteenth century; Theodor Mommsen's *History of Rome* (completed in 1856) extends from Rome's origins to the ascension of Julius Caesar, but stops short of his assassination in 44 BCE; and Ronald Syme's *Roman Revolution* (1939) is focused on the end of the republic and the rise and reign of Augustus, from 60 BCE to 14 CE. Each of these works is marked by great erudition, beautiful prose, and a strong narrative drive. Each, moreover, is shaped by a central thesis or preoccupation that colors the whole: Gibbon, that Christianity undermined the civic and martial spirit of Rome and led to its downfall; Mommsen, that Julius Caesar was the perfect statesman and creative genius who rescued Rome from the chaos of the late days of the republic; and Syme (in direct reaction to Mommsen), that in all ages oligopoly lurks behind the facade of government and that "undue insistence upon the character and exploits of a single person invests history with dramatic unity at the expense of truth." Editions of Gibbon and Syme are readily available. A complete Mommsen requires more searching but repays the effort.

Useful recent histories include the following:

Anthony Everitt, *The Rise of Rome: The Making of the World's Greatest Empire* (New York: Random House, 2012).

Brian Campbell, *The Romans and Their World* (New Haven, CT: Yale University Press, 2011).

Klaus Bringmann, *A History of the Roman Republic* (Cambridge: Polity Press, 2007), translated by W. J. Smyth.

Robin Lane Fox, *The Classical World: An Epic History from Homer to Hadrian* (New York: Basic Books, 2006).

The Oxford History of the Roman World (Oxford: Oxford University Press, 2001), edited by John Boardman, Jasper Griffin, and Oswyn Murray.

Helpful works on specialized aspects of Roman life and knowledge include:

Daryn Lehoux, *What Did the Romans Know? An Inquiry into Science and Worldmaking* (Chicago: University of Chicago Press, 2012).

Peter Garnsey and Richard Saller, *The Roman Empire: Economy, Society, and Culture* (Berkeley: University of California Press, 1987).

Vitruvius Pollio, *Ten Books on Architecture* (New York: Cambridge University Press, 1999), translated by Ingrid D. Rowland.

PLAUTUS AND ROMAN COMEDY

TRANSLATIONS

Plautus, *"The Rope" and Other Plays* (London: Penguin Books, 1964), translated by E. F. Watling.

Plautus, *"The Pot of Gold" and Other Plays* (London: Penguin Books, 1965), translated by E. F. Watling.

Plautus: The Comedies, 4 vols. (Baltimore: Johns Hopkins University Press, 1995), edited by David R. Slavitt and Palmer Bovie, translated by Constance Carrier et al.

Terence: The Comedies (London: Penguin Books, 1976), translated by Betty Radice.

Terence: The Comedies (Baltimore: Johns Hopkins University Press, 1992), edited by Palmer Bovie.

George E. Duckworth, *The Nature of Roman Comedy: A Study in Popular Entertainment*, 2nd ed. (Norman: University of Oklahoma Press, 1994).

Erich Segal, *Roman Laughter: The Comedy of Plautus*, 2nd ed. (New York: Oxford University Press, 1987).

Timothy J. Moore, *The Theater of Plautus: Playing to the Audience* (Austin: University of Texas Press, 1998).

Gian Biagio Conte, *Latin Literature: A History* (Baltimore: Johns Hopkins University Press, 1999), translated by Joseph B. Solodow, revised by Don Fowler and Glenn W. Most, pp. 49–65, 92–104.

CICERO

Cicero, *Tusculan Disputations*, rev. ed. (Cambridge, MA: Harvard University Press, 1945), translated by J. E. King.

Cicero: Selected Letters (New York: Oxford University Press, 2008), translated with an introduction and notes by P. G. Walsh.

Cicero: Selected Political Speeches (1969; repr., London: Penguin Books, 1989), translated with an introduction by Michael Grant.

Cicero: Selected Works (Baltimore: Penguin Books, 1960), translated with an introduction by Michael Grant.

Cicero, *The Republic* and *The Laws* (Oxford: Oxford University Press, 2008), translated by Niall Rudd with an introduction and notes by J. G. F. Powell and Niall Rudd.

Cicero, *On the Commonwealth* and *On the Laws* (Cambridge: Cambridge University Press, 1999), edited by James E. G. Zetzel.

Cicero, *On Duties* (Cambridge: Cambridge University Press, 1991), edited by Miriam T. Griffin and E. M. Atkins.

Cicero, *On Moral Ends* (Cambridge: Cambridge University Press, 2001), edited by Julia Annas, translated by Raphael Woolf.

Cicero: On the Good Life (London: Folio Society, 2003), translated with an introduction and notes by Michael Grant.

SECONDARY SOURCES

Anthony Everitt, *Cicero: The Life and Times of Rome's Greatest Politician* (New York: Random House, 2003).

Elizabeth Rawson, *Cicero: A Portrait* (1975; repr., London: Bristol Classical Press, 2001).

Cicero the Philosopher: Twelve Papers (1995; repr., Oxford: Clarendon Press, 2002), edited with an introduction by J. G. F. Powell.

Neal Wood, *Cicero's Social and Political Thought* (Berkeley: University of California Press, 1988).

LUCRETIUS

TRANSLATIONS

Lucretius, *On the Nature of the Universe* (1994; repr., London: Penguin Books, 2005), translated by R. E. Latham, revised with an introduction and notes by John Godwin.

The Essential Epicurus: Letters, Principal Doctrines, Vatican Sayings, and Fragments (Amherst, NY: Prometheus Books, 1993), translated with an introduction by Eugene O'Connor.

Catullus: The Poems (1966; repr., London: Penguin Books, 2004), translated with an introduction by Peter Whigham.

SECONDARY SOURCES

The Cambridge Companion to Lucretius (New York: Cambridge University Press, 2007), edited by Stuart Gillespie and Philip Hardie.

Martha C. Nussbaum, *The Therapy of Desire: Theory and Practice in Hellenistic Ethics* (Princeton, NJ: Princeton University Press, 1994), chaps. 5–7.

Stephen Greenblatt, *The Swerve: How the World Became Modern* (New York: W. W. Norton, 2011).

George Santayana, *Three Philosophical Poets* (Garden City, NY: Doubleday Anchor Books, 1953).

Introduction to *On the Nature of Things* (Cambridge, MA: Harvard University Press, 1924), translated by W. H. D. Rouse, revised by Martin F. Smith.

VIRGIL

TRANSLATIONS

The Eclogues of Virgil (New York: Farrar, Straus and Giroux, 1999), translated by David Ferry.

The Georgics of Virgil (New York: Farrar, Straus and Giroux, 2005), translated by David Ferry.

Virgil, *Eclogues; Georgics; Aeneid 1–6* (Cambridge, MA: Harvard University Press, 1999), translated by H. R. Fairclough, revised by G. P. Goold.

Virgil, *Aeneid* (New York: Penguin Books, 2010), translated by Robert Fagles.

Theocritus, *Idylls* (New York: Oxford University Press, 2002), translated by Anthony Verity.

SECONDARY SOURCES

L. P. Wilkinson, *The Georgics of Virgil: A Critical Survey* (New York: Cambridge University Press, 1978).

Virgil (New York: Chelsea House, 1986), edited by Harold Bloom.

Paul Alpers, *What Is Pastoral?* (Chicago: University of Chicago Press, 1997).

David R. Slavitt, *Virgil* (New Haven, CT: Yale University Press, 1991).

Virgil: A Collection of Critical Essays (Englewood Cliffs, NJ: Prentice-Hall, 1966), edited by Steele Commager.

The Cambridge Companion to Virgil (New York: Cambridge University Press, 1997), edited by Charles Martindale.

Brooks Otis, *Virgil: A Study in Civilized Poetry* (Norman: University of Oklahoma Press, 1995).

Hermann Broch, *The Death of Virgil*, translated by Jean Starr Untermeyer (San Francisco: North Point Press, 1983).

Bruno Snell, "Arcadia: The Discovery of a Spiritual Landscape," in *The Discovery of the Mind* (New York: Dover Publications, 1982), translated by T. G. Rosenmeyer.

HORACE

TRANSLATIONS

The Odes of Horace (New York: Farrar, Straus and Giroux, 1998), translated by David Ferry.

Horace, *Satires* and *Epistles*, rev. ed. (London: Penguin Books, 2005), translated by Niall Rudd.

Horace: The Complete Odes and Epodes (New York: Oxford University Press, 2008), translated by David West.

The Epistles of Horace (New York: Farrar, Straus and Giroux, 2001), translated by David Ferry.

SECONDARY SOURCES

Edith Hamilton, *The Roman Way to Western Civilization* (New York: New American Library, 1957), chap. 8.

Gian Biagio Conte, *Latin Literature: A History* (Baltimore: Johns Hopkins University Press, 1999), translated by Joseph B. Solodow, revised by Don Fowler and Glenn W. Most, pp. 292–320.

David Armstrong, *Horace* (New Haven, CT: Yale University Press, 1989).

C. M. Bowra, "The Odes of Horace," in *The Golden Horizon* (New York: University Books, 1955), edited by Cyril Connolly.

Steele Commager, *The Odes of Horace: A Critical Study* (New Haven, CT: Yale University Press, 1962).

David West, *Reading Horace* (Edinburgh: Edinburgh University Press, 1967).

OVID

TRANSLATIONS

Ovid: The Erotic Poems (London: Penguin Books, 1982), translated by Peter Green.

Ovid, *Heroides* (London: Penguin Books, 2004), translated by Harold Isbell.

Ovid, *Metamorphoses* (New York: W. W. Norton, 2005), translated by Charles Martin.

Ovid: The Poems of Exile (Berkeley: University of California Press, 2005), translated by Peter Green.

Tibullus: Elegies (New York: Oxford University Press, 2012), translated by A. M. Juster.

Propertius: The Poems (Oxford: Oxford University Press, 1999), translated by Guy Lee.

SECONDARY SOURCES

Sara Mack, *Ovid* (New Haven, CT: Yale University Press, 1988).

Gian Biagio Conte, *Latin Literature: A History* (Baltimore: Johns Hopkins University Press, 1999), translated by Joseph B. Solodow, revised by Don Fowler and Glenn W. Most, pp. 321–66.

Brooks Otis, *Ovid as an Epic Poet* (Cambridge: Cambridge University Press, 1966).

SENECA

TRANSLATIONS

Seneca: Letters from a Stoic and Three Dialogues (London: Folio Society, 2003), translated by Robin Campbell and C. D. N. Costa.

Seneca: Dialogues and Essays (Oxford: Oxford University Press, 2008), translated by John Davie.

Seneca: The Tragedies, vol. 1 (Baltimore: Johns Hopkins University Press, 1992), edited and translated by David R. Slavitt.

Seneca: The Tragedies, vol. 2 (Baltimore: Johns Hopkins University Press, 1995), edited by David R. Slavitt, translated by David R. Slavitt et al.

Seneca: Four Tragedies and Octavia (London: Penguin Books, 1966), translated by E. F. Watling.

Seneca, *The Apocolocyntosis*, rev. ed. (London: Penguin Books, 1986), translated by J. P. Sullivan.

Secondary Sources

C. A. J. Littlewood, *Self-Representation and Illusion in Senecan Tragedy* (New York: Oxford University Press, 2004).

Norman T. Pratt, *Seneca's Drama* (Chapel Hill: University of North Carolina Press, 1983).

Denis Henry and Elisabeth Henry, *The Mask of Power: Seneca's Tragedies and Imperial Rome* (Chicago: Bolchazy-Carducci, 1985).

C. J. Herington, "Senecan Tragedy," in *Essays on Classical Literature* (Cambridge: Heffer, 1972), edited by Niall Rudd.

T. S. Eliot, "Seneca in Elizabethan Translation" and "Shakespeare and the Stoicism of Seneca," in *Selected Essays* (New York: Harcourt, Brace, 1950).

Edith Hamilton, *The Roman Way to Western Civilization* (New York: New American Library, 1957), chap. 11.

A. A. Long, *Hellenistic Philosophy*, 2nd ed. (London: Duckworth, 1986).

Martha C. Nussbaum, *The Therapy of Desire: Theory and Practice in Hellenistic Ethics* (Princeton, NJ: Princeton University Press, 1994), chaps. 9–12.

Donald Russell, "The Arts of Prose: The Early Empire," in *The Oxford History of the Roman World* (Oxford: Oxford University Press, 2001), edited by John Boardman, Jasper Griffin, and Oswyn Murray.

PLUTARCH

Translations

Plutarch: Essays (London: Penguin Books, 1992), translated by Robin Waterfield.

Plutarch's Lives (New York: Modern Library, 2001), edited by Arthur Hugh Clough, translated by John Dryden.

Secondary Sources

Timothy E. Duff, *Plutarch's Lives: Exploring Virtue and Vice* (Oxford: Oxford University Press, 2002).

Robert Lamberton, *Plutarch* (New Haven, CT: Yale University Press, 2001).

TACITUS AND THE ROMAN HISTORIANS

Translations

Polybius, *The Rise of the Roman Empire* (London: Penguin Books, 1979), translated by Ian Scott-Kilvert.

Julius Caesar, *The Gallic and Civil Wars* (London: Folio Society, 2006), edited by Jane F. Gardner, translated by S. A. Handford and Jane F. Gardner.

Sallust, *Catiline's War, The Jugurthine War, Histories* (London: Penguin Books, 2007), translated by A. J. Woodman.

Livy, *The Early History of Rome* (1960; repr., London: Penguin Books, 2002), translated by Aubrey de Sélincourt.

Livy, *Rome and Italy* (London: Penguin Books, 1982), translated by Betty Radice.

Livy, *The War with Hannibal* (1965; repr., London: Penguin Books, 1972), edited by Betty Radice, translated by Aubrey de Sélincourt.

Livy, *Rome and the Mediterranean* (London: Penguin Books, 1976), translated by Henry Bettenson.

Tacitus, *Agricola* and *Germany* (Oxford: Oxford University Press, 2009), translated by Anthony R. Birley.

Tacitus, *The Histories* (Oxford: Oxford University Press, 2008), edited by D. S. Levene, translated by W. H. Fyfe.

Tacitus, *The Annals: The Reigns of Tiberius, Claudius, and Nero* (Oxford: Oxford University Press, 2008), translated by J. C. Yardley.

Suetonius, *The Twelve Caesars*, rev. ed. (1979; repr., London: Penguin Books, 1989), translated by Robert Graves.

Appian, *The Civil Wars* (London: Penguin Books, 1996), translated by John Carter.

Cassius Dio, *The Roman History: The Reign of Augustus* (London: Penguin Books, 1987), translated by Ian Scott-Kilvert.

Ammianus Marcellinus, *The Later Roman Empire* (1986; repr., London: Penguin Books, 2004), translated by Walter Hamilton.

Secondary Sources

Gian Biagio Conte, *Latin Literature: A History* (Baltimore: Johns Hopkins University Press, 1999), translated by Joseph B. Solodow, revised by Don Fowler and Glenn W. Most, pp. 367–76, 530–52.

Ronald Mellor, *Tacitus* (New York: Routledge, 1993).

Ronald Mellor, *The Roman Historians* (New York: Routledge, 1999).

The Oxford History of the Roman World (Oxford: Oxford University Press, 2001), edited by John Boardman, Jasper Griffin, and Oswyn Murray, chap. 10.

The Cambridge Companion to Tacitus (Cambridge: Cambridge University Press, 2009), edited by A. J. Woodman.

Michael Grant, *Greek and Roman Historians: Information and Misinformation* (New York: Routledge, 1995).

John Burrow, *A History of Histories: Epics, Chronicles, Romances and Inquiries from Herodotus and Thucydides to the Twentieth Century* (New York: Vintage Books, 2009).

EPICTETUS AND MARCUS AURELIUS

TRANSLATIONS

Epictetus, *The Discourses of Epictetus, The Handbook, Fragments* (London: Everyman, 1995), edited by Christopher Gill, translated by Robin Hard.

Marcus Aurelius, *Meditations* (1964; repr., London: Folio Society, 2002), translated by Maxwell Staniforth.

SECONDARY SOURCES

A. A. Long, *Epictetus: A Stoic and Socratic Guide to Life* (2002; repr., Oxford: Oxford University Press, 2010).

R. B. Rutherford, *The "Meditations" of Marcus Aurelius: A Study* (Oxford: Clarendon Press, 1989).

Pierre Hadot, *The Inner Citadel: The "Meditations" of Marcus Aurelius* (Cambridge, MA: Harvard University Press, 2001), translated by Michael Chase.

Pierre Hadot, *Philosophy as a Way of Life: Spiritual Exercises from Socrates to Foucault* (Malden, MA: Blackwell, 1995), edited by Arnold I. Davidson, translated by Michael Chase.

NOTES

PREFACE

    1. David Ferry, trans., *The Epistles of Horace* (New York: Farrar, Straus and Giroux, 2001), Epistle 2.1, p. 123.

    2. See Harold Bloom, *The Anxiety of Influence: A Theory of Poetry*, 2nd ed. (New York: Oxford University Press, 1997).

INTRODUCTION: THE GRANDEUR THAT WAS ROME

    1. Up until chapter 7, all dates are BCE (before the Common Era) unless otherwise noted.

    2. Livy, *The Early History of Rome*, trans. Aubrey de Sélincourt (1960; repr., London: Penguin Books, 2002), pp. 29–30.

    3. Ibid., p. 34.

    4. Ibid., p. 104.

    5. Robin Lane Fox, *The Classical World: An Epic History from Homer to Hadrian* (New York: Basic Books, 2006), p. 296.

    6. Suetonius, *The Twelve Caesars*, trans. Robert Graves, rev. ed. (1979; repr., London: Penguin Books, 1989), p. 14.

    7. Ibid., p. 28.

    8. Ronald Syme, *The Roman Revolution* (1939; repr., Oxford: Oxford University Press, 2002), p. 2.

    9. Suetonius, *Twelve Caesars*, p. 69.

    10. Tacitus, *Agricola*, ch. 30, in *Agricola* and *Germany*, trans. Anthony R. Birley (Oxford: Oxford University Press, 2009).

    11. Suetonius, *Twelve Caesars*, p. 33.

    12. Ibid., p. 154.

    13. Ibid., p. 158.

    14. Edward Gibbon, *The Decline and Fall of the Roman Empire*, ed. J. B. Bury, vol. 1 (1909; repr., New York: AMS Press, 1974), pp. 85–86.

    15. Peter Green, trans., *Juvenal: The Sixteen Satires*, 3rd ed. (1998; repr., London: Penguin Books, 2004), 10.80–81. References are to satire and line. (Professor Green translates the phrase as "bread and the Games"; in the text I use the more traditional translation, "bread and circuses.")

16. P. G. Walsh, trans., *Pliny the Younger: Complete Letters* (Oxford: Oxford University Press, 2006), 3.5.16. References are to book, letter, and line.

CHAPTER 1: PLAUTUS AND ROMAN COMEDY

1. Plato, *Laws*, 7.816e, trans. Trevor J. Saunders, in *Plato: Complete Works*, ed. John M. Cooper, 4 vols. (Norwalk, CT: Easton Press, 2001), 4:1318.

2. See Terence, *Hecyra*, in *Terence: The Comedies*, trans. Betty Radice (London: Penguin Books, 1976), pp. 293–94.

3. Terence, *The Self-Tormentor*, trans. Palmer Bovie, in *Terence: The Comedies*, ed. Palmer Bovie (Baltimore: Johns Hopkins University Press, 1992), p. 84.

4. See George E. Duckworth, *The Nature of Roman Comedy: A Study in Popular Entertainment*, 2nd ed. (Norman: University of Oklahoma Press, 1994), pp. 103–109.

5. Plautus, *Amphitryo*, in *"The Rope" and Other Plays*, trans. E. F. Watling (London: Penguin Books, 1964), p. 270.

6. Plautus, *Casina*, trans. Richard Beacham, in *Plautus: The Comedies*, ed. David R. Slavitt and Palmer Bovie, vol. 1 (Baltimore: Johns Hopkins University Press, 1995), p. 317.

7. Plutarch, "Marcus Cato," in *Plutarch's Lives*, ed. Arthur Hugh Clough, trans. John Dryden, vol. 1 (New York: Modern Library, 2001), p. 469.

8. Plautus, *A Three-Dollar Day*, in Watling, *"The Rope" and Other Plays*, p. 165.

9. Ibid., p. 176.

10. Ibid., p. 211.

11. Ibid., p. 167.

12. Ibid., pp. 191–92.

13. Ibid., p. 219.

14. Ibid.

15. Ibid.

16. Plautus, *The Pot of Gold*, in *"The Pot of Gold" and Other Plays*, trans. E. F. Watling (London: Penguin Books, 1965), p. 21.

17. Ibid., p. 37.

18. Ibid., p. 38.

19. William Shakespeare, *The Merchant of Venice*, ed. M. M. Mahood (Cambridge: Cambridge University Press, 2003), 2.8.15.

20. Plautus, *The Pot of Gold*, in Watling, *"The Pot of Gold" and Other Plays*, p. 44.

21. Ibid., pp. 48–49.

22. Aristotle, *Poetics*, 1448b26, trans. Ingram Bywater, in *The Complete Works of Aristotle: The Revised Oxford Translation*, ed. Jonathan Barnes, 2 vols. (Princeton, NJ: Princeton University Press, 1984), 2:2316.

23. Plautus, *Amphitryo*, in Watling, *"The Rope" and Other Plays*, p. 230.

24. Ibid.

25. Ibid., p. 245.

26. Ibid., p. 246.

27. Ibid., p. 254.

28. Ibid., p. 255.

29. Ibid., p. 264.

30. Ibid., p. 283.

31. Ibid., p. 272.

32. Plautus, *The Prisoners*, in Watling, *"The Pot of Gold" and Other Plays*, p. 72.

33. Ibid., p. 93.

34. Ibid., p. 59.

35. Ibid., p. 95.

36. Terence, *The Self-Tormentor*, in Radice, *Terence: The Comedies*, p. 102.

37. Plautus, *A Three-Dollar Day*, in Watling, *"The Rope" and Other Plays*, p. 208.

38. Plautus, *Curculio*, trans. Henry Taylor, in Slavitt and Bovie, *Plautus: The Comedies*, vol. 1, p. 350.

39. Plautus, *Two Sisters Named Bacchis*, trans. James Tatum, in Slavitt and Bovie, *Plautus: The Comedies*, vol. 2, p. 163.

40. Plautus, *Curculio*, in Slavitt and Bovie, *Plautus: The Comedies*, vol. 1, p. 362.

41. Plautus, *The Rope*, in Watling, *"The Rope" and Other Plays*, p. 152.

42. Plautus, *The Little Box*, trans. R. H. W. Dillard, in Slavitt and Bovie, *Plautus: The Comedies*, vol. 4, pp. 184–85.

43. Plautus, *Asinaria*, trans. Fred Chappell, in Slavitt and Bovie, *Plautus: The Comedies*, vol. 3, p. 108.

44. Plautus, *Curculio*, in Slavitt and Bovie, *Plautus: The Comedies*, vol. 1, p. 340.

45. Plautus, *Truculentus*, trans. James Tatum, in Slavitt and Bovie, *Plautus: The Comedies*, vol. 2, p. 363.

46. Ibid., p. 336.

47. Plautus, *The Ghost*, in Watling, *"The Rope" and Other Plays*, p. 36.

48. Ibid.

49. Plautus, *A Three-Dollar Day*, in Watling, *"The Rope" and Other Plays*, p. 165.

50. Ibid., p. 166.

51. Plautus, *Casina*, in Slavitt and Bovie, *Plautus: The Comedies*, vol. 1, p. 269.

52. Plautus, *The Brothers Menaechmus*, in Watling, *"The Pot of Gold" and Other Plays*, pp. 131–32.

53. Erich Segal, *Roman Laughter: The Comedy of Plautus*, 2nd ed. (New York: Oxford University Press, 1987), p. 25.

54. Plautus, *Stichus*, trans. Carol Poster, in Slavitt and Bovie, *Plautus: The Comedies*, vol. 4, p. 327.

55. Plautus, *Casina*, in Slavitt and Bovie, *Plautus: The Comedies*, vol. 1, p. 262.

56. Plautus, *Two Sisters Named Bacchis*, in Slavitt and Bovie, *Plautus: The Comedies*, vol. 2, p. 178.

57. Plautus, *The Little Box*, in Slavitt and Bovie, *Plautus: The Comedies*, vol. 4, p. 192.

58. Plautus, *A Three-Dollar Day*, in Watling, *"The Rope" and Other Plays*, p. 193.

59. Plautus, *Two Sisters Named Bacchis*, in Slavitt and Bovie, *Plautus: The Comedies*, vol. 2, p. 188.

60. Dante writes in a direct translation from Plautus's Latin: *"Lasciate ogne speranza, voi*

ch'entrate" ("Abandon all hope, you who enter here."). Dante, *The Divine Comedy: Inferno*, trans. Allen Mandelbaum (New York: Bantam Books, 2004), canto 3.9, p. 20.

61. Plautus, *The Ghost*, in Watling, *"The Rope" and Other Plays*, p. 82.

62. Gian Biagio Conte, *Latin Literature: A History*, trans. Joseph B. Solodow, rev. Don Fowler and Glenn W. Most (Baltimore: Johns Hopkins University Press, 1999), p. 55.

63. Plautus, *The Ghost*, in Watling, *"The Rope" and Other Plays*, p. 58.

64. Plautus, *Epidicus*, trans. Constance Carrier, in Slavitt and Bovie, *Plautus: The Comedies*, vol. 3, p. 262.

65. Plautus, *The Ghost*, in Watling, *"The Rope" and Other Plays*, p. 78.

66. Ibid., p. 77.

67. Ibid., p. 52.

68. See Duckworth, *Nature of Roman Comedy*, pp. 288–91.

69. Plautus, *The Ghost*, in Watling, *"The Rope" and Other Plays*, p. 45.

70. Plautus, *The Swaggering Soldier*, in Watling, *"The Pot of Gold" and Other Plays*, p. 153.

71. Ibid., p. 155.

72. Ibid., p. 154.

73. Ibid., p. 159.

74. Ibid., p. 170.

75. Ibid.

76. Ibid., p. 182.

77. Ibid., p. 161.

78. Ibid., p. 182.

79. Ibid., p. 188.

80. Ibid., p. 177.

81. Ibid., p. 183.

82. Ibid., p. 188.

83. Ibid., p. 201.

84. Ibid., p. 212.

85. William Shakespeare, *Henry IV, Part I*, ed. Maynard Mack and Sylvan Barnet, rev. ed. (New York: New American Library, 1998), 2.5.437–39.

86. Plautus, *The Swaggering Soldier*, in Watling, *"The Pot of Gold" and Other Plays*, p. 212.

87. See Timothy J. Moore, *The Theater of Plautus: Playing to the Audience* (Austin: University of Texas Press, 1998), p. 72: "Plautus discredits theater as a moral teacher by presenting a moralistic misreading of a play-within-the-play."

88. Cicero, *Cato the Elder: On Old Age*, in *Cicero: On the Good Life*, trans. Michael Grant (London: Folio Society, 2003), p. 179.

89. Plautus, *Pseudolus*, in Watling, *"The Pot of Gold" and Other Plays*, p. 225.

90. Ibid., p. 254.

91. Ibid., p. 234.

92. Ibid., p. 237.

93. Ibid., p. 238.

94. Ibid., p. 237.

95. Ibid., p. 221.

96. Ibid., p. 220.

97. Ibid., p. 232.

98. Ibid., p. 233.

99. Ibid., p. 240.

100. Ibid., p. 245.

101. Ibid., p. 268.

102. Ibid., p. 239.

103. Ibid., p. 243.

104. Plautus, *The Rope*, in Watling, *"The Rope" and Other Plays*, p. 97.

105. Ibid., p. 99.

106. Ibid., p. 141.

107. Ibid., p. 139.

108. Ibid., p. 142.

109. Ibid., p. 147.

110. See Moore, *Theater of Plautus*, p. 78.

CHAPTER 2: MARCUS TULLIUS CICERO, THE GOOD CITIZEN

1. Quoted in Cicero, *On the Commonwealth*, 5.1, in *On the Commonwealth* and *On the Laws*, ed. James E. G. Zetzel (Cambridge: Cambridge University Press, 1999).

2. Michael Grant, trans., *Cicero: Selected Political Speeches* (1969; repr., London: Penguin Books, 1989), p. 159.

3. See Plutarch, "Cicero," in *Plutarch's Lives*, ed. Arthur Hugh Clough, trans. John Dryden, vol. 2 (New York: Modern Library, 2001), p. 423.

4. Peter Whigham, trans., *Catullus: The Poems* (1966; repr., London: Penguin Books, 2004), poem 49, p. 108.

5. See Plutarch, "Caesar," in Clough, *Plutarch's Lives*, vol. 2, p. 206. In text, I use the common translation of Caesar's words rather than the Dryden translation, which reads, "I wished my wife to be not so much as suspected."

6. P. G. Walsh, trans., *Cicero: Selected Letters* (New York: Oxford University Press, 2008), letter 29.5, p. 66.

7. Ibid., letter 19.2, p. 49.

8. Plutarch, "Cicero," in Clough, *Plutarch's Lives*, vol. 2, p. 412.

9. Tacitus, *A Dialogue on Oratory*, sec. 21, quoted in Anthony Everitt, *Cicero: The Life and Times of Rome's Greatest Politician* (New York: Random House, 2003), p. 34.

10. Cicero, *The Republic*, 1.13, in *The Republic* and *The Laws*, trans. Niall Rudd (Oxford: Oxford University Press, 2008).

11. Ibid., 1.12.

12. Ibid., 1.1.

13. Ibid., 1.2.

14. Ibid., 1.8.

15. Ibid.

16. Ibid., 1.27.

17. Ibid., 1.27–28.

18. Cicero, *On the Commonwealth*, 1.1.

19. Cicero, *Republic*, 1.39.

20. Declaration of Independence (U.S. 1776), par. 2: "We hold these truths to be self-evident, that all men are created equal, that they are endowed by their Creator with certain unalienable Rights, that among these are Life, Liberty, and the pursuit of Happiness."

21. Cicero, *Republic*, 2.69.

22. Walsh, *Cicero: Selected Letters*, letter 17.8, p. 44.

23. Cicero, *Republic*, 1.70.

24. Ibid., 4.1.

25. Ibid., 2.30.

26. Ibid., 2.2.

27. Ibid., 3.41.

28. Ibid., 5.2.

29. Ibid., 3.33.

30. Cicero, *The Laws*, 1.17, in Rudd, *The Republic* and *The Laws*.

31. Ibid., 2.11.

32. Ibid., 1.57.

33. Ibid., 2.39.

34. Quoted in Neal Wood, *Cicero's Social and Political Thought* (Berkeley: University of California Press, 1988), p. 131.

35. Cicero, *Laws*, 2.11.

36. Ibid., 3.44.

37. Cicero, *Republic*, 1.49.

38. Ibid., 3.33.

39. Ibid.

40. Cicero, *Laws*, 1.28.

41. Ibid., 1.25.

42. Cicero, *On Moral Ends*, ed. Julia Annas, trans. Raphael Woolf (Cambridge: Cambridge University Press, 2001), 3.67.

43. Cicero, *Laws*, 1.33.

44. *Southern Pac. Co. v. Jensen*, 244 U.S. 205, 222 (1917) (Holmes, J., dissenting).

45. Quoted in *Cicero: On the Good Life*, trans. Michael Grant (London: Folio Society, 2003), p. xvi.

46. Cicero, *On Duties*, ed. Miriam T. Griffin and E. M. Atkins (Cambridge: Cambridge University Press, 1991), 1.4.

47. Ibid., 2.7.

48. Ibid., 1.15.

49. Ibid.

50. Ibid., 1.20.

51. Ibid., 1.15.

52. Ibid., 1.26.

53. Ibid., 1.53.

54. Ibid.

55. Ibid., 1.54–55.

56. Ibid., 1.54.

57. Ibid.

58. Ibid., 1.57.

59. Lionel Trilling, *Sincerity and Authenticity* (London: Oxford University Press, 1972), p. 3.

60. William Shakespeare, *Hamlet*, ed. T. J. B. Spencer, in *Four Tragedies* (London: Penguin Books, 1994), 1.3.78–80, p. 109.

61. Cicero, *On Duties*, 1.111.

62. Friedrich Nietzsche, *Thus Spoke Zarathustra*, in *The Portable Nietzsche*, trans. Walter Kaufmann (New York: Viking Press, 1968), p. 351.

63. Cicero, *On Duties*, 1.117.

64. Ibid., 1.119. Compare Friedrich Nietzsche, *The Gay Science*, trans. Walter Kaufmann (New York: Vintage Books, 1974), sec. 143, p. 191: each individual must "posit his own ideal and . . . derive from it his own law, joys, and rights."

65. Cicero, *On Moral Ends*, 2.86.

66. Cicero, *Discussions at Tusculum (V)*, in Grant, *On the Good Life*, p. 10.

67. Cicero, *On Duties*, 1.90.

68. Eugene O'Connor, trans., *The Essential Epicurus: Letters, Principal Doctrines, Vatican Sayings, and Fragments* (Amherst, NY: Prometheus Books, 1993), Vatican Saying 58, p. 83.

69. Cicero, *On Moral Ends*, 2.44.

70. Ibid., 1.24.

71. Ibid., 2.45.

72. Ibid., 2.59.

73. Ibid., 2.85.

74. Cicero, *Discussions at Tusculum*, in Grant, *On the Good Life*, p. 6.

75. Ibid., pp. 6–7.

76. Ibid., p. 7.

77. Ibid.

78. Ibid., p. 21.

79. Ibid., p. 25.

80. Ibid., p. 15.

81. Cicero, *On Moral Ends*, 4.68.

82. Ibid., 4.36.

83. Cicero, *Laelius: On Friendship*, in Grant, *On the Good Life*, p. 209.

84. Walsh, *Cicero: Selected Letters*, letter 14.1, p. 33.

85. Cicero, *On Friendship*, in Grant, *On the Good Life*, p. 206.

86. Ibid., p. 242.

87. Ibid., p. 230.

88. Ibid., p. 212.

89. Ibid., p. 206.

90. Ibid., p. 208.

91. Ibid., p. 238.

92. Ibid., p. 229.

93. Ibid., p. 236.

94. Cicero, *Cato the Elder: On Old Age*, in Grant, *On the Good Life*, p. 165.

95. Ibid.

96. Cicero, *On Duties*, 1.123.

97. Cicero, *On Old Age*, in Grant, *On the Good Life*, p. 163.

98. Ibid., p. 175.

99. Ibid., p. 173.

100. Ibid.

101. Ibid., p. 184.

102. Ibid., p. 174.

103. Ibid.

104. Ibid., p. 176.

105. Ibid., p. 193.

106. Ibid., p. 186.

107. Ibid., p. 194.

108. Ibid., p. 193.

109. Cicero, *On the Orator (I)*, in Grant, *On the Good Life*, p. 251.

110. Walsh, *Cicero: Selected Letters*, letter 154,1, p. 253.

111. Cicero, "The Second Philippic Against Antony," in *Cicero: Selected Works*, trans. Michael Grant (Baltimore: Penguin Books, 1960), p. 152.

112. Pliny the Elder, *Natural History: A Selection*, trans. John F. Healy (1991; repr., London: Penguin Books, 2004), 7.117.

113. Cicero, *On the Orator*, in Grant, *On the Good Life*, p. 290.

CHAPTER 3: LUCRETIUS AND THE POETRY OF NATURE

1. Despite the dramatic story, the modern text of *De Rerum Natura* is based on two ninth-century manuscripts rather than on the manuscript rediscovered by Bracciolini.

2. Michel de Montaigne, *Essays*, ed. William C. Hazlitt, trans. Charles Cotton, vol. 3 (London: Reeves & Turner, 1902), p. 52.

3. George Santayana, *Three Philosophical Poets* (Garden City, NY: Doubleday Anchor Books, 1953), p. 38.

4. Eugene O'Connor, trans., *The Essential Epicurus: Letters Principal Doctrines, Vatican Sayings, and Fragments* (Amherst, NY: Prometheus Books, 1993), fragment 54, p. 97.

5. Ibid., letter to Pythocles 104, p. 52.

6. Anthony Gottlieb, *The Dream of Reason: A History of Philosophy from the Greeks to the Renaissance* (New York: W. W. Norton, 2000), p. 101.

7. Russel M. Geer, trans., *Epicurus: Letters, Principal Doctrines, and Vatican Sayings* (Indianapolis: Bobbs-Merrill, 1964), letter to Menoeceus 134, p. 58.

8. O'Connor, *Essential Epicurus*, letter to Menoeceus 123, p. 62.

9. Ibid., letter to Herodotus 67, pp. 33–34.

10. Ibid., letter to Herodotus 66, p. 33.

11. Ibid., letter to Menoeceus 124, p. 63.

12. Ibid., letter to Menoeceus 125, p. 63.

13. Ibid., letter to Menoeceus 128, p. 65.

14. Ibid., fragment 10, pp. 89–90.

15. Ibid., Vatican Saying 68, p. 84.

16. Ibid., fragment 48, pp. 96–97.

17. Ibid., letter to Menoeceus 128, pp. 64–65.

18. Ibid., Vatican Saying 58, p. 83.

19. Ibid., Principal Doctrine 21, p. 72.

20. Ibid., letter to Menoeceus 132, p. 67.

21. Ibid., letter to Menoeceus 135, p. 68.

22. Ibid., Principal Doctrine 27, p. 73.

23. Ibid., Vatican Saying 28, p. 79.

24. Ibid., fragment 86, p. 101.

25. Lucretius, *On the Nature of the Universe*, trans. R. E. Latham (1994; repr., London: Penguin Books, 2005), 1.38–43.

26. Ibid., 1.141–44.

27. See Joseph Farrell, "Lucretian Architecture: The Structure and Argument of the *De Rerum Natura*," in *The Cambridge Companion to Lucretius*, ed. Stuart Gillespie and Philip Hardie (New York: Cambridge University Press, 2007), p. 76.

28. Lucretius, *On the Nature of the Universe*, 3.3, 3.322.

29. Ibid., 5.46–49.

30. Ibid., 1.71.

31. Ibid., 1.67–68.

32. Ibid., 6.14–16.

33. Ibid., 6.23–24.

34. Ibid., 1.1–3, 1.22–23.

35. Ibid., 1.7–20.

36. Ibid., 1.23–24.

37. Ibid., 1.731–33.

38. Ibid., 4.14–15, 4.19.

39. Ibid., 2.655–59.

40. Ibid., 2.1030–36.

41. Ibid., 1.157–58.

42. Ibid., 1.151.

43. Ibid., 1.216.

44. Ibid., 2.752.

45. In his poem, Lucretius does not use any direct Latin equivalent of the Greek word *atomos*, but instead adopts various locutions, such as "the seeds of things," that embody the same idea.

46. Ibid., 1.483.

47. Ibid., 1.822–27.

48. Ibid., 1.958.

49. Ibid., 1.1001–1005.

50. Ibid., 1.1017–20.

51. Ibid., 1.458–60.

52. Ibid., 2.1052–58.

53. Ibid., 5.243–44.

54. Ibid., 1.313.

55. Ibid., 2.72–73.

56. Ibid., 2.73–76.

57. Santayana, *Three Philosophical Poets*, pp. 28, 40.

58. Lucretius, *On the Nature of the Universe*, 2.253–54.

59. Ibid., 2.259–60.

60. Marcus Aurelius, *Meditations*, trans. Maxwell Staniforth (London: Folio Society, 2002), 4.3.

61. Lucretius, *On the Nature of the Universe*, 1.1021–23.

62. Ibid., 2.169.

63. Ibid., 1.98.

64. Ibid., 5.1194–1203.

65. Ibid., 3.138–42.

66. Ibid., 3.800–802.

67. Ibid., 3.335–36.

68. Ibid., 3.445–46.

69. Ibid., 3.446–53.

70. Ibid., 3.841–42.

71. Ibid., 3.870–71.

72. Ibid., 3.886–87.

73. Wallace Stevens, "Sunday Morning," quoted in Martha C. Nussbaum, *The Therapy of Desire: Theory and Practice in Hellenistic Ethics* (Princeton, NJ: Princeton University Press, 1994), p. 230.

74. Lucretius, *On the Nature of the Universe*, 3.1088–90.

75. Ibid., 3.978–79.

76. Ibid., 3.1019–20.

77. Ibid., 3.1000.

78. Ibid., 3.993–94.

79. Ibid., 3.1005–1009.

80. Ibid., 3.1060–67.

81. Ibid., 3.1074–75.

82. Ibid., 3.1082–85. Plato develops a similar portrait of a life "always on the gasp" in book 7 of the *Republic*. See Plato, *Republic*, 561c–d, trans. G. M. A. Grube, rev. C. D. C. Reeve, in *Plato: Complete Works*, ed. John M. Cooper, 4 vols. (Norwalk, CT: Easton Press, 2001), 3:971.

83. *Essays of Arthur Schopenhauer* (New York: Walter J. Black, 1932), p. 305.

84. Lucretius, *On the Nature of the Universe*, 5.953–65.

85. Ibid., 5.1011–12.

86. Ibid., 5.1022–23.

87. Ibid., 5.1023–27.

88. See, for example, Martin A. Nowak and Roger Highfield, *The SuperCooperators* (New York: Free Press, 2011).

89. Lucretius, *On the Nature of the Universe*, 5.1144–47.

90. Ibid., 5.1447–56.

91. Ibid., 5.1305–1307.

92. Ibid., 5.1128–30.

93. Ibid., 5.1130–31.

94. Ibid., 4.1059–60.

95. Ibid., 4.1081–83.

96. Plato, *Symposium*, 191a, trans. Alexander Nehamas and Paul Woodruff, in Cooper, *Plato: Complete Works*, 2:457.

97. Lucretius, *On the Nature of the Universe*, 4.1111–13.

98. Ibid., 4.1076–77.

99. Peter Whigham, trans., *Catullus: The Poems* (1966; repr., London: Penguin Books, 2004), poem 51, p. 110.

100. Ibid., poem 70, p. 182.

101. Ibid., poem 85, p. 197.

102. Ibid., poem 75, p. 187.

103. Ibid., poem 76, p. 188.

104. Lucretius, *On the Nature of the Universe*, 4.1070–73.

105. Ibid., 4.1074–76.

106. Ibid., 4.1283.

107. Ibid., 4.1233–35.

108. Whigham, *Catullus: The Poems*, poem 109, p. 221.

109. Lucretius, *On the Nature of the Universe*, 2.7–13.

110. Ibid., 2.16–17.

CHAPTER 4: VIRGIL—POET OF SHADOWS

1. L. P. Wilkinson, *The Georgics of Virgil: A Critical Survey* (New York: Cambridge University Press, 1978), p. 21.

2. Elaine Fantham, *Roman Literary Culture: From Cicero to Apuleius* (Baltimore: Johns Hopkins University Press, 1999), p. 63.

3. David Ferry, trans., *The Georgics of Virgil* (New York: Farrar, Straus and Giroux, 2005), p. xvi. See also Adam Parry, "The Idea of Art in Virgil's *Georgics*," in *Virgil*, ed. Harold Bloom (New York: Chelsea House, 1986), p. 86 ("The *Georgics* may well contain the finest expression of Virgil's poetic art."); W. R. Johnson, "The Broken World: Virgil and His Augustus," in Bloom, *Virgil*, p. 174 ("The *Georgics* is Virgil's masterpiece, not only technically but also emotionally and intellectually.").

4. David Ferry, trans., *The Eclogues of Virgil* (New York: Farrar, Straus and Giroux, 1999), Eclogue 4, p. 29.

5. Theocritus, *Idylls*, trans. Anthony Verity (New York: Oxford University Press, 2002), 1.1–2, 1.64.

6. Ferry, *Eclogues of Virgil*, Eclogue 6, p. 45.

7. Paul Alpers, *What Is Pastoral?* (Chicago: University of Chicago Press, 1997), p. 51.

8. Ferry, *Eclogues of Virgil*, Eclogue 7, p. 57.

9. Bruno Snell, "Arcadia: The Discovery of a Spiritual Landscape," in *The Discovery of the Mind*, trans. T. G. Rosenmeyer (New York: Dover Publications, 1982), p. 284.

10. Ibid., p. 308.

11. Ferry, *Eclogues of Virgil*, Eclogue 5, p. 39.

12. John Milton, "Lycidas," ll. 1–14, in *The Portable Milton*, ed. Douglas Bush (New York: Viking Press, 1949), pp. 107–108.

13. Samuel Johnson, *Life of Milton* (London: George Bell & Sons, 1894), pp. 55–56.

14. Ferry, *Eclogues of Virgil*, Eclogue 1, p. 7.

15. Ibid., p. 9.

16. Ibid., Eclogue 9, p. 71.

17. See Alpers, *What Is Pastoral?* p. 24.

18. Ferry, *Eclogues of Virgil*, Eclogue 9, p. 71.

19. Ibid., p. 75.

20. Ibid., Eclogue 3, p. 27.

21. Ibid., Eclogue 10, p. 85.

22. Ibid., pp. 82–83 (my translation).

23. Virgil, *Georgics*, 1.145–46, in *Eclogues; Georgics; Aeneid 1–6*, trans. H. R. Fairclough, rev. G. P. Goold (Cambridge, MA: Harvard University Press, 1999) (my translation).

24. Ferry, *Georgics of Virgil*, first Georgic, p. 41. Bernard Knox, working with partisans in Italy during World War II, came across a volume of Virgil in a bombed-out house. Following the tradition of the *Sortes Virgilianae*—by which the book is opened at random and whatever passage one happens upon becomes an oracle—he opened it to the passage quoted in text and resolved, if he survived the war, to become a classics scholar. Virgil, *Aeneid*, trans. Robert Fagles (New York: Penguin Books, 2010), pp. 40–41.

25. Ferry, *Georgics of Virgil*, first Georgic, p. 41.

26. Ibid., second Georgic, pp. 83–85.

27. Ibid., first Georgic, p. 3.

28. For a discussion of Hesiod, see Michael K. Kellogg, *The Greek Search for Wisdom* (Amherst, NY: Prometheus Books, 2012), pp. 51–72.

29. Ferry, *Georgics of Virgil*, third Georgic, p. 93.

30. Ibid., second Georgic, p. 87.

31. Ibid., p. 85.

32. Ibid.

33. Ibid., first Georgic, pp. 11–13. Compare Hesiod, *Works and Days*, ll. 118–19, in *Theogony; Works and Days; Shield*, trans. Apostolos N. Athanassakis, 2nd ed. (Baltimore: Johns Hopkins University Press, 2004) ("the barley-giving earth asked for no toil to bring forth / a rich and plentiful harvest").

34. Ferry, *Georgics of Virgil*, first Georgic, p. 11.

35. Ibid., p. 13.

36. David R. Slavitt, *Virgil* (New Haven, CT: Yale University Press, 1991), p. 59.

37. Ibid., p. 56.

38. Ferry, *Georgics of Virgil*, first Georgic, p. 15.

39. Ibid., p. 9.

40. Ibid., second Georgic, p. 87.

41. Ibid., first Georgic, pp. 15–17.

42. Ibid., p. 7.

43. Ibid., second Georgic, p. 49.

44. Ibid., p. 87.

45. Ibid., p. 79.

46. Ibid., p. 59.

47. Ibid., p. 73.

48. Ibid.

49. Ibid., first Georgic, pp. 17–19.

50. Ibid., pp. 31, 37.

51. Ibid., third Georgic, p. 113.

52. James Boswell, *Life of Johnson*, ed. George Birkbeck Hill, vol. 2 (New York: Harper & Brothers, 1891), p. 148.

53. Ferry, *Georgics of Virgil*, third Georgic, pp. 97–99.

54. Ibid., p. 133.

55. Ibid., p. 99.

56. Ibid., second Georgic, p. 89.

57. Ibid., fourth Georgic, p. 179.

58. Ibid., p. 177.

59. Ibid., pp. 179–81.

60. Parry, "The Idea of Art in Virgil's *Georgics*," in Bloom, *Virgil*, p. 87.

61. Ferry, *Georgics of Virgil*, second Georgic, p. 81.

62. Virgil, *Aeneid*, 1.1, in Fairclough, *Eclogues; Georgics; Aeneid 1–6*.

63. Virgil, *Aeneid*, l.342–43 (Fagles translation).

64. Adam Parry, "The Two Voices of Virgil's *Aeneid*," in Bloom, *Virgil*, p. 51.

65. See C. S. Lewis, "Virgil and the Subject of Secondary Epic," in *Virgil: A Collection of Critical Essays*, ed. Steele Commager (Englewood Cliffs, NJ: Prentice-Hall, 1966), pp. 65–66.

66. Virgil, *Aeneid*, 1.113–17 (Fagles translation).

67. Ibid., 2.445.

68. Ibid., 2.343–45.

69. Ibid., 2.789.

70. Ibid., 2.915–19.

71. Ibid., 2.920.

72. Ibid., 2.971–72.

73. Ibid., 2.977.

74. Ibid., 2.979.

75. Ibid., 2.983–86.

76. Ibid., 1.4.

77. Ibid., 3.819–20.

78. Ibid., 1.245–46.

79. Ibid., 1.239.

80. Ibid., 7.365.

81. Ibid., 4.555–62.

82. Ibid., 2.881–82.

83. Ibid., 1.545–46.

84. Ibid., 1.862–63.

85. Ibid., 4.4–7.

86. Ibid., 4.68–69.

87. Ibid., 4.101–102.

88. Ibid., 4.207–18.

89. Virgil, *Aeneid*, 4.361 (Fairclough translation).

90. Virgil, *Aeneid*, 4.498 (Fagles translation).

91. Ibid., 4.552–65.

92. Ibid., 4.623.

93. Ibid., 4.771–84.

94. Ibid., 4.797–803.

95. Ibid., 5.681, 702.

96. Ibid., 5.694.

97. Ibid., 5.792, 834.

98. Ibid., 6.103–104.

99. Ibid., 6.151–52.

100. Ibid., 6.162–77.

101. Charles Martindale, ed., *The Cambridge Companion to Virgil* (New York: Cambridge University Press, 1997), p. 1.

102. Parry, "The Two Voices of Virgil's *Aeneid*," in Bloom, *Virgil*, p. 51.

103. Robert A. Brooks, "*Discolor Aura*: Reflections on the Golden Bough," in Commager, *Virgil: A Collection of Critical Essays*, p. 157.

104. Virgil, *Aeneid*, 6.305–306 (Fagles translation).

105. The Sibyl despairs of describing the full horrors of Tartarus: "No, not if I had a hundred tongues and a hundred mouths and a voice of iron too—I could never capture all the crimes or run through all the torments, doom by doom." Ibid., 6.724–27. That is exactly the task undertaken by Dante in his *Inferno*.

106. Ibid., 6.349–55.

107. Ibid., 6.543–51.

108. Ibid., 6.885–86.

109. Ibid., 6.976–84.

110. Ibid., 6.1033.

111. Ibid., 7.48–49.

112. Ibid., 7.106–109.

113. Ibid., 7.695–96.

114. Ibid., 8.632–38.

115. Ibid., 8.857–58.

116. Ibid., 10.593–94.

117. Ibid., 10.970–80.

118. Ibid., 10.1076–77.

119. Ibid., 11.189.

120. Ibid., 12.969–71.

121. Ibid., 12.1102–13.

122. Wendell Clausen, "An Interpretation of the *Aeneid*," in Commager, *Virgil: A Collection of Critical Essays*, p. 86.

123. Erich Auerbach, *Mimesis: The Representation of Reality in Western Literature* (Princeton, NJ: Princeton University Press, 1973), p. 6.

CHAPTER 5: HORACE—ODES TO A POET

1. Letter from D. S. Carne-Ross to David Ferry, quoted in *The Odes of Horace*, trans. David Ferry (New York: Farrar, Straus and Giroux, 1998), p. ix.

2. See Horace, *Satires*, 1.6.71–81, in *Satires* and *Epistles*, trans. Niall Rudd, rev. ed. (London: Penguin Books, 2005).

3. Ferry, *Odes of Horace*, 2.7.

4. Reprinted in David West, trans., *Horace: The Complete Odes and Epodes* (New York: Oxford University Press, 2008), pp. xxiv–xxvi.

5. Horace, *Satires*, 2.6.1–5.

6. Edith Hamilton, *The Roman Way to Western Civilization* (New York: New American Library, 1957), p. 95.

7. David Ferry, trans., *The Epistles of Horace* (New York: Farrar, Straus and Giroux, 2001), Epistle 2.1, p. 129.

8. Horace, satire 2.1, quoted in Hamilton, *Roman Way*, p. 89.

9. Ferry, *Epistles of Horace*, Epistle 2.2, p. 143.

10. Ibid., Epistle 2.3 (*Ars Poetica*), p. 169.

11. Ferry, *Odes of Horace*, 3.19.

12. Gian Biagio Conte, *Latin Literature: A History*, trans. Joseph B. Solodow, rev. Don Fowler and Glenn W. Most (Baltimore: Johns Hopkins University Press, 1999), p. 299.

13. Horace, *Satires*, 1.4.42.

14. Ibid., 1.1.25.

15. Ibid., 1.1.62.

16. Ibid., 1.1.49–50.

17. Ibid., 1.1.119.

18. Ibid., 1.2.119–21.

19. Ibid., 1.2.127–31.

20. Ibid., 1.6.129–30.

21. Ibid., 2.3.267–71.

22. Ibid., 2.7.93–94.

23. Horace, *Epodes*, 7.17–20, in West, *Complete Odes and Epodes*.

24. Ibid., 16.1–2.

25. Ibid., 2.69–70.

26. Ibid., 13.3–8.

27. David Armstrong, *Horace* (New Haven, CT: Yale University Press, 1989), p. 68.

28. C. M. Bowra, "The Odes of Horace," in *The Golden Horizon*, ed. Cyril Connolly (New York: University Books, 1955), p. 454.

29. Friedrich Nietzsche, *Twilight of the Idols*, in *The Portable Nietzsche*, trans. Walter Kaufmann (New York: Viking Press, 1968), "What I Owe to the Ancients," sec. 1, p. 556.

30. See, for example, "Quintus Horatius Flaccus—*Carmina*: Liber I, IX," LAITS Digital Audio, University of Texas at Austin, last updated September 5, 2006, http://www.laits.utexas.edu/itsaud/series.php?series_name=cc-6-02 (accessed February 1, 2014).

31. Ferry, *Odes of Horace*, 1.9.

32. In preparing this translation I was aided by *Horace Fully Parsed Word by Word* (Wauconda, IL: Bolchazy-Carducci Publishers, 2003), edited by LeaAnn A. Osburn, and by the literal prose translation of Steele Commager in *The Odes of Horace: A Critical Study* (New Haven, CT: Yale University Press, 1962), p. 270.

33. Patrick Leigh Fermor, *A Time of Gifts* (New York: New York Review Books, 2005), quoted in West, *Complete Odes and Epodes*, p. vii.

34. Andrew M. Miller, trans., *Greek Lyric: An Anthology in Translation* (Indianapolis, IN: Hackett, 1996), pp. 47–48.

35. Paul Fussell, *Samuel Johnson and the Life of Writing* (New York: W. W. Norton, 1986), pp. 47–48.

36. Steele Commager, *The Odes of Horace: A Critical Study* (New Haven, CT: Yale University Press, 1962), pp. vii–viii.

37. Ferry, *Odes of Horace*, 2.3.

38. Ibid., 2.13.

39. Ibid., 1.11.

40. Ibid., 2.10.

41. Rudyard Kipling, "If—," in *The Collected Poems of Rudyard Kipling* (Ware, UK: Wordsworth Editions, 1994), p. 605.

42. Ferry, *Odes of Horace*, 2.16.

43. Ibid., 3.1.

44. Ibid., 2.2.

45. Ibid., 2.11.

46. Ibid., 2.14.

47. Ibid., 3.8.

48. Ibid., 2.16.

49. Ibid., 1.36.

50. Ibid., 2.3.

51. Donald M. Frame, trans., *The Complete Essays of Montaigne* (Stanford, CA: Stanford University Press, 1976), p. 857.

52. Ibid.

53. Ferry, *Odes of Horace*, 3.16.

54. Ibid., 2.10.

55. Ibid., 3.28.

56. Ibid., 3.8.

57. Ibid., 1.32.

58. Ibid., 1.7.

59. Ibid., 1.1.

60. Ibid., 3.21.

61. Ibid., 2.8.

62. Ibid., 1.19.

63. Ibid., 1.13.

64. Ibid., 1.5.

65. Ibid.

66. Ibid., 4.12.

67. Ibid., 4.13.

68. Ibid., 3.26.

69. Ibid., 1.4.

70. Ibid., 4.11.

71. Ibid., 4.1.

72. Ibid., 1.34.

73. David West, *Reading Horace* (Edinburgh: Edinburgh University Press, 1967), p. 78.

74. Ferry, *Odes of Horace*, 1.1.

75. Ibid.

76. Ibid., 4.9.

77. Ibid., 3.30.

78. Ferry, *Epistles of Horace*, Epistle 1.1, p. 3.

79. Ibid., p. 11.

80. Ibid., p. 3.

81. Ibid., Epistle 1.18, p. 89.

82. Ibid., p. 95.

83. Ibid., Epistle 2.1, p. 129.

84. Ibid., Epistle 1.7, p. 37.

85. Ferry, *Odes of Horace*, 1.35.

86. Ferry, *Epistles of Horace*, Epistle 1.17, p. 83.

87. Ibid., p. 85.

88. Ferry, *Odes of Horace*, 4.8.

89. Ferry, *Epistles of Horace*, Epistle 1.7, p. 37.

90. Ibid.

91. Hamilton, *Roman Way*, p. 89.

92. Ferry, *Odes of Horace*, 2.17.

93. Ibid., 1.6.

94. Ibid., 2.1.

95. Ibid., 1.37.

96. Ibid.

97. Ibid.

98. Ibid., 3.14.

99. Ibid., 3.5.

100. Ibid.

101. Ferry, *Epistles of Horace*, Epistle 2.1, p. 111.

102. Ibid., p. 123.

103. Ferry, *Odes of Horace*, 4.9.

104. Ferry, *Epistles of Horace*, Epistle 2.3 (*Ars Poetica*), p. 173.

105. Ibid., Epistle 1.3, p. 19.

106. Ibid., Epistle 2.3 (*Ars Poetica*), pp. 173–75.

107. Ibid., p. 153.

108. Ibid.

109. Ibid., p. 151.

110. Ibid., p. 153.

111. Ibid., p. 157.

112. Ibid.

113. Ibid.

114. Ibid., p. 159.

115. Ibid.

116. Ibid., p. 161.

117. Ibid., pp. 162–63.

118. Ibid., pp. 161–63.

119. Ibid., p. 163.

120. Ibid., p. 165.

121. Ibid.

122. Ibid., p. 163.

123. Ibid., Epistle 1.2, p. 15.

124. Ibid., p. 13.

125. Ibid., Epistle 2.3 (*Ars Poetica*), p. 181.

126. Ferry, *Odes of Horace*, 2.2.

127. Ferry, *Epistles of Horace*, Epistle 1.2, p. 15.

128. Ferry, *Odes of Horace*, 4.2.

129. Ferry, *Epistles of Horace*, Epistle 2.2, p. 143.

130. Ibid., Epistle 2.3 (*Ars Poetica*), pp. 176–77.

131. Ibid., Epistle 2.2, p. 141.

132. Ibid., Epistle 2.1, p. 119.

133. Ibid., Epistle 2.2, p. 141.

134. Ibid., Epistle 2.3 (*Ars Poetica*), p. 179.

135. Ibid., p. 181.

136. Ibid., Epistle 2.2, p. 141.

137. Ibid., Epistle 2.3 (*Ars Poetica*), pp. 183–85.

138. Ibid., p. 185.

139. Ibid., Epistle 2.1, p. 113.

140. Ibid., p. 115.

141. Ibid., p. 117.

142. Ibid., Epistle 1.4, p. 23.

143. Ferry, *Odes of Horace*, 4.7.

144. Ibid., 1.24.

145. Ferry, *Epistles of Horace*, Epistle 2.2, p. 137.

146. Horace, *Odes*, 3.29.

CHAPTER 6: OVID—POET OF LOVE AND CHANGE

1. Ovid, *Tristia*, 4.10.21–22, in *The Poems of Exile*, trans. Peter Green (Berkeley: University of California Press, 2005).

2. Ibid., 4.10.38.

3. Ibid., 4.10.51.

4. Ovid, *Black Sea Letters*, 4.2.33–34, in Green, *Poems of Exile*.

5. Ovid, *Tristia*, 4.10.131.

6. Ibid., 4.10.70.

7. Ibid., 4.10.60–61.

8. Ibid., 4.10.71.

9. Ibid., 4.10.71–72.

10. Ibid., 4.10.72–74.

11. Ovid, *Amores*, 2.4.44–48, in *The Erotic Poems*, trans. Peter Green (London: Penguin Books, 1982).

12. Ovid, *Tristia*, 2.353–56.

13. A. M. Juster, trans., *Tibullus: Elegies* (New York: Oxford University Press, 2012), 2.3.86.

14. Guy Lee, trans., *Propertius: The Poems* (Oxford: Oxford University Press, 1999), 1.12.19–20.

15. Ibid., 2.2.5.

16. Ibid., 2.2.5–6.

17. Ibid., 2.8.40.

18. Ovid, *Tristia*, 4.10.54.

19. Quoted in Lionel Trilling, *Sincerity and Authenticity* (London: Oxford University Press, 1974), p. 70.

20. Ovid, *Amores*, 2.1.8.

21. Ibid., 1.1.1–4.

22. Ibid., 1.1.27.

23. Ibid., 1.2.7–8.

24. Ibid., 1.2.31–32.
25. Ibid., 1.3.6, 13.
26. Ibid., 1.3.15.
27. Ibid., 1.4.17–20.
28. Ibid., 2.5.16–20.
29. Ibid., 1.5.9–10.
30. Ibid., 1.6.
31. Ibid., 1.7.21–22.
32. Ibid., 1.8.
33. Ibid., 1.9.27–28.
34. Ibid., 1.10.
35. Ibid., 1.11.
36. Ibid., 1.12.7–9.
37. Ibid., 1.13.5–8.
38. Ibid., 1.14.
39. Ibid., 2.13.5–6.
40. Ibid., 3.7.26–27, 37–38.
41. Ibid., 2.1.29–34.
42. Ibid., 2.4.8–9.
43. Ibid., 2.10.25.
44. Ibid., 2.10.21–23.
45. Ibid., 2.12.2–4.
46. Ibid., 2.19.
47. Ibid., 3.4.31–32.
48. Ibid., 3.4.6.
49. Ibid., 3.4.37–39.
50. Ibid., 2.7.24–28.
51. Ibid., 3.14.1–6.
52. Ibid., 3.14.49–50.
53. Ibid., 2.5.55–56.
54. Ibid., 3.11B.1–2.
55. Ibid., 2.9B.2.
56. Ibid., 2.10.29, 36.
57. Ibid., 3.15.19.
58. Ovid, *Heroides*, trans. Harold Isbell (London: Penguin Books, 2004), letter 6, p. 50.
59. Ibid.
60. Ibid., p. 53.
61. Ibid., letter 12, p. 109.
62. Ibid., p. 110.
63. Ibid., p. 113.
64. Ibid., letter 2, p. 13.
65. Ibid., letter 1, p. 3.
66. Ibid.

67. Ibid.

68. Ibid., p. 5.

69. John Milton, "When I Consider How My Light Is Spent," in *The Portable Milton*, ed. Douglas Bush (New York: Viking Press, 1949), p. 223.

70. Ovid, *Heroides*, letter 1, p. 6.

71. Ibid., letter 13, p. 122.

72. Ibid., letter 3, p. 22.

73. Ibid., letter 4, p. 34.

74. Ibid.

75. Ibid., letter 15, p. 134.

76. Ibid., letter 15, p. 140.

77. Ovid, *Art of Love*, 1.2, in Green, *Erotic Poems*.

78. Ibid., 1.17.

79. Ibid., 1.30.

80. See Ovid, *Amores*, 1.8.

81. Sara Mack, *Ovid* (New Haven, CT: Yale University Press, 1988), p. 90.

82. Ovid, *Art of Love*, 1.126.

83. Ibid., 1.229–32.

84. Ibid., 1.269–70.

85. Ibid., 1.275–76.

86. Ibid., 1.342–43.

87. Ibid., 1.358–59, 365–67.

88. Ibid., 1.385–86.

89. Ibid., 1.453–55.

90. Ibid., 1.468.

91. Ibid., 1.478–79.

92. Ibid., 1.611–14.

93. Ibid., 1.645–46.

94. Ibid., 1.673–79.

95. Ibid., 1.756–57.

96. Ibid., 2.662.

97. Ibid., 2.151–53.

98. Ibid., 2.351–52.

99. Ibid., 2.445.

100. Ibid., 2.453–54.

101. Ibid., 2.725–28.

102. Ibid., 3.291.

103. Ibid., 3.754.

104. Ibid., 3.802–804.

105. Ibid., 3.61–64.

106. Ovid, *Metamorphoses*, trans. Charles Martin (New York: W. W. Norton, 2005), 1.5.

107. Gian Biagio Conte, *Latin Literature: A History*, trans. Joseph B. Solodow, rev. Don Fowler and Glenn W. Most (Baltimore: Johns Hopkins University Press, 1999), p. 354.

108. Brooks Otis, *Ovid as an Epic Poet* (Cambridge: Cambridge University Press, 1966), p. 345.
109. Ovid, *Metamorphoses*, 1.26–29.
110. Ibid., 1.64, 99–100.
111. Ibid., 1.108–17.
112. Ibid., 1.142–43.
113. Ibid., 1.174–77.
114. Ibid., 1.240–42.
115. Ibid., 1.784–953, 998–1037.
116. Ibid., 2.1204.
117. Ibid., 2.549–739.
118. Ibid., 1.735–44.
119. Ibid., 8.575–76.
120. Ibid., 8.584.
121. Ibid., 8.519–20.
122. Ibid., 12.353–60.
123. Ibid., 6.391.
124. Ibid., 6.431–41.
125. Ibid., 8.325–26.
126. Ibid., 11.90–94.
127. Ibid., 10.366–68.
128. Ibid., 4.101.
129. Ibid., 4.227.
130. Ibid., 11.650.
131. Ibid., 11.808–13.
132. Ibid., 11.976–77.
133. Ibid., 11.1060.
134. Ibid., 8.887.
135. Ibid., 8.994–99.
136. Ibid., 9.763–65.
137. Ibid., 9.956–57.
138. Ibid., 10.610–13.
139. Ibid., 9.1044–47.
140. Ibid., 9.1067–71.
141. Ibid., 9.1132–36.
142. Ibid., 15.1095–98.
143. Ibid., 1.3.
144. Otis, *Ovid as an Epic Poet*, p. 323.
145. Ovid, *Metamorphoses*, 15.303–11.
146. Ibid., 15.234.
147. Ovid, *Tristia*, 3.5.53.
148. See, for example, Green, *Erotic Poems*, pp. 49–59.
149. Ovid, *Tristia*, 3.7.46–52.

CHAPTER 7: SENECA AS TRAGEDIAN

1. E. F. Watling, trans., *Seneca: Four Tragedies and Octavia* (London: Penguin Books, 1966), p. 7.

2. T. S. Eliot, "Seneca in Elizabethan Translation," in *Selected Essays* (New York: Harcourt, Brace 1950), p. 51.

3. Ibid., p. 75.

4. Dana Gioia, introduction to David R. Slavitt, ed., *Seneca: The Tragedies*, vol. 2 (Baltimore: Johns Hopkins University Press, 1995), p. xliv.

5. C. J. Herington, "Senecan Tragedy," in *Essays on Classical Literature*, ed. Niall Rudd (Cambridge: Heffer, 1972), pp. 195–96.

6. T. S. Eliot, "Shakespeare and the Stoicism of Seneca," in *Selected Essays*, p. 110.

7. Edith Hamilton, *The Roman Way to Western Civilization* (New York: New American Library, 1957), p. 136.

8. From this point on, all dates are CE (Common Era) unless otherwise specifically noted or if it is obvious from context.

9. Suetonius, *The Twelve Caesars*, trans. Robert Graves, rev. ed. (1979; repr., London: Penguin Books, 1989), p. 180.

10. Tacitus, *The Annals of Imperial Rome*, trans. Michael Grant (London: Folio Society, 2006), 14.52.

11. Suetonius, *Twelve Caesars*, p. 234.

12. Tacitus, *Annals*, 15.62–64.

13. Ibid., 15.63.

14. Ibid.

15. Alexander Pope, "An Essay on Man," quoted in A. A. Long, *Hellenistic Philosophy*, 2nd ed. (London: Duckworth, 1986), p. 170.

16. Aristotle, *Nicomachean Ethics*, 7.1153b19–21, trans. Joe Sachs (Newburyport, MA: Focus Publishing, 2002).

17. Martha C. Nussbaum, *The Therapy of Desire: Theory and Practice in Hellenistic Ethics* (Princeton, NJ: Princeton University Press, 1994), p. 363.

18. Eliot, "Shakespeare and the Stoicism of Seneca," p. 110.

19. Donald Russell, "The Arts of Prose: The Early Empire," in *The Oxford History of the Roman World*, ed. John Boardman, Jasper Griffin, and Oswyn Murray (Oxford: Oxford University Press, 2001), p. 301.

20. Quoted in Watling, *Seneca: Four Tragedies and "Octavia,"* p. 8.

21. Robin Campbell and C. D. N. Costa, trans., *Seneca: Letters from a Stoic and Three Dialogues* (London: Folio Society, 2003), letter 48, p. 66.

22. Ibid., letter 40, p. 52.

23. Seneca, *On Anger, Book 3*, 36, in *Seneca: Dialogues and Essays*, trans. John Davie (Oxford: Oxford University Press, 2008).

24. Campbell and Costa, *Seneca: Letters from a Stoic and Three Dialogues*, letter 16, p. 29.

25. Ibid., letter 48, p. 64.

26. Seneca, *Consolation to Marcia*, 10, in Davie, *Seneca: Dialogues and Essays*.

27. Campbell and Costa, *Seneca: Letters from a Stoic and Three Dialogues*, letter 9, p. 18.

28. Seneca, *On the Happy Life*, 23, in Davie, *Seneca: Dialogues and Essays*.

29. Ibid., 22.

30. Seneca, *Consolation to Marcia*, 10.

31. Seneca, *Consolation to Helvia*, 5, in Davie, *Seneca: Dialogues and Essays*.

32. Campbell and Costa, *Seneca: Letters from a Stoic and Three Dialogues*, letter 16, p. 31.

33. Ibid., letter 123, p. 188.

34. Seneca, *On the Tranquillity of the Mind*, 9, in Davie, *Seneca: Dialogues and Essays*.

35. Campbell and Costa, *Seneca: Letters from a Stoic and Three Dialogues*, letter 12, p. 25.

36. Seneca, *On Anger, Book 3*, 5.

37. Campbell and Costa, *Seneca: Letters from a Stoic and Three Dialogues*, letter 122, p. 187.

38. Ibid., letter 15, p. 29.

39. Seneca, *On the Shortness of Life*, 14, in Davie, *Seneca: Dialogues and Essays*.

40. Campbell and Costa, *Seneca: Letters from a Stoic and Three Dialogues*, letter 88, p. 118.

41. Ibid., letter 90, p. 127.

42. Ibid., letter 5, p. 7.

43. Ibid., letter 6, p. 9.

44. Ibid., letter 33, p. 50.

45. Ibid., letter 7, p. 13.

46. Ibid., letter 107, p. 160.

47. Ibid., letter 63, p. 82.

48. Ibid., letter 91, p. 143.

49. Seneca, *Consolation to Marcia*, 1.

50. Campbell and Costa, *Seneca: Letters from a Stoic and Three Dialogues*, letter 77, p. 93.

51. Ibid., letter 91, p. 146.

52. Seneca, *On the Happy Life*, 17.

53. Campbell and Costa, *Seneca: Letters from a Stoic and Three Dialogues*, letter 90, p. 137; Seneca, *On Providence*, 2, in Davie, *Seneca: Dialogues and Essays*.

54. Seneca, *On the Happy Life*, 20.

55. Norman T. Pratt, *Seneca's Drama* (Chapel Hill: University of North Carolina Press, 1983), p. 94.

56. For example, ibid., p. 10.

57. Herington, "Senecan Tragedy," p. 197.

58. Seneca, *The Trojan Women*, ll. 1–8, in *Seneca: The Tragedies*, ed. and trans. David R. Slavitt, vol. 1 (Baltimore: Johns Hopkins University Press, 1992).

59. Ibid., ll. 54–55.

60. Ibid., ll. 282–86.

61. See Michael K. Kellogg, *The Greek Search for Wisdom* (Amherst, NY: Prometheus Books, 2012), pp. 201–202.

62. Seneca, *Trojan Women*, l. 334.

63. Ibid., ll. 648–49.

64. Ibid., ll. 1011–13.

65. Ibid., ll. 985–91.

66. Ibid., ll. 378–82.

67. Ibid., ll. 760–61.

68. Joseph Kerman, *Opera as Drama* (1956; repr., Berkeley: University of California Press, 2005), p. 205.

69. See Kellogg, *Greek Search for Wisdom*, pp. 85–87.

70. Seneca, *Thyestes*, ll. 895–96, in Slavitt, *Seneca: The Tragedies*, vol. 1.

71. Ibid., ll. 24–27.

72. Ibid., l. 314.

73. Ibid., ll. 197–201.

74. Ibid., ll. 206–18.

75. Ibid., ll. 551–53.

76. Ibid., ll. 760–65.

77. Ibid., ll. 786–87.

78. Ibid., l. 138.

79. Ibid., ll. 793–96.

80. Ibid., ll. 1016–20.

81. Ibid., ll. 1088–90.

82. Ibid., ll. 357–59.

83. Ibid., ll. 927–29.

84. Seneca, *Phaedra*, ll. 544–46, in Slavitt, *Seneca: The Tragedies*, vol. 1.

85. Ibid., ll. 529–30.

86. Ibid., ll. 493–94.

87. Ibid., ll. 98–99.

88. Ibid., ll. 124–26.

89. Ibid., ll. 150–51.

90. Ibid., ll. 130–33.

91. Ibid., l. 184.

92. Ibid., ll. 457–59.

93. Nussbaum, *Therapy of Desire*, pp. 441–42.

94. Seneca, *Medea*, ll. 11–14, in Slavitt, *Seneca: The Tragedies*, vol. 1.

95. Ibid., ll. 420–24.

96. Ibid., ll. 570–71.

97. Ibid., ll. 1030–31.

98. Seneca, *Oedipus*, ll. 787–88, trans. Rachel Hadas, in Slavitt, *Seneca: The Tragedies*, vol. 2.

99. Ibid., l. 694.

100. Ibid., ll. 1030–34.

101. Ibid., ll. 1114–18.

102. Ibid., l. 1111.

103. Seneca, *The Madness of Hercules*, ll. 1213–16, trans. Dana Gioia, in Slavitt, *Seneca: The Tragedies*, vol. 2.

104. Ibid., ll. 263–70.

105. Seneca, *Medea*, ll. 46–48.

CHAPTER 8: PLUTARCH AND THE INVENTION OF BIOGRAPHY

1. Ian Kidd, introduction to *Plutarch: Essays*, trans. Robin Waterfield (London: Penguin Books, 1992), p. 13.

2. Arthur Hugh Clough, ed., John Dryden, trans., *Plutarch's Lives*, vol. 1 (New York: Modern Library, 2001), p. x.

3. Ibid.

4. Plutarch, "Demosthenes," in *Plutarch's Lives*, ed. Arthur Hugh Clough, trans. John Dryden, vol. 2 (New York: Modern Library, 2001), p. 388.

5. Plutarch, "Timoleon," in Clough, *Plutarch's Lives*, vol. 1, p. 325.

6. Plutarch, "Solon," in Clough, *Plutarch's Lives*, vol. 1, p. 124.

7. In the first volume of his masterful biography of Teddy Roosevelt, Morris describes at great length a boxing match at Harvard, which puts Roosevelt's character in high and flattering relief. See Edmund Morris, *The Rise of Theodore Roosevelt* (New York: Modern Library, 2001), pp. 90–91. But the match almost certainly never happened. In his "memoir" of Ronald Reagan, Morris imaginatively inserts himself as a recurrent figure in Reagan's life, the better, he thinks, to reveal the late president's character. See Edmund Morris, *Dutch: A Memoir of Ronald Reagan* (New York: Random House, 1999).

8. Timothy E. Duff, *Plutarch's Lives: Exploring Virtue and Vice* (Oxford: Oxford University Press, 2002), p. 10.

9. Robert Lamberton, *Plutarch* (New Haven, CT: Yale University Press, 2001), p. 69.

10. Plutarch, "Pericles," in Clough, *Plutarch's Lives*, vol. 1, p. 201.

11. Ibid.

12. Ibid., p. 202.

13. Ibid.

14. Plutarch, "Timoleon," in Clough, *Plutarch's Lives*, vol. 1, p. 325.

15. Ibid.

16. Plutarch, "Alexander," in Clough, *Plutarch's Lives*, vol. 2, p. 139.

17. Plutarch, "Demetrius," in Clough, *Plutarch's Lives*, vol. 2, p. 446.

18. Ibid., p. 445.

19. Ibid.

20. Donald M. Frame, trans., *The Complete Essays of Montaigne* (Stanford, CA: Stanford University Press, 1976), pp. 703–704.

21. Plutarch, "Cimon," in Clough, *Plutarch's Lives*, vol. 1, p. 643.

22. Ibid., pp. 643–44.

23. Plutarch, "Theseus," in Clough, *Plutarch's Lives*, vol. 1, p. 1.

24. Ibid.

25. Ibid.

26. Plutarch, "The Comparison of Romulus with Theseus," in Clough, *Plutarch's Lives*, vol. 1, p. 49.

27. Plutarch, "Romulus," in Clough, *Plutarch's Lives*, vol. 1, p. 30.

28. Ibid., p. 48.

29. Ibid.

30. Plutarch, "Lycurgus," in Clough, *Plutarch's Lives*, vol. 1, p. 79.

31. Plutarch, "Numa Pompilius," in Clough, *Plutarch's Lives*, vol. 1, p. 85.

32. Ibid., p. 87.

33. Ibid., p. 95.

34. Plutarch, "The Comparison of Numa with Lycurgus," in Clough, *Plutarch's Lives*, vol. 1, p. 102 (emphasis added).

35. Ibid., p. 103.

36. Plutarch, "Numa Pompilius," in Clough, *Plutarch's Lives*, vol. 1, p. 99.

37. Plutarch, "Poplicola," in Clough, *Plutarch's Lives*, vol. 1, p. 135.

38. Ibid.

39. Plutarch, "Coriolanus," in Clough, *Plutarch's Lives*, vol. 1, p. 291.

40. Ibid.

41. Plutarch, "The Comparison of Alcibiades with Coriolanus," in Clough, *Plutarch's Lives*, vol. 1, pp. 324–25.

42. Plutarch, "Fabius," in Clough, *Plutarch's Lives*, vol. 1, p. 239.

43. Ibid., p. 235.

44. Ibid., p. 250.

45. Plutarch, "Themistocles," in Clough, *Plutarch's Lives*, vol. 1, p. 147.

46. Plutarch, "Coriolanus," in Clough, *Plutarch's Lives*, vol. 1, p. 291.

47. Plutarch, "The Comparison of Tiberius and Gaius Gracchus with Agis and Cleomenes," in Clough, *Plutarch's Lives*, vol. 2, p. 384.

48. Plutarch, "Tiberius Gracchus," in Clough, *Plutarch's Lives*, vol. 2, p. 360.

49. Ibid., p. 357.

50. Ibid., p. 361.

51. Plutarch, "Gaius Gracchus," in Clough, *Plutarch's Lives*, vol. 2, p. 375.

52. The Dryden translation of Plutarch's *Lives* gives his name as Sylla, rather than Sulla. I follow here the standard Anglicization of the name.

53. Plutarch, "Gaius Marius," in Clough, *Plutarch's Lives*, vol. 1, p. 549.

54. Ibid., p. 554.

55. Plutarch, "Sulla," in Clough, *Plutarch's Lives*, vol. 1, p. 609.

56. Ibid., p. 633.

57. Ibid., p. 634.

58. Plutarch, "Pompey," in Clough, *Plutarch's Lives*, vol. 2, p. 113.

59. Ibid., p. 87.

60. Ibid., p. 88.

61. Ibid., p. 89.

62. Ibid., p. 94.

63. Plutarch, "Caesar," in Clough, *Plutarch's Lives*, vol. 2, p. 206.

64. Ibid., p. 202.

65. Ibid., p. 210.

66. Ibid., p. 201.

67. Ibid., p. 207.

68. Ibid., p. 221.

69. Plutarch, "Pompey," in Clough, *Plutarch's Lives*, vol. 2, p. 124.

70. Ibid., p. 129.

71. Ibid., p. 127.

72. Plutarch, "Caesar," in Clough, *Plutarch's Lives*, vol. 2, p. 235.

73. Ibid., pp. 243–44.

74. William Shakespeare, *Julius Caesar*, in *Tragedies*, ed. Sylvan Barnet, vol. 2 (New York: Alfred A. Knopf, 1993), 3.1.148–50.

75. Plutarch, "Antony," in Clough, *Plutarch's Lives*, vol. 2, p. 497.

76. Plutarch, "Cato the Younger," in Clough, *Plutarch's Lives*, vol. 2, p. 270.

77. Ibid., p. 282.

78. Ibid., p. 299.

79. Ibid., p. 286.

80. Ibid., p. 314.

81. Ibid., p. 316.

82. Plutarch, "Marcus Brutus," in Clough, *Plutarch's Lives*, vol. 2, p. 575.

83. Ibid., p. 572.

84. Ibid., p. 592.

85. Compare ibid., p. 577.

86. Shakespeare, *Julius Caesar*, 5.1.92.

87. Ibid., 3.1.182.

88. Ibid., 4.3.19.

89. Plutarch, "Marcus Brutus," in Clough, *Plutarch's Lives*, vol. 2, p. 586.

90. Ibid., p. 608.

91. Shakespeare, *Julius Caesar*, 5.5.34–38.

92. Quoted in Clough, *Plutarch's Lives*, vol. 1, p. xxxvi.

CHAPTER 9: TACITUS AND THE ROMAN HISTORIANS

1. Edward Gibbon, *The Decline and Fall of the Roman Empire*, ed. J. B. Bury, vol. 1 (1909; repr., New York: AMS Press, 1974), p. 87 (footnotes omitted).

2. Tacitus, *The Annals: The Reigns of Tiberius, Claudius, and Nero*, trans. J. C. Yardley (Oxford: Oxford University Press, 2008), 3.65.

3. Polybius, *The Rise of the Roman Empire*, trans. Ian Scott-Kilvert (London: Penguin Books, 1979), 1.1.

4. Ibid., 1.3.

5. Ibid., 1.14.

6. Ibid.

7. Ibid., 2.56.

8. Ibid., 1.35.

9. Ibid., 1.37.

10. Ibid., 6.57.

11. Ibid., 6.9.

12. Ibid., 6.10.

13. Ibid., 6.18.

14. Sallust, *Catiline's War*, 3.3–5, in *Catiline's War, The Jugurthine War, Histories*, trans. A. J. Woodman (London: Penguin Books, 2007). Woodman translates the Latin word *uirtus* as "prowess" (see p. xxx). But, although "prowess" captures the elements of strength and valor, it ignores the moral component of the term *uirtus*, which is essential to Sallust's use of it.

15. Sallust, *Catiline's War*, 4.1–2; see also Sallust, *The Jugurthine War*, 4.4, in Woodman, *Catiline's War, The Jugurthine War, Histories*.

16. Sallust, *Catiline's War*, 8.3–5.

17. Ibid., 4.2.

18. Ibid., 10.4.

19. Ibid., 53.6.

20. Quintilian, *Institutio Oratoria*, trans. H. E. Butler, vol. 4 (London: William Heinemann, 1922), 10.1.32.

21. Livy, *The Early History of Rome*, trans. Aubrey de Sélincourt (1960; repr., London: Penguin Books, 2002), 1.1, p. 30.

22. Ibid., 1.1, p. 29.

23. Livy, *Rome and the Mediterranean*, trans. Henry Bettenson (London: Penguin Books, 1976), 31.1.

24. Livy, *The War with Hannibal*, ed. Betty Radice, trans. Aubrey de Sélincourt (1965; repr., London: Penguin Books, 1972), 21.1.

25. Ibid., 21.57.

26. Livy, *Early History of Rome*, 1.1, p. 30.

27. Ibid., 1.1, pp. 29–30.

28. Ibid., 1.1, p. 30.

29. Livy, *War with Hannibal*, p. 19.

30. Livy, *Early History of Rome*, 2.1, p. 107.

31. Tacitus, *Agricola*, chap. 46, in *Agricola* and *Germany*, trans. Anthony R. Birley (Oxford: Oxford University Press, 2009).

32. Ibid., chap. 45.

33. Ibid., chap. 2.

34. Ibid., chap. 45.

35. Ibid., chap. 42.

36. Ibid., chap. 13.

37. Ibid., chap. 40.

38. Ibid., chap. 12.

39. William Shakespeare, *Richard II*, ed. Barbara A. Mowat and Paul Werstine (New York: Washington Square Press, 1996), 2.1.55–56.

40. Tacitus, *Agricola*, chap. 30.

41. Tacitus, *Germany*, chap. 4, in Birley, *Agricola* and *Germany*.

42. Ibid., chap. 19.

43. Tacitus, *The Histories*, ed. D. S. Levene, trans. W. H. Fyfe (Oxford: Oxford University Press, 2008), 1.2.

44. William Shakespeare, *Macbeth*, in *Tragedies*, ed. Sylvan Barnet, vol. 1 (New York: Alfred A. Knopf, 1992), 1.4.7–8, p. 451. See Tacitus, *Annals*, 1.53: "In the resolute manner of his death he was not unworthy of the name Sempronius; it was in his life that he had fallen short of it."

45. Tacitus, *Histories*, 2.89.

46. Ibid., 2.74.

47. Ibid., 3.84.

48. Ibid., 3.71–72.

49. Ibid., 2.12.

50. Ibid., 2.13.

51. Ibid., 4.1.

52. Ibid., 1.1.

53. Ibid., 1.2.

54. Ibid., 1.12.

55. Ibid., 1.19.

56. Ibid., 1.36.

57. Ibid., 1.39.

58. Ibid., 1.45.

59. Ibid., 1.49.

60. Ibid., 1.74.

61. Ibid., 3.56.

62. Ibid., 4.57.

63. Ibid., 4.70.

64. Tacitus, *Annals*, 1.1.

65. Ibid.

66. Gian Biagio Conte, *Latin Literature: A History*, trans. Joseph B. Solodow, rev. Don Fowler and Glenn W. Most (Baltimore: Johns Hopkins University Press, 1999), p. 550.

67. Suetonius, *The Twelve Caesars*, trans. Robert Graves, rev. ed. (1979; repr., London: Penguin Books, 1989), pp. 136, 141.

68. Tacitus, *Annals*, 1.4.

69. Ibid., 4.30.

70. Ibid., 4.69.

71. Ibid., 6.19.

72. Ibid., 4.33.

73. Ibid., 4.32.

74. Ibid.

75. Ibid., 4.20.

76. Ibid., 4.35.

77. Ibid., 4.1.

78. Ibid., 6.20.

79. Ibid., 6.6.

80. Ibid., 3.18.

81. Ibid., 12.67.

82. Ibid., 13.45.

83. Ibid., 15.39.

84. Ibid., 15.63.

85. Ibid.

86. Ibid., 16.18.

87. Ibid., 16.19.

88. Ibid.

89. Ronald Mellor, *Tacitus* (New York: Routledge, 1993), p. 28.

90. Tacitus, *Annals*, 4.33.

CHAPTER 10: THE EMPEROR AND THE SLAVE

1. Epictetus, *Discourses*, 4.1.1, in *The Discourses, The Handbook, Fragments*, ed. Christopher Gill, trans. Robin Hard (London: Everyman, 1995).

2. Ibid., 4.1.34.

3. Ibid., 4.1.35, 77.

4. Ibid., 4.1.57.

5. Ibid., 4.4.21.

6. Friedrich Nietzsche, *On the Genealogy of Morals*, trans. Walter Kaufmann and R. J. Hollingdale, in *On the Genealogy of Morals / Ecce Homo* (New York: Vintage Books, 1969), first essay, sec. 10, p. 36.

7. Gill, *Discourses of Epictetus, The Handbook, Fragments*, p. 1.

8. Epictetus, *Discourses*, 1.4.17.

9. Ibid., 1.15.2.

10. Ibid., 1.4.18.

11. Epictetus, *Handbook*, in *Discourses of Epictetus, The Handbook, Fragments*, 1.

12. Epictetus, *Discourses*, 2.2.26.

13. Epictetus, *Handbook*, 14.

14. Epictetus, *Discourses*, 1.1.17.

15. Ibid., 1.1.30.

16. Epictetus, *Handbook*, 1.

17. Epictetus, *Discourses*, 1.19.8–9.

18. Ibid., 4.7.24.

19. Epictetus, *Handbook*, 19.

20. Epictetus, *Discourses*, 2.17.29.

21. Ibid., 2.16.47.

22. Epictetus, fragment 9, in *Discourses of Epictetus, The Handbook, Fragments*.

23. Epictetus, *Handbook*, 31.

24. Epictetus, *Discourses*, 1.19.7–8.

25. A. A. Long, *Epictetus: A Stoic and Socratic Guide to Life* (2002; repr., Oxford: Oxford University Press, 2010), p. 92.

26. Epictetus, *Discourses*, 1.8.16.

27. Ibid., 2.20.7.

28. Long, *Epictetus*, p. 228.

29. Ibid., pp. 236–37.

30. Epictetus, *Discourses*, 3.2.4.

31. Long, *Epictetus*, p. 249.

32. Epictetus, *Discourses*, 2.13.17.

33. Ibid., 2.8.11.

34. Ibid., 2.18.19, 2.19.26.

35. Ibid., 2.17.22.

36. Ibid., 2.5.12.

37. Ibid., 1.6.21.

38. Epictetus, *Handbook*, 8.

39. Epictetus, *Discourses*, 1.12.15.

40. Henry James, quoted in Long, *Epictetus*, p. 272.

41. Friedrich Nietzsche, *Ecce Homo*, trans. Walter Kaufmann, in *On the Genealogy of Morals / Ecce Homo*, "Why I Am So Clever," sec. 10, p. 258.

42. Epictetus, *Discourses*, 1.18.21.

43. Ibid., 1.18.16.

44. Ibid., 3.23.1.

45. Epictetus, *Handbook*, 51.

46. Ibid.

47. See William B. Irvine, *A Guide to the Good Life* (New York: Oxford University Press, 2009), p. 65.

48. Epictetus, *Discourses*, 1.1.25.

49. Marcus Aurelius, *Meditations*, trans. Maxwell Staniforth (1964; repr., London: Folio Society, 2002), 1.17.

50. Edward Gibbon, *The Decline and Fall of the Roman Empire*, ed. J. B. Bury, vol. 1 (1909; repr., New York: AMS Press, 1974), p. 85.

51. Ibid., p. 84.

52. Henry James, *Collected Travel Writings: The Continent: A Little Tour in France, Italian Hours, Other Travels* (New York: Library of America, 1993), p. 418.

53. William Shakespeare, sonnet 111.6–7, in *Shakespeare's Sonnets*, ed. Stephen Booth (New Haven, CT: Yale University Press, 2000), p. 96.

54. Marcus Aurelius, *Meditations*, 5.16.

55. Ibid., 7.54.

56. Ibid., 8.5.

57. Ibid., 3.6.

58. Ibid., 4.25.

59. See Pierre Hadot, *The Inner Citadel: The "Meditations" of Marcus Aurelius*, trans. Michael Chase (Cambridge, MA: Harvard University Press, 2001), p. 47.

60. Marcus Aurelius, *Meditations*, 6.32.

61. Ibid., 12.17.

62. Ibid., 7.2.

63. Ibid., 6.13.

64. Ibid., 4.48, 7.1.

65. Ibid., 5.33.

66. Ibid., 9.14.

67. William Shakespeare, *Hamlet*, ed. T. J. B. Spencer, in *Four Tragedies* (London: Penguin Books, 1994), 1.2.133–34, p. 97.

68. R. B. Rutherford, *The "Meditations" of Marcus Aurelius: A Study* (Oxford: Clarendon Press, 1989), pp. 123–24.

69. Marcus Aurelius, *Meditations*, trans. A. S. L. Farquharson (New York: Alfred A. Knopf, 1992), p. xvii.

70. Pierre Hadot, *Philosophy as a Way of Life: Spiritual Exercises from Socrates to Foucault*, ed. Arnold I. Davidson, trans. Michael Chase (Malden, MA: Blackwell, 1995), p. 186.

71. Marcus Aurelius, *Meditations*, 10.17.

72. Ibid., 2.7.

73. Ibid., 5.10.

74. Ibid., 4.3.

75. Ibid., 6.10.

76. Ibid., 12.24.

77. Ibid., 9.28.

78. Ibid., 4.27.

79. Ibid., 10.6.

80. W. F. Trotter, trans., *Pascal's Pensées* (New York: E. P. Dutton, 1958), p. 68; see Marcus Aurelius, *Meditations*, 10.6.

81. Marcus Aurelius, *Meditations*, 4.40.

82. Ibid., 4.10.

83. Ibid., 12.21.

84. Ibid., 6.15.

85. Ibid., 2.3.

86. Ibid., 2.16.

87. Ibid., 3.5.

88. Ibid., 2.17.

89. Ibid., 1.1–10.

90. Ibid., 6.47.

91. Ibid., 8.26, 8.32.

92. Ibid., 10.21.

93. Ibid., 6.30.

94. Hadot, *Philosophy as a Way of Life*, pp. 201–202.

95. Long, *Epictetus*, p. 144.

INDEX